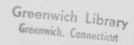

THE POET IN THE
IMAGINARY MUSEUM

DONALD DAVIE

The Poet in the Imaginary Museum

ESSAYS OF TWO DECADES

edited by

BARRY ALPERT

Persea Books, Inc./New York

For information, address the publisher:

Persea Books, Inc.

Box 804 Madison Square Station, New York, N. Y. 10010

International Standard Book Number: 0-89255-029-5
Library of Congress Catalog Card Number: 77-85356

First American Edition

Printed in Great Britain

CONTENTS

FOREWORD

THESE PIECES were chosen from Donald Davie's uncollected prose criticism. A primary focus on twentieth-century poetry and poetics narrowed the possibilities. Though the rubric *The Poet in the Imaginary Museum*, liberally interpreted, might embrace most of what Davie has written during the past twenty-five years, this volume was not designed to prove that point. Rather, I first took substantial essays whose intrinsic quality compelled me. That selection bore an odd relation to the publishing career as documented bibliographically. It did not constitute an historical record comparable to Davie's *Collected Poems*. Nor did it possess the connective tissue present in his five previous full-length critical volumes. Davie asked that the essays be printed in chronological order and he refused to alter history by rewriting or revision, preferring to register second thoughts in the form of postscripts.

After reconsidering the matter, I shifted to a supplementary editorial perspective emphasizing choice representation of his various critical modes. Coverage of significant figures was also taken into account. Davie's articulation of a developing critical position shows itself more prominently than if this had been a Collected Essays. One regrets that arguments are advanced intermittently rather than systematically, and that the sole consideration of certain writers is occasioned by reviews, but these 'flaws' typify Davie's empirical sensibility. Perceptual traffic runs almost entirely from the external world to his mind. Books came (or were brought) to his attention and he responded to them, often writing with great distinction when it was feasible to relate the object of discussion to his lifelong radical probing into the parameters of the poetic event. Poems came in a manner suggested by the following passage from 'The Rhetoric of Emotion': 'Just so, surely, does a good poem or story explore, respectfully and patiently, the somehow foreign body which has provoked it.' In fact, as I will be at pains to point out in my introduction, Davie's poems often initiate exploration which he extends in his critical writing. And I dare say that the 'criticism' included in this volume merits as much claim to be considered 'literature' as Davie argues is the right of the critical essays of F. R. Leavis.

It would be unwise to ride a thesis through an entire book when the author has not chosen to do so. Donald Davie's criticism stands up well enough as it is: no other British poet to emerge since 1945 has a comparable record. Does it not seem odd that literary critics tend to neglect what for them must be the most immediately germane aspect of a poet's *oeuvre* (his literary criticism) when ultimate evaluations are made?

B. A.

INTRODUCTION

OF PREVIOUS approaches to Donald Davie's work, I like Christopher Ricks's invocation of the 'presiding spirit'. Though as Ricks himself admits, Davie is not monotheistic, there exists empirical evidence in both the poetry and prose that George Berkeley has been present, *along with* other figures. Manifesting themselves first as authors of books worth considering, claiming the poet's attention and becoming subjects for discussion in critical prose, these presences richly reward the poet-critic who attends to them. Davie has ranged widely and yet has been so articulate about the quality of his interest that singling out his most promising engagements for further critical discussion precludes the usual lame speculation about nearly intangible 'sources and influences'.

I hope to trace scrupulously the overlapping 'fields of force' which resonate from Davie's work when one evokes Pushkin, Berkeley, Adrian Stokes and Carl Sauer. This may seem a narrow selection to some, but it locates my critical operation on grounds which Davie has not covered thoroughly from a selfconscious direction, while allowing for exact correlation between poems and prose which take up the same presence. A literary critic can't help but be intrigued by notes such as the following which Davie appends to his *Collected Poems*:

Hawkshead and Dachau in a Christmas Glass. I seem to remember that this poem is connected with an essay I contributed to the Dublin periodical *The Bell*, entitled rather quaintly 'Professor Heller and the Boots'. The poem was written in imitation of Coleridge's 'Dejection. An Ode'.

The 'Sculpture' of Rhyme. The title comes from Pound's *Hugh Selwyn Mauberley*. Some of the notions and sentiments packed into this little epitome were teased out by me years later in an essay on Michael Ayrton's 'The Maze Maker', in *The Southern Review*, Summer 1969.

If he's interested enough, this critic can gather the appropriate documents, read them in one sitting, consider how Davie has articulated the relationship and how he in turn can discuss it. There seem to be roomier possibilities for a secondhand critical operation upon the situation suggested by the first example above, but when one meditates upon the matter, Davie's tenuous language in the note appropriately reflects the quality of the interaction. It might deserve brief examination in a chapter on *Brides of Reason* within a book-length study of Davie's work, but the momentary convergence does not resonate precisely or with much energy. The second note, on the other hand, designates the temporal range of a major field of force sparked by thinking about poetry's analogies with the other arts. Stokes is a convenient exemplar, but Davie immediately considers Pound from that sculptural perspective, and much later, as he specifically indicates, the work of Michael Ayrton. The symbolist musical analogy is much less open to treatment because Davie has so convincingly argued his position without hinting at an unarticulated relationship between a poem and an essay.

Judging from the frequency of his appearance within Davie's writing, Pushkin seems an unlikely candidate for 'presiding spirit'. Yet Davie forthrightly terms him a 'constantly abiding presence'. Those modifiers 'constantly abiding' tell the story: Davie must have first encountered Pushkin in the forties while researching his unpublished doctoral thesis on the impact of nineteenth-century Russian literature in England. He reviewed two books about Pushkin in 1971. Twenty-odd years of involvement in which the visible evidence is the earliest written poem retained in *Collected Poems* ('Pushkin. A Didactic Poem'), a poem from the middle fifties entitled 'Dream Forest', a chapter on *The Captain's Daughter* in his unjustly neglected book *The Heyday of Sir Walter Scott* published in 1961, and the above-mentioned review ten years later. What can be ascertained from these clues? First, one must remember that Davie (as critic) cautions historians of ideas that the relationship between a poet's poetry and his ideas is not as direct as they often assume; in fact, it is indirect. Davie does emphasize, however, that *Purity of Diction in English Verse*, published in 1952, was an attempt to understand the poems he had been writing. Though a notion like 'didactic diction' doesn't seem to offer much help with 'Pushkin. A Didactic Poem'. Rather, Pushkin emerges as a personal example despite the very evident fact that they don't share the same language. Ascending to the lectern, Davie points out a shared reality:

> . . . The poet exhibits here
> How to be conscious in every direction
> But that of the self, where deception starts.
> This is nobility; not lost
> Wholly perhaps, if lost to art.

So thorough and explicit is his 'discussion' of Pushkin in this poem that one wonders if any qualities remain to be 'teased out' in later evocations. In fact, 'Dream Forest' essentially works with a metaphor drawn from Adrian Stokes and prefiguring Michael Ayrton. Davie overtakes this emblematic rendering of Pushkin's sculptured bust as one of the 'types of ideal virtue' (the Romantic) when he discerns 'the consciousness in Pushkin of the two traditions ['Romantic' and 'Classical'], and of the necessity of judging between them' while writing about Pushkin's novel in *The Heyday of Sir Walter Scott*. Such an awareness has ample resonance for Davie's consciousness. He's reminded of Pushkin's procedures for warding off 'spleen' and his morbid diagnoses of those infected with it, but the writing is much more memorable in Davie's early poem than on the later prose occasion:

> . . . we assume the truth
> That for life to be tolerable, man must
> Be wary, ingenious, quick to change
> Among diversions, grave or frivolous,
> . . .

> (Schiller and Dostoievsky, oysters
> Pearling their own disease, the saints
> Full of self-help)
> . . .
> What need dissection of the thrust
> Which motivates the skating feet?
> Skating with friends in the winter,
> He foretold our defeat.

That gloomy conclusion remains unshaken when twenty years later
Davie reassesses Pushkin's reception in England:

> The times, as I read them, could hardly be less propitious for a recog-
> nition among us of the radiant paradox that Pushkin embodies: the
> union of impregnable impersonality and reserve as an artist with eager
> and vulnerable frankness as a person.

At this time, however, the strict syntax and fine diction of Davie's prose
render Pushkin's exact character more incisively than ever before. Certainly one aspect of the 'radiant paradox' must be that the two presences
(Pushkin's and Davie's) rhymed for an instant.

The admittedly 'vulnerable' note which Davie appends to the poem
'With the Grain' helps us out in turn with the first poem specifically
taking up the figure of George Berkeley. He remarks:

> As in 'The Fountain' and 'Killala', the idea and the sensuous experience
> struck me independently, and only in the process of writing did I
> recognize a harmony between them, and a rightness about splicing
> them together in the poem.

That 'The Fountain' had its earliest origins in his reading of Berkeley
becomes clear when one consults the succinct note to that poem: 'Berkeley uses the figure of a fountain at the end of his *Dialogues of Hylas and
Philonous.*' It takes relatively little effort to locate this particular metaphor and read it before rereading Davie's poem:

> You see, Hylas, the water of yonder fountain, how it is forced up-
> wards, in a round column, to a certain height; at which it breaks and
> falls back into the basin from whence it rose: its ascent, as well as
> descent, proceeding from the same uniform law or principle of *gravi-
> tation.* Just so, the same principles which at first view lead to scepti-
> cism, pursued to a certain point, bring me back to common sense.

While the first stanza of 'The Fountain' may indeed register Davie's empirical apprehension of a very specific fountain, its syntax deliberately
approximates Berkeley's. Philonous encloses the literal description within the beginnings of an argument but Davie refrains from following his
source that closely. The metaphor no longer convinces him. In the second stanza therefore, Davie distances himself from language which
allows a rhetorical turn to replace civil and scrupulous argument.

> The Fountain
>
> Feathers up fast, and steeples; then in clods

Thuds into its first basin; thence as surf
Smokes up and hangs; irregularly slops
Into its second, tattered like a shawl;
There, chill as rain, stipples a danker green,
Where urgent tritons lob their heavy jets.

For Berkeley this was human thought, that mounts
From bland assumptions to inquiring skies,
There glints with wit, fumes into fancies, plays
With its negations, and at last descends,
As by a law of nature, to its bowl
Of thus enlightened but still common sense.

However indulgent it may seem to extend Berkeley's terms so fully,
Davie explodes the metaphor by overinflating it. Scrutinized closely, the
sensuous experience worked into the poem as almost an afterthought
offers more entertainment than the dubious idea which began it. This is
not a didactic poem, although its witty one-line rejoinder (separated
from the last of three six-line stanzas by a comma *and* a stanza break)
prefigures the reservations Davie was to express in his prose criticism:

We ask of fountains only that they play,

Though that was not what Berkeley meant at all.

Quite a few eighteenth-century stylists, Berkeley among them, serve
Donald Davie as resources for dead metaphors which he can enliven
should a situation occur which warrants such action. Let me cite a remarkable passage from *Articulate Energy*, a passage written, I imagine,
not long after 'The Fountain':

If the mind is a bag into which Locke put a lot of apparently external
'things', then Berkeley gathers up the things that Locke left outside
and pops them in also. But this is to halt midway. Having got everything into the bag, he puts his fist to the bottom; the bag turns inside out and there everything is, outside the bag again, once more an
external reality.

This is not offered as an argument, only as the statement of a position. The case has been argued elsewhere.

Davie asks our indulgence for a moment as he steps out of the philosopher's character into the poet's. What we are offered is an amusing and
stimulating metaphor, fairly labelled as no more than that. In *The Language of Science and the Language of Literature, 1700-1740* (published
in 1963) Davie treats Berkeley's *Siris*, arguing that even metaphors which
hover ambiguously between a scientific and spiritual significance, nearly
out of the writer's control, are 'legitimate' when the context is poetry,
though their presence in a philosophical argument makes him feel uncomfortable. 'The Fountain' suggests that ambiguous metaphors are *rarely*
legitimate when a truthful statement is the object. Perhaps the very
*un*ambiguous 'figure' mediating Locke and Berkeley is an early prose

realization of formal linguistic aspirations candidly articulated in the valuable note to 'With the Grain':

> What takes my interest is something behind the ideas, something which can be expressed only, as in 'Obiter Dicta', by finding a concrete fantasy which not only expresses but truly *is* the common element in the ideas which attract me.

Despite his very evident value in sparking Davie to tangible and rhetorically compelling enactments, George Berkeley has so far been observed to lack the deeper values signalled by the term 'Candour'. It seems a bit odd that Berkeley should be Davie's primary example in his essay towards an understanding of the Augustan idea of Candour, 'Berkeley and the Style of Dialogue'. But we have encountered George Berkeley in his weaker moments. Although Davie refers to the *Three Dialogues of Hylas and Philonous* as 'an exemplification of the virtue of candour', he finds Philonous 'less sympathetic because always on the winning side'. Philonous is the character responsible for the metaphor of the fountain which Davie challenges, perhaps partly because Hylas ('the more engaging and attractive of the speakers') isn't given his usual fair chance. *Three Dialogues* ends with Philonous' metaphor. Davie reopens the discussion some two hundred years later by writing 'The Fountain'.

Typically, Candour manifested itself in two poems composed well before the essay on the subject. Davie's note on the first of these poems suggests to me why I have always found his essays more compelling than the early surfacings:

> 'Under St Paul's' by contrast conceals the true movement of my mind, presenting as a deduction from concrete experience what was in fact the source of the poem (the idea of Candour), to which the concrete experience of the cathedral as a building was subsequently attached, not without difficulty.

As I read 'Under St Paul's', neither line works itself out lucidly. The experiential realm in which Candour is situated does not invigorate an abstraction which (as Davie admits in his essay) survives only with considerably reduced amplitude. The present understanding of the term competes with Davie's attempt to revive its expanded eighteenth-century significance. Certain individuals might consult the OED, but I'd maintain that a reading of 'Berkeley and the Style of Dialogue' provides a more precise registration of Davie's understanding of Candour and the ethical value he apprehends in its operation. The concrete fantasies provoked by the fountain and the bag are more successful attempts to work against the grain, perhaps because the transformation of the abstract into the concrete occurs within such a short span. Far too much gets incorporated in 'Under St Paul's'. We glimpse Adrian Stokes shortly after the poem begins: '. . . the dome/Of stone-revetted crystal swung and hung/Its wealth of waters . . .' Davie recently decided that Pushkin enters 'Under St Paul's' as well, since candour is really what he was praising in 'Pushkin. A Didactic Poem', though he didn't then have the term at hand. It's not surprising that Davie experienced difficulty attaching the elements of the poem one to another, nor that the relationships remain unclear in this realization.

'Against Confidences' is a much more straightforward, a more natural poem for Davie to write. Though again, Berkeley's presence in the poem can only be detected from the perspective gained from reading Davie's later essay. Commencing with the idea of Candour, Donald Davie on this occasion continues with it through to the end. The title suggests an ethical significance which doesn't require the particular experience on which it rests in order to be understood. By animating Candour within the bounds of the poem and defining this personified figure by its activity, Davie obliquely presents his own values without distorting what we will later recognize as Berkeley's understanding of Candour:

> Not to dispense
> With privacies,
> But reticence
> His practice is;
>
> Agreeing where
> Is no denial,
> Not to spare
> One truth from trial,
>
> But to respect
> Conviction's plight
> In Intellect's
> Hard equal light.

Terse iambic dimeter allows numerous distinctions without garrulousness, as Davie's mind walks naturally among abstractions. Still, though memorably expressed, this passage is only a partial definition in the light cast by 'Berkeley and the Style of Dialogue'. I can only refer you to that essay here (and perhaps single out Davie's lucid discrimination between Berkeley's relatively candid style in the *Three Dialogues* and his uncandid later practice in *Alciphron*). Finally, Berkeley as moral example supersedes the practical resource his writings represent for Davie and this last major encounter concludes by elevating Berkeley to a sort of spiritual pantheon on very much the same grounds as in the case of Pushkin:

> In the Augustan age as in any other, to deal candidly with oneself, still more to give a lively and edifying image of candour in others— these achievements were won by the lonely and exacting labour of distinguished individuals who were not carried by the current of their times but strove against it.

I have noted how Davie in 'Under St Paul's' compresses into a single perception Stokes's complex discussion of the interrelationship between water, stone and glass, but this is not to suggest that the fields of force resonating from Berkeley and Stokes overlap easily. Rather, Pushkin and

Berkeley came to Davie's attention early on in his career and remained
with him as supportive identities, supporting each other as well. Stokes
appeared later, provoking a prolonged consideration of poetry in relationship to the other arts. Moving from such concerns towards poetry
vis-à-vis history and geography does not seem an unnatural step. Indeed,
one passage from the poem 'With the Grain' underlies the remarkable
reading of Hardy's *Poems 1912-1913* which Davie published some fifteen
years after completing the poem:

> Love, a condition of such fixed colour,
>> Cornwall indeed, or Wales
>> Might foster . . .

Compare these lines to Davie's critical demonstration that for Hardy
love's fixed colour is purple, its quality dependent on geography: 'North
Cornwall is a landscape of loyalty; thereabouts he will be true to her, she
will be true to him. The use of landscape is as starkly emblematic as that.'
'With the Grain' was completed after his essay 'Adrian Stokes and Pound's
Cantos' and his lecture 'The Poet in the Imaginary Museum' had appeared. It continues the discussion, as it were, in lieu of an essay:

> Now I am meditating an essay on the relationship between poetry
> and painting. Yet I feel that I shall not express in the essay what
> makes this complex of ideas so interesting to me. What takes my in-
> terest is something behind the ideas, something which can be expressed
> only, as in 'Obiter Dicta', by finding a concrete fantasy which not
> only expresses but truly *is* the common element in the ideas which
> attract me. I have a hunch that this common element has something
> to do with the distinction in painting between hue and tone. This dis-
> tinction is still a distinction between ideas, but the ideas are a good
> deal less abstract than those I started with . . .

Well, the essay didn't get written, but three days later a poem comes to
him going on as follows:

> The purest hue, let only the light be sufficient
>> Turns colour. And I was told
> If painters frequent St Ives
>> It is because the light
> There, under the cliff, is merciful. I dream
>> Of an equable light upon words
> And as painters paint in St Ives, the poets speaking.

Davie's understanding of hue and its bearing for poetry is not unlike the
viewpoint he was to express in *Ezra Pound: Poet as Sculptor*, though one
might suspect the 'concrete fantasy' imagined in 'With the Grain' to be
Thomas Hardy speaking to his wife Emma. Thus the speaker in the
passage just quoted is not necessarily Donald Davie, but perhaps the
self-made craftsman Hardy, whose working against the grain may have
seemed relevant to Davie at the time. By the early sixties, Davie had located a slightly more rigorous distinction between hue and tone in a
poem by Ezra Pound ('A Song of the Degrees') and a hitherto unremarked

discussion of the subject in a book by Adrian Stokes. He formulated it in this way: 'hue is the "intrinsic" colour, tone that colour which is imparted to objects by the light as it strikes them this way or that, with this or that degree of intensity . . .' 'For an Age of Plastics', a poem apparently written not too long after 'With the Grain', takes up an analogous distinction in sculpture.

The intellectual experience is largely reconsideration, in this case, because Davie had fully discussed the implications in his essay on Stokes and Pound. One should recall, however, that 'For an Age of Plastics' came at a time when Davie was experimenting with the relationship between experience and idea in a poem. I'm inclined to think that the poem was primarily prompted by a visit home for a funeral. Ideas which had lately preoccupied him naturally entered in during the process of composition, but they don't dominate the poem. Experiential light shades such ideas so that while the earlier manifestation can be discovered in the later articulation, one can also detect a difference. Consider Davie's explication of a passage from Pound's Canto 47:

> But if the mountain is the female body ('By prong have I entered these hills'), it is also literally the mountain from which the sculptor quarries his marble block ('Yet hast thou gnawed through the mountain'), the quarrying being itself a sort of sculpture, a first stage in the carving. It is also ('Begin thy plowing . . . Think thus of thy plowing'— out of Hesiod in this same canto) the mountain that the farmer scores with his plough. And in *The Stones of Rimini* Adrian Stokes makes this analogy too: carving is not only like a man's way with a woman, it is also like a ploughman's way with the land.

Compare it to this passage from 'For an Age of Plastics':

> Annoyed to take a gloomy sort of pride
>   In numbering our losses, I suppose
> The ploughman ceased his carving of the hillside
>   And all the coulters and the chisels broke
> When he was young whom we come home to bury,
>   A man like clay in the hands of his womenfolk.
>
> A ploughman carved three harvests, each a son,
>   Upon the flesh of Wales . . .

Having earned for himself what we might term 'metaphorical economy', Davie can register the emotional state of the speaker, detail the sculptural tools, offer up in a simile the antithetical sculptural possibility (moulding), and incorporate the ideas broached within the prose passage—all in fewer words. The title of the poem apparently derives from an elegiac passage by Stokes (which Davie quotes in his criticism), on the accelerating retreat of hewn stone from the continued onslaught of plastic material, but the experience of visiting Plymouth and being startled by the chance juxtaposition of homes carved from stone with those 'moulded in bakelite' is just as convincing a source. I doubt whether the conclusion

of 'For an Age of Plastics' owes any direct indebtedness to earlier critical
discussion, but the oddly anecdotal, almost Frostian manner (not without its rustic charm, however) doesn't distort a respect and liking for
'stony' qualities which aren't washed away despite the nearly all-encom-
pasing flux in which we're now situated:
>   Still he would flow, himself, from mould to mould.

>   Whatever he showed of something in the rough,
>   Sluggish in flow and unadaptable,
>   I liked him for; affecting to be gruff,
>   An awkward customer—so much was due,
>   He seemed to think, to what a man was, once:
>   Something to build with, take a chisel to.

If, as Davie insists, his criticism is a spin-off from his poetry, then the
connections between a poem composed in the late fifties, 'The "Sculpture" of Rhyme' and an essay written some ten years later, 'Michael
Ayrton's *The Maze Maker*', should be a prime exhibit. He tells us in a
note on the poem, 'Some of the notions and sentiments packed into this
little epitome were teased out by me years later . . .' The title's overt
Poundian glance and, internally, insects 'borrowed' from the Pisan cantos, suggest that the poem arose out of a matrix of ideas which Davie
had located (around the time of its composition) in the writings of
Stokes and Pound. In fact, Davie's characteristic welding of specific
personal experience and abstract ideas cannot be observed in 'The
"Sculpture" of Rhyme'. Its weighing of aesthetic alternatives resembles
more closely the procedure of 'Against Confidences' than that of 'With
the Grain' and 'For an Age of Plastics'. Traffic doesn't always move
from poems to criticism, or, as most critics of Davie's work believe,
from criticism to poetry. Examination of the documents which chart
the traffic suggests, instead, that Davie's mind can move in either direction, depending on unpredictable circumstances. He didn't sit down to
expand 'The "Sculpture" of Rhyme' into a critical essay; the occasion
of reading Ayrton's novel led him further into the paradox of bronze
casting than the mere notion of a less attractive value implied by the
first three lines of the poem:
>   Potter nor iron-founder
> Nor caster of bronze will he cherish,
>   But the monumental mason;

Bronze possesses qualities which can be cherished by a devotee of stone:
>   For those cast bronzes which Gautier and Pound respond to so eagerly,
>   as showing how art can be durable and rigid, in fact are fashioned out
>   of the most fluid material; the molten bronze is *poured* into the
>   mould. The rigidity and hardness of the end product is in direct propor-
>   tion to the fluid malleability in the process of production. For a carving
>   in stone is usually softer than cast bronze. Moreover, in both cases the
>   process of artistic creation mimics a process of natural creation.

Furthermore (and here Davie almost convinces himself that he has been in error about the proper analogy for his own poetic processes):

> For if we believe that an art is more than a rhetoric, more than a compassing of certain effects by whatever means; if we believe that on the contrary the morality of art has everything to do with a congruence between process and product, between means and ends—then we must argue that for the rendering of metamorphic flux as a profound reality, nothing will serve but an act that itself comprehends metamorphosis centrally in its processes. And bronze casting is such an art whereas stone carving is not.

Finally, however, Donald Davie decides that the valuation registered in the poem still holds for him on this later occasion, and will hold in the future:

> Not in those subterranean wynds and galleries, nor in the kneaded wax and the poured bronze which seem their natural concomitants, shall we find that which some of us will always want more than anything else—the resistant and persisting, the rigid and the hard, everything that poets have yearned for naively in the image of the stone that resists the chisel and confronts the sunlight.

Certain considerations deriving from another field of force which had been forming during the temporal gap between the poem and the essay contributed to the reassertion of his earlier values. The significance which Ayrton attributes to the maze provokes Davie to a rejoinder:

> For is it the whole truth—that man, and the artist in particular, can explore nothing beyond the confines of his own personality? For that is what it means surely: that the artist explores, cognizes, not Nature but only his own nature; that the truths he discovers are neither physical nor metaphysical, but merely, when you come down to it, psychological.

I detect the presence of Pushkin here. But also, when Davie proceeds to praise the stone carver for apprehending with scrupulous feeling the particular qualities of his medium instead of giving way before the objective means of the scientist, I recall the geographer Carl Sauer implicitly inviting artists to enter his physical realm: 'A good deal of the meaning of area lies beyond scientific regimentation. The best geography has never disregarded the asethetic qualities of landscape, to which we know no approach other than the subjective.' Davie had cited this passage within an essay entitled 'Landscape as Poetic Focus', published a year earlier than the Ayrton piece in the same magazine. It seems more instructive, in this case, to trace out how Davie accepted Sauer's invitation and consequently wrote some of his finest poems, than to show how earlier poems argue the need for a guiding spirit like that represented by Carl Sauer. One instance of prefiguration should suffice, though even here one can't be sure that 'convergence' isn't the proper term. A poem entitled 'Behind the North Wind', part of *More Essex Poems (1964-8)*, contains the following passage:

> More than ever I need
> Places where nothing happened,
> Where history is silent,

'Landscape as Poetic Focus' concludes in a more tentative, yet nearly identical vein: 'It begins to seem as if a focus upon scenery, upon landscape and the areal, relations in space, are a necessary check and control upon the poet's manipulation of the historical record.' There is an unidentified prose quotation (which could have been written by Carl Sauer) serving as a preface to 'Behind the North Wind': 'the Arctic Ocean was open during glacial stages and its margins would have been habitable for man'. Davie begins the poem by instructing himself, 'Envisage it:'. Imaginative speculation preoccupies the first stanza, and then Davie's personal experience in that area during the Second World War enters the poem almost as a check upon the theoretical. It's a procedure he later offers to others in his critical prose.

Donald Davie's 'Fifth Epistle to Eva Hesse' was written 'light-heartedly, between September 1969 and March 1970'. His literary-historical essay ('John Ledyard: The American Traveller and His Sentimental Journeys') on the individual who preoccupies his attention in the poem, appeared in the autumn of 1970. Though the two pieces could have been written side-by-side, as it were (the development is occasionally parallel), I suspect that the Muse of Comedy first exacted her demands and then Scholarship tidied up the matter. Approximately ten years earlier, *A Sequence for Francis Parkman* had articulated his first response to North America while *The Heyday of Sir Walter Scott* brought together related critical concerns. The research into eighteenth-century exploration of the New World which nourishes the writing stems from Davie's personal investigation of this world, mediated by the presence of Sauer and those American poets who saw Sauer's worth, Charles Olson and Edward Dorn. When reading converges with experience, Davie's writing is particularly compelling. Dorn's poem 'Ledyard. The Exhaustion of Sheer Distance' must have rhymed with Davie's naval experience in the Arctic during the Second World War, as did the geographer's proposition which yielded 'Behind the North Wind'. Discovering that Captain James Cook hailed from Yorkshire couldn't help but interest Davie further. All he needed was a vehicle ('Not poetry, nor yet discourse . . .') which he stumbled upon when the need arose to write a personal letter, and he's convinced me that 'as much variety of time, space and action can be encompassed in one of the traditional forms of English verse as in the much vaunted "free form" of an American tradition originating in Pound's *Cantos*.' The verse epistle permits a productive intermingling of Davie's critical and creative faculties which the formal demands of each discipline had not quite allowed in the past.

One can observe Davie researching subsequent poems, for example in his note to 'Trevenen', but also, as in the past, writing essays which extrapolate from poems or poems which arise out of essays. I can't quite determine the direction of his mental traffic in the case of his essay 'The Cantos: Towards a Pedestrian Reading' and his poem 'Reticulations'. Again the dates of publication are so close as to offer no help in ascertaining which was written first. I suspect however that the poem with its programmatic subtitle '(Guide Michelin)' is a spin-off from the critical viewpoint he proffers in the essay:

> And indeed I would insist on this: the first requirement for a study of Pound is a set of maps . . . of at any rate certain regions of France, Italy and England; the second requirement is a set of Michelin Green Guides for France and Italy . . .

No doubt Davie took his own advice; indeed, the essay shows him comparing Pound's geographical detail to what can be ascertained from maps and what can only be learned from first-hand exploration of particular areas. Davie literally followed Pound's footsteps, and readers of 'Reticulations' may in turn want to retrace Davie's path after they have exhausted what help the appropriate Michelin guides and maps can offer. In fact, they had better make the trip, since Davie records in the poem his experience of discovering that the printed matter is not quite enough, that it must be constantly checked against personal experience: 'And he does not need even to go there!/yet will, he will discover'.

How is this situation altered when a poet records unearthly or supernatural experience? In his book *Thomas Hardy and British Poetry*, Donald Davie asks critics to

> pause long enough to say explicitly whether from their own experience they know what it means to 'meet Artemis', to 'turn into a tree', to 'walk sheer into nonsense'. I will confess at once that my own experience provides me with not an inkling of what these expressions mean.

This confession makes me almost certain that the visions and ghostly apparitions which occasionally crop up in Davie's poetry are literary devices concocted for certain effects. Yet when I read 'Widowers' I am less certain. Davie published this poem in the Thomas Hardy number of *Agenda* he guest-edited, and positioned it immediately after his essay 'Hardy's Virgilian Purples'. Note the following passage:

> . . . all of us have the thought
> That states of soul in some uncertain sort
> Survive us—sealed, it could be, in locations:
> A yard, a coomb, an inn, a Cornish tor.

Despite the qualified manner in which Davie offers up this proposition, a literal 'metaphysical landscape' (one that can be mapped) must be a more attractive possibility than subjective fantasies. Three years earlier, in his essay on Michael Ayrton, Davie's language ('the truths he discovers are neither physical nor metaphysical but merely when you come down to it, psychological') intimated the direction in which his mind would move, but the mapping was much more tentative: 'No one can blame Ayrton, or any other twentieth-century man, for not having decided

how wide a margin we ought to leave for the supernatural in our experience.' Still, the supernatural *is* acknowledged. After tracing the physical *and* metaphysical journey of a poet of similar temperament (Thomas
Hardy), Davie fulfils the condition he set for 'the poet' within his critical essay by affirming with Hardy the literal presence of spirits: '. . . There
she dwells, we think . . ./She does, although our need to think so passes.'
It is too much to ask Davie to 'decide the mode in which the quality will
persist after his death'. We should be satisfied with the registration of
those presences which come to mind when he invokes each of the shires
of England, a landscape from which he has removed himself.

BARRY ALPERT

THE SPOKEN WORD

Poems for Speaking: An Anthology, with an Essay on Reading Aloud,
Richard Church, Dent.
Poets of the Pacific, Second Series, ed. Yvor Winters, Stanford University Press, 1949.

WHEN W. B. Yeats was experimenting with verse-speaking to the psaltery, Wilfrid Blunt commented on the practice that 'it reduced the verse to the position it holds in an opera libretto.' Something of this may have been in the mind of Ezra Pound when he introduced into Canto LXXXI a short lyric which is headed 'libretto'. That lovely piece of writing demonstrates the beautiful and surely valuable effects that can be obtained from verse written in this way. And it is not hard to think of other famous pieces which could be described as 'libretti' in the same way—'Alexander's Feast', for example, or 'The Leaden Echo and the Golden Echo'. And more candidates are provided by Mr Church in his anthology, especially in his first section, headed 'Ballad', and his last, headed 'Ceremonial or Choral Speaking'. In such poetry, it seems that the poet's experience is so simple or so simplified that he can allow the speaking voice to exploit his words as a libretto while running no risk that attention will thus be diverted from what he has to say.

Poems which deal with more complicated experience require the speaking voice no less than the 'libretti' but in a different way. Examples of such poetry are, on the one hand, the sonnets of Shakespeare and Donne; on the other, those 'pure' lyrics of which Mr Church writes:

A story to tell always means a more obvious basic structure. Where a poem is built of pure air and fire, out of the mood of the human spirit, or maybe from something even more impersonal, some momentary visitation of spiritual insight, then the rhythm of this strange impulse is likely to be difficult to anatomize. To speak such a poem is comparable to the task of a surgeon operating on the brain or the eye. Delicately does it, with a hand as light as the air after which it is reaching . . .

Plainly, Mr Church is not concerned only with poems as excuses for displaying the speaker's repertoire of tone and pitch and volume. And he reprobates that attitude in his remarks on the old-fashioned 'elocutionist'. He makes sufficient room for poems in which 'the music' is not openly called for or imposed by the poet, but can only be derived from a strenuous understanding. Part IV (Sonnet) and Part V (Lyric) are devoted to these other sorts of verse.

Nevertheless, the attitude required of the verse-speaker by verse of this sort is so different from that required of him by the 'libretti' that we may well wonder how there can be framed any notion of verse-speaking which will embrace two such different kinds of activity. Mr Church goes far towards framing such a notion. He sees clearly that the danger lies in regarding verse-speaking merely as a technique, however expert and arduous;

and so, in an urgent and eloquent essay, he argues for proper speaking of verse as in some sort a spiritual discipline, an activity of the whole being which can heal the human sensibility of the conflict between ear and eye brought about by the invention of the printing-press. When Mr Church sees in the speaking of verse something so momentous as this, he disarms our suspicions. And yet—

> I believe that every poem should be composed to be heard. It should therefore aim at such simplicity of expression that its meaning, however profound or subtle, can be instantly and in some degree apprehended. Its phrasing should admit neither of confusion of meanings nor clumsiness of sounds. And the meaning and the sound should live together like man and wife.

The meaning we note, should be only *'in some degree* apprehended' at a first hearing; and what is in question is not ambiguity but 'confusion of meanings'. It may be true that many of the 'ambiguities' beloved of Mr Empson and his American adherents should properly be called 'confusions'. On the other hand it may be that some of what Mr Church sees as 'confusions' could be justified as 'ambiguities'. At any rate, it is on points such as these that many readers will fall out among themselves in interpreting the excellent principles that Mr Church puts forward.

And such disagreements will become sharper when the readers turn to the selection of poems, to see how Mr Church interprets his own principles in practice. It may surprise some, for example, to find Donne represented by two sonnets, and not by any of the love-songs, such as 'Aire and Angells', which might seem to present to the verse-speaker some most challenging but also most rewarding problems; for these are the poems which seem full of 'clumsiness of sounds' until the speaker, by strenuous understanding, can draw out the melody only revealed when he grasps fully the sense of what is said. A sonnet, even a sonnet by Donne, is a relatively easy undertaking, since the reader has, from the first, the guidance of what Mr Church calls the 'architecture' of the sonnet-form. Again, it might seem to some that nothing is to be gained, for verse-speaking or anything else, by placing 'Sailing to Byzantium' and Cory's 'Heraclitus' in the same section of the same anthology. If the speaker must enter into the spirit of each poem he reads, it could be argued that the speaker who can enter into Cory's world of vulgar emotion will be so much less able to 'enter into' the world of Yeats.

In the end, it is always pointless to disagree with the selection of poems for anthologies. And yet Mr Church's book, being designedly provocative, deserves to be argued about. Perhaps one criticizes it most sharply by saying that it will not be argued about enough. For the selection of poems is so catholic that there is something to please every taste. From one point of view that is a back-handed compliment, and yet it is hard not to be disappointed at finding such an orthodox and catholic selection, after a stirring introduction which seemed to promise a new perspective and a new departure.

A special case is presented to the speaker of verse by poetry in which the movement imposed upon the reader seems at variance with the sense of what is said. Some have argued that the rhythm in some of Milton's verse-paragraphs is of this sort, not following and reflecting the sense, but hiding and gliding over inconsistencies in what is said. I find such a poem in Mr MacNeice's 'Streets of Laredo', included by Mr Church, where a jaunty emphatic rhythm seems, especially at the end, to impose a false simplification on the complex issues raised by theme and diction. This, I suppose, is the besetting sin of most Georgian verse, in which one feels that the movement, whether regular or cunningly various, and the rhyming, whether in echoing chimes or cunningly imperfect, are contrived for their own sake and not under pressure from what is to be conveyed.

From time to time, in *Poets of the Pacific*, the British reader may be offended by evidence of this Georgian trick. And the poets represented do in fact belong to a group which holds that certain Georgian poets, notably T. Sturge Moore and Robert Bridges, are today under-rated. But this is by no means the guiding principle of the school, and they are not to be regarded as in any way neo-Georgians nor as related to such American 'traditionalists' as the late William Rose Benet. The group, centred upon the Californian University of Stanford, differs from the poets and critics of the Eastern States in believing that a poem is none the worse for being built around a structure of rational discourse, and that a poet's intelligence can be brought into play as effectively when he follows a rational argument as when he has recourse to witty metaphor or juxtaposition. These poets are not afraid, when convenient, to distinguish between what a poet says and the way he says it. There is all the more reason, in their view, for supposing that a poet cannot write in a void; and that, other things being equal, he will write better poetry if he has philosophical training, and if his philosophical standpoint is rationally sound. They recognize the achievement of French symbolists, and of post-symbolists and experimentalists such as Eliot, Pound, Wallace Stevens and Hart Crane; but they think that this vein is now worked out and that healthy poetry today must find again a basis in rational philosophy. In general they eschew free verse and write in strict metre and in rhyme.

The British poet today is so nearly insulated from his American colleagues that he hardly knows the work of such established poets as Stevens, Ransom, Tate, Williams, even Hart Crane. Still less does he know the work of these Western poets. Yet this Western school has already passed, as it were, through one generation, and some of those older poets, notably J. V. Cunningham, Howard Baker and Yvor Winters, are regarded in some quarters as among the most important American poets of the day. It is high time some of this work was made available to the British public. Meanwhile it seems worthwhile to take notice of this American publication, for it presents a shift of direction in American poetry analogous in some ways to certain tentative movements over here.

The 'Georgianism' is an issue which must be faced. I find it here:

> Green growing bush, compounded elements,
> The clean excrescence of the earth, the first
> To rift the stony desert face and burst
> The rigid outline with a foliage dense,
> Your latest leaf against my garden fence
> Is older than the silent man you nursed;
> But silent too with only mortal thirst—
> Is younger than the man whom man invents.

The notions here are sufficiently difficult, especially in the last three lines. And the rhymes, I find, do not help the reader to grapple with the difficulty; they only distract him. Thus the second and third lines, which lean forward breathlessly over their rhymes (perhaps *to get* the rhymes) do not reflect, as they might in Donne, a strenuous urgency of thought and feeling. On the other hand, when, in the sixth and seventh lines, some such effort is called for, the emphatic rhymes thump home as if the difficult sense they carry were self-evident. And once we begin to suspect that the rhymes dictate the arrangement, we notice and dislike the inversion, 'foliage dense'. We are right, I think, to call this 'Georgian' and dislike it. Yet this is the poet, Helen Pinkerton, who contributes what are perhaps the most distinguished poems in the whole collection, her two sonnets, 'To a Spiritual Entity'.

The Georgian manner (if that is what it is) crops up in her poems and in others to spoil them. A better convention, which they use, I should tend to identify with the example of some other neglected poets who have been admired by Yvor Winters. These are the Elizabethan epigrammatists, Turberville, Gascoigne and Googe; and theirs may be the influence behind such a poem as the following by W. Wesley Trimpi, 'Phlegm':

> The body is not spent;
> The mind is complement
> To but a little lust:
> We do but what we must.
> Our only will is want,
> And it is sheathed in gaunt
> Complacent gauze of flesh,
> Alive nor full nor fresh.
> The mind is but a waste
> Of thought, inert, defaced;
> And doubt, the slow dissembling
> Loss of intent, the trembling
> Choice without willing choice,
> Echoes illusion's voice.

This tough, taut verse gives nothing away. And it is difficult. From his other poems here, notably 'Affliction' and 'Contingency', it seems that, for this poet, 'will', 'thought', 'intent', 'doubt' are recurrent terms in an argument which is carried on in more than one poem. At any rate it is hard not to feel that this is an important achievement in a convention which may be less restricted than it seems. From the same hand comes a sonnet, 'The Glass Swan', which is beautifully managed up to a baffling final couplet. This poetry, like Helen Pinkerton's, aims at major status. So does that of Pearce Young, who achieves that status precariously in 'The Winter Flood', and triumphantly in 'October Garden'. And so does Edgar Bowers, notably in the first of 'Two Poems on the Catholic Bavarians', 'The Mountain Cemetery', and in 'The Stoic', the last of which contains the beautiful image, 'Eternal Venice sinking by degrees/Into the very water that she lights . . .' It is natural to talk of Mr Bowers's poetry in terms of 'images'; for it is richer in texture than Mr Trimpi's, richer and yet looser, more what we are used to. Nevertheless, a different discipline sustains it. The poet does not care if what he has to say about Catholic Bavaria can be paraphrased, without total loss, into prose; he does care that such a paraphrase should be logical and accurate, as observation and analysis. This is a poetry no longer worried about securing a territory free from the encroachments of science; plainly poetry must do things science cannot do—otherwise it need not exist—but there can be fruitful and un-flurried interchange between the two, at least on some levels. Indeed, it could be argued that thus to draw upon scientific or philosophical disci-pline would give to poetry a framework to stop it sprawling, the sort of frame which some have argued is to be contrived by the poet only out of a galvanized mythology such as that of Yeats.

Not that there isn't sprawling here—Donald F. Drummond seems a poet of talent who still spreads himself unduly; that is a phenomenon com-mon to all schools of poetry. In Mr Drummond's best pieces—'The Fro-ward Gull', 'On a Book by John Milton, Annotated'—the sprawl is con-trolled and he achieves a minor distinction. In others, such as 'Epitaph for a Reno Woman', the matter is allowed to dissipate itself, not being tightened into the form of epigram. There are other excellent minor pieces by L. F. Gerlach ('Death of a Teacher') and Ann Louise Hayes ('Desolation').

For the young English poet resentful of the tyranny of the 'image' in the restricted sense of 'metaphor' (whether inflated into symbols, worried into conceits, or compressed into 'striking' epithets), this American anthology points in a direction which may provide a wholesome alterna-tive; i.e. it points to a renewed poetry of statement, openly didactic but saved by a sedulously noble diction, from prosiness. Mr Church's book, while it claims to provide some such alternative, seems rather to point in too many directions at once.

Postscript: In a letter to me Yvor Winters demurred at my liking for Wesley Trimpi's poem ('pretty soggy') and at my use of 'Georgian'—'I understand the dynastic reference . . . but am vague about the rest.'

THE POETIC DICTION OF JOHN M. SYNGE

IT HAS recently been argued that the literary achievement of J. M. Synge is meretricious; that his use of Irish speech in his writing was entirely a literary manoeuvre; that, in using that speech, he betrayed his lack of sympathy with the concerns and aspirations of the Irish people; and that his concern with their speech was therefore only superficial. This is a controversy into which I need not enter. In the first place, it is a matter which can be decided only by Irishmen, in which the word of a foreigner such as myself can carry no weight. In the second place, such claims as are made for Synge as a great artist must rest upon his achievement in drama; and here I am only concerned with his volume of *Poems and Translations*, first published in 1909 and recently reprinted. No one, I think, makes any great claims for the intrinsic importance of this part of Synge's work. It is of great historical importance, as a sort of challenge and manifesto, and as such, its significance in the history of the Irish literary movement has been examined by Mr Robert Farren and others. I want to look at it in another light. For Synge's volume is a challenge not only to the Irish poets of his time, but to everyone who tries to write poetry in English at any time. This is what interests me most in his verse, and it is from this point of view that I want to consider him.

This sort of interest was invited by Synge himself. In his preface he wrote as follows:

I have often thought that at the side of the poetic diction, which everyone condemns, modern verse contains a great deal of poetic material, using poetic in the same special sense. The poetry of exaltation will be always the highest; but when men lose their poetic feeling for ordinary life, and cannot write poetry of ordinary things, their exalted poetry is likely to lose its strength of exaltation, in the way men cease to build beautiful churches when they have lost happiness in building shops.

Many of the older poets, such as Villon and Herrick and Burns, used the whole of their personal life as their material, and the verse written in this way was read by strong men, and thieves, and deacons, not by little cliques only. Then, in the town writing of the eighteenth century, ordinary life was put into verse that was not poetry, and when poetry came back with Coleridge and Shelley, it went into verse that was not always human.

In these days poetry is usually a flower of evil or good; but it is the timber of poetry that wears most surely, and there is no timber that has not strong roots among the clay and worms.

Even if we grant that exalted poetry can be kept successful by itself, the strong things of life are needed in poetry also, to show that what is exalted or tender is not made by feeble blood. It may almost be said that before verse can be human again it must learn to be brutal.

The poems which follow were written at different times during the last sixteen or seventeen years, most of them before the views just

stated, with which they have little to do, had come into my head.
I do not agree that 'in the town writing of the eighteenth century, ordinary life was put into verse that was not poetry'. That was a view common enough when Synge wrote, but discredited today. And I think that Dean Swift, for instance, wrote *poetry*, not merely verse. But that is another argument into which it would be idle to enter now. And I mention it only for this reason: that if Synge had wanted traditional authority for his views on poetry, he would have had to go back just to those eighteenth-century poets whom he condemns. For instance, the distinction which he makes, between 'the poetry of exaltation' and 'the poetry of ordinary things', between poetry which is 'exalted' and poetry which is 'tender', is just the distinction habitually made in the eighteenth century between 'the sublime' and 'the pathetic'. And the eighteenth century would have agreed with Synge that sublime poems require a different sort of diction from pathetic poems.

About this question of poetic diction we have very confused ideas. Many readers of poetry, and many poets even, still believe that poetic diction is '*a bad thing*'. They think it is the name for a poetic vice, connected with the false idea that only 'poetical' words can be used in poetry, and that ugly or common words should not be used by poets. Most people today would argue that poetry can be made out of any words, however common or ugly; and that to speak of 'poetic diction' implies that this is not the case. On the other hand the fashion for regarding 'poetic diction' in this way was set by Wordsworth; and people are beginning to realize that what Wordsworth said about this, in his famous preface to *Lyrical Ballads*, was wrong or, at any rate, incomplete. Oliver Goldsmith, for instance, believed in poetic diction. We know from his criticism, and we see from his poetry, that however many poems he wrote he would never have used certain common or ugly words, which he thought too undignified and coarse. Yet 'The Deserted Village' is a great poem, and a poem about ordinary things; and some of the pleasure we get from reading the poem derives from our sense that the language the poet uses is carefully selected, a 'choice' language. It is as if words from the English language were beating at the walls of the poem, asking to be let in, and the poet is keeping them out; we enjoy and appreciate the skill with which he does this, for by using dignified language he gives dignity to the ordinary things of life. We can see, therefore, that poetic diction is not necessarily a bad thing; for certain poets can only make the worthwhile effects they want, by using a careful selection from the language, instead of the whole of it.

If we read Synge's poems with this in mind we see, in fact, that he is using a poetic diction as much as Goldsmith is: ('The Passing of the Shee')

> Adieu, sweet Angus, Maeve, and Fand,
> Ye plumed yet skinny Shee,
> That poets played with hand in hand
> To learn their ecstasy.

> We'll stretch in Red Dan Sally's ditch,
> And drink in Tubber fair,
> Or poach with Red Dan Philly's bitch
> The badger and the hare.

This poem was written 'After looking at one of Æ's pictures'. It expresses Synge's dissatisfaction with the practice of writing poetry about the ancient mythology, and his determination to write about the real life of Ireland in his time. It means too (what amounts to the same thing) that he will avoid the poetic diction of Irish poets at that time, a diction which, as he says, is different from that condemned in eighteenth-century poetry, but no less restricted. And so he uses common or ugly words like 'skinny', 'ditch', 'poach', 'bitch'. The point I am trying to make is that, in doing this, Synge is not, as he seems to think, avoiding poetic diction altogether, but only substituting one sort of diction for another. He is still refusing to use certain words, the words of romantic glamour; he has only chosen to exclude a different set of words. He is still using a poetic diction, a selection of words; he is only making his selection on different principles.

It is true that Synge in his preface warns us against trying to trace in his poems the principles which he lays down. And it is obvious that, as he says, many of his poems were written without those principles in mind. For instance 'In Kerry':

> We heard the thrushes by the shore and sea,
> And saw the golden stars' nativity,
> Then round we went the lane by Thomas Flynn,
> Across the church where bones lie out and in;
> And there I asked beneath a lonely cloud
> Of strange delight, with one bird singing loud,
> What change you'd wrought in graveyard, rock and sea,
> This new wild paradise to wake for me . . .
> Yet knew no more than knew those merry sins
> Had built this stack of thigh-bones, jaws and shins.

Here such words as 'a lonely cloud of strange delight' are just those romantically glamorous words which Synge was later determined not to use. They belong to the poetic diction which he refused. And very many of his poems are of this kind.

Now, as I pointed out, a poetic diction is used because it lends dignity to ordinary things and common human activities. Therefore, the question of what diction a poet shall use depends upon the poet's idea of what it is that gives man his dignity. What, for instance, distinguishes man from the brute? What is the noblest human faculty? Is it man's will, or the force of his emotions, or the discrimination of his senses, or his control of himself by reason? In the eighteenth century, most poets believed that what dignified man and distinguished him from the brute was his faculty of reasoning; so the poetry they wrote was reasonable and intellectual; and the diction they chose included many words for operations of the reason, such as generalization and analysis. In the nineteenth century most poets glorified man's will or his passion or his sensibility, rather than his reason; and their diction changed accordingly. Synge had the novel idea of seeing human dignity not in what distinguishes man from the brute, but in what he and the brute had in common, in a word, in man's brutality: 'It may almost be said that before verse can be human again it must learn to be brutal.'

The clearest example of this deliberate brutality is the ballad 'Danny':

> One night a score of Erris men,
> A score I'm told and nine,
> Said, 'We'll get shut of Danny's noise
> Of girls and widows dyin'.
>
> There's not his like from Binghamstown
> To Boyle and Ballycroy,
> At playing hell on decent girls,
> At beating man and boy.
>
> He's left two pairs of female twins
> Beyond in Killacreest,
> And twice in Crossmolina fair
> He's struck the parish priest.
>
> But we'll come round him in the night
> A mile beyond the Mullet;
> Ten will quench his bloody eyes,
> And ten will choke his gullet.'
>
> It wasn't long till Danny came,
> From Bangor making way,
> And he was damning moon and stars
> And whistling grand and gay.
>
> Till in a gap of hazel glen—
> And not a hare in sight—
> Out lepped the nine-and-twenty lads
> Along his left and right.
>
> Then Danny smashed the nose on Byrne,
> He split the lips on three,
> And bit across the right hand thumb
> Of one Red Shawn Magee.
>
> But seven tripped him up behind,
> And seven kicked before,

And seven squeezed around his throat,
Till Danny kicked no more.

Then some destroyed him with their heels
Some tramped him in the mud,
Some stole his purse and timber pipe,
And some washed off his blood.
    . . . .
And when you're walking out the way
From Bangor to Belmullet,
You'll see a flat cross on a stone
Where men choked Danny's gullet.

To do Synge justice, he proposes this brutality in poetry only as a temporary expedient. He wants to shock the inhumanly exalted poetry of his time by writing poems of all too human degradation; but only in hopes that between the two extremes poetry may come to rest in a central area of human interest and compassion. By thus seeing the poetic tradition in terms of action and reaction, Synge proves himself a thoroughly modern mind. He is taking the same position as Mr T. S. Eliot who is now recanting all his critical pronouncements of twenty years ago, because they were made in a period when poetry had to be brought close to colloquial English, whereas now the situation is quite different and poetry needs to move away from the colloquial once more.

All the same one may doubt whether these changes come about quite as Synge and Mr Eliot would have us believe. I doubt whether poetry is such an independent activity that its language changes according to laws and by a rhythm of its own. After all, words have meaning. And the poets choose among words by reference to their meanings. Therefore, the words chosen by a poet, his diction, will vary according to what he believes about such questions as the nature, the dignity and the destiny of man. For poetry to be semi-permanently concerned with the pathos of common life, the language of poetry must be chosen by reference to a reasoned body of traditional belief about human nature and destiny. Such was the poetry of Goldsmith and his contemporaries, written in a diction which was part and parcel of the religious and philosophical convictions of the age. A poetic diction which acknowledges no authority outside poetry can never produce poems so assured and humane as 'The Deserted Village'. For all Synge may say, his best poems remain illustrations and examples of a critical theory about the language of poetry. Parts of his theory are questionable. But he remains one of the very few poets, writing in English since the end of the eighteenth century, who have talked sense about the question of diction in poetry.

'ESSENTIAL GAUDINESS': THE POEMS
OF WALLACE STEVENS

FOR NEARLY thirty years the Americans have been claiming, in Wallace Stevens, one of the great poets of our age. It seems inexcusable that the English reader has had to wait so long before he could judge the poet for himself. It is especially exasperating when one discovers that Stevens deserves nearly everything that his admirers have claimed for him. He is indeed a poet to be mentioned in the same breath as Eliot and Yeats and Pound. That is his place, and that is the company he must keep. We are called upon now not to assign a status but to define an excellence. And now, at last, generous selections from his work come at the same time from two different publishers. (1) What a pity one or other of them did not appear fifteen years ago.

The third poem in the Fortune Press selection, one of the most important works of Stevens's early period, is entitled 'Le Monocle de Mon Oncle'. (The title is a silly one, like many of Stevens's titles.) The second stanza runs as follows:

A red bird flies across the golden floor.
It is a red bird that seeks out his choir
Among the choirs of wind and wet and wing.
A torrent will fall from him when he finds.
Shall I uncrumple this much-crumpled thing?
I am a man of fortune greeting heirs;
For it has come that thus I greet the spring.
These choirs of welcome choir for me farewell.
No spring can follow past meridian.
Yet you persist with anecdotal bliss
To make believe a starry *connaissance*.

I think it was Yvor Winters who first drew attention to the felicities here. 'Much-crumpled', for instance, gives us (1) a sensuous impression of the wet woods, (2) the difficulty of distinguishing the bird-song from its accompaniments of sounding rain and wind, (3) the staleness for the poet of the hackneyed theme that the bird represents—'Spring', the topic handled so many times by so many poets before.

But now consider a stanza, later in the same poem:

If sex were all, then every trembling hand
Could make us squeak, like dolls, the wished-for words.
But note the unconscionable treachery of fate,
That makes us weep, laugh, grunt and groan, and shout
Doleful heroics, pinching gestures forth
From madness or delight, without regard
To that first, foremost law. Anguishing hour!
Last night, we sat beside a pool of pink,
Clippered with lilies scudding the bright chromes,
Keen to the point of starlight, while a frog
Boomed from his very belly odious chords.

This is thoroughly late-Victorian, poor Browning or poor Meredith. Activity masquerades as agility; violence as energy; it is hectic and monotonous. Refusal to use abstractions brings about locutions neither abstract nor concrete, but fussy blunt gestures—'pinching gestures forth . . .', 'to that first, foremost law'. And the point is that this stanza differs from the stanza about the red bird, only in degree. The stuff is the same, and in the later stanza it has been worn threadbare, that's all.

In fact, 'Le Monocle de Mon Oncle', for all its precious title and a few jazzy superficialities ('connaissance'), is a strikingly old-fashioned poem. This is as true of the movement of thought, as of the versification. 'At forty', the poet asks, 'is it time to grow "spiritual" or "platonic"?' To abjure the world of sense now that in so many ways (e.g. sex) that world is becoming easier to abjure, because it is less insistent and intoxicating? He answers that this is not the case, because the imagination does not decay with the senses, but can create a world as 'real' as the actual world. The poet thinks in Keatsian terms throughout, and the movement of thought is Keatsian too. For instance, between stanzas viii and ix the thought turns upon itself and abdicates the path it had embarked upon, in just the fashion of—'Forlorn! The very word is like a bell. . .' We can imagine the student's painstaking account: 'The poet's mood suddenly changes . . .' It hardly needs to be pointed out that one cannot read *The Waste Land* in this way, or *Hugh Selwyn Mauberley*. When we try to understand 'Le Monocle de Mon Oncle' or 'Sunday Morning', it is a question of 'Do you follow? Have you hold of the thread?' Eliot does not ask us to 'follow' in this way. The process of understanding *The Waste Land* is not a process of pursuit, but of harking back and forth. In short, Stevens's poem, like an ode by Keats, is still *discursive*; it moves from point to point, always forward from first to last. Lose the thread, and you may go back and look for it. In *The Waste Land*, by contrast, it is only when the poem is grasped as a whole that each part of it falls into place.

The difference between 'Sunday Morning' and 'Le Monocle' on the one hand, *The Waste Land* and *Mauberley* on the other, can be put in another way. Except at certain key-points, like the image at the very end of 'Le Monocle' ('That fluttering things have so distinct a shade'), the poetry and the meaning do not coincide. To get at the meaning, you have to go *behind* the poetry, whereas if you go behind Eliot's poetry you have gone behind the meaning too. Understanding 'Le Monocle' is a matter of groping through a dazzle, or stripping off the caparisons, until you come behind the rhetorical magnificence, at a structure of plain sense that is quite lean and skeletal. It is possible to write a prose paraphrase of the poem, without quoting from it more than once; it is not possible to do this with *The Waste Land* or *Mauberley* or Yeats's 'Byzantium'. The gorgeousness, we cannot help but feel, was laid on afterwards, the flesh upon the skeleton, the clothes on top of that. So, if this verse at its best recalls the Keats of the Odes, it is not surprising that at its worst it sounds like some uninspired Victorian imitating the Keatsian manner:

Death is the mother of beauty; hence from her,
Alone, shall come fulfilment to our dreams
And our desires.

Stevens has written, of his poem 'The Emperor of Ice Cream': 'This wears
a deliberately commonplace costume, and yet seems to me to contain
something of the essential gaudiness of poetry; that is the reason why I
like it. . . . I dislike niggling, and like letting myself go.' Once again, the
echo is there. For this recalls nothing so much as the Keatsian tag about
how poetry should 'surprise by a fine excess'. Stevens has insisted repeatedly that he is a 'Romantic' poet. This, together with what we find in the
verse of 'Le Monocle de Mon Oncle', for instance, advises us of one way
in which 'Romantic' may be understood. Stevens is a Romantic in the
sense that Keats was a Romantic—his is to be a poetry of excess, among
other things of rhetoric in excess of meaning, rhetoric for its own sake,
for its 'essential gaudiness'.

Consider, for instance, this poet's thoroughly oldfashioned concern for
the beautiful. It is surely plain that his poems are, or aspire to be, 'beautiful' in a quite straightforward way, winning and seductive. If we were
pressed, presumably we should have to maintain that *Hugh Selwyn Mauberley* is as 'beautiful' as Stevens's 'Sunday Morning'; but in saying that
of Pound's poem we need to use quotation marks, while in applying the
word to Stevens's poem we can let it stand unqualified. Stevens, like
Keats, is saying something and also 'being beautiful'; Pound and Eliot
are saying something as exactly as possible, and the beauty is in the exactness. The beauty of their poetry is in the relation of rhetoric to meaning;
in Stevens the rhetoric aspires to be beautiful for its own sake. So Stevens's
obscurity is of a kind familiar to readers of Keats; it derives from what he
puts into the poem. Pound's and Eliot's obscurity derives from what they
leave out.

Marius Bewley remarks, (2) of a poem called 'Bantams in Pine-Woods',
'The rather brassy appeal of this poem exists at a more superficial level
than its meaning which is extremely difficult to excerpt.' This is no more
than I have argued for; in Stevens's poetry, the meaning and the 'appeal'
are on different levels. The 'appeal' is the appeal of 'beauty' and it exists
in the rhetoric; the meaning is somewhere else, behind or below. The
question is, of course, whether this is typical of Stevens's procedure in
general, or peculiar to this poem and a few others which are less than his
best. I differ from Mr Bewley in finding this feature typical of all Stevens,
even at his best. But then I am not so shocked by it as Mr Bewley is.
'Brassy' and 'superficial', taken together, show that the critic is rather
contemptuous or afraid of this sort of 'appeal'. I am simply grateful for
it. Marius Bewley, being more of a purist, has to draw attention to 'the
ultimate failure of this poem', and to decide 'if the poem means what I
think it does, the meaning fails to be realized in the body of the verse. It
is disowned by the very images that proclaim it.' That 'the meaning fails
to be realized in the body of the verse' is true; that 'it is disowned by the

very images that proclaim it' is another matter, and not true at all. The images will serve, they serve splendidly, and proclaim loudly. They 'own' the meaning all right. All one feels is that they were not the only images, the inevitable choice, to proclaim this meaning: the poet chose these rather than others, and chose well—still, he chose; the images did not choose themselves.

Perhaps the most striking thing about the poetry of Stevens is its metrical conservatism. 'To break the pentameter,' said Pound, 'that was the first heave.' Stevens has never made the break; the greater part of his poetry is written in quite regular iambic pentameters. One can read critic after critic without finding this really striking feature even acknowledged. Yet there can be no adequate account of Stevens that does not take note of one of his most striking eccentricities—his extreme metrical conservatism in an age of revolutionary metrical experiment. If I am right in thinking that a Keatsian allegiance is the clue to Stevens, then his metres are accounted for—his conservatism in this department is part and parcel with his conservatism in structure and in rhetoric. It used to be said that Stevens's poetry could only be appreciated if one were familiar with the poetic experiments of French symbolism. But I do not think that Stevens is 'post-symbolist' in this sense, as T. S. Eliot is. His novelty is all on the surface; he is really very conservative.

By 'Keatsian allegiance' I mean nothing so crass as Keatsian 'influence'; nor do I mean that, for Stevens, Keats is the poet of poets. I take him only as the most distinguished representative of the kind of poetry that Stevens seems to favour. And perhaps, after all, Keats is not the most distinguished name that can be found. It has been said of a line from 'Le Monocle de Mon Oncle' that it has 'the Shakespearean note': 'I am a man of fortune greeting heirs'. This sounds like a line from a play, but this should not make us suppose that it recalls, in its context, Shakespeare the dramatist. If it is true that Stevens at his best can compass 'the Shakespearean note' (and I think it is), what he gets is the note of the sonnets, not of the plays. It is the note of: '. . . the prophetic soul/Of the wide world dreaming on things to come.' F. W. Bateson says that what this means is 'professional soothsayers'. If he is right, then surely the splendour of the language is something in excess of the sense, adding enormously to our pleasure but not assisting (rather, obstructing) our understanding. The same can be said of Stevens at his most splendid: 'We live in an old chaos of the sun/Or old dependency of day and night.' To twist and reverse T. S. Eliot's remark on Dryden, this is poetry that suggests enormously but states little. Consider just the repeated 'old'. Is the repetition necessary to the sense? Or can we say of 'dependency', even, that on scrutiny, it yields as much by way of meaning as it does in terms of euphony and rhythm? This is florid poetry, a poetry of excess; but in saying so, we are saying no more than must be said sometimes of Shakespeare.

And Stevens needs no sponsors. To defend his methods, we need appeal to no authority beyond the poet himself. His view of life is comprehensive and consistent. As critic and as poet, he defines this one inclusive vision. Up to this point, we have examined that part of his vision which may be called his aesthetic, arriving at it in the surest way by seeing how it works out in his artistic practice. But he has, too, a metaphysic, an ethic, an epistemology; and the aesthetic can be seen truly only when it finds its place in the whole structure of the poet's thought. If we see it in that way, we see that his rhetoric of excess corresponds to an ethic of excess, even (the expression is a queer one but may be clearer later) an epistemology of excess. As according to him the best language is excessive language, so the best, the noblest sort of conduct is action in excess. And so the clearest, the truest sort of perception is the perception that exceeds its object, elaborating upon it.

We do not think of Stevens as an ethical poet. William Van O'Connor (3) agrees with Marius Bewley in finding Stevens's central preoccupation to be with imagination, with the role that imagination plays, or should play in the apprehending of reality. That is, they see him first and foremost as epistemologist, and I think they are right—this is indeed the point of leverage. But as one can speak of imaginative perception and imaginative language, so one speaks of 'imaginative' behaviour. And if we understand what Stevens means by 'imagination', we may understand not only what perception he trusts and what language he tries for, but also what behaviour he recommends. Marius Bewley has brilliantly demonstrated how Stevens has gradually built up for himself in his earlier poems a vocabulary of personal symbols which is, by the time he does his later work, astonishingly copious, and finely articulated. One advantage of such a symbolic vocabulary is in the way it provides the poet with deliberate ambiguities. When he has perfected such a personal symbolism, he can write sentences which have meaning on more than one level, so that a statement about the conditions of human perception is also a statement about the conditions of human action.

Both Mr Bewley and Mr O'Connor compare Stevens's view of imagination with Coleridge's. Mr O'Connor throws out, apparently at random, a valuable observation: 'Coleridge believes the power of imagination is denied to "the sensual and the proud"; there is no reason to think that Stevens does.'

Indeed, there is not. There is, on the contrary, every reason to think that Stevens takes one sort of pride as the surest evidence of imagination. For him, as for many Romantics, the imaginative man is the proud man. He esteems in men the quality of *panache*, the capacity for making large gestures, conspicuous self-expression, in manner and clothes as in language. The grand manner expresses itself in action as in speech. One may live with style, as one may write with style, and Stevens in his criticism has set great store by this fruitful ambiguity. As Mr O'Connor remarks, of a poem called 'The Weeping Burgher': 'The verities are "sorry verities". We are reconciled to them by "excess", by style.' Yes, we come to terms with the world by going beyond it, by wearing our hat at a rakish angle,

by elaborate movements of the arm or wrist. It is only so that we perceive it truly, by letting our imagination colour our perceptions. In the
same way it is only so that we act in the world with dignity, by letting
our imagination colour our actions in excess of what circumstances force
upon us. And it is only so that we recreate it in the beauty of poetry, by
letting our imagination colour our words in excess of what bare meaning
demands of us. Style, imagination, rhetoric, excess—these are the basic
terms of Stevens's ethic, as of his epistemology and his aesthetics.

We see this in Stevens's own life. Mr O'Connor heads his first chapter
'Stevens as Legend'. Precisely. Stevens is a legendary figure; he has taken
care that he should be, as Byron and Yeats did before him. Perhaps some
of the legend was built up around him, wished upon him by others. But
not all. It is surely clear, for instance, that some of the early poems that
have not worn well, the selfconsciously cryptic or culpably ambiguous
pieces like 'Anecdote of the Jar', 'Metaphors of a Magnifico', even 'Bantams
in Pine-Woods', are Stevens's contributions to the legend. They are good
for the legend, if they are not good poems—again, like many poems by
Byron. Each of these poems is 'a grand gesture', a too deliberate bow, a
too exquisite formality; they are Stevens's substitutes for the cape and
the flowing tie.

At this point I must take issue with Marius Bewley. He quotes himself,
and analyses, 'The Pastor Caballero', where—

> The sweeping brim of the hat
> Makes of the form Most Merciful Capitan

> If the observer says so: grandiloquent
> Locution of a hand in rhapsody.

He quotes from 'Infanta Marina':

> She made of the motions of her wrist
> The grandiose gestures
> Of her thought.

And yet he can write of the jar in 'Anecdote of the Jar', 'It had style (more
properly, manner or affectation) rather than reality.' This diminuendo,
from 'style' through 'manner' to 'affectation', seems to me at variance
with the whole course of Stevens's thought, as of his poetic practice. For
Stevens, 'style', whether in life or literature, is only 'affectation' or 'man-
nerism' that succeeds. Admittedly the splendid hat of 'The Pastor Caballero'
is examined from the point of view of the beholder, not the wearer. But
observe that 'Infanta Marina' makes gestures of thought not *with* the motions of her wrist, but *of* those motions. The movement of the wrist does
not express the motions of the mind; it invokes them and creates them.
She behaves grandly not because she thinks grandly, but in order to do so.
So, in 'Le Monocle de Mon Oncle', the poet's solution for the drabness
and sterility that comes upon him, is 'bravura', 'the music and manner of
the paladins'. If a man can no longer think and feel grandiosely, then he
acts grandiosely or he makes a grandiose speech, and this renovates and

exalts his thinking and his feeling. The cure for sterility is to act and speak as if it did not exist; by so doing, one destroys it.

Stevens is always mannered and affected. The affectation of his poorer poems reflects back out of the poetry upon Stevens the private individual; in his better pieces the affectation succeeds and becomes style because it stays in the poetry and builds up the public and representative figure of the poet. Where the affectation is a way of dealing with experience, with the theme of the poem, it justifies itself as poetic style; where it is a way of dealing with society, represented by the reader, it may be justified in terms of social behaviour, but not in terms of poetry.

This account, I fear, will appear laboured. And yet it is the merest scratching of the surface, oversimplifying at every point a weave so rich and ramifying that it calls for volumes of explication. I hope that at least it will show I am nothing if not profoundly grateful for the significant beauty that Stevens so generously provides. Only if that point is taken, can I go on to admit that, for my own part, I think the very greatest poetry is more chaste, less florid than this. It would seem to follow that I prefer an ethic more austere, a heroism less confounded with 'panache'. That inference, too, I do not refuse. Yet it is Stevens's achievement that whenever we pick up his poems, he makes such reservations seem graceless and niggling. He is a great poet indeed.

Postscript: This reads oddly now, because it was addressed to a public that thought 'the modern', whatever else it was, was 'unromantic'. For many years now on the contrary American critics like Harold Bloom have contended that the (American) 'modern' is continuous with the (American, i.e. Emersonian) 'romantic'; and so they find Stevens much less in need of excuses than for instance Eliot. Accordingly I should now probably be more captious about Stevens than I was when I wrote this.

PROFESSOR HELLER AND THE BOOTS

I CANNOT read German. And I was the more surprised to find that one of the best books of criticism I read last year—I mean one of those that gave me the most pleasure—was Erich Heller's *The Disinherited Mind*, which deals exclusively with German authors. That my ignorance, in great measure, of these authors did not prevent me from enjoying Heller's book, seems to me the best proof of how good it is. Some purists of course might object that criticism is only good in so far as it demands recourse to the texts it offers to deal with. For my own part I think that is a good rule of thumb, in fact indispensable, but that there is a certain rare kind of criticism which transcends it. And *The Disinherited Mind* belongs, for me, in that rare class.

For the sake of argument, though, I want to take Heller at his least impressive, where the apocalyptic undertow of his thought becomes too rapid and insistent, so that he rides his thesis too hard:

The predicament of the symbol in our age is caused by a split between 'reality' and what it signifies. There is no more any commonly accepted symbolic or transcendent order of things. What the modern mind perceives as order is established through the tidy relationship between things themselves. In one word: the only conceivable order is positivist-scientific. If there is still a—no doubt, diminishing—demand for the fuller reality of the symbol, then it must be provided for by the unsolicited gifts of art. But in the sphere of art the symbolic substance, dismissed from its disciplined commitments to 'reality', dissolves into incoherence, ready to attach itself to any fragment of experience, invading it with irresistible power, so that a pair of boots, or a chair in the painter's attic, or a single tree on a slope which the poet passes, or an obscure inscription in a Venetian church, may suddenly become the precariously unstable centre of an otherwise unfocused universe. Since 'the great words from the time when what *really* happened was still visible, are no longer for us' (as Rilke once put it in a Requiem for a young poet), the 'little words' have to carry an excessive freight of symbolic significance. No wonder that they are slow in delivering it. They are all but incommunicable private symbols, established beyond any doubt as symbols by the quality and intensity of artistic experience behind them, but lacking in any representative properties. Such is the economy of human consciousness that the positivist impoverishment of the one region produces anarchy in the other. In the end, atomic lawlessness is bound to prevail in both.

The point of taking Heller at his worst is that then he becomes representative. And it requires no extensive acquaintance with contemporary British and American criticism, especially academic criticism, to recognize that the view Heller puts forward here is by now almost commonplace. The prevailing tone of criticism today is elegiac, even nostalgic. It is taken for granted that the literature of our own day stands in need of some excuse. And the excuse found for it is the absence of any coherent symbolism, and unified or 'integrated' world-picture, such as Dante had, and Shakespeare. It is explained that as the ambitious writer cannot get on without some mythology or symbolic system of this kind, the really great creative minds nowadays have to construct, by some prodigious effort of imagination, a whole private 'world-picture' or mythology or 'religion' of their own. This is what Heller finds in Rilke, and others have found the same sort of thing nearer home, in Yeats. It is crudely 'Science', that is to say a spread of positivist-scientific habits and attitudes, and the great prestige these now enjoy, that is blamed for this additional and unprecedented burden nowadays laid on the shoulders of the poet. And after all the pains that the Rilkes and Yeatses take, it appears that what they get out of it is even so only a second-best. For their mythologies, it is pointed out, however elaborate and persuasive their formulation, remain to some extent private, not just obscure but arbitrary and provisional; they can never be so compelling as the world-pictures of the past, secured by the common consent of an age or of many ages.

Now it cannot be denied that there is some truth in this. It is obvious that the modern poet is at a disadvantage in lacking any one mythology, whether Christian, classical or whatever else, to which he knows he may safely allude in confidence that the majority of his readers will pick up the allusion. And the historical perspectives opened up by this sort of argument are frequently illuminating or at least challenging. Nevertheless it contains too many confusions to merit the sort of orthodoxy it has achieved in literary circles.

For instance, the crucial confusion in Heller's statement of the position is between poetry and poems. He admits that the 'little words', by which I understand the names of objects and situations encountered by chance and taking on for the poet a symbolic weight not sanctioned by tradition, are 'established beyond any doubt as symbols by the quality and intensity of artistic experience behind them.' But is it not disingenuous to link together in this way 'quality' and 'intensity'? The critic is careful not to imply that quality is determined by intensity, but one certainly gets the impression, at least on a careless reading, that a poem is better the more heady and exciting it is. (The better the poem, the bigger the thrill.) At any rate 'quality' begs the question, whether it is not recognized in any work of art as *communicated order*. Even 'intensity', if we free it from its associations of 'thrill' and of the poem as something analogous to an injection, a shot in the arm, surely presupposes, in the same way, an ordering of experience. We know we have 'quality and intensity of artistic experience' in a poem, only when we have the sense of an ordering of experience. It is not the quality and intensity that validates the symbols from the reader's point of view; it is the symbols that, by establishing order, testify to the intensity not so much behind as in them. In pretending that a non-traditional symbol requires to be justified by something else in or behind the poem, Heller shows his hand. He is asking for order in the world of poetry, and is not satisfied with order in the world of each poem. Indeed, it is not at all clear that he is even aware of the latter, or capable of responding to it. For it is characteristic of all such speculations that they consider the world of poetry as if it were something else than a world of poems. It is not even true that we no longer have 'representative symbols' in our poetry—consider the symbols of the 'mirror' and the 'island' in the poetry of the thirties; what *is* true is that we no longer have a representative *system* of such symbols. And this means that we can no longer hope for a poem whose world will be coterminous with the world of poetry and the world of thought, as the *Divine Comedy* is.

This suggests the other objection, that Heller's historical perspective is foreshortened. If we take over and apply to English poetry the scheme that Heller draws out of German poetry (and this is fair, for it is not suggested that what he finds is a peculiarly German phenomenon), I think we find that the apocalyptic state of affairs he paints for us has obtained for a very long time indeed, much longer than he allows for. For it is Newton that he takes to mark the point at which all the earlier 'world-pictures' gave way to the positivist-scientific. But surely, long before Newton and before Bacon even, in Wyatt and in Chaucer, we can already see the 'little words' taking over the function of the 'great words'.

This point has been recently made by Miss Kathleen Nott in her very controversial book, *The Emperor's Clothes*. What it amounts to, as she shows, is that in so far as the scientific method is a matter of observation followed by inference and guided by hypothesis, it has a much longer history than is allowed for by Professor Willey, for instance, when he treats the demand for scientific explanation as a seventeenth-century novelty. Miss Nott maintains that the scientific habits of thought are as old as the human mind itself, and she argues further that the poet's characteristic attitudes are much nearer to the scientist's than to the theologian's—a contention with which I sympathize. Unfortunately *The Emperor's Clothes* suffers, to my mind, from concentrating too exclusively on those who adapt views like Professor Heller's to serve the ends of instituted Christianity. I, too, dislike Christian apologetics masquerading as literary criticism, but the literary missionaries have no monopoly in either dislike for science or nostalgia for lost symbolic structures. Moreover, while it may be true that Professor Willey and Mr Eliot are ignorant of the true nature of that scientific method they dislike, Miss Nott knows just as little about the true nature of Christian dogma and about what goes on in the minds of professing Christians. Finally she has, I think, an inadequate idea of the problems of poetic style, all of which she boils down to the hard and fast principle, also maintained apparently by W. R. Rodgers, that in poetry the concrete word is always and everywhere better than the abstraction.

For all these reasons I prefer to set against Professor Heller some admittedly cryptic sentences from the German poet Gottfried Benn, writing against 'Rilkeism':

A great new tidal wave sweeps across the continent: Döblin, Toynbee,

Eliot, Jünger: all of it retrogression, noble bearing but a slackening
of style, conformism. God, I wrote once, is bad as a principle of style.
To me, prayer and humility seem arrogant pretensions; they presuppose
my existence, which is precisely what I doubt: something passes through
me, that is all.

Man must be reassembled on a broad basis—out of idioms, pointless
reference, niceties. His 'act' will be kept going by formal tricks, the repetition of words and motifs—whims will be driven in like nails and
whole trains of thought suspended therefrom. Now they are marshalled, geography invoked, reveries indulged and abandoned. No
longer are things woven into a psychological fabric; everything is
touched upon, nothing followed through . . .

I agree with Gottfried Benn, if I understand him properly, in being dis-
satisfied with even such representative symbols as we have. When in a
modern English poem I encounter 'the island' or 'the mirrors' I fear the
worst, for in proportion as these are 'representative', they are not freshly
lived and felt, but rhetorical reach-me-down. What I most like in poetry
are what Benn calls 'whims driven in like nails and whole trains of thought
suspended therefrom', or, in Heller's terms, the 'pair of boots' that 'suddenly become the precariously unstable centre of an otherwise unfocused
universe.' And in what sense is this centre 'unstable' (and not just that,
but precariously that, i.e., 'precariously precarious')? Certainly it is less
stable than Dante's centre, but is it any less stable than the old leech-
gatherer that stands at the centre of Wordsworth's 'Resolution and Independence', or the charred paper flapping in the grate at the centre of
Coleridge's 'Frost at Midnight'? 'The centre cannot hold . . .' Any number
of centres can hold for any number of poems; no centre can hold together the whole fabric of poetry, as Dante's centre could. If in saying this I
am concerned for poems rather than poetry, I can't see that that would
justify Professor Heller in thinking me fatally infected with 'positivist-
scientific' habits. Dr Tillyard himself, it seems, would not now maintain
that even Shakespeare had, in the sense that Heller wants, a centre for his
poetic world: in his world the crystal spheres revolved musically round a
centre, but that centre would not hold the Machiavellian novelties that
Shakespeare knew and was concerned about.

The trouble is that, in looking for a centre for poetry, a system of
symbols, too many poets seem to leave out the centres from each of their
poems, the symbol that is true for that poem, and perhaps for that poem
only. This is what Benn means, I take it, by saying that Heller's sort of
concern leads to a slackening of style. And he is quite right. A slackening
of style in that crucial sense comes of arrogance, of too much concern
for style in the other sense of 'noble bearing', that is, for consistency, for
cutting a self-consistent 'great figure'. A concern for poetry turns out too
often to be a concern for the poet and the effect he is making; but a concern for *poems* leads the poet to an image like the Romantic image of the
Aeolian harp, a view of the poet as no more than the instrument through

which the wind of inspiration intermittently plays. If every poem the poet writes is a new visitation, it is highly unlikely that the poems will be consistent one with another, whether in terms of a single symbolic structure, or as stages in an interesting development of vision, to be traced admiringly by later commentators. 'Something passes through me, that is.all.'

Up to a point, what Gottfried Benn is demanding, what for Erich Heller is not good enough, is the poetry that can be called in the fullest sense 'occasional' as opposed to mythological or mythopoeic. And it is in accordance with Benn's feeling that in demanding this he is swimming against the tide, that W. H. Auden should see at the present time a marked swing away from the occasional and the anecdotal in verse to the mythopoeic. (He remarks on this in his preface to the poems of W. S. Merwin.) And I think it is obvious that, as regards English poetry at any rate, Auden is right. Edith Sitwell, that reliable barometer of changing fashions, shows in all her recent writing an attempt to build up a private vocabulary of traditional symbols given new meanings or interrelated in a new way; Kathleen Raine, a better poet, is doing the same; while there are any number of selfconsciously 'Christian' poets. Indeed there is now widely entertained a new hope, which Heller, to do him justice, apparently does not share, that the private mythologies may turn out to be public after all. For from Jung the poet learns about the hypothetical 'collective unconscious'; and an uncritical reading of some of the older anthropologists or of Robert Graves's *White Goddess* suggests that if the poet, looking for symbols, can dredge deep enough in his own mind, he comes across the archetypes, eternally recurrent myths and symbols which underlie all Christian and other mythologies just as they underlie the dreams of the sleeping individual.

We have to be careful here. For my part I am not maintaining that all poetry nowadays has to be occasional, that traditional symbols should never be used. What matters is that the poet, in using them, should have his eye on the particular poem he is making as for the moment an end in itself, and not as one more brick laid in the construction of a private or a public temple. This would make room, for instance, for the best poems of Edwin Muir, in which the traditional symbols are used as valid only for one poem at a time. A good poem by Muir is thus an emblem, in which the symbol is immobilized in a selfsufficient heraldic stance; it is not one more fable to go with the rest towards the creation of a pantheon.

The danger with any poetic programme that puts its faith in the collective unconscious and goes in hopes of reaching the archetypes is the view which it encourages of poetic composition as coming out of a willed suspension of the waking faculties. Those who hold by this view often subscribe themselves Romantics, and stick the label 'anti-Romantic' on all who insist on the necessity for the poet to remain not less but infinitely more wide-awake that other people. 'Kubla Khan' notwithstanding (Coleridge, it will be remembered, called that 'a psychological curiosity'), the great Romantic poets seem to me to stand for an attitude of humility at the opposite pole from the arrogance of the mythopoeic poet of today. I have pointed to the Romantic image of the Aeolian harp as a case in point.

At first glance, Yeats seems a very clear case of most of the attitudes I have tried to tilt against. And as I have remarked he is in fact often called in evidence by people who make a similar diagnosis to Heller's. He constructed a private pantheon and even created a sacred book for the cult before he began to write poems with the symbols thus made and organized. He tried to be, very deliberately, a 'great figure'. And he disliked Newton and Locke, using Berkeley as a stick to beat them with. And yet people seem to forget, especially if they are critics with an axe to grind, that he wrote many other poems besides 'Byzantium'. Even in the oldfashioned sense, he was a great occasional poet; and even his mythopoeic poems are drawing continually upon common experience, on whims, on quirks and oddities like the girl doing a tinker's shuffle picked up on the street, or on things he merely *happened* to see or to remember, like Loie Fuller's Chinese dancers.

Certainly it is unfair to ask the poet to put into each poem everything that is required for the understanding of it, though that is the position forced upon any poet today who seriously wants to communicate with his readers. This demand has never been made of poets before. There was always hitherto a field of common knowledge on which the poet could draw for allusions, to give his work an extra dimension. That has gone now, and it is a serious matter. But the way out of it is not for the poet either to refuse to acknowledge the fact that old myths and symbols are dead (and they are dead poetically even if people still know them, as soon as they are unable to respond to them imaginatively), or to construct a private range of symbols of his own. The way out of the impasse is to make up for the lost dimension.

The situation is not unprecedented. It occurred once before, at any rate so far as English poetry is concerned, in 1798. When poets and critics nowadays appeal to the Romantics, it is safe to assume nearly always that they do not mean by that the Wordsworth of *Lyrical Ballads* or the Coleridge of 'Frost at Midnight' and the other conversation-poems. This is certainly true if the appeal comes, as it often does, in the midst of an elegiac argument about lost mythologies or 'world-pictures' or systems of representative symbols. For it was Wordsworth, surely, and Coleridge, who showed how poets could do without these things if they had to, merely by keeping their eyes skinned and noting how they themselves responded to the crassest and tritest features in the world about them. In a word, they showed how poetry could afford to be realistic in the most obvious and straightforward way. For the eighteenth century, so often taken to be essentially unpoetical because (so the argument runs) infected with Newtonian and Lockean habits, had in fact a singularly coherent and stable mythology on which to draw in poetry. This mythology or 'world-picture' is the one we allude to, usually without noticing it, whenever we call this the Augustan age. The field of force (as it has been called) that lay behind almost every eighteenth-century poem before Blake, was the age of Augustan Rome, an ideally civilized state of society against which their own age could be measured and found, usually, wanting. The literature and history of Augustan Rome was so well known to the poetry-reading public of the eighteenth century that the eighteenth-century English poet could make the sketchiest, most unobtrusive allusion to it, by perhaps no more than a Virgilian or Horatian turn of phrase, and rest assured that most of his readers would pick it up. Wordsworth and Coleridge threw overboard all this classical machinery. What we have instead in a poem such as 'Frost at Midnight' is the homely feature made strange, the apparently random and accidental made inevitable and just, the apparently wayward development coming round in a significant curve. What we have in fact is Professor Heller's 'pair of boots', which can never be the centre of a world of poetry but can be the centre of the world of a poem.

I will admit that I am for my own part so enamoured of the quirky occasional in poetry that I am never fully satisfied by even so fine a poem as David Gascoyne's 'Ecce Homo'. It is not of course that it does not move me, Christ hanging on the cross. The symbol moves me too much, in and by itself. I am almost as much moved by a hymn like 'There is a green hill far away'. It is the symbol that is doing all the work; all the poetry can do is to make itself scarce. And that, of course, is not so easy as it sounds. In fact this may be just a blind spot on my part. But it only adds point to my main disagreement with Professor Heller. I will state it again for the last time by saying that, while Dante is no doubt a classic in the strict sense of a permanent model from whom all poets at all times have something to learn, he is doing us no good if he teaches us to reach after what can no longer be grasped, if in fact he teaches us to be too—well, too big for our boots.

Postscript: Since writing this I have been at least half persuaded by Donald Greene's contention that we might stop calling our eighteenth century 'Augustan' and call it instead 'Augustinian'; in other words that the world-picture which held together for that century, as it held together no longer for Wordsworth and Coleridge, was much less 'Roman' than it was *Christian*.

POETRY, OR POEMS?

FOR THE young man of my generation who was interested at all keenly in poetry, to discover the criticism of R. F. Blackmur was a turning-point and something of a revelation. But ten or fifteen years ago the revelation was partial and in some ways frustrating, because many of the poets by whom Mr Blackmur laid most store, such as Wallace Stevens and Hart Crane and Allen Tate, were known to us only by a couple of poems in the *Faber Book of Modern Verse*. Moreover, our discovery of Mr Blackmur himself was partial too, and usually belated; for he, like the poets he talked about, had not at that time found a British publisher, and we came across his work only in the few copies of his American publications that came our way. His two books were especially hard to come by, and more often we knew him only from articles in American magazines like the *Kenyon Review* or the *Sewanee Review*, to which as undergraduates we could not afford to subscribe. At long last he has now appeared from a London publishing house, (1) and in the meantime the American poets he wrote about have also found British publishers—though, incidentally, we still await a British edition of the poems of Hart Crane.

The time-lag is still regrettable, for the enthusiast who now encounters Mr Blackmur for the first time will hardly welcome him as we did. Partly this is because the poets whom he wrote of in the thirties were then the latest thing, whereas now they almost have the status of accepted classics. The poetic situations to which they responded were very different from those that the contemporary poet is faced with; and so they seem already quite remote. But, more important, Mr Blackmur as a critic has not improved with the years. The volume that now appears contains much of his recent writing as well as his earlier work, and this later material shows such a falling away from the earlier that a new reader will find himself at best forced to take the rough with the smooth. To me, this falling away is so obvious that the most pressing task seems to be to define it and if possible to account for it.

This is unfortunate, however, because to insist on the limitations and (more than that) the perversities of the later essays is likely to dissuade the new reader from looking even at the earlier ones. And so it is in place to say at once that the essays here reprinted from the two earlier volumes are as good as ever they were and only improve with keeping. In fact this is not quite true of all of them: the account of Ezra Pound which was acceptable in 1933, when only *A Draft of Thirty Cantos* had appeared, is now, since Hugh Kenner's book on Pound, thoroughly out of date; and it is not easy to excuse Mr Blackmur for reprinting it. But the essays on Wallace Stevens, on Marianne Moore, on Hart Crane, are still much the best introductions to the work of these poets. Best of all is the mildly debunking essay of 1937 on Emily Dickinson, which looks as if it ought to be definitive. All in all, the best advice one can give to a reader meeting Mr Blackmur for the first time in this volume is to urge him to take particular notice of the dates usefully printed at the end of each section.

There is much to be said for taking these not in their printed order but in their chronological order, trusting most the Blackmur of the thirties, taking ever larger pinches of salt as he progresses through the forties up to the present time.

The question of Mr Blackmur's deterioration is of particular interest and importance because there are grounds for thinking that it is part and parcel of a larger tendency. Some would maintain that this falling away can be paralleled in the work of other critics whose names have been often associated with Mr Blackmur's as co-workers with him in a fairly conscious movement, the movement, already too much argued over, labelled 'The New Criticism'. As the New Criticism becomes the Old Criticism, it seems as if for many people it is belying its earlier promise. It is easy to dismiss this as just a swing of the pendulum of fashion, as a case of familiarity breeding contempt. But I do not think this is the case—not, at least, as it concerns Mr Blackmur in particular. Mr Blackmur seems to have gone off the rails. I am content to leave it an open question whether New Criticism as a whole has gone off the rails in the same way and roughly the same place.

The change in Mr Blackmur can be seen most obviously in his own prose-style; and the opacity of his later style is what has attracted most attention, so far as I can see, from his American reviewers. But just because a radical change in style is nearly always the symptom of a change in the attitudes of the writer, it may be just as well to bypass the style for the moment and strike at once to the heart of the matter. Now the heart of the matter where literary criticism is concerned is, in my view, always *in practice*, in the manner of approach to a specific text. In a critic so conscious of his role as Mr Blackmur these changes in approach always arise from or else are buttressed by changes in theory—in his theories about what poetry is and what criticism is. And, sure enough, there are to be noted far-reaching changes in Mr Blackmur's theories about literature. But these too I will defer for later attention and give a concrete example of how he has changed his ways of dealing with a poem or rather, as it happens, with a line of poetry.

The line is Ezra Pound's: 'In the gloom, the gold gathers the light against it.' In 1931, discussing the line by the way in the course of an essay on Wallace Stevens (p. 234 of the present volume), Mr Blackmur noted that the line presents a visual image, yet 'not physical observation, but something to be seen in the mind's eye'; and that it is differentiated from physical observation by 'the non-visual associations of a single word —*gathers*, which in the active voice has an air of intention.' In 1946, in a short essay specifically on Pound (pp. 155-6 of this volume), Mr Blackmur asks:

> . . . does it not commit itself in the memory by coming as an absolute image, good anywhere the writs of language run, by the most ordinary possible means, the fused sequences of two trains of alliteration, the one guttural and the other dental? Does it not also, and more important,

clinch the alliteration and the image by displaying itself, as Pound used
to argue all verse ought to display itself, in the sequence, not of the
metronome, but of the musical phrase? Do we not come, thus, on a
true blank verse line where something, which we here call music, lasts
when the words have stopped, and which locks, or gears, the words
together when they are spoken?

The differences, I submit, are striking. And the most obvious difference is
quite simply that in 1931 Mr Blackmur was looking for poetry in a play
of meanings; fifteen years later he is looking for it in a play of sounds.

He is quite deliberate about this, as we see if we refer to an essay falling
between the two considered. In 'W. B. Yeats: Between Myth and Philosophy' (1942), he quotes from Yeats's 'Under Ben Bulben':

> Measurement began our might;
> Forms a stark Egyptian thought,
> Forms that gentler Phidias wrought.
> Michael Angelo left a proof
> On the Sistine Chapel roof,
> Where but half-awakened Adam
> Can disturb globe-trotting Madam
> Till her bowels are in heat,
> *Proof that there's a purpose set*
> *Before the secret working mind:*
> *Profane perfection of mankind.*

Mr Blackmur is led to 'insist' (p. 115) that all the lines here, with the exception of the three italicized, 'could have as well been different, most of
all could have been their own opposite without injury to the meaning
which is under the lines.' So, earlier in the same essay, he has played
about with the last stanza of another late poem by Yeats, 'The Apparitions', reversing the meaning of line after line and maintaining that to
these lines of his, no less than to the lines of Yeats, the two-line refrain
is appropriate. And he concludes (pp. 111, 112):

> Is not the precision of the poem for the most part a long way under
> the precision of the words? Do not the words involve their own oppo-
> sites, indeed drag after them into being their own opposites, not for
> contradiction but for development? After such queries we can return
> to the poem as it is, and know it all the better so, and know that we
> have not altered, even tentatively, anything of its actual character by
> playing with what is after all merely its notation. We have come nearer,
> rather, to the cry, the gesture, the metaphor of identity, which as it
> invades the words, and whichever words, is the poem we want.

Now it is less than fair to Mr Blackmur thus to tear his audacious conclu-
sions out of the fabric of very subtle and close argument. This essay on
Yeats, I am inclined to think, was the turning-point for him. And he
ought to get credit for trying to deal with these wayward late lyrics by
Yeats which a critic more circumspect would have disingenuously avoided.
His phrasing is less pretentious than it seems; 'metaphor of identity', for

instance, refers back to a discussion on the significance of refrain in general. Moreover, Yeats may be a special case; to say that 'the lines could
have been their own opposites without injury to the meaning' appears
less outrageous when we remember how Yeats's mind moved naturally
in terms of paradoxes, of mask and anti-mask, of gyrations through
phases, from dark to light and back again. Yet, when all is said and done,
this view that in a poem, in *any* poem, the words are 'merely its notation'
—how can we describe it as anything but outrageous?

Some may not agree. Plenty of people are ready to believe that the soul
of a poem, its true value and life, is unutterable, escapes analysis, is magic
and mystery. Perhaps, in fact, there is hardly anyone who, being really
honest with himself, would deny this. Yet if we feel that in the normal
way we would go to almost any lengths rather than admit it, we are
not thereby being inconsistent or dishonest. For we have every reason to
be suspicious. Yes, we would all agree of course that something escapes
analysis, is mysterious. But where, how soon in our reflections, how near
the surface of the poem, does the magic start, the mystery supervene?
And nearly always one finds, when people take up this position, that
they mean the magic starts from the word go. The magic and the mystery
are the smoke-screen for the enemies of criticism and of poetry. They
start by asking us to admit that somewhere in the poem there is mystery;
but always what they really mean is that it is a mystery all through. If it
is, then all critics are parasites and charlatans. And this is always the conclusion they drive at. For it nearly always turns out that the smoke-screen
is really covering the getaway of some poet or poets whose work, as their
apologists know very well, won't stand up to the critic's scrutiny.

I am not imputing these motives to Mr Blackmur. On the contrary, he
knows the tactic of old and he knows how to deal with it—he can be seen
dispersing just such a smoke-screen so as to get within range of Emily
Dickinson. Thirty years ago hardly anybody could do more before a
poem than (in all sincerity, often enough) throw up his arms and sigh
'Unaccountable' or 'Sheer magic'. Twenty years ago Mr Blackmur was
one of the critics—Richards was another, Empson, Leavis, Ransom, no
need to call the roll—who, in their different ways, and each within his
own limitations, showed us how to penetrate a great deal further than
that. They rolled back the frontier of magic, and in doing so provided
some clues how to distinguish white magic from black, the honest mystery from the dishonest one. Yet now Mr Blackmur is rolling the magic
forward again until it broods over every inch of the poem.

Few would deny that the enormous improvement in critical techniques,
the advance made in the last few decades, has cost something. The study
of ambiguity in poetry has not kept count of the virtues of plainness and
clarity, and this disproportion is only now perhaps being corrected. In
the same way there is no doubt that the attention paid to the semantics
of poetry, to the poem as a structure of meanings, has meant that another
aspect, the poem as a structure of sounds and rhythms, has sometimes

been neglected. And probably this is the disproportion that Mr Blackmur is trying to redress. But after all some techniques are available even here. Prosody, for instance, may be rusty (though at least one good critic, Mr Yvor Winters, has kept it in repair), but it is traditionally the tool for getting somewhere on the side of poetry that slopes towards music. Mr Blackmur, however, disdains it and will let us get no nearer to the mystery than a ritual incantation of Pound's 'composing in the sequence of the musical phrase'. And here we can hardly think anything but the worst, especially when he presents 'In the gloom, the gold gathers the light against it' as 'a true blank verse line'. If this is a sample of Mr Blackmur's prosody, there is no wonder he is chary of resorting to it.

Yet there is more to it than that. This keeping of the reader at a distance seems to be the essential motive behind all Mr Blackmur's later writing. It informs his style. This was always difficult, chiefly because it was so copious. But lately, influenced by the prefaces of Henry James, it is more full than ever of elegant variation. Mr Blackmur can always 'put it another way', and always does so. 'To put it another way,' or 'What I have been saying is this,' are almost his trademarks. And it is this which enables him to circle his subject time and again, in very nearly the same track, while giving the illusion that he is moving in for a kill which never comes. The incantations—of certain lines of verse as well as of certain critical pronouncements—are offered as 'keys', but really they are only the same old landmarks coming round into sight again as we complete one more tedious circuit. The thing at the centre—thus the implication—is unutterable. The hush which falls, the ceremonious invocations of great names, the general impression that what goes on is terribly important and terribly difficult (one false step and we are done for)—all this creates the effect of a devotional act. And indeed Mr Blackmur, who is so respectful to the authority of Mr Eliot, seems perilously close sometimes to falling foul of the gibes that his master has cast at Matthew Arnold. For him too, as on Mr Eliot's showing for Arnold, poetry seems to be attracting to itself the emotions and expectations proper only to religion. We remember Mr Eliot's warning that the one cannot be substituted for the other, and that to try to do this is to do justice to neither.

For him too, as for Arnold, it is poetry that has to carry this burden of religious feeling deflected from its proper object. Poetry, not poems; poetry, that is, considered not as the body of poems that have been or may be achieved, but as a quality or a condition of language never exemplified without some adulteration in even the greatest poems, seen there only by glimpses, by fits and starts, a fortunate visitation on some one line or snatch of lines. This comes out very clearly if we return to the line of Pound with which we started, and compare again Mr Blackmur's two treatments of it, early and late. In the early essay the line from Pound, together with other extracts from his work, is presented, alongside similar examples from Mr Eliot and from Wallace Stevens, precisely for limited comparison—to isolate what is unique to Stevens. In the later essay the line is used as a tuning-fork, to ring out the true poetic note by which, while it rings in our minds, other lines can be heard as sharp or flat. It is used in fact precisely in the manner of Arnold's by now notorious 'touchstones', and it begs the same question—whether it can be anything but misleading thus, for other than strictly limited purposes, to tear poetic lines out of their contexts. We can be sure that Mr Blackmur has taken note of the question and has decided to take the risk—or rather has decided that no risk is involved. For he declares flatly (p. 206): 'The point is, the poem is not as near full response as the language the poem uses. All poems are imperfect.'

It is from this point of view that we see the logic of the critic's development. For in the thirties, following I. A. Richards, he was much concerned with the relationship between poetry and belief. And this concern took the form of disentangling, for instance, in Yeats's later poems, the unacceptable structure of magical belief from the grandly acceptable poetry that structure made possible; or, for another instance, deciding how a non-Christian reader could respond to Christian poetry. Already, that is, the poetry in the poem was being separated out from the other things in it—the doctrines, for example. Once the critic had decided he could cut away without loss some of the meaning of the poem (for that is what it amounts to), it was only logical that he should go on to cut away the meaning altogether, in the conviction that the poetry would still be left mysteriously standing. Poetry became style. Poetry became 'language as gesture'.

We may now be in a position to understand this last slogan which Mr Blackmur calls out from his title page. The last hundred years of poetic theory afford many examples of critics arriving at the point where poetry, for them, becomes style and nothing else. There is only one route forward from there, and that is by way of analogies between poetry and the other arts. Poetry must 'aspire to the condition of music'. Mr Blackmur is no exception. He too aspires to make the match with music, and this is what 'language as gesture' means. 'Gesture' seems to take us to the art of the dance rather than music, but the distinction, if it exists, is so fine as not to matter. Mr Blackmur seems to admit as much when he tells us that the essential poetry in a poem of Yeats is that for which the words are only the notation, and that it is 'the cry, the gesture' —the cry of the singer, the gesture of the dancer. So too when he asks us to attend, in another poem by Yeats, to 'the meaning which is under the lines', we are reminded of Suzanne Langer's judgement on music:

> Articulation is its life, but not assertion; expressiveness not expression. The actual function of meaning, which calls for permanent contents, is not fulfilled; for the *assignment* of one rather than another possible meaning to each form is never explicitly made.

And at this stage of Mr Blackmur's argument the incantation which is most efficacious—more important even than Pound's 'composing in the sequence of the musical phrase'—is an observation by Mr Eliot to the effect that the poet must see 'beneath the beauty and the ugliness, the boredom, the horror and the glory.' This spatial metaphor of beneath or under or below—this is a recurrent feature of Mr Blackmur's writing.

It would be idle now to embark on a discussion of the relationship between poetry and music. For my own part I believe that critics should be concerned with poems not with poetry; above all, with dividing the sheep from the goats, good poems from bad ones. This has the advantage of keeping the critic in his place. For the odd thing is that, as poetry becomes more and more unspeakable and untouchable, more and more of a sacred mystery, criticism of a certain sort, far from withering away, grows ever more pretentious. Presuming no longer to judge and discriminate, it presumes instead to direct our obeisances. As the poet becomes a god, the critic becomes his high priest and partakes of his sanctity. So Mr Blackmur speaks (p. 420) of 'the professional critics, a race hitherto more ornamental than necessary':

But now, in the first society of the western world not based upon the religious imagination but based directly and precariously upon the secular and experimental imagination, so far as it is based at all, it is a race that seems more necessary than it is possible.

This is surely a criticism grown too big for its boots.

Postscript: The suggestion that 'criticism . . . grows ever more pretentious' has, I dare to think, been proved right in the years since this essay was printed. It is nowadays French voices, more than British or American ones, which assert or assume (in words that I take from a recent academic study of Coleridge) that 'we do not wish to maintain the centrality or efficaciousness of our own myths, except through criticism itself'. I am proud to subscribe myself 'critic', no less than 'poet'; but am that much the more horrified when the critic takes on the sanctity, and the visionary authority, which belong not to him, but to the poet.

T. S. ELIOT: THE END OF AN ERA

I

I FIND it very surprising that all readers seem to either accept or reject the *Four Quartets* as a whole—and yet not really surprising, since the cleavage comes plainly not along any line of literary fact, but is flagrantly ideological: the religiously inclined applaud the Quartets, the more or less militantly secular and 'humanist' decry them. As simple as that.

At any rate, I find it still surprising (and depressing) that no one should yet have remarked to my knowledge how the third Quartet, 'The Dry Salvages', sticks out among the rest like a sore thumb. At first sight it is not only incongruous with the others, strikingly different in conception and procedure, but different unaccountably and disastrously. One could take it by itself and prove convincingly that it is quite simply *rather a bad poem*. It amazes me that, so far as I know, no one has yet done this; and until very lately I thought I was the person to do it. In fact, I aim to do it here and now—but now with the proviso that all I can say against it is true only so far as it goes, that from another point of view all the vices become virtues and fall into place. It is possible, of course, that all other readers have been clever enough to see the thing aright from the start. But it goes without saying that I don't think so. Here at any rate, to begin with, is my case against 'The Dry Salvages'.

II

Leavis and Rajan have both applauded the opening lines of the poem, and Helen Gardner was so misguided as to choose them for the basis of her claims for Eliot specifically as a manipulator of language:

> I do not know much about gods; but I think that the river
> Is a strong brown god—sullen, untamed and intractable,
> Patient to some degree, at first recognized as a frontier;

Miss Gardner says that the 'strong brown god' is 'a personification which the poet's tone makes no more than a suggestion, a piece of only half-serious myth-making'. But the first line has not sufficiently defined the tone (a single line hardly could) for this to be true; and indeed it is to my ear still too uncertain, eight lines later, to carry the journalistic cliché, 'worshippers of the machine', by giving it the invisible quote-marks which, as Miss Gardner allows, such an inert and faded locution requires. What in any case, we may well ask, is the tone in which we could hear without embarrassment the first line spoken? 'I do not know much about gods'—who could conceivably start a conversation like that without condemning himself from the start as an uncomfortable poseur? Is it not rather like 'Poems are made by fools like me/But only God can make a tree'? What is it but a gaucherie? and yet there *is* a tone in which we have been addressed, which hovers here in the offing, a tone familiar enough but still far from acceptable, a tone which has indeed become a byword as a type of strident uncertainty in the speaker and of correspondingly acute embarrassment in the hearer—it is the tone of Whitman.

But what is Eliot thinking of, that he should talk like Whitman? And our bewilderment deepens:

> Unhonoured, unpropitiated
> By worshippers of the machine, but waiting, watching and waiting,
> His rhythm was present in the nursery bedroom,
> In the rank ailanthus of the April dooryard,
> In the smell of grapes on the autumn table,
> And the evening circle in the winter gaslight.

'Worshippers of the machine'; then the incredibly limp 'watching and waiting'; and finally, limpest of all, 'his rhythm was present'. 'His rhythm was present in the nursery bedroom'—could anything be more vague and woolly? After this statement has been issued, we know not a tittle more about the relation between river and bedroom than we did before. And the poetry is not just bad, but unaccountably so. For 'His rhythm was present in' represents just that bridgework, that filling in and faking of transitions, which Eliot as a post-symbolist poet has always contrived to do without. From first to last his procedure has been the symbolist procedure of 'juxtaposition without copula', the setting down of images side by side with a space between them, a space that does not need to be bridged. There is an example just over the page in 'The Dry Salvages': 'The salt is on the briar rose,/The fog is in the fir trees.' For now, from 'The river is within us' through to the end of the first section, the poetry picks up, the diction becomes distinctively Eliotic and fine; and only an unwonted straightforwardness, the vulnerable stance face to face with the subject, the overtness of the evocation, are there to trouble us with something pre-symbolist and oldfashioned.

But, then, what shall be said of the famous sestina of the second section, which Rajan calls 'as intricately organized as anything Eliot has written'? Shall I be thought laughably naïve for calling attention to the rhymes? In the first sestine comes an extremely beautiful perception:

> The silent withering of autumn flowers
> Dropping their petals and remaining motionless;

The rhymes found to correspond to these in the later sestines are as follows, in order:

> ... the trailing
> Consequence of further days and hours,
> While emotion takes to itself the emotionless .
> Years of living among the breakage . . .
>   ... the failing
> Pride or resentment at failing powers,
> The unattached devotion which might pass for devotionless . . .
> Where is the end of them, the fishermen sailing
> Into the wind's tail, where the fog cowers?
> We cannot think of a time that is oceanless . . .
> Setting and hauling, while the North East lowers
> Over shallow banks unchanging and erosionless . . .

No end to the withering of withered flowers,
To the movement of pain that is painless and motionless . . .

Should we not be justified in seeing here a case of sheer incompetence? Is it not plain that the trouvaille at the head of the page, 'Dropping their petals and remaining motionless', gets the poet into more and more patent difficulties (and dishonesties) once the rhyme on it has been taken up as a determining feature of his stanza-form? 'Emotionless'—how? 'Oceanless' —grotesque! 'Erosionless'—does he mean 'uneroded'? And 'movement . . . pain . . . painless . . . motionless'—our confidence in the poet has by this time been so undermined that we cannot, in justice to ourselves, take this as anything but incantatory gibberish. Faced with this, we have to feel a momentary sympathy with the rancour even of a Robert Graves—who, whatever his limitations, would never allow such slapdash inefficiency into his own verses.

The next passage reads:

It seems, as one becomes older,
That the past has another pattern, and ceases to be a mere sequence
Or even development: the latter a partial fallacy
Encouraged by superficial notions of evolution
Which becomes, in the popular mind, a means of disowning the past

Is this the poet who wove to and fro the close and lively syntax at the beginning of 'East Coker', or the passage from 'Burnt Norton' beginning 'The inner freedom from the practical desire'? How can we explain that the same poet should now proffer, in such stumbling trundling rhythms, these inarticulate ejaculations of reach-me-down phrases, the debased currency of the study circle? And worse is to come—Possum's little joke:

The moments of happiness—not the sense of well-being,
Fruition, fulfilment, security or affection,
Or even a very good dinner . . .

At the dismal jocularity of that 'very good dinner', we throw in our hands. The tone that Miss Gardner thought established in the very first line can now, we realize, never be established at all. Or else, if we prefer to put it this way—it has been very thoroughly established, as excruciatingly unsettled, off-key. To be sure, the diction now picks up again for a while, though still liable to such upsets as the lame gabble, 'not forgetting/ Something that is probably quite ineffable: . . .' But section III begins with *Krishna*, which sticks in the throat even of Dr Rajan (who for the most part seems to be reading a different poem): 'Mr Eliot is never happy in "the maze of Oriental metaphysics" and his wanderings this time are uncomfortably sinuous.' And there is, as Rajan further notes, a self-advertising virtuosity, almost Euphuistic, about 'the future is a faded song, a Royal Rose or a lavender spray . . .'

At this point re-enter Whitman, conspicuously. S. Musgrove, author of *T. S. Eliot and Walt Whitman*, compares with this passage turning on 'Fare forward, travellers', Whitman's 'Song of the Open Road'; and he comments (p. 55):

Once again, Eliot has employed Whitman's material and manner in order to reject his philosophy. For Whitman, time stretches away in one infinite linear direction, towards a positive and perfect future, in which the possession of something actual, something better than the present, awaits the growing spirit of man. For Eliot, the sense of a direction is illusory; time is an eternal present which can never yield more than is now known, in which the only kind of possession conceivable is one alike in kind to dispossession from the demands of the self . . .

This is a good deal less than fair to Whitman, who is at pains in 'Song of the Open Road' to make it clear that there is no destination to the voyaging, no end to it, no perfection to be aimed at or achieved except in the process of still and still going on. Thus Eliot, with his 'Fare neither well nor ill, so it be forward' (my words, of course, but a fair summary of Eliot's drift), has dropped from Whitman only his optimism, substituting for it the Chekhovian compassion which strips its objects of all dignity: 'Fare forward, you who think that you are voyaging; . . .' And to be sure, Musgrove talks as if the one unforgivable thing about Whitman, what proves his vulgarity, is precisely his optimism—a good example of that rigid neo-Augustinian temper among Eliot's adherents which very properly enrages a secular liberal like Kathleen Nott. For Whitman's optimism is not by any means the worst thing about him. There is beneath and beside it what Lawrence pointed out—'Always wanting to merge himself into the womb of something or other'; that is, the drive to 'transcend' the self by losing it in identification with some inhuman process, of which, as Wyndham Lewis pointed out long ago, the process of time is perhaps the most obvious and popular. Moreover, as Lawrence and, following him, Yvor Winters have shown, this drive is especially marked in the American literary tradition, from Emerson and Melville to Hart Crane (1)—its obsessive symbol very frequently, as here in 'The Dry Salvages', the sea. And, sure enough, Rajan comes aptly in once more with the suggestion that section IV, 'Lady, whose shrine stands on the promontory', 'perhaps owes something to the sermon in *Moby Dick*'. Even the Hinduism fits in, if one recalls Yeats's remark about 'those translations of the Upanishads, which it is so much harder to study by the sinking flame of Indian tradition than by the serviceable lamp of Emerson and Walt Whitman'. And yet, when one recalls also Yeats's verdict on Emerson and Whitman, 'writers who have come to seem superficial precisely because they lack the Vision of Evil', one finds it unaccountable that Eliot, the author of the essay on Baudelaire, however American, should have fallen into this trap of ecstatic merging with the process.

The last section begins with an admirable new departure, in the vigour of 'To communicate with Mars, converse with spirits . . .;' but then it modulates, through a very beautiful yet again strangely uncritical treatment of the Bergsonian *durée* in music ('but you are the music/While the music lasts'), into the inhuman conclusion that human life for all but the

saints is mere purposeless *movement*, scurrying activity, only at fleeting
uncontrollable moments elevated into the meaning and dignity of true
action. We realize that the poet indeed meant the shocking 'emotionless'
of the sestina; and if that helps to validate the poetry of that passage,
it only makes the poet seem even less humane.

III

If we are to turn the force of these various objections we have to go a
long way round—and yet in a way we need to go no further than Hugh
Kenner's essay on 'Eliot's Moral Dialectic' (*Hudson Review*, 1949),
which relegates to the status of curio every other piece of criticism on
the *Quartets*. Kenner there distinguishes the predominant structural principle of this poetry as a diagram in which two terms (life and death, beginning and end) are first opposed, then falsely reconciled in a third term,
and then truly reconciled in a fourth term, a metaphysical conception.
His examples are section III of 'Burnt Norton', where the opposed terms
light and darkness are combined in the parody-reconciliation of the
'flicker' in the twilit murk of London, only to be truly reconciled para-
doxically in the metaphysical Dark Night of the Soul; and section III of
'Little Gidding', where the opposing terms attachment and detachment
are reconciled in parody in 'indifference', only to be truly reconciled in
Love.

  Section III of 'East Coker' yields up the same pattern:
  . . . So the darkness shall be the light, and the stillness the dancing.
  Whisper of running streams, and winter lightning,
  The wild thyme unseen and the wild strawberry.
  The laughter in the garden, echoed ecstasy
  Not lost, but requiring, pointing to the agony
  Of death and birth.
                   You say I am repeating
  Something I have said before. I shall say it again.
  Shall I say it again? In order to arrive there,
  To arrive where you are, to get from where you are not,
      You must go by a way wherein there is no ecstasy.
  In order to arrive at what you do not know
      You must go by a way which is the way of ignorance . . .
Darkness and light, stillness and dancing, are two pairs of opposed terms.
They are reconciled in 'the agony/Of death and birth'. Birth, coming
from the dark to the light, is a sort of death, for as soon as we are born
we begin to die; and death, going from the light to the dark, is a sort of
birth—into eternal life. And the stillness of a seizure, the dance of pain,
are reconciled in agony. But this is a false reconciliation which is at once
abandoned for the true one carried in the borrowings from St John of
the Cross. Thus, 'I shall say it again/Shall I say it again?' is an ironical
trap. Musgrove suggests an allusion to Whitman's 'Do I contradict myself? Very well, I contradict myself'. This points it up even more; for the

point is that Eliot *is* contradicting himself even as he *seems* to repeat
himself—inevitably, because it is characteristic of the terms he is thinking
in that the false reconciliation, being a parody of the true one, is very
hard—all but impossible—to distinguish from it in words, even in words
charged to the utmost, as in poetry.

Since the third sections of 'Burnt Norton', 'East Coker' and 'Little
Gidding' are thus broadly parallel in structure, one would expect to discern the same structure in section III of 'The Dry Salvages', which is the
Whitmanesque passage I have just quoted. But 'The Dry Salvages', as we
noted at the start, is the odd one out in all sorts of ways; and though the
pattern is there, it is there only with a difference, and is hard to discern.
'And the way up is the way down, the way forward is the way back'—
here are the terms opposed, right enough. But we look in vain for the
false reconciliation, though the image of the traveller is obviously apt for
it—since travelling is the same state whether one travels from here to
there, or there to here. But this parody-reconciliation is ruled out of
court when the poet jumps at once to his insight (a restatement, as Kenner has noted, of the insight of 'Tradition and the Individual Talent'):
'You cannot face it steadily, but this thing is sure,/That time is no healer:
the patient is no longer here.' Yet the parody-reconciliation *is* present in
the lines that follow, though never overtly offered—it is there precisely
in the shade of Whitman that haunts the passage, the Whitmanesque tone
that hovers here as an overtone.

But we can, and must, go further. This diagram that Kenner has brilliantly
extricated he does not offer to us merely as the structural principle informing these passages and others like them. He hints that the same
diagram informs the *Four Quartets* as a whole. If this is so, then 'The
Dry Salvages', the third of them, should appear to be the false reconciliation, the parody. And here it seems we may at last be coming near to
understanding, and forgiving, its peculiarities.

It is generally recognized that parody is to be found in the *Four Quartets*, that in 'East Coker', for instance, when the poet says, of the lyric at
the start of section II, 'That was a way of putting it—not very satisfactory:/A periphrastic study in a worn-out poetical fashion', we are meant
to take this at its face value and to agree that the passage referred to is,
therefore, a parody. But when Kenner asks us to compare 'Down the
passage which we did not take' at the start of 'Burnt Norton' with the
'cunning passages, contrived corridors' of Gerontion (himself, as Kenner
argues, a living parody of the true self-surrender that we find in Simeon),
we are advised that we must look for parody elsewhere in the *Four Quartets*, where it is not explicitly pointed out to us by the poet. For instance, the false reconciliation which I have pointed out in 'East Coker',
'the agony/Of death and birth', while it looks back to the significantly
theatrical image, 'With a hollow rumble of wings, with a movement of
darkness on darkness', looks forward surely to 'The wounded surgeon
plies the steel' and the much-elaborated skull-and-crossbones conceit

which occupies the whole of section IV of the poem. Several readers have
objected to this as strained and laboured; and since the necrophily
which informs it has already been shown as a parody of the true reconciliation between dark and light, should we not take it that the strain and
the labouring are deliberate, a conscious forcing of the tone, a *conscious*
movement towards self-parody? What is it in fact but what we were
warned of in the typically opalescent lines from 'Burnt Norton'—'The
crying shadow in the funeral dance,/The loud lament of the disconsolate
chimera?'

It is my argument, then, that in the sense and to the degree in which
section IV of 'East Coker' is a parody the whole of 'The Dry Salvages' is
a parody. It is hardly too much to say that the whole of this third quartet is spoken by a nameless persona; certainly it is spoken through a mask,
spoken *in character*, spoken in character as the American. This, and nothing else, can explain the approximations to Whitmanesque and other
pre-symbolist American verse-procedures; and the insistent Americanism,
of course, as all the commentators have noted, is a quality also of the
locale persistently evoked by the images—of the Mississippi and the New
England coast for instance. It is thus that the incompetence turns out to
be dazzling virtuosity; and the inhumanity of the conclusion reached
turns out to be only a parody of the true conclusion reached in 'Little
Gidding', which is thoroughly humane in its insistence that all varieties
of human folly and imperfection are the conditions for apprehending
perfection, that the world is therefore necessary and to that extent—
even the worst of it—good.

IV

There remains only one question. Admitting, as we have had to admit,
that the *Four Quartets*—and 'The Dry Salvages' no less than every other
part—represent a superbly controlled achievement of its kind, what are
we to say of that kind? What kind of poetry is this, in which loose and
woolly incoherent language can be seen to be—in its place and for special
purposes—better than clear and closely-articulated language? This is a
question raised not just by the *Quartets* but by Eliot's work as a whole.
The opening paragraph of the fifth section of 'Ash Wednesday' is what
Leavis says it is—a magnificent acting out in verse-movement and word-
play of 'both the agonized effort to seize the unseizable, and the elusive
equivocations of the thing grasped.' But it is also, from another point of
view, what Max Eastman says it is—an 'oily puddle of emotional noises'.
It is easy to say that Leavis's point of view is right, and Eastman's wrong
—that any poetic effect can be seen and judged only as it plays its part
in the economy of the whole poem, and that any amount of violence
done to language, any amount of sheer ugliness, can be justified as means
to a justifiable poetic end. But this is to assert that Eastman's pang of
angry discomfort, which I suppose is shared by every sensitive reader at
least at a first reading, is not a protest against ugliness on behalf of beauty,

but only a protest against the functional in favour of the pretty. Are we in fact prepared to waive the claim 'beautiful' which we make for those lines of poetry which move us to applause as surely as the lines from 'Ash Wednesday' move us to rebellion? And are we, moreover (for this too is implied), prepared to waive the claim 'poetry' for those lines we applaud —unless, that is, their engagingness can be seen as functional?

Well, we—you and I, dear reader—may be prepared to waive these claims. What is quite certain is that not only that legendary figure, the common reader, but the enthusiast and the specialist—a person like Dr Rajan—is not prepared to do so; not prepared because he has not realized it is what is required. More, the poet himself—a poet like Robert Graves— is not prepared to do so. And (what perhaps should make us pause) younger poets than either Graves or Eliot *have* realized what is required of them by poetry like Eliot's and have refused—at least where their own writing is concerned—to waive their claims to poetry and to beauty in the oldfashioned pre-symbolist sense.

'Pre-symbolist', yes. For it is pre-eminently symbolist and post-symbolist poetry that waives these claims and insists that the reader waive them also. Eliot waives them when he says, in 'East Coker', 'The poetry does not matter'. The exegetes cushion the shock of this by taking it to mean '*That sort* of poetry doesn't . . .', the sort which we have just heard called 'A periphrastic study in a worn-out poetical fashion', which we have agreed to consider as parody. Well, that interpretation can be allowed to stand for classroom consumption. But it isn't what Eliot means, or it isn't all that he means. He means what he says: the poetry doesn't matter, the beauty doesn't matter—for no verse can be judged either poetic or beautiful except in so far as it is seen to be expressive; and what it has to express may demand, as it does in 'The Dry Salvages', rather the false note than the true one, the faded and shop-soiled locution rather than the phrase new-minted, the trundling rhythm rather than the cut, woolliness rather than clarity—'See now they vanish,/The faces and places, with the self which, as it could, loved them.' Woolliness becomes the only sort of clarity, the wrong note is the right note, and nothing is so beautiful as what is hideous—in certain (not uncommon) poetic circumstances.

If it is true that Kenner's essay has made everything else on the *Quartets* (and not on them only but on Eliot's work in general) seem like literary curiosities, none of these curios is so appealing to me as Anthony Thorlby's essay, 'The Poetry of Four Quartets', which was published after Kenner's (in the *Cambridge Journal*, 1952) but was obviously not written in the light of it. Thorlby is seriously wrong about the *Quartets*; nothing could be further from the truth than his assertion, 'What is remarkable in Mr Eliot's use of imagery is not that it is symbolic or capable of interpretation, but that the interpretation is essential to its poetic coherence.' Or rather, if this is true in one sense, if we take 'interpretation' to mean 'seeing the place of any part in relation to the whole', it is certainly untrue if we take it to mean, as Thorlby does, that each image as we come to it must be construed, like the images of allegory. What is appealing and important about Thorlby's essay is that it represents a man recognizing that the symbolist revolution in poetry has happened, and trying to come to grips with it. To be sure, Thorlby does not acknowledge that the revolution he perceives is the symbolist revolution; indeed, he writes as if it were inaugurated specifically by *Four Quartets*, seemingly unaware that the revolution was over, and successfully over, long before Eliot began to write, and that all Eliot's poems, the earliest as well as the latest, are constructed on that assumption—that the symbolist procedures have arrived and supplanted all others. Then, again, Thorlby's objections to the procedure as he detects it could be easily countered by anyone versed even a little in symbolist theory; for his argument rests upon a hard and fast distinction between 'having an experience' and 'seeing the significance of that experience'—a distinction made untenable by Bergson. Nevertheless, Thorlby at least perceives the essentially post-symbolist nature of the poetry of the *Quartets*—which is more than can be said for most of the commentators—even if he hasn't the label to tie on to it. And he grasps quite a lot of the implications of the symbolist revolution in terms of the revised expectations that the reader must now entertain— a matter of crucial importance which is hardly ever touched upon.

Thus it is very nearly correct—it is entirely correct from most points of view—to say with Thorlby: 'Mr Eliot's poetry is *about* the many forms in which the life of poetry has flourished; which is a very different thing from simply accepting one form and creating within it a poetry of life.' And it is entirely correct to say, as he does:

> Mr Eliot, then, is not standing outside his material looking in upon the experience he is writing about, composing it into one form; he is himself at the centre . . . looking around him upon so many of the problems of today which he hopes to illumine by its light.

This last point is the vital one. If no one has made it before Thorlby, that was (I suspect) for fear of falling foul of the master's own propaganda for impersonality in poetry, on the gap between the man who suffers and the poet who creates. Eliot was always perfectly fair on this, and one can hardly resent his insistence when one finds critics, deaf to all his warnings, reading 'Gerontion' as a *cri de coeur* rather than what it is—the rendering of the state of mind of an imagined persona, from which the poet is wholly detached. From this point of view Eliot is indeed impersonal, standing quite aside and apart from his creation—my diagnosis of 'The Dry Salvages' as parody makes the point all over again. And yet Thorlby is right too: in another sense Eliot is never outside and apart from his poems. No post-symbolist poet can be outside his poems as Milton was outside 'Lycidas', and no post-symbolist poem can ever be as impersonal as 'Lycidas' was for John Crowe Ransom when he called it 'a poem nearly anonymous'. If Eliot enters his poems only disguised as a persona, wearing a mask, at least he enters them. Reading a parody, we are inevitably aware (though as it were at one remove) of the parodist. Perhaps no other kind of poet is so much in evidence in his own poems as the parodist is, the histrionic virtuoso, always tipping the wink. And if Eliot thus enters into his own poems, his reader must do likewise, changing his focus as the poem changes focus, knowing when to give almost full credence to what the poetry says, when to make reservations according as he detects the voice of now one persona, now another parodying the first.

I share Thorlby's preference for a kind of poetry which stands on its own feet, without my help, as an independent creation, a thing to be walked round, and as satisfying from one standpoint as from another. And so I hope not to be thought lacking in gratitude to Eliot for the *Four Quartets*, nor lacking in respect for the prodigious achievement of that poem, if I say that I hope for quite a different sort of poem in the future, a sort of poem more in harmony with what was written in Europe before symbolism was thought of, even (since symbolist procedures are only the logical development of Romantic procedures) before Romanticism was thought of. I am not forgetting the lesson of 'Tradition and the Individual Talent'. I know that history cannot be unwritten, that there can be no question of putting the clock back; the post-post-symbolist poetry I look for may be more in harmony with pre-Romantic poetry, it can never be the same. There cannot be a conspiracy to pretend that the symbolist revolution never happened. (The annoying thing of course is that, because Eliot has been seen by the influential critics most often in the perspective of the specifically English tradition rather than in the perspective of Europe as a whole, it is commonly held that he has done just what I seem to ask for, has re-established continuity with the poetry of the seventeenth and eighteenth centuries. And he has really done so—but only in relatively superficial ways.)

If I hope for a different sort of poetry, that hope is reasonably confident— not because I give much weight to the younger poets of today who, when they think in these terms at all (they seldom do), declare that the post-symbolist tradition is 'worked out'; nor even because the respectable poetry written in England and America by poets younger than Eliot is plainly not written according to his prescription; but simply because the *Four Quartets* represent a stage of such subtlety and intricacy in the post-symbolist tradition that it is impossible to think of its ever being taken a stage further. Surely no poet, unless it be Eliot himself, can elaborate further this procedure in which the true key is never sounded, but exists in the poem only as the norm by which all the voices that speak are heard as delicately off-key, as the voices of parody. It is, at any rate, in this hope and this confidence of something quite different in the offing, that I have written the second half of my title: 'T. S. Eliot: *The End of an Era*'.

COMMON-MANNERISM

Collected Poems, Randall Jarrell, Faber.
Bread rather than Blossoms, D. J. Enright, Secker & Warburg.

JARRELL'S CASE is very like that of the early Wordsworth. For instance, his 'The Night before the Night before Christmas' is a dramatic monologue open to the same surely conclusive objections as those Coleridge and Jeffrey brought against Wordsworth's 'The Thorn' (cf. Jarrell's explanatory preface to his poem with Wordsworth's to his). The objection is that by being dramatic monologues written so wholeheartedly 'in character', both Jarrell's poem and Wordsworth's depend for their interest upon the extent to which the imagined character and the imagined situation of that character can be universalized. Wordsworth's imagined persona is too idiosyncratic, and the situation in which Jarrell places his persona is too special, for either poem to have the sort of general relevance that one asks of art. Jarrell's poem is about pain and loss first as recognized by the child, then as accommodated never with complete success into the psyche of the grown-up; and this is certainly a theme of general interest. But its interest is severely narrowed when the protagonist is made a person of a very special type in an intellectual situation possible or general, even to persons of that type, only at the precise date Jarrell specifies, 1934.

A much more exact and obvious analogy is between Jarrell's 'The Black Swan' and Wordsworth's 'We are Seven'. But here the comparison works all in Wordsworth's favour—not only because his poem is self-explanatory where Jarrell's is impenetrable except by reference to his explanatory note; but because Wordsworth's poem can yield a general law of child-psychology (that the child's psyche refuses to accept the fact of death), whereas Jarrell's presents only one child's specific way of evading the fact of death through fantasy.

Jarrell's poems of this kind seem to invite the same sort of interest as extracts from a psychoanalyst's casebook; Wordsworth's *Lyrical Ballads*, though they contain material rather like this (e.g., 'The Thorn'), yet as a whole provide the higher because more universal interest of the systematic theory of child-psychology written by such a psychologist, drawing upon his casebook but generalizing from the particulars there noted. And there is the further difference that Wordsworth's poems have the excitement and conviction of personally-intuited entirely novel discoveries, where Jarrell's too often are just particular illustrations of discoveries made by Freud or hypotheses made by Jung.

Sister Bernetta Quin, for whom Jarrell is 'perhaps the most likely candidate among the younger writers for a permanent place in American letters' (*The Metamorphic Tradition in Modern Poetry*, p. 168), insists that the Jungian collective unconscious is only a hypothesis, but when she goes on to elucidate Jarrell's Jungian attitude to dreams and folklore she does not pause to wonder what difference it makes to her valuation of Jarrell's poems if we find ourselves out of sympathy with their Jungian basis. So far as I can see, it makes more difference than it should if Jarrell's poetry were properly achieved art.

Jarrell in fact (and this again is Wordsworthian), while asking an act of faith in psychological hypotheses, himself is incapable of an act of faith in poetic as distinct from factual truth, in the validity of the poem as arte-fact rather than document. His poems make their claims on our attention too exclusively on the basis of the supposedly intrinsic importance of the raw materials they are made from; hardly at all on the basis of the *making*, the artificer's manipulating and organizing of his materials. And in fact such manipulation and organization has apparently been reduced to a minimum, or else exerted to the paradoxical end of giving that impression. In the latter case, if this is a question of the art that conceals art, it is only too successful. The poem looks only too spontaneous and formless, being innocent—not only of discursive logic (this was inevitable, given the nature of the chosen material)—but also of all the traditional disciplines, rhyming, rhythmical, and (for the most part) stanzaic. This unlicked nakedness is particularly apparent in what is to the English reader Jarrell's best-known work, though it is certainly not his best; I mean, his war-poems such as the much-anthologized 'Death of the Ball-turret Gunner'. (Three better poems are 'The Knight, Death, and the Devil', 'A Sick Child' and 'The Marchen'.)

All this is to put the best face on the matter. One could instead remember Jarrell's cheerful and ingratiating criticism; and think of his respect for 'fact' and disrespect for art as simply philistine. Perhaps he is just trying to be the poet of the common man.

This brings me to the other book under review. For the most disconcerting thing about D. J. Enright's second collection is what I privately think of as 'common-mannerism'. This has always been an element in the make-up of 'The Movement', though up to now it's been apparent chiefly in criticism, notably in some of the pronouncements of Mr Amis. Here it shows up in poetry, where it seems to me a very ugly phenomenon. Enright when he wrote these poems was lecturing on English in a Japanese university; and yet poem after poem follows the same pattern, elevating a structure of references to traditional culture, Oriental or European or both, only to tear it down again with snarls of disgust. To be sure the poet juxtaposes his cultural references with images of the squalor and physical destitution of contemporary Japanese life, and would have us believe—what in a few cases we *can* believe—that his revulsion against the culture came from his feeling that, for all its riches, it had nothing to say to the down-and-out Geisha-girl or the peasant in the paddy-field. All the same, there seems to be a genuine danger that impatience with cultural pretentiousness is turning into impatience with culture; and that humane indignation is dissolving into a ready-made sentimentality. The book has been duly applauded by the reviewers for its 'humanity'.

There is a sort of perverse heroism about Jarrell's endeavours. But if we cannot withhold a kind of admiration for a wrong-headedness so thorough, this also means that his case seems incurable where Enright's doesn't. It's not just that Jarrell's book represents the author's selection from no less than four previous volumes, where Enright's is by comparison only an interim report. It should also be noted that *Bread rather than Blossoms*, though it contains sixty pieces, is really a very light-weight volume, consisting for the most part of what may be called verse-journalism. Like some of the collections of MacNeice it asks to be read only at that level, and this blunts the edge of the criticism I've levelled at it. What's more, it profits by being keyed so low and asking to be taken so casually; it can be read through at a sitting without strain yet without giving too much away. One laughs outright time and again, notes the clever wisecracks for subsequent use at sherry-parties, and turns the page eagerly for the next piece of calculated impudence. I agree with those admirers of MacNeice who argue that it's a good thing when poetry can do this. And personally I get more pleasure when Enright does it than when MacNeice does it, because Enright always remembers—as MacNeice often doesn't, and of course as Jarrell doesn't want to—that the poem is an artefact, not just a sample section of animated conversation. All the same I cling to the hope that Enright has been composing poems more ambitious and deliberate than any here; and that he's not so out of patience with artiness and cultural window-dressing that he's forsworn for good the deeper reaches (and so the deeper humanity) of the art he practises.

THE IMAGINARY museum in my title is taken from the brilliant book of that name published a few years ago by André Malraux. The central insight of that book is well known and widely accepted as a true and penetrating statement of an element, a basic assumption, common to all the arts in the present century. This perception is at bottom a simple one; and this means—luckily, for my present purposes—that it can be re-stated in summary fashion without being damaged too much. M. Malraux' contention, then, is this: that it is no accident that what we recognize as 'the modern movement' in the arts appears on the historical scene at roughly the same time as certain techniques of reproduction, like gramophone recording in the case of music and colour-photography in the cases of painting, sculpture, and architecture.

The perfection of these techniques—and the long-playing record, which has appeared in the last few years, may be taken to consummate this achievement—means that the modern painter, or sculptor, or architect, or musical composer differs from all his predecessors in one enormously important respect: he has immediately at his disposal, in a way his predecessors had not, the whole achievement of worldwide artistic endeavour over the centuries. In his library of art books or of long-playing gramophone records the modern artist has an imaginary museum infinitely more comprehensive and convenient than even the finest of actual museums and galleries. Where a painter or art-critic less than a hundred years ago—say Baudelaire—would have had to travel across Europe from Madrid to Leningrad in order to compare two paintings by Rembrandt, having to keep in his memory the image of what he had seen in Madrid to set beside what he was going to see in Russia, today such a painter or critic can open his art-book to see the two pictures, both reproduced with unprecedented fidelity, on opposite pages of the one volume.

Moreover he is not limited—as for practical purposes Baudelaire was limited—to the continent of Europe. He can have to hand the sculptures of Easter Island or the devil-masks of Nigeria or the rock-paintings of ancient China, no less than Giotto, Rembrandt or Turner. The whole of the artistic past is available to painter, sculptor, architect, musician, as never before. He is free to wander about in the past, to pick and choose from among the styles of the past, in a way his predecessors never dreamed of. And M. Malraux maintains—conclusively, as I think—that this unprecedented attitude to the past—to artistic and cultural 'tradition' in the broadest sense—accounts for and makes inevitable some of the features of modern painting and music in which they differ most strikingly from the painting and music of all other periods and all other cultures.

It is natural to ask: what about the art of literature, or, more narrowly, of poetry? Malraux says nothing of this: and for obvious reasons. For if one thinks about it at all, it is easy to realize that the perfection of techniques of reproduction came, for poetry, five centuries earlier than for music and painting. The invention of printing in the fifteenth century did for poetry what the invention of gramophone recordings did for music, and the invention of colour photography did for painting, only in the last fifty years.

So it would seem, if M. Malraux' contention is correct, that the poet and his reader have been inhabiting the imaginary museum for the past four hundred and fifty years. This reflection—although so obvious—is yet sufficiently arresting. For it seems to mean that poetry is strikingly 'out of step' with the other arts. And it may well be asked whether in our approach to poetry we pay sufficient attention to the special position of this art among the rest. It is commonly assumed, for instance, that 'the modern movement' is something which manifests itself equally in all the arts; that there is, to take one example, a significant connection between the cubist perspective of Picasso and Juan Gris and the exactly contemporary telescoping of historical perspective in the first lines of *The Waste Land*. Or we may recall the symbolist contention, at the start of 'the modern movement', that poetry should 'approach the condition of music'.

Yet if Malraux is right, and modern painting and music owe their modernity to a changed attitude towards the artistic past, then it would seem that poetry, whose attitude towards the past has not been revolutionized by technical inventions, should not share in this 'modernity'. One comes to think that those critics who explain and justify novel features in modern poetry by appeal to what seems to be analogous innovation in the other arts are guilty of an elementary error in historical perspective. Further, since it is indubitable that many poets of our period have conceived themselves to be sharing in a modern movement equally manifest in the other arts, it seems we may have to say that not only those poets' critics, but the poets themselves, have fallen into the error of supposing an affinity where none exists or can exist.

Yet surely, printing had a different and much less far-reaching effect on poetry than colour-reproduction has had on painting. For the medium of painting, like the medium of music, is an international language as the language of poetry is not. After the invention of printing, as before, a poem was written in some one of the languages of the world; whereas pigment and line, a musical chord, the interplay of space and solid in buildings and sculptures—these artistic vocabularies are truly international.

Worse still, we may recall that the literary arts once had such a *lingua franca* which they have now lost. Until only a hundred and fifty years ago, Latin and to a less extent Greek were still international literary languages, in that all but a very few of the serious literary works in all the languages of Europe were written with Latin and Greek models in mind, employing a common vocabulary of Latin and Greek mythology and symbolism. This literary heritage possessed and exploited by Russian as by Spaniard, by Norwegian as by Greek, constituted something like an international language for poetry. This international language still survives indeed, though it is spoken and understood only by a calamitously depleted number. It fell out of general use ('general' I mean among even the numerically tiny minority that at any given time cares for the arts) at precisely the time when the gramophone and colour photography were being invented.

In other words, at precisely the time when the inherently international media of painting and music were becoming (thanks to the technicians) *effectively* international, the medium of poetry was losing even that degree of international currency which it had enjoyed. At just the time when musician and music-lover, painter and art-enthusiast, are able to leap over the limitations of being born to one nation and one culture rather than another, the poet and his reader find themselves locked more securely than ever before inside one national milieu. This raises the possibility that poetry is and will be 'the odd one out' among the arts in the worst possible way. Poetry becomes ever more parochial and provincial, while painting and music and sculpture become ever more international. Is there not a real danger that poetry will become, among the arts, of only marginal importance?

It is this possibility, surely, which lies behind a remarkable work, Mr Hugh MacDiarmid's *In Memoriam James Joyce*, which appeared a couple of years ago. This enormous poem is itself only an extract from another yet more enormous, to be called *Towards a World Language*. That title in itself explains how this fits in with what I am discussing. Yet, so far as I can see, Mr MacDiarmid throughout this poem is for the moment merely trying to bring home to us the necessity for such an international medium for poetry. He is not trying to create such a language by manifesting it in action.

Another writer has done just that; and I do not mean the writer whom Mr MacDiarmid apparently has in mind, the James Joyce of *Finnegans Wake*. I mean Ezra Pound in his *Cantos*. I do not suppose that Mr Pound had this purpose in mind when, forty years ago, he began his poem. But now, when the poem is almost completed, it seems clear that this is at any rate one of the things this great poem has done. It has created and put into action a language which is literally international, a language to which Chinese, Greek and many other languages have contributed nearly as much as Anglo-American. It becomes clear that, though English is laid under heavier contribution than any other national tongue, yet Pound's *Cantos* cannot properly be described as 'a poem in English'.

I do not pretend that this is the central significance of Pound's poem, and indeed I do not really share Mr MacDiarmid's anxiety about a language for poetry which shall be 'international' in this obvious perhaps superficial sense. But it is only the extreme statement of a problem which is indeed crucial. For if we set aside these two poems, together with the work of Mr Eliot, surely the English poetic scene presents us with just what I foresaw above—a poetry that has committed itself to the status of being no more than a marginal pleasure, a deliberately and self-confessedly *provincial* utterance. I do not mean by this just that Mr Amis, say, or Mr Philip Larkin, does not lard his verse with tags from the

Greek or with Chinese characters. We should have every right to be dismayed if they did. But just look at their attitude to what we call the cultural heritage. Here is Mr Kingsley Amis, writing a brief manifesto: '. . . Nobody wants any more poems about philosophers or paintings or novelists or art galleries or mythology or foreign cities or other poems. At least I hope nobody wants them.' 'Nobody wants any more poems about . . . foreign cities'. So much for Goethe and Spenser and Du Bellay and Vyacheslav Ivanov and so many other poets down the ages to whom, for instance, the name and the actuality of Rome have been an inspiration, standing for a cultural and moral standard. Or here is Mr Philip Larkin: '[I] have no belief in "tradition" or a common myth-kitty or casual allusions in poems to other poems or poets, which last I find unpleasantly like the talk of literary understrappers letting you see they know the right people.' 'Tradition' here in Mr Larkin's mouth carries derisive quotation marks, as it does (to take a third example) when Mr D. J. Enright speaks of finding in one of his predecessors: 'The shadow of "Tradition", which apparently takes the form of tasteful quotations from the Greek with an odd nymph or two thrown in: a weary world of "culture" borne away from the battlefield on one man's shoulders.'

Here 'culture' no less than 'tradition' gets inverted commas. And if someone protests that Enright and Larkin only put the quote-marks to show that they mean *fake*-culture, *fake*-tradition, I still demand to be shown what they mean in that case by true 'culture', true 'tradition'. My impression is, from their often admirable poems as from their criticism, that there is no place for either concept in their view of the world and of the art which they practise.

These poets are my friends and I think I know perfectly well what makes them, being finely civilized men, pretend to be barbarians; why, though they are humane persons and responsible citizens, they pretend sometimes to be cultural teddy-boys. They are putting the house of English poetry in order: not before time, too. Or rather they are trying to build it afresh, an altogether humbler structure on a far narrower basis. On all sides, our good poets are 'pulling in their horns'. They are getting rid of pretentiousness and cultural window-dressing and arrogant self-expression, by creating an English poetry which is severely limited in its aims, painfully modest in its pretensions, deliberately provincial in its scope. I do not think they would be very offended or even make demur if one added: 'inevitably marginal in importance'.

The problem is: what in the present age should be the poet's attitude to past poetry? There are good reasons why the poet's attitude to the poetry of the past çannot be like the painter's attitude to past painting, or the musician's to past music: because most past poetry is not available to the poet in the same way as all past painting is now available to the painter. By writing as if past poetry did not exist, Mr Amis and Mr Larkin and Mr Enright solve this problem to their own satisfaction. It is one way out, at any rate—but at what a cost!

Yet, why should this be a problem for the poet at all? It seems that the poet has escaped the problem and the opportunity that were presented to the painter by the recent perfecting of the means of reproduction. If that is so, why does the modern poet need to have an attitude to the past any different from Tennyson's attitude or Keats's? To answer this I have had to look at M. Malraux again and to supplement him a little. For he is surely wrong to lay such exclusive stress on the revolution in mechanics of reproduction. The techniques of reproduction—colour photography and musical recording—were discovered, as perhaps all such techniques are discovered, to answer to a need.

This need is the true source of the eclecticism of the modern movement, for it came out of an ethnological and anthropological temper of mind, which was then first appearing on the stage of history. This temper of mind was prepared and eager to investigate exotic cultures without prejudice, and from no preconceived position of cultural superiority. The modern sculptor can learn from Polynesian sculptures partly because the corpus of Polynesian sculpture is readily available to him in reproductions, but ultimately he can do so because of a new attitude of humility or anyway open-mindedness towards such supposedly 'primitive' cultures as those of Polynesia. If that attitude had not been inculcated by the first scientific anthropologists, the volumes of reproductions would never have come into existence.

The point is that at this level of attitude, temper, and need, the imaginary museum is as much the habitat of the poet today as of the sculptor. From this point of view, then, the poet finds himself—no less than sculptor, painter and musician—in what we may call 'the imaginary museum situation' but it is the poet's peculiar misfortune that his medium, being so much less international than the media of those other arts, is much less able to cope with the situation.

The modern poet's attitude to the poetic past must differ from Keats's attitude or Tennyson's simply because he has felt the impact, as the painter has, and the sculptor, and the man in the street, of the characteristic temper of scientific anthropology. We have all come to see, thanks to the anthropologist, that the artistic past of the human race is far richer and far more various than Tennyson or any poet before him realized. The masterpieces of the past do not constitute one order, derived from Greece and Rome; nor two orders, Nordic-Gothic on the one hand, classical-mediterranean on the other; nor even three orders or four. There are innumerable orders. We know this to be true of painting, architecture, sculpture, music; it is doubtless true of poetry also—with this awkward difference, that the poet is much less capable than the other artists of facing up to this knowledge and exploiting it. In short, whatever weight we give to the realization that poetry in Europe is chronologically 'out of step' with the other arts—nevertheless, poetry does participate in 'the modern movement' in the arts. As indeed we knew it did—for, after all, it does help to be reminded of cubist perspectives when faced with the first page of *The Waste Land*.

The position, then, is this: that we are not faced with a simple Either:Or. It is not a question of *either* internationalism *or* provincialism, *either* inside *or* outside the museum. Poetry finds itself in an uncomfortable betwixt-and-between; it inherits the imaginary museum and participates in the modern movement to the extent that poets and their readers share a modern sensibility determined and coloured by scientific anthropology and by practice in the other arts; it is outside the imaginary museum and outside the modern movement to the extent that its medium—language— is not international as other artistic media are. In my next talk I shall look from this point of view at the theory and practice of some modern poets.

IN MY last talk I discussed the modern poet's attitude to his art, and in particular to the past history of poetry. The intelligent poet today finds himself in a certain situation *vis-à-vis* poetry and past poetry; and I tried to define this, by asking how the poet's situation differs from the painter's, the sculptor's, and the musical composer's.

The situation in which these practitioners of the other arts find themselves has been defined by M. André Malraux as 'the imaginary museum'. What M. Malraux means is that the modern painter, for instance, differs from painters of all previous ages precisely in his relation to the past achievements of painting. Thanks in the first place to technicians who evolved modern methods of colour-reproduction, but thanks also to modern anthropologists who have shown how many and various are the cultural and artistic traditions of mankind, the painter today has at his immediate disposal virtually the whole corpus of paintings of all ages and localities. The same is true in some degree of the sculptor and, thanks to gramophone-recordings, of the musician. All these artists find themselves free to pick and choose among all the artistic styles of the past, in a way their predecessors could not.

The same is not true of the modern poet. For in relation to the art of poetry there has been no technical revolution in the medium of reproduction—nothing since the invention of printing in the fifteenth century. Neither that revolution, nor any other that one can conceive, in the reproduction of poetry, could have effects as far-reaching on poetry as revolutions in techniques of reproduction have had on painting and on music; this is so, because the medium of all the other arts is international as the medium of poetry is not. A poem is written in some one of the languages of the world, and is available (leaving aside the vexed question of poetic translation) only to readers who know that language.

So it comes about that the poet's situation is peculiarly difficult; in so far as poetry shares in 'a modern movement' common to all the arts (and it seems plain that to some extent it does so share, feeling the impact, no less than the other arts, of modern anthropology, for instance), the poet shares with the other artists a new attitude towards the cultural and artistic past of the race, a new freedom in picking and choosing among the styles of the past. Yet in so far as the medium of poetry is not international as the other media are, the poet finds himself less free of the riches of the past than the painter is, if only because most of the poems of the past are in languages he does not understand. Thus the poet stands awkwardly with one foot inside the imaginary museum, and one foot out of it.

It seems to me that you have to grasp this before you can understand the procedures and achievements of the great American, Irish and English poets of this century. First I will look at their theories, then at what is more important, their practice—their styles. Obviously the theories we are after are those that have to do with 'tradition', the theories to be found in Mr Eliot's essay on 'Tradition and the Individual Talent' and Pound's essay *How to Read* and the *A.B.C. of Reading*; and I would like to add Dr Leavis's rejoinder to Pound, his 'How to Teach Reading'. To take the last one first, it seems to me that Dr Leavis's essay has had the effect of swinging academic criticism away from Pound's solution of the problem, away from Pound's understanding of tradition, and behind Mr Eliot's—or rather behind what Dr Leavis took to be Mr Eliot's position, for Mr Eliot's essay is evasive and self-contradictory in the extreme.

Dr Leavis, being like almost all academic critics vowed to the principle and the fact of independent schools of English in our universities, has in effect and perhaps without knowing it committed his followers—which is to say, in varying degrees, nearly all the best critics in these islands—to an extreme provincialism, which assumes (what is in fact wildly improbable) that the poetry extant in our own language affords a paradigm or microcosm of poetry as a whole. As for the evasiveness of Mr Eliot's essay, let me remind you only of the passage quoted *ad nauseam* which says the poet must feel 'that the whole of the literature of Europe from Homer and within it the whole of the literature of his own country has a simultaneous existence and composes a simultaneous order'. There is also that other passage where we learn that 'The poet must be very conscious of the main current, which does not at all flow invariably through the most distinguished reputations'. The thousand-dollar question, as it seems to me, is 'How do you detect a main current through a simultaneous order?'

What is more interesting is to ask why Mr Eliot is so evasive; and I believe the answer is that he is struggling towards a perception of what I have called the betwixt-and-between situation of modern poetry, trying to accommodate a perception of the imaginary museum, of any number of different traditions and different styles all equally available, with the incompatible notion of *one* tradition, a central tradition. Some of his later criticism (for instance 'What is a Classic') shows him solving this deadlock by discriminating between those styles such as Milton's which are usefully available at one period and not at another, and those others such as Dante's and Virgil's which are available at all times and are thereby truly 'classic'.

But this was precisely the position which Pound had reached years before. His *A.B.C. of Reading* shows him as aware as Mr Eliot of how poetry stands with one foot in the museum and one foot out of it. And with admirable directness Pound there specifies, out of all the traditions hung on the walls of the museum, which it is absolutely necessary for the modern poet to take account of, which of them are—as Mr Eliot would put it—perpetually available and thereby 'classic'. Pound's list of required reading is not 'out of the question'; it is not 'more than any one man can cope with'. One may cavil at this name or that, supplement the list here or cut it back there, but it is no good turning away with a gibe just because the pedagogue includes in his list one of the traditions of Chinese poetry, and the tradition of Provençal. After all, he is prepared to consi-der reading in translations, as his critic Dr Leavis (aligning himself with the huffiest academic opinion) is not.

But the poet's attitude to the poetic past, his understanding of what 'tradition' is as a fact of his experience, manifests itself far more certainly in the way he writes, in his style, than in any theoretical formulations. The chief advantage of looking at modern poetry from the point of view of the imaginary museum is that only from this standpoint do poetic styles as various as those of Wallace Stevens and T. S. Eliot, of Ezra Pound and W. B. Yeats, appear as so many different (yet related) answers to one and the same problem—the problem of a radically changed rela-tionship to the poetic past, a relationship which must be different from Tennyson's or Pope's, yet also from that of a Matisse or a Mestrovic, a Stravinsky or a Corbusier.

This seems to me the radical problem facing the modern poet. Much has been made of the challenge presented to modern poetry by the new sciences of psychology, for instance, and sociology; but the real challenge is that of anthropology, which underpins those others. Or again one hears of the disadvantage for the poet of having no one coherent system of mythology and symbolism on which to draw and in terms of which to communicate; but this too is only an aspect of the same thing—because the problem for the poet is not that he has no mythology to use, but that he has no one such mythology, in other words, that he has too many mythologies to choose among and nothing to direct him which one to choose in any given case, nothing to tell him which of the innumerable galleries in the imaginary museum are those he should frequent.

Take one example: our still general distaste, as critics, for archaism in poetic diction. If we are asked to justify this aversion of ours, we say that poetry should 'express its age', not escape into some age of the past. And we quote the judgement of Gerard Manley Hopkins that the language of poetry should be 'the current language heightened', based on the spoken language of its time.

Yet if (as Malraux has argued) what is specifically 'modern' about the modern age is its changed attitude to the past, then the modern poet will express his age, express the modern sensibility, precisely by picking and choosing, manipulating and adapting, among the poetic styles of the past. Faced with a work out of the imaginary museum like Ezra Pound's translation (version, imitation, whatever) of the Confucian Classic Antho-logy of Chinese poetry, our distaste for archaism in diction is worse than useless; for the poet's achievement there is precisely in choosing now this, now that style from the English past in order to convey now this, now that mode of ancient Chinese sensibility. We cannot any more—though we still do, I am afraid—endorse without large qualifications Hopkins's famous manifesto in favour of 'the current language heightened'. We shall have to learn to take this as part of Hopkins's Victorianism, not his 'modernity'; it was a position possible only before the advent of the imaginary museum.

Yet we do not have to relinquish our conviction that there is indeed a sort of archaism in poetic diction which, other things being equal, is 'a bad thing'. Often, still, we encounter poems which we know to be bad just because they advertise, in their diction and style, an elaborate pretence or a mistaken conviction that nothing has changed since the death of Keats. In these cases, what we get, instead of the original poem which the poet thought he was writing, is an unconscious pastiche or sometimes an unconscious parody of poems by Keats. But it is just here that the modern poet can cut in: our objections are silenced as soon as the poet, when he uses a style from the past, makes it plain to the reader that he knows what he is doing—that his is a conscious pastiche or a conscious parody. Pastiche and parody, from this point of view, are matters of degree; and we have to say that there is an element of pastiche or of parody whenever a poet gives the merest indication—as it were a slightly lifted eyebrow—to show that he is well aware, even as he writes Keatsian verse, that a lot of water has flowed under the bridge since Keats wrote as he did. An elementary device of this kind—rather a heavy-handed one—is the use by Ezra Pound in *Hugh Selwyn Mauberly*, of hovering quotation marks:

> For three years, out of key with his time,
> He strove to resuscitate the dead art
> Of poetry; to maintain 'the sublime'
> In the old sense . . .

Here the quotation marks about 'the sublime', no less than the phrase 'In the old sense', show the poet is aware that the concept of 'the sublime', once a serious principle informing a poetic style of the past, is no longer viable, though not for that reason to be laughed entirely out of court. Or again, far more deftly and unobtrusively, a modern poet may acknowledge the element of pastiche in his writing after an archaic manner, by carrying his archaic language on a just slightly inappropriate metre. Or, yet again, the poet's awareness of the element of parody may be made as plain as it is by Eliot in the *Four Quartets* when, after a passage in delicately wrought seventeenth-century manner, he begins a new paragraph with 'That was a way of putting it; not very satisfactory.'

But, as that last example should have indicated, the most delicate way of acknowledging an element of parody or pastiche in a passage of writing is simply to set it beside something deliberately incongruous, so that the incongruity effects an ironic detachment from both. When the passages chosen are slightly adapted quotations from specific poems of the past, what we get is a modification of an ancient poetic genre, the *cento*.

But the principle is just the same when the items juxtaposed are not quotations from specific past poems, but careful imitations of specific past styles. By writing in this way the poets acknowledge, on the one hand that, like the painter, they are free to pick and choose as never before among the styles of the past; on the other hand that this unprecedented freedom is bought at a cost—the cost of never feeling entirely at home in any one of the styles they adopt. The modern style in poetry is the arrangement in new patterns of the styles of the past. To try to forge a style independent of the past can only produce poems which are, if not bad, at best minor and provincial achievements, for the good or paradoxical reason that what is specifically modern about the modern age in art is precisely its catholic and uncommitted attitude to all the ages of the past.

I have been doing no more than just glancing over the surface, indicating without really exploring some of the ways in which an apprehension of the imaginary museum situation can be made to serve analysis and evaluation of modern poetic procedures. There are other ways, just as there are other devices than those of Eliot and Pound for acknowledging the element of parody or pastiche; Wallace Stevens, for instance, has perfected a whole range of other most delicate stylistic devices to the same purpose. At some point it might be necessary and I think possible, though difficult, to distinguish parody from pastiche.

Again I throw out the suggestion for what is is worth—I believe it could be shown that whereas English poets younger than Eliot have failed by not realizing that the imaginary museum situation bears on poetry at all, American poets of those generations have mostly failed by accepting the imaginary museum too wholeheartedly, not realizing poetry's partially special position. Or again there is the interesting question of those poets in English--Robert Graves and Edwin Muir are examples—who have taken abundant note of modern anthropological researches; I believe it could be shown that this does not redeem them from provincialism, if only because they have applied themselves to distinguishing one or two archetypal patterns underlying apparent cultural diversity: and this is the sort of thing that older anthropologists, such as Frazer, did, whereas modern anthropology insists, as Malraux insists, on a diversity which is irreducible, of any number of culture-patterns each of them *sui generis*.

There is one more point that is worth making, because it is important— at least, to some people. If the modern style in poetry is as I have defined it, one can say of it that it precludes formal perfection. At some point, it appears, there must always be a flaw in the mirror, a deliberately contrived maladjustment between content and form; the modern poem can never speak for itself as completely as, say, a poem by Dryden. The illusion must, if only for an instant, be broken; the convention at some point must be deliberately transgressed. The modern poet must always, as it were, peep round from behind his poem, to advise the reader—if by no more than a lifted eyebrow or a sidelong glance—that the poem is not to be trusted all the way, that there are modes of experience or ways of saying things which the poet is aware of though his poem on its own account is not.

To be sure this is to understand 'form' in an inadequate, even a rather mechanical way; for in a more sophisticated understanding of poetic form the very breaking of illusion and convention, the very flaw of the surface, is itself a formal artifice of a delicate kind. All the same the point remains that a poem by Dryden enjoys a kind of formal beauty and completeness that no poem by Mr Eliot enjoys, that (we have got as far as this) no truly modern poem *can* enjoy.

If I am right, before the imaginary museum situation arose, poems could be complete in themselves, self-dependent, cut loose from the poet who wrote them, in a way no modern poem can be. That sort of pleasure can be afforded by modern poems only when they are minor, even provincial achievements. I have sympathy with those poets (such as Robert Graves, I suspect) who care so much for this kind of poetic pleasure that they choose to write minor poems possessing it, rather than major poems which must do without it; and equally I sympathize with those modern readers who for the same reason would rather read the minor poems of our age than the major ones.

Postscript: The argument pursued in these two broadcasts on the Imaginary Museum is so disconcerting in its implications, not to say *unnerving*, that I no less than others have tried to forget about it, or to pretend that somehow, somewhere, the argument is flawed. Yet no one to my knowledge has found that flaw. Some have complained—reasonably enough—that at the end of my argument I use the terms 'major' and 'minor' as if they had firm and definite meanings, whereas in fact of course they are very approximate words indeed. It may placate such critics to tell them that, in the sense I give to 'minor' and in the terms of this argument as a whole, all the poems I have written myself have to be called, at best, *minor* poems.

AN ALTERNATIVE TO POUND?

The Form of Loss, Edgar Bowers, Alan Swallow.

THE STANFORD school of poets, grouped around and schooled by Yvor Winters, seems to me perhaps the most interesting feature of the poetic scene in the U.S. Where other masters—British as well as American—have tried to come to terms with the challenge of the Poundian-Eliotic poetic mostly by diluting, muffling, taking what they want and evading the harder truths, Winters has met the challenge by offering a considered and coherent alternative, an alternative poetic theory grounded in an alternative morality driving through to an alternative practice. And so, while most talent can and does spring up in other quarters of the poetic scene, it is only from the Poundian wing (and by that I mean rather Charles Tomlinson, say, than Louis Zukofsky) or else from this other extreme at Stanford, that one can expect talent, when it appears, not to have to save itself by *ad hoc* improvisations, hairsbreadth escapes from eleventh-hour expedients. It is especially good, if also ironical, that this most traditional and forbiddingly 'classical' of current schools should be, at Palo Alto, within the orbit of that San Francisco bohemianism which, in its naïve reliance on the generous impulse, spells death to any poetic whatever.

Edgar Bowers has been hailed by Winters and others as exemplifying at last the Stanford poetic in the service of a major talent. In fact, he is not so good as that—hardly so good as Winters himself, certainly less good than an older hand, Howard Baker. All the same, his first collection is impressive—impressive, and also puzzling, in a way that is characteristic, more or less, of the whole school. The puzzle is how so much licence can exist along with so much discipline. On the one hand Alan Swallow, in an unusually educated blurb, is right to invoke the name (unexpectedly recondite) of Fulke Greville:

> O sages,
> Of whom we are the merest shades, you are
> The undemanding whom indifference
> Has least defiled, those few whose innocence
> Is earned by long distraction with minute
> And slow corruption proving all they know,
> Till patience, young in what may come to pass,
> Is reconciled to what its love permits,
> And is not proud that knowledge must be so.

It is quite quite true that if we look for precedents for this close and abstract ratiocination in verse, the grotesquely neglected Fulke Greville is one of the few names that can be invoked. (A less remote and therefore perhaps more tactful precedent is in some unfashionable poems by Edwin Arlington Robinson.) And the whole of the poem from which these lines are taken—it is called 'The Prince', and is a dramatic monologue analysing human evil in the shape of intellectual perversity—manifests

the same virtues of close and scrupulous thought in verse, virtues for so
long out of fashion that they strike with all the shock of absolute novelty.
It is always possible to argue of course (though I wouldn't) that these are
not virtues at all, at any rate not in poetry, which has its own and quite
different ways of thinking—as we say, 'through images'. That would make
the poem a perverse achievement; but an achievement none the less.

Not an unflawed one, however. Alongside the forbiddingly strict discipline of ratiocination and the no less strict (though perhaps equally
perverse) discipline of metre still bound to the iambic, both diction and
syntax are permitted unusual freedoms. Diction for instance is free to in-
dulge an occasional melancholy blast on the Tennysonian organ: 'Austere
old lonely grandeur's complete pride' (where the dryness of 'complete'
can't mop up the sogginess of 'austere' and 'old' and 'lonely'—three
words very long on suggestion but short on sense). More generally,
Bowers's diction is at all points very far from the usages (i.e., the word-
order) of either modern prose or modern conversation; its lean compactness cannot disguise the fact that it is very *poetical* diction, and sounds a
muffled note in consequence.

Syntax goes along with, and is a part of, diction:

> Despite erratic fires which chance
> In self-consuming, bright array
> Hurls from our gaze, let us advance
> Desire that puts despair away,
>
> In loving keeps the hope for love,
> And, though inconstant and perverse,
> Conform to law in how we move
> Like lucid stars: let love coerce.

This is really very bad, especially from a poet whom Winters names with
six others as signalizing a formal recovery to set against 'the decay of
form . . . in men such as Pound and Eliot.' (1) The poeticisms ('Desire
that puts despair away') are part and parcel of the one inefficiency that,
for instance, invites us to take 'chance', isolated at the line-ending, as a
verb—a misapprehension corrected with extreme discomfort only when
we reach line 3. But there is worse though similar discomfort inherent in
the syntax: 'puts' and 'keeps' are both governed by 'desire'; since there is no
'and' at the start of the second stanza, we inevitably expect that the 'And'
at the start of the next line will introduce yet a third verb governed by 'desire'; when the next verb arrives, however, it is 'conform', and the unexpected plural form jolts us right back to 'let us', in order to find its antecedent.
The only possible explanation of this is the sheer inability, within the exi-
gencies of rigid metre, to find room, between 'puts' and 'keeps', for the 'and'
that would make all clear. Admittedly this is as bad as Bowers ever gets. And
yet the same looseness shows up elsewhere, in more distinguished contexts:

> His nerves have left his figure loose, as mine
> Must let it go, and with it memories

> So violent they dominate the sense,
> Lest mind should settle like soft dust in trees . . .

Is it memories that should dominate, or nerves that must 'let it go', lest mind should settle? There is no way of deciding, except by the logic of the poem's argument as a whole; and though this reveals that the second alternative is the right one, we understand this only when we study the poem, not as we read it, however many times we do so. This syntactical uncertainty (cf. lines 32-7 of 'The Prince') is especially important of course, and especially betraying, in poetry like this which offers a surface of close discursive reasoning.

No, it's no good. The alternative to a Poundian poetic—it exists in theory (though the theory too needs trimming and extending—notably into a rationale of poetic diction); it does not exist as a proven alternative in practice. At least, Bowers's poems have not supplied that proof. It's a pity they have been asked to carry that responsibility; for considered simply as a first collection of poems *The Form of Loss* is a very distinguished performance. After all, what Pound and Winters have in common is an unremitting moral concern, driving through their poems to acts of judgement which nourish programmes of right action. And it is this urgency and seriousness which lift Bowers out of the ruck. His poems are never merely accomplished. Not one, for instance, of his poems about Europe is a glossy picture-postcard in verse, such as the Guggenheim Fellows so incessantly dispatch to the folks back home; his poems are written out of genuine inwardness with the European (mostly German) mind and destiny, a true commitment of intelligent sympathy. In fact he is that rarest bird, a new poet more interested in what he has to say than in himself saying it.

KINDS OF COMEDY

All That Fall, Samuel Beckett, Grove Press.

BECKETT—HOW absurd to start this way, yet this is never said—Beckett is a comic writer. He has yet to write a book that is not a funny book:

> *Mrs. Rooney*: . . . It's like the sparrows, than many of which we are of more value, they weren't sparrows at all.
>
> *Mr. Rooney*: Than many of which . . . You exaggerate, Maddy.

What Mrs Rooney exaggerates isn't in the first place man's dignity (his price in terms of sparrows), but the dignity of his language. By the meticulous correctness of her syntax ('than many of which') she achieves an elegance so conscious of itself that it becomes absurd, a parody of all stylistic elegance whatever, insinuating the suspicion that all the elegances of language, which seem so superbly to articulate experience, in fact articulate nothing but themselves. Mrs Rooney knows that her own faith in language is excessive:

> *Mrs. Rooney*: Do you find anything . . . bizarre about my way of speaking? (*Pause*.) I do not mean the voice. (*Pause*.) No, I mean the words. (*Pause. More to herself*.) I use none but the simplest words, I hope, and yet I sometimes find my way of speaking very . . . bizarre.

As Mr Rooney says, 'Do you know, Maddy, sometimes one would think you were struggling with a dead language.'

> *Mrs. Rooney*: Yes indeed, Dan, I know full well what you mean, I often have that feeling, it is unspeakably excruciating.
>
> *Mr. Rooney*: I confess I have it sometimes myself, when I happen to overhear what I am saying.
>
> *Mrs. Rooney*: Well, you know, it will be dead in time, just like our own poor dear Gaelic, there is that to be said.

'I know full well . . .', the very expression by which Mrs Rooney admits herself at the mercy of clichés, is itself a cliché. And in this state, the language can express the speaker only by betraying him, as in 'There is that to be said', the hopeful and consolatory cliché here applied to the chance of death.

One could be forgiven for thinking that Beckett has been reading Mr Kenner on Joyce's use of parody. (The radio-play is a new genre for Beckett, and it's notable how, by a comic use of sound-effects, he at once exploits the medium by parodying it.) At all events, every reader of Mr Kenner's book on Joyce will know what to make of the evidence so far presented. Joyce was forced to use parody as his central literary device because his subject dictated it. Simon Dedalus speaks involuntary parody of eighteenth-century Ciceronianism, and acts a parody of eighteenth-century manners, because these are the only norms of speech and behaviour which his milieu affords, and those only in an ossified form. Molly Bloom has access to different norms, those of nineteenth-century Romanticism; but these are just as dead as Simon's, and serve her no better—rather worse, in fact, since they were less efficient symbols for feeling even when they were alive. Mrs Rooney's formulae are from the same stock as Molly's, and indeed she is a sort of parody of Molly, grieving, as Molly did for her dead son, over a dead daughter—'In her forties now she'd be, I don't know, fifty, girding up her lovely little loins, getting ready for the change . . .' But Mrs Rooney differs from both Mrs Bloom and Mr Dedalus in knowing that the formulae cannot be trusted, even though she uses them. In other words she speaks by formula, but she does not live and feel by formula—or she strives not to, though her language continually traps her into it. From this point of view there is more hope for her, and it may be quite true that the hope will indeed be consummated when her language is as dead as 'our own poor dear Gaelic', that is to say, without the sort of zombie life it now has, which suffices to thwart her feelings while good for nothing else. 'There is that to be said.'

Here as elsewhere Beckett stakes new ground away from Joyce by applying Joycean perceptions of parody to a different dimension of language. Like Mrs Rooney, he uses 'none but the simplest words', and accordingly his quarry is not Joyce's, the word, but the sentence, not in the first place vocabulary but syntax. It is syntax, rather than the word in isolation, which parodies itself. Though language may betray the speaker in a Joycean pun ('Nip some young doom in the bud'), more often for Beckett it does so by syntactical over-elegance. This is what happens to Maddy with her 'than many of which', as here to her husband:

Mrs. Rooney: There is nothing to be done for those people!

Mr. Rooney: For which is there? (*Pause.*) That does not sound right somehow.

Or else there is a thoroughly dramatic and Wildean reversal of the expected, as in Maddy's 'There is that to be said', or in 'I saved his life once. (*Pause.*) I have not forgotten it.'

For Joyce, what began as a perception about the use of English by Irishmen became a perception about man and his language everywhere. Beckett's work up to *All That Fall* showed a similar very steady movement towards abstraction and generalization. From Murphy through to Molloy, the central figures which give their names to his novels are steadily stripped of particularity, losing first their ties with other persons, then (symbolically) their limbs, finally, with *L'Innommable*, even that badge of residual individuality, a name. In tune with this, the milieu became less and less distinguishable, from the London and Dublin of *Murphy* to the nowhere and everywhere of *Waiting for Godot*. Most people who have noticed this have supposed that it meant an ever bleaker pessimism about the human person and human destiny, but it could equally well be explained as an attempt, like Wordsworth's in his progress from articulate men through peasants and children to idiots and lunatics, to strip from the human being all attributes save precisely that of *being*—a common ground on which (who knows?) Beckett might stand, as Wordsworth did, to utter a hurrah for the human race. However that may be, *All That Fall* represents a disconcerting break or harking back in the middle of this development. It is sited so firmly in a particular milieu, that some of the jokes need for their appreciation a first-hand knowledge of the Republic of Ireland today. As usual in these cases, the jokes when disentangled are not very good ones, not for export. (For instance, 'Our own poor dear Gaelic'—if it was ever anybody's own, it certainly wasn't the shabby-genteel Maddy Rooney's; but to get this you need to know very exactly the significance, to the Catholic majority in present-day Ireland, of Mrs Rooney's allegiance to the Church of Ireland.) Similarly, some of the minor characters are only too clearly just that. The reviewer in the London *Daily Telegraph* spoke of 'Shrewd character sketches reminiscent of *Under Milk Wood*'. And while no author can be held responsible for the vagaries of his reviewers, this was a misapprehension which Beckett could have avoided; it is in fact hard to see any point to a figure like his Miss Fitt (note the schoolboy joke) except something like Dylan Thomas's assumption that 'a broad humanity' means copiousness of unrelated particulars:

There she goes, they say, there goes the dark Miss Fitt, alone with her Maker, take no notice of her. And they step down off the path to avoid my running into them. (*Pause.*) Ah yes, I am distray, very distray, even on weekdays. Ask Mother, if you do not believe me. Hetty, she says, when I start eating my doily instead of the thin bread and butter, Hetty, how can you be so distray? (*Sighs.*) I suppose the truth is I am not there, Mrs. Rooney, just not really there at all.

The dark Miss Fitt . . . dark lady of the sonnets . . . Mary Fytton . . . alone with her Maker (Shakespeare, lament for the makaris) . . . Mary Fytton without meaning for any but her creator, his language so decayed he can no longer communicate . . . Shakespeare and his language dead or half-dead . . . hence, 'not there, Mrs. Rooney, just not really there at all.' And, 'doily'? D'Oyly Carte? Perhaps not. But once started on this, where do we stop? Shall we say that this is not *Under Milk Wood*, but a parody of that? Not derivative slapstick but its parody? This having it both ways is Joycean indeed—throw the exegete a red herring to keep him quiet, and then on with the motley. Common sense demands that we ignore the lure, and call this derivative slapstick, just that.

And the play never recovers from the point, less than halfway through, where Miss Fitt appears. Up to that point it has been a joy, and its drama has all been in the language. From this point on, it is only partly in land-slips of language, syntax yawning suddenly in crevasses under the speaker's feet. More and more significance is pumped into the text in the manner of the dark lady nonsense, and the piece ends with ambiguities flying off in all directions, and a tediously insoluble whodunnit question-mark over whatever it was unspeakable that the blind Mr Rooney did to a child in the train. There is also a fascination with blasphemy, which most non-Irish readers will find childish and trivial. The thing to hold on to is the comedy:

Mrs. Rooney: I remember once attending a lecture by one of those new mind doctors, I forget what you call them. He spoke—

Mr. Rooney: A lunatic specialist?

Mrs. Rooney: No, no, just the troubled mind. I was hoping he might shed a little light on my lifelong preoccupation with horses' buttocks.

Mr. Rooney: A neurologist.

Mrs. Rooney: No, no, just mental distress, the name will come back to me in the night.

The gratuitous zaniness—'horses' buttocks'—is of all jokes the last that can afford to fall flat. And when a comedian so delicate and resourceful as Beckett does something as lame as this, it is a sign that something is wrong.

The play goes to pieces. But in the light of Beckett's other achievements, the handsome thing to do is to remember how comic he is, and how serious, when he is really in control:

Mrs. Rooney: . . . It's like the sparrows, than many of which we are of more value, they weren't sparrows at all.

Mr. Rooney: Than many of which . . . You exaggerate, Maddy.

Mrs. Rooney: (*with emotion*). They weren't sparrows at all!

Mr. Rooney: Does that put our price up?

A concern with the dignity or the decrepitude of language is, after all, a concern for the dignity or decrepitude of man. To a writer of the twentieth century who, like his contemporaries the painters and sculptors, disdains to do with his art anything more questionable than explore the nature of his own medium, words in arrangements, the question of human dignity cannot present itself in any other terms than those of the dignity of human language. But in those terms it cannot *but* present itself. And Beckett, when he is not stooping to trick-endings and symbolic puns, is of those modern writers who have withdrawn into a sheerly verbal universe, not in order to exclude the more troublous worlds of experience, but precisely to see all those wider troubles at work in language as in a microcosm.

And in any case what survives is, formidable and affecting, the figure of Mrs Rooney. In *All That Fall*, for the first time in Beckett's career, it is not a man who is at the centre of attention. And this makes a great difference. The advent of Maddy Rooney was signalled perhaps in *Malone Dies*, by the dying Malone, who obviously speaks more than any of Beckett's other creations with his master's voice: 'Unfortunately our concern here is not with Moll, who after all is only a female, but with MacMann . . .' This refers to the sustained episode of MacMann's grotesque amour with Moll as told by Malone. Just as MacMann's name (son of man) is a pun of a different order from the name of Miss Fitt, so this whole episode in *Malone Dies* is a good example of how delicately and seriously Beckett can use allegory. What the allegory shadows forth, in a blasphemous parody of marriage as a Christian sacrament (and here the blasphemy too has point and force), is the divorce of body from mind in post-Cartesian man. (I'm sorry to use this cant phrase, but there is abundant evidence that these are the terms, and this is the historical perspective, of Beckett himself.) Moll—like that other Molly, Mrs Bloom—'stands for' the body, MacMann for the mind; and Moll's only demand is that she shall die at the same time as her equally decrepit and impotent lover. It is little to ask, for of course body and mind should die together. But in fact Moll dies first. And accordingly MacMann, like Malone himself, becomes a mind without a body as he waits for death. In Mr and Mrs Rooney mind and body live on together, bound together by mutual needs which, acknowledged, become affections. And in Mrs Rooney, for the first time since the Celia of *Murphy* but here far more centrally, Beckett presents the wisdom of the body and its claims.

   Similarly, some light is thrown on the still irritating and gratuitous conundrum of what happened in the train between Dan Rooney and the child, by Malone's maudlin reverie on his deathbed:

   Or I might be able to catch one, a little girl for example, and half strangle her, three quarters, until she promises to give me my stick, give me soup, empty my pots, kiss me, fondle me, smile to me, give me my hat, stay with me, follow the hearse weeping into her handkerchief, that would be nice. I am such a good man at bottom, such a good man, how is it nobody ever noticed it? A little girl would be into my barrow, she would undress before me, sleep beside me, have nobody but me, I would jam the bed against the door to prevent her running away, but then she would throw herself out of the window. . .

This has far more logic and point in *Malone Dies* than in *All That Fall*, because in the novel the allegory has established a historical perspective in which the reader may naturally recall how a cult of the immature and the virginal has been a feature of ages which made an absolute gulf between the physical and the spiritual conceived of as mental, between the body and the mind. But if Mr Rooney, being male, has something in common with Malone, it is worth recalling what the latter has to say of himself: 'The aeroplane . . . has just passed over at two hundred miles an hour perhaps. It is a good speed, for the present day. I am with it in spirit, naturally. All the things I was always with in spirit. In body no. Not such a fool.' Mrs Rooney *is* such a fool, who takes all the risks of being with things in body; that is why we like and admire her, as surely her author meant that we should. And from this point of view his comment on her earlier avatar Moll, that she was 'only a female', carries plenty of irony. And when he says in the novel that our concern is not with Moll but with MacMann 'unfortunately', *that* word—so most readers will feel—need carry no irony at all.

   All the same, Beckett avoids the easy dishonesty of presenting Mrs Rooney's indomitable carnality as a panacea. The questions which disabled Watt and Molloy and Malone—how to know the world, how to know the self—are no nearer being answered after we have seen Mrs Rooney contriving not to worry about them. Her husband's refusal to retire from business into domesticity represents, in *All That Fall*, Beckett's renewed acknowledgement of the right of the masculine intellect to ask questions, which, being unanswerable, may disable the mind and the body both.

Beckett's wit has never been in question. But in calling him a comic writer one credits him with something else—humour, with whatever that may or must imply of affirmation, and pleasure in the human spectacle. If it is hard to believe in the humour beneath the more bleakly witty passages of *Molloy* and *Malone Dies, All That Fall* is quite plainly humorous, at least in all that immediately concerns Mrs Rooney. It would be pleasant to suppose that in future work by Beckett the humour will continue to come to the surface in that way, and that the unfortunate elements in *All That Fall* only tell of the strains of transition to this more humorous mode.

Postscript: Some of the ideas in this piece appear also in a poem, 'Samuel Beckett's Dublin', which last however, as the title implies, originated in the immediate sensuous experience of the city of Dublin in wintertime. I cannot now remember which came first—the poem (*Collected Poems*, p. 51), or this review-article.

SEE, AND BELIEVE

Seeing is Believing, Charles Tomlinson, McDowell, Obolensky.

THIS IS Tomlinson's third collection of poems, but the first that is both substantial and representative. His first, published quite some years ago by the Hand & Flower Press, contains, as they say, 'prentice-work', promising, intelligent and various, but now interesting chiefly because it shows the poet casting about for the style he wanted. In *The Necklace*, fifteen poems published four years ago by the Fantasy Press, the style has been achieved completely, but appears a specialized instrument for very special purposes. Special, and limited. Of course. But not at all so limited as people thought. The proof is in this collection, where what is recognizably the same style has been adapted, refined and elaborated so as to serve a much wider range of experience—as wide a range, in fact, as anyone has the right to demand of any poets except the greatest.

The word which the reviewers found for *The Necklace* was 'imagist'. But it was the wrong word, as Geoffrey Strickland pointed out in this journal; for Tomlinson had entered into his landscapes with far more of himself than an Imagist poet could ever afford to deploy. What he aimed at and achieved was a sensuous apprehension more comprehensive and more comprehending than the Imagist programme, bound to the one sense of sight and the one stance of cool observer, could allow for. Tomlinson's attitude, as distinct from his techniques, was far nearer to Lawrence's (in a poem like 'Snake') than to Pound's or Hulme's. What prompted the word 'imagist' was the one thing no one could deny, however little he might value it: the exquisitely accurate register of sense-impressions. What wasn't realized was that this scrupulous exactness wasn't there for its own sake, but as a discipline and a control; controlling an exceptionally passionate and whole-hearted response to the world, to a world that bore in, not just on the five senses, but also on a man's sentiments, a man's convictions. The American reviewers seem, some of them, to be making the same mistake with this collection.

But for heaven's sake let's not carp at the Americans. They have published, first in their magazines and now in this very elegant book, poems which (as I know) have for years been hawked in vain round the British magazines, the British anthologists and the London publishing houses. All honour to Miss Erica Marx and Mr Oscar Mellor, and to those editors who have published Tomlinson in British magazines, even if they did choose to print mostly pieces which were marginal and untypical. The blunt fact remains: that *The Necklace* was unavoidably a slight and fugitive publication, and that otherwise this most original and accomplished of all our postwar poets, profoundly English as he is in his attitudes and nowadays his landscapes, had to wait for a transatlantic critic, Hugh Kenner, to discover him; for transatlantic magazines to publish him in bulk, pay him, and award him prizes; and for a transatlantic publisher to bring him out between hard covers. Your withers, of course, remain

unwrung. Am I trying to pretend that this is a national disgrace? Nothing
less. But anyhow, the case is no special one: the publication of this volume
gives point to desultory arguments that have gone on for some time,
about whether New Provincial isn't Old Parochial, whether the glibly cosmopolitan is any worse than the aggressively insular. For Tomlinson's
models are largely French and American; that is, he refuses to join the
silent conspiracy which now unites all the English poets from Robert
Graves down to Philip Larkin, and all the critics, editors and publishers
too, the conspiracy to pretend that Eliot and Pound never happened.
Tomlinson refuses to put the clock back, to pretend that after Pound and
Eliot, Marianne Moore and Wallace Stevens have written in English, the
English poetic tradition remains unaffected. He refuses to honour even
the first rule of the club, by sheltering snugly under the skirts of 'the
genius of the language'; instead he appears to believe, as Pound and Eliot
did before him, that a Valéry and a Mallarmé change the landscape of
poetry in languages other than their own. No wonder he doesn't appeal
to our Little Englanders.

   This, the debt to the French, is the subject of the elaborate tail-piece to
this volume, an eight-page poem in six parts entitled 'Antecedents'. It is
the only lineal descendent of Pound's *Mauberley*, and worthy of that great
original, limited only as that is limited, by offending against Sidney's in-
junction that the poet should not confound himself with the historian.
The hero is Jules Laforgue, introduced in the second section after a
brilliant capsulated history of French symbolism as the logical consequence of the Romantic Movement, the whole orchestrated in terms of
two arch-Romantic images, sunset and the call of a horn, conflated in a
series of synaesthetic perceptions like those of the symbolists themselves
('Slow horn pouring through dusk an orange twilight'). After Byron,
Tennyson, Nietzsche, Wagner, Mallarmé, Baudelaire, enter Laforgue:

> We had our laureates, they
> Their full orchestra and its various music. To that
>   Enter
> On an ice-drift
> A white bear, the grand Chancellor
> From Analyse, uncertain
> Of whom he should bow to, or whether
> No one is present. It started with Byron, and
> Liszt, says Heine, bowed to the ladies. But Jules . . .
> Outside,
>
>   De la musique avant toute chose
> The thin horns gone glacial
> And behind blinds, partitioning Paris
> Into the rose-stained mist,
> He bows to the looking-glass. Sunsets.

Will Tomlinson be told to bear his learning more lightly? But where do we find a lighter touch than in the elegant fantasy (adapted from La-forgue himself) which makes the blank white page and the blank space on the page a polar bear on an icefloe? Mallarmé said, 'L'armature intel-lectuelle du poème se dissimule et tient—a lieu—dans l'espace qui isole les strophes et parmi le blanc du papier: significatif silence qu'il n'est pas moins beau de composer que les vers.' If this is one of the most percep-tive things said about the art of poetry in the last hundred years, how can we maintain that a professional poet should not know this, or that, if he does, he should conceal the fact? But he answers such objections himself:

> Our innate
> Perspicacity for the moderate
> Is a national armory. 'I have not
> Read him: I have read about him':
> In usum delphini—for the use
> Of the common man. After Nietzsche
> (Downwards) Sartre, for whom
> Anouilh, dauphin's delight. And thus
> Rimbaud the incendiary,
> Gamin contemporary
> With Gosse, the gentleman
> Arrived late. He was dressed
> In the skin of a Welsh lion, or the lion
> Wore his—for the light
> Was dubious, the marsh softening
> And the company, willing to be led
> Back to the forsaken garden by a route
> Unfamiliar—yet as it wound
> Dimly among the fetishes, a bewilderment
> Of reminiscence. The force
> That through the green dark, drove them
> Muffled dissatisfactions. Last light, low among tempests
> Of restless brass. Last music
> For the sable throne (She comes, she comes!)
> As the horns, one by one
> Extinguish under the wave
> Rising into the level darkness.'

Except for the strident and typically Poundian pun ('delphini'/'dau-phin's'), this is more Eliotic than Poundian, in the interlarded quotations of course, but more importantly in the Mallarméan syntax which acts out, for instance, the anachronism of Dylan Thomas playing in 1940 the Rimbaud game for which the right time was 1870:

> And thus
> Rimbaud the incendiary,
> Gamin contemporary
> With Gosse, the gentleman
> Arrived late.

This is wit that is something better than deprecating, because this is a poet with something better to write about than himself. Laforgue had nothing better—'He bows to the looking-glass'; and so 'Antecedents' is, as the title says, at once 'A homage and a valediction'. Tomlinson is a post-symbolist poet, not a symbolist absurdly belated. And he is not going to make the mistake he diagnoses in Thomas, of playing Laforgue as Thomas played Rimbaud, a half-century too late.

How to utilize the Symbolist disciplines and procedures while escaping from the Symbolists' solipsistic trap—this is spelled out in the last section of 'Antecedents', as well as at other points. But Tomlinson's style (and I don't mean the specially contrived style of 'Antecedents') does better than spell out the answer; it exhibits it in living action. For the style which Tomlinson discovered in *The Necklace* and has here developed so flexibly is not just a way of writing, not at all a way of writing in any sense that is not also a way of perceiving, a way of responding. Central to this style of perceiving is a symbolist idea generally known to us only in the rather special version that Eliot gave of it when he spoke of the objective correlative. It is the idea that an arrangement of objects or events in the apparently external world may so correspond to a pattern of thought and feeling in the mind, that the latter may be expressed and defined in terms of the former. It is against the background of this conviction that Tomlinson can speak (as, to be sure, others have spoken) of 'a certain mental climate', of 'the moral landscape of my poetry in general'. These are something better than metaphors or, if they are metaphors, these metaphors underpin everything Tomlinson writes. Now it is obvious that the idea as just outlined permits of a two-way traffic between the poet's mind and the world: he may proceed from himself outward, starting with a state of feeling in himself and seeking an objective correlative for it; or he may start with perceptions of the objective world, and move inward to find a subjective correlative for them in a state of feeling he induces or imagines. Symbolist poetry characteristically seems to have run the traffic all the first way, to the point indeed at which the reality of the supposedly objective world, as anything but a phantasmal reflection of the subjective, becomes highly questionable. Tomlinson too may run the traffic this way, as when he answers Amis's notorious 'Nobody wants any more poems about foreign cities', by conjuring up cities imagined so as to correspond to states of mind:

> Not forgetting Ko-jen, that
> Musical city (it has
> Few buildings and annexes
> Space by combating silence),
> There is Fiordiligi, its sun-changes
> Against walls of transparent stone
> Unsettling all preconception—a city
> For architects (they are taught
> By casting their nets
> Into those moving shoals); . . .

But far more characteristically (and specifically so as to escape the Symbolist vertigo about whether the objective exists), Tomlinson runs the
traffic the other way, insisting upon the irreducible Otherness of the non-
human world, its Presence in the sense of its being present, its being
bodied against the senses, as the irreplaceable first principle of all sanity
and all morality. Of many statements of this (for it is after all what gives
the book its title), I take 'Cézanne at Aix':

> And the mountain: each day
> Immobile like fruit. Unlike, also
> --Because irreducible, because
> Neither a component of the delicious
> And therefore questionable,
> Nor distracted (as the sitter)
> By his own pose and, therefore,
> Doubly to be questioned: it is not
> Posed. It is. Untaught
> Unalterable, a stone bridgehead
> To that which is tangible
> Because unfelt before. There
> In its weathered weight
> Its silence silences, a presence
> Which does not present itself.

Some objections may here be anticipated, and a concession made at no
cost (which is that, yes, there are about five unsuccessful poems here, out
of thirty-five). It will be objected that the poems are inhuman, that they
never deal with people, human relations, human sentiments. In fact, the
great advance on *The Necklace* is precisely here, in commenting (but by implication, always by implication from arrangements of sense-perceptions)
on the life of man in history, especially on his communal life as registered
by his buildings, by the nature and quality of his tools, by the landscapes
he has modified. Secondly, it appears that readers have difficulty
with Tomlinson's metres. Like most of Eliot (and how much else?), the
metre is on the uncertain borderline between *vers libre* and loose (basical-
ly four-stress) accentual verse. For my part, I am sure that to count
syllables as well as stresses is to have an instrument more delicate and
various. But it is disingenuous to object to Tomlinson's metre while accepting Hopkins and Eliot—he is less emphatically muscle-bound than the
one, more alert and vigorous than the other. The stops and starts of syntax play over against, and tauten, the runs and pauses of rhythm; and
there is a Hopkinsian (but again less emphatic, and so more flexible) richness of orchestration in internal echoes and half-echoes of consonance
and assonance, lacing clauses and lines together.

When I turn from these poems to work by highly and justly commended
writers, such as R. S. Thomas, say, or even Edwin Muir, what dismays me
about these is a pervasive slackness—not in perception nor in seriousness
(for both are commonly as honest and truthful as Tomlinson), but simply

in artistic ambition. In their hands the medium is used scrupulously and well, to good and important ends; but it is *not wrought up to the highest pitch*. They do not say a thing once and for all, then move on fast to another thing. Their expressions could be, not more true, but more forcibly, more brilliantly and compactly true. What people don't realize is that in poetry there can be no question of choosing between the thing well done and the thing done consummately, conclusively. The art imposes its own laws: it demands to be pushed to the extreme, to be wrought up to the highest pitch it is capable of. There are degrees of meritorious performance, certainly, but there can be no question—not for the poet nor for the responsible reader—of preferring the less degree to the greater, as one may prefer weak tea to strong. Thus it is nonsense to say of Tomlinson, as some have said, that of course his diction and his music are choice and distinguished beyond the reach of his contemporaries, but nevertheless a coarser music may be better, a diction more vulgar may be more vigorous and so more valuable. The muse is not to be fooled, and vigour bought at that cost will soon be exhausted. As an art, poetry cannot juggle with its own hierarchies. This is also the reason why it cannot stand still; why a poet who writes as if Pound and Mallarmé had never written may have merit, certainly, but other things being equal he can never have equal merit with a poet whose writing acknowledges the heights to which the art was wrought at those hands. This book, I am sure, is a landmark. What a pity it should mark a new peak in the obtuseness of the English to their own poets, as well as a new height gained in the long struggle back to English poetry considered by the poet as a way of spiritual knowledge.

REMEMBERING THE MOVEMENT

I'VE BEEN thinking for some time that I ought to set down my recollections and impressions of the last few years, so far as they may amount to a chapter of literary history. But I've never seen myself putting this straight into print. Always it seemed that the time for that wasn't ripe, the occasion disreputable. Now that I find myself writing for print after all, I feel impatient with all the crippling embarrassment and Simon-Pure evasiveness that prevented me from doing so before, and still obstructs me now. And this wasn't peculiar to me: nothing now strikes me as so significant and so queer about 'the Movement', as the way all of us who were supposed to be 'in' it still spoke of it among ourselves inside invisible quotation-marks. We ridiculed and deprecated 'the Movement' even as we kept it going. I don't know, but I should imagine that this would have been the most baffling thing about us, to any Frenchman (say) or American, who got into company with two or three of us. For in their countries, so far as I can see, writers who set out in concert to write a chapter of literary history don't have to pretend elaborately to be doing something else. Why should they? We in the Movement did so, for the same reasons which brought the whole thing to a halt and broke it up before it was under way —out of pusillanimity; from the unforgivable literary sin of going much further than halfway to meet our readers, forestalling their objections, trying to keep in their good books. Ours was writing which apologized insistently for its own existence, which squirmed in agonies of embarrassment at being there in print on the page at all. In the interstices of our poems—in the metrical places wasted on inert gestures of social adaptiveness—'no doubt', 'I suppose', 'of course', 'almost', 'perhaps'—you can see the same craven defensiveness which led us, when we were challenged or flattered or simply interviewed, to pretend that the Movement didn't exist, that it was an invention of journalists, that we had never noticed how Larkin and Gunn and Amis had something in common, or that, if we had noticed, it didn't interest or excite us.

Other people have said this before, have pointed out for instance how Amis's and Larkin's dislike of foreign travel and foreign languages seems meant to ingratiate them with aggressively insular philistines among their readers. But I have in mind something else. There are insular philistines among readers of the *Sunday Times*, and John Betjeman knows how to tap their prejudices to good purpose. Just as insular, just as philistine, are their political enemies, the readers of *Tribune* whom Amis seems to be wooing. But there is insularity and philistinism—the first, and therefore the second—among the readers of *Essays in Criticism* and the ex-readers of *Scrutiny*; among, in fact, just the selfconscious élite which is first to leap on 'the Movement' for selling out to the middlebrows. The longer I look at it, the more it seems to me that it was the selling out to *this* public, the attempts to placate in advance *these* readers, which crippled 'the Movement' from the start. What did for us was conceding too much, not to the insularity which orders baked beans on toast in Pavia and thinks all foreigners are dirty, but to the insularity which has ready its well-documented and conclusive sneer at Colette and Marianne Moore, Cocteau and Gide and Hart Crane. This is probably the time to speak only for myself, and to admit that while I hadn't hope of many readers from the *Tribune* or the *Sunday Times*, I had hopes of readers from among this highbrow élite; and now when I reread my poems of those years it seems all too obvious how far I was ready to go to woo and placate these bodies of feeling and opinion.

This isn't just to concede everything to the gibe which was flung at us from the beginning, that we were 'academic'. Academic is no bad thing to be, and in any case becomes inescapable, as the philistinism of Anglo-American society forces all artists—not just writers—back into the campus as a last stronghold. It is a question whether the universities can rise to this emergency. But it has been normal at every period for the poet to be a learned man; and if universities exist for or provide for the pursuit of learning, it is proper and natural that the poets should cluster round the campuses. In any case, in so far as academicism is a besetting danger for the poet, the most full-blooded and best-informed campaigns against that academicism have always come from inside the academic body. I foresaw and intended that some of the dons I knew would be affronted and offended by what I wrote, and many more would ignore it. I addressed myself hopefully not to the academic profession but to a group within the profession, very consciously at odds with the rest and more or less committed, appropriately enough, to the idea of 'a minority culture'. In so far as the others shared my hopes of these readers (and I think they did, up to a point), we were all disillusioned. The radicals of yesteryear were now the guardians of the law; and those who had once fought to get Eliot and Lawrence on students' reading-lists were now the most determined that no later writer should figure there, the most careful not to risk a good opinion of a contemporary.

Meanwhile all of us in the Movement had read the articles in *Scrutiny* about how the reputations of Auden and Spender and Day Lewis were made by skilful promotion and publicity; and it was to placate *Scrutiny* readers that we pretended (and sometimes deceived ourselves as well as others) that the Movement was not being 'sold' to the public in the same way; that John Wain on the B.B.C., and later Bob Conquest with his anthology *New Lines* weren't just touching the pitch with which we others wouldn't be defiled. Again I limit myself to my own case: I remember nothing so distastefully as the maidenly shudders with which I wished to know nothing of the machinery of publicity, even as I liked publicity and profited by it. Of course, once the machinery was set going, there was no controlling it; and Wain, Gunn and Larkin figured in a series of 'profiles' in *The Times Educational Supplement*, lately almost duplicated in the *Sunday Times*, from which I can in all honesty rejoice to have been excluded. And of course there is a quite drastic coarsening and simplification that goes on even at the hands of a sophisticated publicity-agent like

G. S. Fraser. But for heaven's sake publicity is what in some degree we all want, quite legitimately; and the prissiness which won't pay any of the price, won't use any of the channels which it knows are available, only brings about the sort of half-hearted falling between two stools which made the Movement abortive. The writer's job, I now think, is to make sure that the wares are good; and then to be as cynical and ingenious as possible in marketing them by the only channels that are open.

There's a lot more than this to be said about publicity. Too much of it, for instance, is certainly worse than too little. Kingsley Amis suffered from this far more than the rest of us; and his staying in his academic job in the provinces, as well as his refusal to contribute to some of the Angry Young Man book-making, were brave and level-headed attempts to resist the publicity that came to him. These were acts of integrity and of a very just perception of where publicity begins to do too much damage—to the writer, and to his relations with the public.

But it's just there—in the relations with the public (not with this public or that one, but with 'the reader' in general, however conceived of)—that the Movement seems to me to be most instructive. I come back to my first point—it wasn't so much that we addressed the wrong set of readers, as that we addressed *any* reader too humbly. We were deprecating, ingratiating. What we all shared to begin with was a hatred for writing considered as self-expression; but all we put in its place was writing as self-adjustment, a getting on the right terms with our reader (that is, with our society), a hitting on the right tone and attitude towards him. And in fact, this was the only alternative to exhibitionism, to 'self-expression', which our education and the climate of ideas presented us with. It's still true that literary criticism in Britain cannot conceive of anything else. Just consider how much of an okay word 'tone' is, and has been ever since I. A. Richards put it into general currency; and how difficult we find it to conceive of or approve any 'tone' that isn't ironical, and ironical in a limited way, defensive and deprecating, a way of looking at ourselves and our pretensions, not a way of looking at the world. Hardly ever did we seem to write our poems out of an idea of poetry as a way of knowing the world we were in, apprehending it, learning it; instead we conceived of it as an act of private and public therapy, the poet resolving his conflicts by expressing them and proffering them to the reader so that vicariously he should do the same. The most obvious register of this is the striking absence from 'Movement' poetry of outward and non-human things apprehended crisply for their own sakes. I'm not asking for 'nature poetry', but simply for an end to attitudinizing. In 'Movement' poetry the poet is never so surrendered to his experience, never so far gone out of himself in his response, as not to be aware of the attitudes he is taking up. It is as if experience, as if the world, could be permitted to impinge on the poet only if he had first defined the terms in which it may present itself; as if the world never imposes its own conditions, but must wait cap-in-hand until the writer is prepared to entertain it (with the lighting and the angles previously arranged). This imperiousness towards the non-human goes along with the excessive humility towards the human, represented by the reader; you can be as arrogant as this towards the natural only if you assume (as I think we all assumed) that the sole function of the natural is to provide a vocabulary of terms—'symbols', 'images'—by which people, poet and reader, can get in touch with each other.

Instead of now trying to find good things to say of the Movement (I could say plenty) or finding creditable exceptions among Movement writers, I prefer to point out that what I've just said against it applies equally well to most English and a great deal of American poetry in the present century and at the present day. Auden and Empson woo their readers as blatantly as Movement poets do; the manipulation of 'tone' plays as big a part in their poems as in Amis and Larkin. Yeats has as little interest in alien modes of being, as imperiously makes of a swan or a tree only a symbol for something in himself, as Thom Gunn does. The younger Eliot, manipulating the defensive ironies of Laforgue and reducing the various liveliness of the natural world to a repertoire of objective correlatives for states of mind, is just as little interested in poetry as a way of knowing that world in its multifarious otherness. As for the Americans—certainly it is harder for them, faced with the impersonal plenitude of landscapes in Utah, Nevada, California, to relegate the world to a mere vocabulary of communication. Yet William Carlos Williams, for instance, honoured father-figure of avant-garde Americans on the West Coast and elsewhere, who has tried to keep his eye on the subject instead of on the reader, seems to have failed most of the time: his 'tone', his way of playing for the reader's attention and getting the reader on his side, is very obvious indeed—it is the excruciating tone of the *faux-naïf*, and it survives into most of the poems of his followers, just as distractingly as the tone of ironical urbanity in us or in the Americans from the Eastern campuses.

Postscript: The occasion for this piece determined its tone. The anger—with myself, as well as with others—is designedly unbuttoned and topical. But it is not for that reason to be dismissed as 'dated', as of 'only historical interest'.

IMPERSONAL AND EMBLEMATIC

AFTER READING through Robert Graves's *Collected Poems* (not the first Graves 'Collected', nor perhaps the last), I am confirmed in my sense of where his surest achievement lies, though my sense of it is enriched by examples I hadn't noticed. His natural and characteristic form is the epigram. I think of such poems as 'Love without Hope', 'Flying Crooked', 'On Portents', 'Woman and Tree' and (a new one to me) 'New Legends'; it seems that this sort of achievement has been possible for Graves at every stage of his career. And it would be easy to elaborate this into a view of Graves as the Landor of his age. Not only the addiction to epigram (in the fullest Greek-Anthology sense, with a special place for the sumptuous love-compliment in this form), but also the self-imposed long exile by the Mediterranean, and the face turned to the public at large (irascible, scornful, selfconsciously independent) are things that Graves and Landor have in common. What's more, the difficulty we have in making Landor fit (into his age, that is, with Wordsworth and Coleridge, Shelley and Keats) is just the difficulty we have seeing where Graves fits in with Eliot and Pound and Yeats, Auden and Thomas. As historians forget about Landor, so, I suspect, they will try to forget Graves. Each poet seems to be the exception that proves the rule about his time, the case which belies the generalization but cannot disprove it because the case is so clearly a special one. Yet this last limitation (for that's what it is) is not at all so clear in Graves's case as in Landor's; and that's why the comparison shouldn't be pressed—not because it is 'academic' but because it prejudges the issue.

To begin with, the epigrams are only a small part of Landor's work as a whole, from which moreover they stand apart in a category of their own. And this isn't true of Graves: it is recognizably the virtues of the epigram which inform much work by Graves that is ampler and more relaxed than the epigram proper. And this means that to do him justice we have either to extend the term 'epigram' to a point where it's meaningless or else find a term more comprehensive. I believe the right term is 'emblem'. This can be applied to a poem like 'Vain and Careless', which develops in very leisurely fashion indeed (such as the strict epigram can never afford) through six quatrains which nevertheless stand to the moral discovery in the final quatrain—'Water will not mix with oil,/Nor vain with careless heart'—in precisely the same relation as the body of an epigram to its pay-off line. The story of the lady so careless she mislaid her child and the man so vain he walked on stilts is an emblematic fable, as 'The Glutton' is an emblematic image:

> Beyond the Atlas roams a glutton
> Lusty and sleek, a shameless robber,
> Sacred to Aethiopian Aphrodite;
> The aborigines harry it with darts,
> And its flesh is esteemed, though of a fishy tang
> Tainting the eater's mouth and lips.

> Ourselves once, wandering in mid-wilderness
> And by despair drawn to this diet,
> Before the meal was over sat apart
> Loathing each other's carrion company.

This is the emblem in the form of riddle. (The answer to the riddle seems to be 'Lust'.) Graves has been much interested in poetic riddles, and in those bodies of literature (e.g. Celtic poetry, and English and Irish folk-lore) which are especially rich in them. Not many of his own riddles are so easy to solve as 'The Glutton'; one of the finest and most extended is also one of the hardest, 'Warning to Children', which I now take to be just about the most ambitious poem Graves has ever written.

It is common, and reasonable, to define 'emblem' by distinguishing it from 'symbol'. And part of the difficulty we have with Graves has to do with his being an emblematic poet in an age when symbol has been most practised and most highly esteemed. It seems important to insist that the one is not an inferior version of the other; every image in George Herbert, for instance, is an emblem. One can define the difference by saying that the symbol casts a shadow, where the emblem doesn't; the symbol aims to be suggestive, the emblem to be, even in its guise as riddle, ultimately explicit. Another difference might be that the emblem is made, fabricated, where the symbol is *found*; or rather, since it seems plain that both 'making' and 'finding' are involved in any act of imagination, let us say that the symbol aims to give the effect of having been discovered, where the emblem aims at the effect of having been constructed. This is an important distinction, for it means that part of the impressiveness of the good symbol lies in the place and circumstances of its finding, whereas with the emblem this isn't true. We think the better of Eliot and Baude-laire for finding their symbols in the unexpected because largely unex-plored life of the industrial metropolis; but this is no warrant for thinking worse of Graves because he finds his emblems most often in a rural and agrarian England which has vanished. (It's not here that the label 'Geor-gian' can be made to stick, but rather on an occasional ponderous whimsy, like 'The General Elliott'.) Who can doubt that the rustic image of 'Love without Hope' was specifically constructed (perhaps out of memory, but perhaps not) to stand as full and explicit counterpart to the abstractions of its title?

> Love without hope, as when the young bird-catcher
> Swept off his tall hat to the Squire's own daughter,
> So let the imprisoned larks escape and fly
> Singing about her head, as she rode by.

The fullness and explicitness, the dry sharp unshadowed silhouette, the lack of resonance and overtone—these are the virtues of this emblematic writing; and the air of fabrication, even of contrivance (but not laboured contrivance), the evidence of forethought, plan and design—these will dis-please only the reader who comes to this verse for what it never offered to supply.

Sometimes, it's true, Graves seems not to understand the nature of his own gift. We have implied that the emblem is fitted to deal with those experiences which can be made explicit, whereas the symbol exists to deal with just those experiences which cannot be grasped, which can only be hinted at, seen askance out of the corner of the eye, part of the penumbra which in our mental life hangs densely about the cleared area of experience which we can formulate. When Graves tries, as he does quite often, to render experiences of nightmare obsession and anxiety, of self-disgust or the fear of madness, his dry and definite technique fails him; and we get the disconcerting effect of a nicely adjusted and chiselled frame about a vaporous centre. The much admired 'Nature's Lineaments' seems a case of this, and 'Welsh Incident' virtually admits as much. Another example, and an instructive one, is 'The Pier-Glass', a piece which could certainly be spared, bearing as it does every evidence of being very early work. This is almost entirely parasitical on early Tennyson ('Mariana' and 'The Lady of Shalott'), and it is interesting chiefly for being so much less 'modern' and 'symbolist', so much more explicit (on a theme which defies explicitness) than Tennyson was in the last century.

One great advantage of emblematic writing is its impersonality. A poet who deals with symbols, a Mallarmé or an Eliot, has to struggle much harder to cut the umbilical cord between poet and poem, so that the poem will stand free and independent. Of course there are those, like Yeats and his admirers, to whom impersonality seems not worth striving for. They find nothing attractive or valuable in the illusion which other poets seek to create, by which the poem shall seem to be a product of the language, and the poet merely a medium through which the language becomes articulate. For them poetry-making is inevitably a histrionic faculty, and they are quite happy to see poetry as the vehicle of personality. It's worth making this point because of a curious passage in Graves's Foreword where, after pointing out that he has lived and written in many countries, he remarks, 'But somehow these poems have never adopted a foreign accent or colouring; they remain true to the Anglo-Irish poetic tradition into which I was born.' What is the Anglo-Irish tradition? It's true we may think of Father Prout and 'The Groves of Blarney', the Irish tradition of comic and macaronic verse, when Graves turns the delicious joke of a poem written in the pidgin idiom of a Mallorcan pamphlet for English-speaking tourists. But there isn't enough of this sort of thing for Graves to have had it principally in mind. In view of what we know to be his opinion of Yeats, he can hardly mean that either. And yet, to the English reader (rightly or wrongly) the Anglo-Irish poetic tradition means Yeats first and the rest nowhere. Is there any point in comparing Graves with Yeats?

The comparison could be sustained about as far as the comparison with Landor (*The White Goddess*, for instance is a parallel case to Yeats's source-book, *A Vision*), but in the end it is no more fruitful. Yet the word 'histrionic', as it comes to mind in relation to Yeats particularly and the Anglo-Irish in general, is worth pondering. Graves has shown himself thoroughly at home in the world of the TV screen and the news-reel cameraman; he is not at all reluctant or maladroit in projecting a public image of himself. And this goes along with a self-regarding element in his own poetry, as in poems about his own name or about his own face in a mirror. This is very Yeatsian. Yet in general it's true that Graves uses other media than poetry in which to project his public image. The poems are impersonal in effect, even when they are on very personal themes. And it is the emblematic style which brings this about, whether the poet intended it or not. The histrionic attitude shows through in some of the early poems, notably the much-anthologized 'Rocky Acres', which I was sorry to see had been chosen by George Hartley for his long-playing disc of Graves reading:

> Yet this is my country, beloved by me best,
> The first land that rose from Chaos and the Flood,
> Nursing no valleys for comfort or rest,
> Trampled by no shod hooves, bought with no blood.
> Sempiternal country whose barrows have stood
> Stronghold for demigods when on earth they go,
> Terror for fat burghers on far plains below.

What can the last lines mean except that the poet is himself one of the demigods, poised at the verge of his harsh and craggy kingdom, prepared to harry and pillage bourgeois society? And is this not indeed very like the talk and boastful rant of Yeats in many poems, and of the professional Irishman everywhere? And if Yeats is frequently superior to this, isn't it in so piling on the extravagance as to show that he's not taken in by his own performance, but can ironically recognize blarney even when he speaks it himself? It will be interesting to hear how Graves reads this poem, for his very idiosyncratic reading manner, flat and casual, seems designed specifically to avoid rant of any kind.

The precautions he takes against rant aren't characteristically ironical; one sees them almost at once when, a few pages after 'Rocky Acres', that poem is as it were rewritten in a much terser mode, as 'Angry Samson':

> Are they blind, the lords of Gaza
>   In their strong towers,
> Who declare Samson pillow-smothered
>   And stripped of his powers?
>
> O stolid Philistines,
>   Stare now in amaze
> At my foxes running in your cornfields
>   With their tails ablaze,
>
> At swung jaw-bone, at bees swarming
>   In the stark lion's hide,
> At these, the gates of well-walled Gaza
>   A-clank to my stride.

This isn't an important poem, but it has all the impersonality of the emblem, of a medallion; and it seems that not the poet but the English language wrote it, out of the range of meanings that, for instance, 'Philistine' has taken on between the Authorized Version and Matthew Arnold. A good way to see the de-personalizing virtue of the emblem is to compare 'The Reader over My Shoulder' (direct and personal, with accordingly a disastrous thumping of the chest in the last lines) with 'The Legs', which stands beside it and treats the same subject—the poet's attitude to his readers, his public, i.e. his society at large—with completely assured and telling control, only possible after he had objectified it fully, in a contrived fable. Hereabouts in the collection—in sections II and III—the fine poems come thick and fast: 'Full Moon', 'Pure Death', the incomparable 'Sick Love', 'Saint', 'Gardener', 'In Broken Images', 'Flying Crooked'—nearly all of these are emblems. 'Flying Crooked' is one such, in which the poet distinguishes himself from other sorts of thinkers, such as logicians; 'In Broken Images', constructed in propositions in couplets, has the same theme, and thus mimics very effectively that very discourse, the logician's, from which it distinguishes itself—and this neatness attained by other means has just the distancing de-personalizing effect of the emblems.

In section IV there are abundant signs of enormous bitterness, seldom defined and as seldom mastered: such emblems as 'Hell', or 'Nature's Lineaments' or 'Ogres and Pygmies' are off-centre, registering an experience they cannot comprehend. This shows up in minutiae like the word 'raffish' in the penultimate line of 'Nature's Lineaments', which would certainly have been another word if the poet hadn't wanted a rhyme for 'fish'. The effect of thin shallowness in these pieces seems the product not of writing that is superficial, insufficiently engaged, but of writing that is engaged in the wrong way, produced out of the jangle of raw nerves not from perturbation of imagination. In 'With Her Lips Only', the shallowness shows up in another way, as knowledgeable glibness. In different ways two poems do establish imaginative control over the screaming nerves: they are 'Down, Wanton, Down!' and the admirable 'Certain Mercies', and George Hartley takes them both for the disc. He's to be complimented also on choosing 'To Evoke Posterity', a less familiar poem which provides a text to hang in the study of every poet and still more of every poetry-reader.

> To evoke Posterity
> Is to weep on your own grave,
> Ventriloquizing for the unborn.

Another body of work that hangs together usefully is section VII, where Graves seems to have herded together most of his poems that can be described as marginalia, witty but trivial pieces like 'The Persian Version', 'Apollo of the Physiologists' and '1805'. These are the graceful trivia with which he now appears every few weeks or so, in the weekly magazines; one wishes one could be sure that editors and readers are as aware as their author is, of how marginal such pieces are to his and poetry's central and exacting concerns.

EZRA POUND'S *HUGH SELWYN MAUBERLEY*

THE NAME of Ezra Pound (born 1885) undoubtedly belongs in the first place to the history of American rather than English poetry. Nevertheless his personality and his activities during at least one phase of his long career, together with the poems he then wrote, cannot be ignored in any survey, however selective, of twentieth-century English poetry. From 1908 until 1920, he made London his headquarters, playing a militant and decisive part in the crucial literary and artistic battles then being fought out on the English scene; in particular over several of these years he acted as at once mentor and sponsor of the youthful T. S. Eliot. Moreover, two of his major works of that period, *Homage to Sextus Propertius* (1917) and *Hugh Selwyn Mauberley* (1920), are explicitly attempts to portray and diagnose the state of British (not at all of American) culture at the historical moment which, for instance, D. H. Lawrence in *Women in Love* similarly took to be for England a tragically momentous turning-point. But the conclusive reason why Pound cannot be ignored is that *Hugh Selwyn Mauberley* at any rate has been accepted into the English poetic tradition, in the sense that every subsequent British poet at all serious about his vocation has found it necessary to come to terms with this work, accepting or else quarrelling with its conclusions about British culture no less than with its revolutionary strategies and methods.

Because Eliot has thrown in his lot with Britain as Pound has not, the British reader will probably come to *Hugh Selwyn Mauberley* only after reading Eliot's poetry up to and including *The Waste Land*. Yet as Eliot has been the first to insist, in respect of many of the poetic methods common to both poets it was Pound who was the pioneer. Moreover, where the poets make use of a device common to both, there is every danger of not realizing that Pound's intention is different from Eliot's in profoundly important ways.

A conspicuous example of this is the strategy which is common to *Hugh Selwyn Mauberley* and to *The Waste Land*—the extensive use of interlarded and unacknowledged quotations from poets and poems of the past, and of more or less devious references and allusions to these sources. When the reader recognizes that in Pound's poem such references are sown more thickly than in *The Waste Land*, and that the allusions are sometimes more devious, it is easy to decide irritably that Pound's use of the device is less serious than Eliot's, and open to objections which Eliot escapes:

> Turned from the 'eau-forte
> Par Jacquemart'
> To the strait head
> Of Messalina:
>
> 'His true Penelope
> Was Flaubert',
> And his tool
> The engraver's.

Firmness,
Not the full smile,
His art, but an art
In profile;

Colourless
Pier Francesca,
Pisanello lacking the skill
To forge Achaia.

A good French dictionary will reveal that 'eau-forte' means an etching;
and the context then makes it clear that the fictitious minor poet, Mauberley (whose career we are following as in a biography), is at this point
turning .in his art from the relatively full and detailed richness of the
etcher's rendering of reality to the severely selective art 'In profile' of the
engraver of medallions. A very little knowledge of Flaubert will reveal
that the French novelist differs from his English contemporaries, at least
in intention, in rather the same way, as throwing his emphasis upon selection of the one telling detail rather than on accumulation of many details
and instances. And in the art of the Italian Renaissance, the medallist
Pisanello can be opposed in just the same way to the painter Piero della
Francesca, master of composition and colour. This is entirely and sufficiently intelligible. But the reader may well protest that the point could
have been made more directly, without all this 'name-dropping'. It is easy
to protest that this is pretentious, a parade of recondite expertise for its
own sake—a charge which at one time was often brought against Eliot.
In fact, in the course of answering this objection, we not only distinguish Pound's attitude and achievement from Eliot's, we uncover what is
uniquely valuable in Pound's work as a whole, and in this poem in
particular.

In the first place Pound would say that to talk of 'recondite expertise'
begs the whole question: if knowledge of the art of the medallion, of
paintings by Piero della Francesca, and of novels by Flaubert, is out-of-
the-way knowledge for us, it shouldn't be. For Pound these names represent experiences which should be familiar to any educated man, and he is
arguing, in particular, that neither we nor the Americans can see our own
cultural traditions in proper perspective except in the context of achievements in other languages or by other cultures. He would be happy if our
reading of these lines sent us to the Victoria and Albert Museum, the
British Museum and the National Gallery to look at the late Roman or
Italian Renaissance coins, and at Italian paintings. Pound in fact, while he
shares with Eliot a wish to attain by these vivid juxtapositions an unex-
ampled conciseness of especially ironic expression, has a further intention which Eliot does not share. He has never ceased to be the pedagogue.
Just as in his London years he sought to instruct (apparently to good
effect) all of his contemporaries whom he respected—Eliot, the novelists
Percy Wyndham Lewis and James Joyce, even the much older and already

illustrious W. B. Yeats—so in all his writings he is trying to instruct his readers, telling them what buildings and paintings they should look at and what books they ought to read. For instance, concealed behind the cryptic reference to the etching by Jacquemart is the name of the French poet Théophile Gautier, who is pointed to much more explicitly elsewhere in the poem. Pound alludes to Gautier as Eliot does, because Gautier suits his purposes, but also because he is sure he fits ours too, if we only knew it.

In fact Pound is much more interested than Eliot in the spectacle of human events and affairs for their own sake, nor merely as somehow reflecting his own predicament. It is this interest which he shares with Robert Browning, whom he has consistently honoured as his own first master; and it is what distinguishes him not only from Eliot but from his other great contemporary and associate, W. B. Yeats. Whereas Eliot's diagnosis of the state of western Christian culture is not of the sort that can be abstracted from *The Waste Land* and argued over, Pound's diagnosis in *Hugh Selwyn Mauberley* asks to be treated, and *can* be treated, in just this way. Pound's view of history is put forward in all seriousness: so in *Hugh Selwyn Mauberley*, if Pound has misgauged the temper of the period he is dealing with, the poem must suffer thereby, as Yeats's poem 'The Second Coming' doesn't suffer for all its very odd view of history. In fact, Pound's reading of English cultural history from about 1860 to 1920 is a wonderfully accurate register of the temper of those times, and squares with the facts as we know them from other sources.

And yet, so far are we from conceiving of a poetry that asks to be measured against commonly observable reality, that even those readers who recognize and applaud Pound's historical insight will not rest content with this, but probe further to find in *Hugh Selwyn Mauberley* a diagnosis by the poet of his own state of mind and his own predicament. Though Pound has said, 'Of course I'm no more Mauberley than Eliot is Prufrock', (1) the poem is commonly read as if H. S. Mauberley, the fictitious poet whose representative biography the poem presents, is no more than a transparent disguise for Pound himself. Yet Mauberley, as the poem presents him, an apprehensive and diffident aesthete, all too tremulously aware of the various artistic achievements of the past (herein, incidentally, another reason—a dramatic one—for the 'name-dropping' in the poem) and of niceties of nuance in social encounters, ever less capable (as the poem proceeds) of coming to terms with the vulgarity of his age, and therefore defensively withdrawing into an always more restricted world of exquisite private perceptions—what has this figure in common with Pound, the poet, who alone among his associates and contemporaries had Browning's (or Chaucer's) zestful appetite for the multifarious variety of human personality and human activity?

The misreading arises from the first five stanzas of the poem. For this poem about Mauberley begins with a section not about Mauberley, but about E.P., that is, Pound himself ('E.P. Ode pour l'Élection de son sépulcre'):

> For three years, out of key with his time,
> He strove to resuscitate the dead art
> Of poetry: to maintain 'the sublime'
> In the old sense. Wrong from the start—
>
> No, hardly, but seeing he had been born
> In a half-savage country, out of date;
> Bent resolutely on wringing lilies from the acorn;
> Capaneus; trout for factitious bait;
>
> Ἴδμεν γάρ τοι πανθ' ὅσ' ἐνὶ Τροίῃ
> Caught in the unstopped ear;
> Giving the rocks small lee-way
> The chopped seas held him, therefore, that year.
>
> His true Penelope was Flaubert,
> He fished by obstinate isles;
> Observed the elegance of Circe's hair
> Rather than the mottoes on sun-dials.
>
> Unaffected by 'the march of events',
> He passed from men's memory in *l'an trentiesme*
> *De son eage*; the case presents
> No adjunct to the Muses' diadem.

This has been taken as Pound's judgement upon himself, but in fact it presents Pound as he knows he must appear to some others. It was the French poet of the Middle Ages, François Villon, a most distinguished 'adjunct to the Muses' diadem', who in the first line of his *Grand Testament* described himself as passing from sight in his thirtieth year, '*l'an trentiesme/De son eage*'; Pound, in his ironic and entirely characteristic use of this inserted quotation, is deriding, in effect, the confidence with which the speaker so conclusively consigns him also to oblivion. Similarly, the earlier reference to Pound's native America as 'a half-savage country' is an example of the Englishman's misplaced condescension. All the same, this fictitious Englishman is no fool. By introducing the line from Homer's *Odyssey*, 'For we know all the things that are in Troy', the speaker of this poem wittily makes Odysseus's own story of Troy into the siren-song which Pound heard and was seduced by. And in fact Pound had already started his version of the story of Odysseus, the long epic poem which has occupied him ever since. In the speaker's view, Circe, representing Pound's epic aspirations, had beguiled him from pursuing his voyage home to his faithful wife, Penelope, to his true objective, which was Flaubertian. The irony of this famous line 'His true Penelope was Flaubert' (which is echoed, as we have seen, in a later section) has been well disentangled by a transatlantic critic. For Pound, he says,

Flaubert represents the ideal of disciplined self-immolation from which English poetry has been too long estranged, only to be rejoined by apparently circuitous voyaging. For the writer of the epitaph, on the other hand, Flaubert is conceded to be E.P.'s 'true' (=equivalent) Penelope only in deprecation: Flaubert being for the English literary mind of the first quarter of the present century a foreign, feminine, rather comically earnest indulger in quite un-British preciosity; . . . a suitable Penelope for this energetic American. (2)

Thus the speaker of the poem says what is true while meaning to say (in identical words) what is false.

Pound has lately said, of commentators on *Hugh Selwyn Mauberley*, 'The worst muddle they make is in failing to see that Mauberley buries E.P. in the first poem; gets rid of all his troublesome energies.' (3) But though we have been obtuse if we suppose that the speaker of this epitaph is Pound himself, there is no way of knowing that the speaker in fact is Mauberley. Moreover Pound's comment implies, what it is not easy to discover within the poetry itself, that subsequent sections of the poem are also to be understood as spoken not by Pound himself but by the imaginary Mauberley. This is indicated by further examples of the same stilted and precious diction as 'the case presents/No adjunct to the Muses' diadem.' (The model for this sort of language, incidentally, is another Frenchman, Jules Laforgue.) Section III, for instance, is written in this style and expresses the views of Walter Pater in one place and of Swinburne in others, more wholeheartedly than Pound himself might choose to do. But this mannered language can be taken, and has been taken, as indicating a degree of ironical detachment in the poet, without supposing that the detachment goes so far as to require another speaker altogether. Again, section V, the beautiful and bitter comment on the First World War, reduces the value of European civilization to 'two gross of broken statues', in a way that doubtless Pound would not endorse, though he might sympathize with the anger at waste and loss which thus expresses itself. But from a lyric one doesn't anyway expect considered judgements; so that the dramatic fiction, Mauberley, isn't necessary here, either. The section where it is essential to realize that Mauberley and not Pound is speaking is section II, where Mauberley acknowledges that if Pound's epic pretensions were not what 'The age demanded', still less does it demand his own 'Attic grace', his 'inward gaze', his 'classics in paraphrase'. Having talked of how Pound is out of step with his age, he now talks of how he himself is out of step with it, though in a quite different way. If readers have found themselves incapable of this rapid change of stance (preferring instead an impossible compound poet, of epic and sublime pretensions in section I yet vowed in section II to Attic grace and Gautier's 'sculpture of rhyme'), the poet is partly to blame; he is trying to make ironical detachment and slight shifts of tone do more than they can do, by way of directing and redirecting the reader's attention.

The admirable sixth and seventh sections, entitled respectively 'Yeux Glauques' and (a line from Dante) 'Siena mi fe'; disfecemi Maremma', are those which provide a tart and yet indulgent capsulated history of late-Victorian literary culture. 'Yeux Glauques' establishes the milieu of, for instance, D. G. Rossetti, in the 1870s:

> The Burne-Jones cartons
> Have preserved her eyes;
> Still, at the Tate, they teach
> Cophetua to rhapsodize;
>
> Thin like brook-water,
> With a vacant gaze.
> The English Rubaiyat was still-born
> In those days.

The masterly compression here is all a matter of punctuation and grammar played against the structure of the quatrain. Grammar makes 'Thin like brook-water,/With a vacant gaze' refer to the distinctively Pre-Raphaelite ideal of feminine beauty, as embodied in several women (the most famous is Rossetti's Elizabeth Eleanor Siddall) who were at once these painters' models and their mistresses, but embodied also in the paintings of the school, of which one of the most famous is 'King Cophetua and the Beggar Maid'. But metre and rhyme make 'Thin like brook-water' refer also, in defiance of grammar, to Edward Fitzgerald's translation of Omar Khayyám's *Rubaiyat,* which went unnoticed for years until discovered by Rossetti, remaindered on a bookstall. Such ('Thin like brook-water') is Mauberley's view of the Pre-Raphaelite ideals, of the painting and poetry in which those ideals were embodied, and of the public taste which indiscriminately overlooked or applauded them. In the next poem, the focus has shifted to the later literary generation of 'the nineties', and it covers the same ground as the chapter 'The Tragic Generation' from *The Trembling of the Veil,* among Yeats's *Autobiographies;* Pound's immediate source is a more obscure book, *Ernest Dowson* by Victor Gustave Plarr, who is concealed in the poem under the fictitious name, 'Monsieur Verog'. To read these two poems as spoken by Mauberley rather than Pound turns the edge of the otherwise weighty objections (4) that Pound's irony here is of the unfocused kind which enables him to have it both ways, so that the tartness and the indulgence, the mockery and the affection, lie side by side without modifying each other. If Mauberley is the speaker, however, this unresolved attitude is dramatically appropriate and effective, and helps to account for his own subsequent failure.

After this sketch of a historical development comes a survey of the state of affairs it produced, concentrated into five acrid portraits—of 'Brennbaum' (perhaps Max Beerbohm); of 'Mr Nixon', the successful best-seller (perhaps Arnold Bennett); of 'the stylist'; of modern woman; and of the patron, 'The Lady Valentine'. Again Mauberley is speaking, for in section

XII the speaker, waiting upon the Lady Valentine, describes himself in
terms more appropriate to Eliot's Prufrock than to the ebullient and
assertive Pound. The first stanza of this poem is another splendid
example of Pound's witty compactness:

'Daphne with her thighs in bark
Stretches toward me her leafy hands'—
Subjectively. In the stuffed-satin drawing-room
I await The Lady Valentine's commands.

The quotation marks are Pound's acknowledgement that the first two
lines are an adaptation from *Le Château du Souvenir* by Gautier. But the
borrowing is made utterly Poundian by the deflating word 'Subjectively',
which meets the reader as he swings around the line-ending, thus achieving the maximum surprise and shock. In the Greek legend the river-nymph
Daphne was saved from ravishment by the amorous god Apollo, when
her father, the river-deity, transformed her on the instant into a laurel-
tree. The sexual connotation is present here, as in other episodes of Mauberley's career. But more important is the allegorical meaning by which
Apollo the god of poetry figures, sensationally diminished, as the poet
waiting humbly upon his patroness. What the poet wants from her is the
traditional acknowledgement of poetic prowess, the laurel-wreath; but
when she seems to hold this out to him ('her leafy hands') he reminds
himself that she does so only 'subjectively', only in his private fantasy,
for in objective fact she represents no such respectable body or principle
of taste as could permit the poet to value her approval. It would require
nothing less than a divine miracle to metamorphose her in this way, from
a false patroness to a true one!

We have to say that this whole sequence of twelve short poems reads
better, that several difficulties are ironed out, if they are taken as spoken
by the fictional Mauberley. Yet many of them can be read as if spoken
directly by Pound. The limitation involved here is inherent in any use of a
created character standing between the poet and the reader. This device,
by which the poet speaks in an assumed character, was first exploited
consistently by Browning in his dramatic monologues. What Pound called
the 'persona' and what Yeats called the 'mask' are refinements upon
Browning's model. Eliot's Prufrock and Gerontion, and his Tiresias who
speaks *The Waste Land*, correspond to Pound's Mauberley, and so (though
with certain important differences) do Yeats's Michael Robartes, his
Ribh and his Crazy Jane. To all three poets the device recommended itself because it helped them to what, at different times and perhaps for
different reasons, they all desired, the effect of impersonality. But the
device appears to work only if the persona is sufficiently differentiated
from the poet himself—otherwise the irony lapses, and the reader over-
looks the presence of the persona. If this happens with Pound's Mauberley, it seems to me to happen too, and more calamitously, with Eliot's
Gerontion.

How closely at this period Pound and Eliot were working in concert can be seen from a comment made by Pound many years later (in 1932, in *The Criterion*):

> at a particular time in a particular room, two authors, neither engaged in picking the other's pocket, decided that the dilutation of *vers libre* . . . had gone too far and that some counter-current must be set going. Parallel situation years ago in China. Remedy prescribed *'Émaux et Camées'* (or the Bay State Hymn Book). Rhyme and regular strophes.
> Results: Poems in Mr Eliot's *second* volume, not contained in his first . . . also H. S. Mauberley.

Pound the pedagogue is characteristically evident. But the central point is clear: Pound and Eliot, the two poets who had done most to familiarize free verse in English, had seen the necessity, at least as early as 1918, to revert to writing in rhyming stanzas, and if necessary to find their models in something so unfashionable as a provincial hymn-book. The model they adopted (Gautier, author of *Émaux et Camées*) was not much less unfashionable.

To be sure, there could be no question of simply putting the clock back. The large-scale rhythms of free verse, with its roving stresses, inform Pound's quatrains, which cannot be scanned by traditional principles, and similarly the rhymes are only approximate rhymes much of the time; still, the pattern of the rhyming stanza imposes itself, and the result is, to the ear, a peculiarly pleasant one—powerful surges of expansive rhythm never quite given their head, but reined back and cut short. On the other hand, there are quite different patterns, as in one of the sections on the Great War:

> These fought in any case
> and some believing,
>> pro domo, in any case . . .

> Some quick to arm,
> some for adventure,
> some from fear of weakness,
> some from fear of censure,
> some for love of slaughter, in imagination,
> learning later . . .
> some in fear, learning love of slaughter;

This may look like free verse; in fact it is a learned imitation of the measures of the late-Greek pastoral poet, Bion.

On the list of contents in the first English and American printings of *Hugh Selwyn Mauberley*, the first and much the longer part of the poem, specifically sub-titled 'Part I', consists of the pieces we have so far considered. Standing on its own, between Part I and Part II, is the poem headed 'Envoi (1919)'. This is one place where there is no doubt who is speaking. It is Pound himself, suddenly stepping from behind the wavering figure of Mauberley and all the veils of irony, to speak out personally, even confessionally, into a situation which he had seemed to contrive just so as not to speak in his own person at all. This wonderfully dramatic moment is signalized by the sudden appearance of a wholly unexpected metre and style, flowing, plangent and *cantabile*, so wholly traditional in every respect that the voice of the poet seems to be the anonymous voice of the tradition of English song:

Go, dumb-born book,
Tell her that sang me once that song of Lawes:
Hadst thou but song
As thou hast subjects known,
Then were there cause in thee that should condone
Even my faults that heavy upon me lie,
And build her glories their longevity.

The tradition that here utters itself is the tradition that is invoked in the name of Henry Lawes, who composed the music for Milton's *Comus*; it is the tradition not of English poetry, but of English song, English poetry for singing.

Tell her that sheds
Such treasure in the air,
Recking naught else but that her graces give
Life to the moment,
I would bid them live
As roses might, in magic amber laid,
Red overwrought with orange and all made
One substance and one colour
Braving time.

We are now enough acclimatized to this unexpected, poignantly archaic convention, to perceive that in its different way it is still dealing with matters that the earlier sections, out of their chilly smiling poise, have already canvassed. The last section of Part I, for instance, spoke of 'Fleet St. where/Dr. Johnson flourished', and remarked:

Beside this thoroughfare
The sale of half-hose has
Long since superseded the cultivation
Of Pierian roses.

These Pierian roses have become the roses which, if sealed in amber, would be 'Red overwrought with orange' and saved from the ravages of time. Thus, the 'she' whom the book must address is surely the England that Pound is preparing to leave. In an American edition of *Hugh Selwyn Mauberley*, the title-page carried a note, reading, 'The sequence is so distinctly a farewell to London that the reader who chooses to regard this as an exclusively American edition may as well omit it . . .' It seems plain that this second stanza of the 'Envoi' conveys with beautiful tenderness Pound's ambiguous attitude to an England which he sees as full of poetic beauties yet regardless of them:

Tell her that goes
With song upon her lips

> But sings not out the song, nor knows
> The maker of it, some other mouth
> May be as fair as hers,
> Might, in new ages, gain her worshippers,
> When our two dusts with Waller's shall be laid,
> Sifvings on siftings in oblivion,
> Till change hath broken down
> All things save Beauty alone.

It is impossible to read this, if one is an Englishman, without real distress. Only Lawrence, in letters written about this time, registers the death of England as a live cultural tradition with such sorrow and with the added poignancy that comes of being English. (Nearly thirty years later, in Canto LXXX written in the Pisan prison-camp, Pound reverts to the theme, using the same imagery, in three beautiful quatrains beginning, 'Tudor indeed is gone and every rose . . .') The name of Waller locks in with that of Lawes, as one who wrote words for the other's music. The 'two dusts' that will lie with Waller's are those of the poet and of his book. And the 'other mouth' than England's, which may in new ages gain England new worshippers, may well be the mouth of the English-speaking nations in North America. The ambitious and poignant perspectives which have been opened before us underline the irony by which the poet who was so conclusively dismissed at the end of the 'Ode pour l'élection de son sépulcre' is the same who, twelve poems later, here recaptures the tradition of English song at its most sonorous and plangent.

Only now, with Part II, does Mauberley, the titular hero of the whole work, emerge for our scrutiny, his emergence signalized by a new cross-heading 'Mauberley (1920)'. As with Eliot's Prufrock, so with Mauberley, the inability to come to grips with the world for the sake of art is symbolized in the inability to meet the sexual challenge, to 'force the moment to its crisis'. Mauberley, like (apparently) Prufrock, allows the moment of choice to drift by without recognizing it, and is left with 'mandate/Of Eros, a retrospect.' The last stanza of this section—about 'The still stone dogs'—is a reference to a story from Ovid's *Metamorphoses*, but for once this doesn't matter, since the biting mouths immobilized in stone are an obviously apt metaphor for impotence which is partly but not exclusively sexual.

Sections III and IV of Part II trace Mauberley's degeneration, his gradual withdrawal into an ever more private world, until he becomes

> Incapable of the least utterance or composition,
> Emendation, conservation of the 'better tradition',
> Refinement of medium, elimination of superfluities,
> August attraction or concentration.

> Nothing, in brief, but maudlin confession,
> Irresponse to human aggression,
> Amid the precipitation, down-float

> Of insubstantial manna,
> Lifting the faint susurrus
> Of his subjective hosannah.

As Mauberley in the very first section of the poem damned Pound with compassionate condescension as Flaubertian, and used Homeric parallels to do it with, so here Pound takes his revenge. The Simoon and 'the juridical Flamingoes' (that epithet a Flaubertian *mot juste*) are taken from Flaubert's exotic novel *Salammbô*, and used (with lordly disregard for geography, which would protest that they are inappropriate to the Moluccas) to stand as metaphors from the physical world for the spiritual state of abstracted passivity which is now Mauberley's condition. As for Homer:

> Coracle of Pacific voyages,
> The unforecasted beach;
> Then on an oar
> Read this:

> 'I was
> And I no more exist;
> Here drifted
> An hedonist.'

In the *Odyssey* one of Odysseus's ship-mates, Elpenor, killed by accident, is buried on the seashore, and his oar is set in the sand to mark his grave, with a noble inscription which Pound, in Canto I, renders as 'a man of no fortune, and with a name to come'. The contrast with Mauberley's epitaph is clear and damning.

The troublesome question of who is to be imagined as the speaker does not arise with these first four poems of section II. It crops up again, however, in respect of the last section of the whole poem. Since we have learned that Mauberley, at a relatively early stage of his disastrous career, attempted in poetry something analogous to the severe and limited art of the medallist, the title 'Medallion' given to these last quatrains must mean that here again Mauberley is speaking, that this is one of his poems, closing the sequence just as another of his poems opened it. The poem is symptomatic of Mauberley's degeneration in its externality, its fixity and rhythmical inertness. It shows too how Pound was aware of just these dangers in a too unqualified acceptance of the Flaubertian doctrine of *'le mot juste'*, as also in the programmes of the Imagists. The poem is not without distinction; it shows exactness of observation, clarity of order, and compact economy in the phrasing. For Mauberley is no fool, as we realized from the first; he is a man of principle, as well as a man of true poetic ability. The judgement is all the more damning: his principles and his abilities go for nothing because they are not informed by any vitality. All his scrupulous search for *le mot juste* to describe the braids of hair only transforms the hair with all its organic expressiveness into the inertness of metal. Venus Anadyomene, the mythological expression of how sexual and other vitality is renewed, hardens under Mauberley's hand into the glazed frontispiece to a book on Comparative Religion. (We note that it is the head which, for Mauberley, is rising Venus-like from the sea, not the breasts or the loins.) And not just the 'amber' but also the 'clear soprano' invite a damning comparison with the 'Envoi', a poem just as formal, but with a formality expressive of vital response. Mauberley's deficiencies as a writer are identical with his deficiencies as a human being. For there appears no reason to doubt that the woman here described is the same figure whose challenge earlier Mauberley could only evade. Everything that is hard, metallic and ominous in Mauberley's description of her as an image in a poem symbolizes his fear of her as a person, and his inability to meet her with any sort of human response.

But the most chastening reflection for a British reader is what Pound implies very plainly, that in a culture so riddled with commercialism and false values as English culture is (or was, in 1920), no English artist is likely to do any better than Mauberley did.

Postscript: This essay was commissioned by Boris Ford for *The Modern Age*, the last volume of the *Pelican History of English Literature*—a commission which I actively sought, for fear that otherwise Pound's achievement would go unremarked. Accordingly it envisages a reader less well informed than the reader addressed in most of my other pieces. I have changed my mind about *Hugh Selwyn Mauberley* over the years, and my revised opinions may be found in *Ezra Pound; Poet as Sculptor* (1964) and in the Fontana Modern Masters *Pound* (1975). In particular I no longer stand over the account given above, of the concluding section, 'Medallion'. In the case of a work of such authority as *Hugh Selwyn Mauberley*, and yet so ambiguous (with an ambiguity that I now believe to be ultimately insoluble), a change of mind is not anything that I think calls for excuse, though I'm aware of many who think it irritating, if not indeed unpardonable. Though I've required that the essay be dropped from future reprintings of *The Modern Age*, I'm glad and impenitent about having it given a new lease of life in print because on balance I think it still a great deal more right than wrong. Pound's poem is so memorable, and speaks still with such authority, that I by no means preclude the possibility that, after three attempts to give an account of it, I may yet some time venture on a fourth!

THE RELATION BETWEEN SYNTAX AND MUSIC IN SOME MODERN POEMS IN ENGLISH

IN THIS paper I shall try to understand and explore one aspect of the poetic theory of the symbolist movement in European poetry; a movement born in France in the last decades of the nineteenth century, which has no effect on poetry written in English until the twentieth. In 1920 Paul Valéry, last of the French symbolists, indulged his memories of that movement:

> What was baptized Symbolism can be very simply described as the common intention of several groups of poets (otherwise mutually inimical) to 'reclaim their own from Music'. The secret of that movement is nothing else. The obscurities and peculiarities with which it was so often reproached; the apparently overintimate relations with English, Slavic, or Germanic literature; the syntactical disorders, the irregular rhythms, the curiosities of vocabulary, the continual images . . . this is all easily deduced, once the principle is acknowledged. In vain did those who watched these experiments, and even those who put them into practice, attack the poor word Symbol. It means only what one wants it to; if someone fastens his own hopes upon it, he will find them there!—But we were nourished on music, and our literary minds dreamed only of extracting from language the same effects, almost, as were produced on our nervous systems by sound alone. Some cherished Wagner, others Schumann. I could as well say that they hated them. In the heat of passionate interest these two states are indistinguishable. (1)

Now, this is not at first sight very promising. We may remember that English poet of the nineties who decided that the letter 'v' stands for the most beautiful sound in the English language. And we have been schooled by the youthful Mr Eliot so that when we hear of the music of poetry we think first of the drugged insistent rhythms of Swinburne, in which patterns of sound are elaborated and sustained at the expense of sense. It seems that this isn't, however, what Valéry understands by the music, or the musicality, of poetry. In the essay from which I've just quoted, he acknowledges that some of the symbolist poets tried to meet the Wagnerian challenge this way: 'For some of them color in sound and the combinative art of alliteration seemed to hold no further secrets; they deliberately transposed the tones of the orchestra to their verse: they were not always wrong'. It is hard to interpret the urbanity of 'they were not always wrong' except by taking Valéry to mean that mostly, of course, they were. But there is firmer evidence, in a foreword which Valéry wrote at the end of his life to some translations from the Latin:

> Latin is, in general, a more compact language than our own. It has no articles; it is chary of auxiliaries (at least during the classical period); it is sparing of prepositions. It can say the same things in fewer words and, moreover, is able to arrange these with an enviable freedom almost completely denied to us. This latitude is most favorable to

poetry, which is an art of continuously constraining language to interest the ear directly (and through the ear, everything sounds may pro-
voke of themselves) at least as much as it does the mind. A line is both
a succession of syllables and a combination of words; and just as the
latter ought to form a probable meaning, so the succession of syllables
ought to form for the ear a kind of audible shape, which, with a special and as it were peculiar compulsion, should impress itself simultaneously on both voice and memory. The poet must therefore constantly fulfill two separate demands, just as the painter must present
to the simple vision a harmony, but to the understanding a likeness of
things or people. It is clear that freedom in arranging the words of a
sentence, to which French is curiously hostile, is essential to the game
of verse-making. The French poet does what he can within the very
narrow limits of our syntax; the Latin poet, within the much wider
bounds of his own, does almost what he will. (2)

Now we must certainly recognize that among the poetic devices 'to interest the ear directly' are all the Swinburnian instruments of alliteration,
consonance and assonance, terminal and internal rhyme and chime and
half-rhyme; Valéry's own poetry is orchestrated very richly—some have
thought, too richly—in these ways. But after all what is Swinburnian is
not this array of devices (since they are used by every poet one can think
of), but only a degree of coarseness and lack of subtlety in their deploy-
ment. And by the time Valéry comes to speak of syntax, especially when
he speaks with envy of Latin syntax, of course the English poet who
comes to mind is not Swinburne, but Milton. And it is Milton's 'linkèd
sweetness long drawn out', not any Sitwellian or Swinburnian 'vowel-
music', which we should bear in mind when we consider Valéry's insistence on the musicality of poetry, on the duty it has to the ear as well as
to the intelligence.

For it would be wrong to suppose that Valéry's experiments in poetic
syntax are undertaken solely to distort word-order so as to get assonantal
or alliterative clusters—as wrong as to explain in the same way the analogous syntactical experiments of Milton. 'Linkèd sweetness long drawn
out'—it is the linking and the drawing out which attracts Milton, just as it
attracts the poet who first envisaged his own poem, *La Jeune Parque*,
as 'an operatic recitative, à la Gluck: thirty or forty lines in one long
phrase almost; and for contralto voice' (*Lettres à quelqu'un*). What they
envy music for is its continuity, its sustained fluency, its never stopping
but to start again.

This is a most important matter, and it is worth dwelling on some of its
implications. In the first place, as the citation from Valéry has shown already, this is an understanding of the musicality of poetry which immediately issues, not in manipulation of vowels and consonants, but in manipulation of syntax. Perhaps the supreme masterpieces of this sort of
musicality in English poetry are the two marriage-hymns of Spenser,
where the music resides just here—in the draping of the sentences, the

syntactical units, over the lines, the metrical units, so that the stops and starts of the grammar are played off, with bewildering and glorious variety, against the stops and starts of metre. Secondly, as the name of Spenser demonstrates, this is a time-honoured aspiration and objective in poetry, stretching back beyond Spenser into the history of the Italian *canzone*, out of which he may have learned it. It is so ancient in fact, and the pleasure of it is (one would have thought) so marked a feature of the experience of enjoying poetry, that it is absurd I should find it necessary to emphasize and define it. That I nevertheless do find it necessary is the third and most alarming implication in the whole matter: how on earth have we got into a position where, if this is indeed still a source of pleasure to us in our reading (and I certainly hope for that at least), yet we look in vain to literary criticism for any examination of it or indeed, much of the time, for any acknowledgement that it exists?

For the most influential criticism of our time in English does not merely ignore this feature of poetry; its whole tendency is to preclude the possibility of it. I have in mind not at all the objections that have been raised to *Paradise Lost* (some of which I find unanswerable), nor the fairly general preference for the rough and broken cadences of Donne over the different music of Spenser and Milton (for that is rather a sign of grace, being an understandable preference for one kind of music over another). I think rather of the critical habit of speaking of a poem as a structure, or as a delimited field in which forces are balanced against each other to set up a tension, of our speaking of planes or levels of meaning, and of, for instance, Professor Wilson Knight's definition of the Shakespearean play as 'an extended metaphor'. When one first encountered this formula, one took it that the extension was an extension in time, in the time taken to see the play acted, or to read it. But no. Professor Knight said, it was extended in space like a carpet, and the pattern of it was not a pattern developing in time but should be seen every part of it at once, like the pattern in a carpet. When Mr John Holloway protested that the play, like it or not, does occupy a duration of time, when he pointed out that therefore to recognize a reference as harking back to an earlier one is a very different and more obviously legitimate activity than recognizing the first reference as looking forward to the later one, he was making a point as almost foolishly elementary as the point I have just made about syntax and music. It is a point like mine, and related to it. For to see the music of poetry in the way Milton and Valéry see it, as 'linked sweetness long drawn out', is to emphasize how poetry, like music, erects its structures in the lapse of time. The experience of reading or hearing a poem, much more than the experience of looking at a painting, goes on; it inhabits a duration. A poem, we see, is a sequence of verbal events, a train of actions, of preparations, crises, denouements. And this is the truth about poetry which many of the metaphors most favoured nowadays by English and American critics, metaphors taken from geometry or architecture, seem designed to obscure.

Of the stanzas in Spenser's 'Prothalamion', it has been justly said, 'the elaborate canzone is sustained by the structure of the sentence'. And indeed a stanza from the poem exemplifies better than anything else in English what I take to be Valéry's ideal of poetic music as a function of poetic syntax—a single sentence seventeen lines long, its grammatical ordering never in doubt, grammatical pause played off against metrical pause with such delicate resourcefulness as always to give the reader time to draw breath just before he needs to. The taking of a new breath—whether actually in reading aloud, or in imagination when reading with the eye—corresponds to the equally unflurried rapid sorting out by the mind of grammatical relationships, in such a way that the physical act, the drawing of breath, embodies and makes immediate, as an intimate physical sensation, the intellectual act of apprehending a relationship. As the breath launches out upon a new access of rhythm, so the mind launches out upon an added curve of meaning. Yet this is not for sound to echo sense; it would be merely fanciful and arbitrary to pretend to hear in the voice's sweet lapse from line to line the plash and ripple of the Thames or even the breathing of the zephyr-wind. And similarly, though the rhyme comes home so pleasantly and the sounds are such as to delight the ear and the mouth with the various quantities of the vowels, the interplay of fricatives and sibilants in consonants, this orchestration is subdued to the melodic unwinding of the syntax. What is this if it is not all that Valéry asked for? And am I therefore proposing Edmund Spenser as a symbolist *avant la lettre*? Plainly, the specifically symbolist version of this ancient resource is still to be inquired for.

We find it, I think, if we revert to the recognition that poetry conceived of as musical in this way has the merit, particularly to be valued at the present time, of insisting on a poem as an artefact which unrolls in time, imposes its shape on time as a peculiarly meaningful duration. Coming from this direction to a Shakespeare play, we shall cease to see it (as we are now asked to do rather often) as simultaneously present in all its parts, extended in imagined space. On the contrary, common sense is given its way and we remember *Julius Caesar* or *Othello* as a shape cut out of time, occupying the time necessary for its performance.

But we cannot fail to remember also, as soon as we think about it, that *Julius Caesar* or *Othello* on this showing still differs from a symphony or a piece of chamber music in the way it carves itself out of lapsing time, making a duration for itself. For of course the Shakespeare play occupies two distinct times, the time it takes for its performance but also the quite different time of several days or weeks or (in the case of *A Winter's Tale*) of more than twenty years, which we are to imagine as necessary for the sequence of events portrayed. So important, indeed, is this second time, that a measure of the dramatist's skill in creating his illusion is precisely his capacity for making this second imagined time supersede, in our own awareness as spectators, the first time actually elapsing. The rule of the unity of time in neo-classical drama was applied in order to make the gap between these two times as narrow as possible—an objective which now-adays we think not worth the trouble, pointless, not worth any trouble at all. And so it is; for so long as the gap remains, it doesn't matter how wide or narrow it is. But suppose the gap could be eliminated altogether, suppose the two times could be made identical, so that what the actors do on the stage should not 'stand for' certain events but should them-selves *be* those events, the only happenings there are. This might indeed be worth doing, and would collapse the two times of literature into the one time of music. This appears to be what the symbolists attempted.

Drama of course is a special case, yet the post-symbolist plays of Yeats are there to show how drama can be made to approach in this way, through ritual and dance, the condition of music. My concern, however, is with non-theatrical verse, in which the only events are verbal events. What if these verbal events could be made not to stand for other imagined events which they tell us about, but should themselves become the only occurrences there are, the succession of words themselves the sequence of events which constitutes the action of the poem? As a matter of fact this has always been a possibility in a kind of poem sometimes called 'the pure lyric', of which indeed Spenser's marriage-hymns might be thought to be especially elaborate examples. But in fact, in the stanza from 'Pro-thalamion' Spenser is telling a story, the story of what he did; and he did it, of course, in a different time from the time which the poem itself occupies. Most of what passes for lyric verse has a substantial narrative element:

> I wandered lonely as a cloud
> Which floats on high o'er vales and hills
> When all at once I saw a crowd,
> A host, of golden daffodils;

The verb 'saw', coming where it does in the poem, is an event in the se-quence of events which is our experience of the poem. But nothing is made of its character as an event in the time-span which is the duration of our reading. On the contrary, the verbal event is at once drained of all its eventfulness by our realizing that it merely 'stands for' an event which is quite other than itself, an event occurring in quite another time, the time that Wordsworth took on the walk he is telling us about. It would regain much of its eventfulness, its character as an event in its own right would be exploited, if it were (in defiance of all the logic governing tense-sequence in prose) put in the present tense: 'When all at once I see a crowd'. And the sudden introduction of a present tense, in defiance of all prosaic logic, is a marked feature of symbolist narration, as here in Mallarmé's 'Prose pour des Esseintes':

> Mais cette soeur sensée et tendre
> Ne porta son regard plus loin
> Que sourire et, comme à l'entendre
> J'occupe mon antique soin

(But this sensible and tender sister/Did not go farther/Than smile, and as

I heard her/I capture my ancient care.) A verb in the present tense necessarily 'stands for' an event which occupies the same time, the present
time, as the event of the word's own occurrence in the poem. Thus the
event it is is simultaneous with the event it describes; and simultaneity
thus achieved, it is a none too difficult task—largely a matter of dis-
creetly ambiguous imagery throughout—to make the two events identical
or at least indistinguishable. It's worth noting that to have all the verbs in
the present tense, from first to last of a poem, would fail of this effect or
at least make the effect much less surely and strongly, because of the
well-known phenomenon of 'the historic present', according to which the
reader, once he has caught on to the convention, automatically translates
every present tense into a past tense even as he apprehends it. It is essential to surprise the reader because surprisingness is a feature of eventfulness. Moreover, it is not a matter of just buying the surprising present
tense by an outlay of past tenses; for once the logical sequence of tenses
is broken, the sequence itself is compromised, so that the past tenses become immediately suspect also. None of the past tenses thereafter can be
trusted. The order of time in which they would make sense is disrupted
from within, and quite discredited. And the only order of time which
the reader is left with, the only order of time he can trust, is the one time
which the tale takes in the telling, the time which the poem takes to be
spoken or read. The two times of literary narrative have been collapsed
into the one time, the pure duration, of music.

This thoroughly simple trick is an elementary example of the reason
why, whatever else symbolist poems may describe or adumbrate, one
thing they always describe is themselves, their own way of coming into
being, comporting themselves, and coming to an end. Thus Edmund
Wilson has to say of a poem by Valéry:

> In such a poem as *Le Cimetière Marin*, there is no simple second
> meaning: there is a marvellously close reproduction of the very com-
> plex and continually changing relation of human consciousness to the
> things of which it is conscious. The noonday is inorganic Nature, but
> it is also the absolute in the poet's mind, it is also his twenty years of
> inaction—and it is also merely the noonday itself, which in a moment
> will no longer exist, which will be no longer either tranquil or noon. And
> the sea, which, during those moments of calm, forms a part of that great
> diamond of nature in which the poet finds himself the single blemish, be-
> cause the single change, is also the image of the poet's silence, which in a
> moment, as the wind comes up to lash the sea, will give way to a sudden
> gust of utterance, the utterance of the poem itself.

And this is why Boris Pasternak, the only post-symbolist poet in Russia,
can declare: 'The clearest, most memorable and important fact about art
is its conception, and the world's best creations, those which tell of
the most diverse things, in reality describe their own birth'. How can
it be otherwise, if the events which the poem narrates are the events of its
own words occurring in it, one by one?

*

But it is high time that I gave some examples of this feature of symbolist
poetry surviving into English poetry. Look, then, at the sequence of
tenses in Yeats's 'Coole Park and Ballylee':

> Under my window-ledge the waters race,
> Otters below and moor-hens on the top,
> Run for a mile undimmed in Heaven's face
> Then darkening through 'dark' Raftery's 'cellar' drop,
> Run underground, rise in a rocky place
> In Coole demesne, and there to finish up
> Spread to a lake and drop into a hole.
> What's water but the generated soul?
>
> Upon the border of that lake's a wood
> Now all dry sticks under a wintry sun,
> And in a copse of beeches there I stood,
> For Nature's pulled her tragic buskin on
> And all the rant's a mirror of my mood:
> At sudden thunder of the mounting swan
> I turned about and looked where branches break
> The glittering reaches of the flooded lake.
>
> Another emblem there! That stormy white
> But seems a concentration of the sky;
> And, like the soul, it sails into the sight
> And in the morning's gone, no man knows why;
> And is so lovely that it sets to right
> What knowledge or its lack had set awry,
> So arrogantly pure, a child might think
> It can be murdered with a spot of ink.

The bibliographical history of this poem is interesting, in a way which
bears upon what I am saying. The present point is sufficiently made by
the baffling changes from past to present tense and back again, in the
second stanza; and in particular by the outrageous, the impossible sequence of tenses 'a child might think/It can . . .', instead of 'It could'.
The effect of this is that a decisive event has taken place in between the
end of the penultimate line and the beginning of the last line. What has
happened is concealed behind the cryptic whiteness of that blank space
on the page. Yet we know it by its effect, the dislocation it has effected
in the tense-sequence; what has happened in that white space is that
poet and reader have become the children they began by only talking
about, so that what began as a potentiality ('they could') has turned into
an actuality by the time it arrives (we 'can'). And of course what arrives,
what is actualized, is a word—not the word we expected, its arrival
therefore all the more actual, all the more an event.

But it is the use of the white space of the page which is more worth insisting on, for this too figures in symbolist theory, in Mallarmé for instance: 'L'armature intellectuelle du poème se dissimule et tient—a lieu—dans l'espace qui isole les strophes et parmi le blanc du papier: significatif silence qu'il n'est pas moins beau de composer que les vers.' I am suggesting that this too, so remote as it seems from any matter of poetic syntax, in fact is or at least may be the simple consequence of certain syntactical usages, such as dislocated sequence of tenses. I shall hope to find other examples.

There is, for instance, the opening of 'A Game of Chess', section II of Eliot's *The Waste Land*:

The Chair she sat in, like a burnished throne,
Glowed on the marble, where the glass
Held up by standards wrought with fruited vines
From which a golden Cupidon peeped out
(Another hid his eyes behind his wing)
Doubled the flames of sevenbranched candelabra
Reflecting light upon the table as
The glitter of her jewels rose to meet it,
From satin cases poured in rich profusion;
In vials of ivory and coloured glass
Unstoppered, lurked her strange synthetic perfumes,
Unguent, powdered, or liquid—troubled, confused
And drowned the sense in odours; stirred by the air
That freshened from the window, these ascended
In fattening the prolonged candle-flames,
Flung their smoke into the laquearia,
Stirring the pattern on the coffered ceiling.
Huge sea-wood fed with copper
Burned green and orange, framed by the coloured stone,
In which sad light a carvèd dolphin swam.
Above the antique mantel was displayed
The change of Philomel, by the barbarous king
So rudely forced; yet there the nightingale
Filled all the desert with inviolable voice
And still she cried, and still the world pursues,
'Jug Jug' to dirty ears.

It is necessary to quote the whole passage, so as to illustrate the repeated insistence upon the past tense, and hence the force of the expectation which is denied by the vicious snarl of the present tense 'pursues'. The poem returns to the past tense at once:

And other withered stumps of time
Were told upon the walls; staring forms
Leaned out, leaning, hushing the room enclosed.
Footsteps shuffled on the stair.
Under the firelight, under the brush, her hair
Spread out in fiery points
Glowed into words, then would be savagely still.

But the single present tense has done its damage, and it is irremediable. The past tense which to begin with was the vehicle of a rapt if morbid interest in what it recorded, after the interruption is flat and weary, limply recording. And again, surely, there is sense in saying that the momentous event, which transforms the speaker from the fascinated historian *temporis acti* to the jaundiced reporter of *moeurs contempo-raines*, takes place nowhere in the verse—not even in 'pursues' itself, shattering event as that is, but somewhere unstated between 'cried' and 'pursues', somewhere in or under 'and still the world', *parmi le blanc du papier*.

Of equal interest in this passage is the wonderfully contrived and sustained ambiguity between the past participle and the past indicative:

> In vials of ivory and coloured glass
> Unstoppered, lurked her strange synthetic perfumes,
> Unguent, powdered, or liquid—troubled, confused
> And drowned the sense in odours; . . .

Is it fanciful to think that the reader hesitates a moment over 'unstopper-ed', half taking it for a past indicative because of its juxtaposition with the indeed indicative 'lurked', which is identical in grammatical form? The same could be said of 'powdered', again by infection from 'lurked'. Perhaps these are too ingenious. But there can at least be no question of the ambiguity of 'troubled, confused . . .', both in the first place surely are taken as adjectival participles like 'powdered'. It is only after swinging round the line-ending and coming upon 'drowned', that the reader realizes them for what they are, past indicatives. Yet of course this is to mis-state the situation: what they are is both things at once, participles in the first line, active verbs (retrospectively) when we get to the second. So much we have learned from William Empson, who gives examples of this kind of ambiguity from poetry much older than the symbolist movement—a recognition which may give us pause. But at least I think he never drew from such cases the moral that now seems in order—the observation that such ambiguities as these operate powerfully to drive the reader on from line to line, to force home to him just how poetry moves and must move always forward through time. For it is only by 'going on' with the poem, that the reader can perceive the ambiguity and to that extent resolve it.

This, as I now think, is the appropriate context in which to consider an observation of Valéry's, for which I have in the past, and in another place, created a context quite different:

> . . . you have surely noticed the curious fact that a certain word which is perfectly clear when you hear or use it in everyday speech, and which presents no difficulty when caught up in the rapidity of an or-dinary sentence, becomes mysteriously cumbersome, offers a strange resistance, defeats all efforts at definition, the moment you withdraw it from circulation for separate study and try to find its meaning after taking away its temporary function. It is almost comic to inquire the exact meaning of a term, that one uses constantly with complete

satisfaction. For example: I stop the word Time in its flight. This word was utterly limpid, precise, honest and faithful in its service as long as it was part of a remark and was uttered by someone who wished to say something. But here it is, isolated, caught on the wing. It takes its revenge. It makes us believe that it has more meanings than uses. It was only a means, and it has become an end, the object of a terrible philosophical desire. It turns into an enigma, an abyss, a torment of thought . . .

It is the same with the word Life and all the rest.

This readily observed phenomenon has taken on great critical value for me. Moreover, I have drawn from it an illustration that, for me, nicely conveys this strange property of our verbal material.

Each and every word that enables us to leap so rapidly across the chasm of thought, and to follow the prompting of an idea that constructs its own expression, appears to me like one of those light planks which one throws across a ditch or a mountain crevasse and which will bear a man crossing it rapidly. But he must pass without weighing on it, without stopping—above all, he must not take it into his head to dance on the slender plank to test its resistance! . . . Otherwise the fragile bridge tips or breaks immediately, and all is hurled into the depths. Consult your own experience; and you will find that we understand each other, and ourselves, only thanks to our rapid passage over words. We must not lay stress upon them, or we shall see the clearest discourse dissolve into enigmas and more or less learned illusions. (3)

This, as I understand, is the observation about language which has particularly occupied philosophers of our time who have engaged in linguistic analysis; and, so far as I can see, Valéry proceeds from this observation to much the same conclusion as Wittgenstein and others have come to—that it is of the nature of words that they should be taken on the run, that only when so taken are they serviceable. It's worth saying this in passing, because it has been claimed for some recently written English poetry which offers to supersede the poetry with affinities to symbolism, that in doing so it takes note of philosophers' worryings about how far language can be trusted; yet the symbolist Valéry appears to be thinking much more nearly than any of these newer poets, about the same problems as the philosophers.

But if we may affect for a moment a condescending indifference to the philosophers' dilemmas, what has Valéry said here, that is novel for literary theory and the practice of literary criticism? Is he saying any more than what we all knew already, that in all discourse and pre-eminently in literature a word is defined by its context? I think he is. For again I suspect that when we think of context in this way, we use a spatial image, seeing the context of a word as an ambience surrounding it, a field in which it lies. When Valéry speaks of 'our rapid passage over words', he forces us to realize how a context unrolls in time, successively. In fact, it would be more accurate to say that any word in any discourse has two contexts—first, what leads up to it, second, what leads away from it. And the grammatical ambiguity of Eliot's 'troubled, confused' forces us to the same recognition: in the context of what leads up to them, these words mean one thing, being past participles used adjectivally to qualify 'perfumes'; in the context of what leads away from them, they mean something else, being active verbs describing what the perfumes do to the observer. In their character as the culmination of what leads up to them, what lies behind them in their past, they are one thing; in their character as starting-points of what leads away from them, what is before them in their future, they are something else. And this, which is true of all words everywhere, is forced home on us in respect of these words in particular by the poet's turning to use two accidents, first the paucity of terminal inflections in modern English (which brings it about that the past participle and the past indicative have the same form), and secondly the rhythmical necessity of the line-ending.

Since I have hinted at one cross-reference into philosophy, I will risk another. E. A. Burtt, in his *Metaphysical Foundations of Modern Physical Science*, after demonstrating how it was necessary for scientific thought to abandon the Aristotelean analysis of time in terms of potentiality and actuality, observes that as a result 'We are forced to view the movement of time as passing from the past into the future, the present being merely that moving limit between the two'. Is that not precisely the perception of time's inexorable lapse to which we are compelled by a syntactical ambiguity like Eliot's? If so, we may be brought up with a jolt by Burtt's next sentence, 'Time as something lived we have banished from our metaphysics, hence it constitutes for modern philosophy an unsolved problem'. But it is precisely here that we need to remember Mr Empson's principle that in the case of such ambiguities the words are the two meanings at one and the same time. We need to insist, at whatever cost to logic and prosaic conventions, that the words are *both* participles *and* active verbs. Only by doing so, by refusing to accept an Either/Or, do we force in between 'what the words have meant' and 'what the words are going to mean', the condition in which we appreciate what they do mean, now, as verbal events actually occurring and occupying the present time. We do this when we recognize the ambiguity, or the possibility of it, and hesitate between the two possible meanings or else embrace them both. Thus syntactical manipulations of this sort, at the same time as they make of the present only a moving limit between past and future, also make the present time something to be dwelt upon and dwelt in, something lived. Mrs Susanne Langer has analysed the effect of music in precisely these terms, as something which so shapes time as to make us live its elapsing, its duration, with unusual attention to each present moment.

NIGHTINGALES, ANANGKE

Collected Poems, Ronald Bottrall, Sidgwick & Jackson.
Poems in English, Samuel Beckett, Calder.
The Nature of Cold Weather, Peter Redgrove, Routledge.
The Bright Cloud, Christopher Lee, Gemini, Cambridge.

IN MY copy of Ronald Bottrall's *Festivals of Fire*, a bookplate says that
it was given to me as a school prize in 1939. I know why: a sixth-former
with my eyes on a Cambridge Entrance Scholarship in English, I had had
pressed upon me by an alert headmaster Dr Leavis's *New Bearings*, where
I had read of 'a very considerable poet indeed', one 'whose achieved work
leaves no room for doubt about his future'. I had enough humility twenty-
two years ago, when I read *Festivals of Fire* with admiration for their
author's knowingness but in bewildered disappointment at their cacophonous obscurity, to suppose that it was I who was wrong. Now I am not
so sure. The cacophony, for instance: I still take no pleasure in Mr Bottrall's rhythms. And yet it's just there that his admirers ground their
claims. 'His rhythms may be found difficult at first; but they are subtle,
varied and sure: he uses the body and sinew of the language'—thus F. R.
Leavis thirty years ago. In 1946 Edith Sitwell was detecting 'a remarkable
ease of movement . . . no hesitation or timidity of movement'. And now
here is Charles Tomlinson talking of 'a muscular and rhythmic strength, a
characteristic weight'. For 'rhythmic tact and muscular drive', Tomlinson
sends us to 'The Thyrsus Retipped', which was admired by Dr Leavis also:

> Nightingales, Anangke, a sunset or the meanest flower
> Were formerly the potentialities of poetry
> But now what have they to do with one another
> With Dionysus or with me?
>
> Drawn for a time towards inept vivisection
> I learned to air profundity in a comment
> As well by understudying Joyce as Valéry,
> Both sorting ill with my bent.
>
> Too bewildered to seek anew my element
> I have lain supine, as Shelley lay questing truth on
> The cool bottom of an untrampled pool,
> Oddly enamoured of his marine prison.
>
> Microscopic anatomy of ephemerides,
> Power-house stacks, girder-ribs, provide a crude base
> But man is what he eats, and they are not bred
> Flesh of our flesh, being unrelated
> Experientially, fused in no emotive furnace.
>
> Hints for a prosthesis
> Are, finding once more half-shivered laughs

> In the suspense of a key turned in a corridor lock,
> Or the strangeness of a snatched kiss—
> These not to be read as epitaphs.

Undoubtedly the first three quatrains here have each a pleasing rhythmical shape; but the shaping had been done long before, in the quatrains of *Hugh Selwyn Mauberley*. And for Bottrall's reproduction of those shapes (the relationship is as close and deliberate as that), the word is not 'tactful' but 'adroit'. In fact even the adroitness can be faulted, for Pound would not have written 'potentialities of', when he meant 'potential with' or 'potent for'; nor would he have used 'questing' without quotation-marks. In any case, if poetic tact is a feeling for experience through and with words, not just a feeling *for* words, this surely is a tactless poem. For when in the fourth stanza it tries to deal with experience not mediated through Pound, all the feeling for Pound's words and Pound's shapes falls away: Bottrall cannot even hold on to the quatrain as such; the eight stresses crammed into the cacophonous second line ('no hesitation or timidity of movement'—no indeed!) belong to some rhythmical convention quite out of keeping with what has been so far established; and the polysyllabic diction is no longer delicately over-ponderous and thus deprecating, but meant to be taken all too nakedly at face-value—'experientially'.

What is it but two distinct poems crammed meaninglessly end to end—the first three stanzas damning the last two as inelegant, the last two damning the first three as elegant at no cost, and to no end? And yet it was in relation to this piece that Dr Leavis could declare, 'Mr Bottrall's use of a technical idiom and manner owes a great deal to Mr Pound, but in Mr Bottrall idiom and manner *have a great deal more behind them*.' (The incredulous italics mine.)

Humility is always in order, before the Collected Poems of a living poet. Let me not seem to say that no case can be made for any of Bottrall's work. 'On a Grave of the Drowned', for instance, is an early poem which stands up very well. But the case that has been made so far, excusably by Dr Leavis, less excusably because lately by Mr Tomlinson—this won't wash. Bottrall's dealings with Pound, and also with Eliot, have been superficial—or so it seems to me; if he deserves our respect, it is for achievements much more modest than theirs.

Let it be clear how hard it is to write well; how the captious reviewer, allowances made for obtuseness and sometimes malice, is in the right if he is hard to please. Here is Samuel Beckett, bold and seminal intelligence that has convulsed the novel and the drama, offering in verse a mish-mash of Joyce and Eliot out of English, and from French moody abstractions and nonce-words to baffle translators; making a lucky strike now and again (mostly with images from Dublin), and yet in the end merely unprofessional, too much at the mercy of whim, risking everything between one line and the next, and over it all the stale whiff of yesterday's avant-garde:

        Ah the banner
        the banner of meat bleeding
        on the silk of the seas and the arctic flowers
        that do not exist.
(The answer is: a sunset.)

   This stale pretentiousness is the price that boldness pays, when it is not
backed by professionalism. Even when it is properly professional, pretension is a price that the best British taste (in contrast to American taste, or
French) is unwilling to pay: we like our poet in a roomy old jacket, not
in his singing-robes. We are surely right to this extent—that the very
greatest poetry of our time, for instance late as distinct from early Pasternak, is completely unpretentious; but much more of the time we are
wrong—wrong because we mistake for pretentiousness in the artist what
is often the just pretension of the art he practises. And so nowadays,
when one of our own poets shoulders clear of the ruck, as Peter Redgrove now does, what one notices and applauds first is his boldness, his
taking the risk of having pretensions. He pays the price: 'Prelude and History', to take one example, seems a group of poems spoilt by their pretentiousness. In the title-piece, an ambitious sequence of twenty-one
short poems, the pretentiousness is in a mostly ill-advised use of italics,
and (more important, for it is an endemic oddity of current British writing)
a selfconsciously muscular barging-about of rhythms. But this is a small
price to pay for the ambitiousness of the undertaking, and the imaginative stamina. Yet not every one will agree; for the subject is accurately
defined by its title, and there will be those to say that this means it is
merely descriptive and therefore cannot be important.

   It sags into description now and then, but by and large it is something
else, a re-creation of what cold weather is, a response to nature in that
guise. And indeed this is the other thing which distinguishes Peter Redgrove among his contemporaries: by comparison with him nearly all of
them inhabit a strikingly *unfurnished* world, a world of very scanty properties in which there are no beings but human beings. Description becomes recreation when furnishings and properties become presences, become beings; and so Redgrove's world, being fully furnished, is by that
token densely peopled also. In fact it is a main focus of attention for him,
through much of this collection, to make serious use of the ideas of
'ghost' and 'shadow', so as to apprehend other modes of being than the
human; we move from the touchingly *human* being of a fat man ('Disguise'), through the other than human being of a place's atmosphere
('Corposant') or of a particular season in time, towards more spiritual
presences still ('Genius Loci'), and yet stop short ('The Ghostly Father')
of the fully spiritual beings affirmed by dogma.

   Description, on the other hand, is what we get in many poems by
Christopher Lee:

        In the harbour nothing stirs, no-one moves:
        but light glances and dances, and below

this cliff the sea rolls in the rocks, a flow
breaking in foam and ebbing off the drowned
ledges, sliding in grooves
of silence graven by incessant sound.

In the last two lines the place becomes more than an aggregate of items inertly registered (I haven't quoted the whole of course), and becomes a presence. For the poet thus to work up to his breakthrough reveals that he knows the difference, and abides by it in his perceptions; but a bolder, more ambitious poet would have made the last two lines his first, and tried to go on from there. That bolder poem, of course, would have been less insinuating, less engagingly modest; for reading Christopher Lee we are back with a very British writer, the singing-robes tucked up under the old jacket, low-voiced and beautifully tactful. This way has its rewards; and indeed, since *The Bright Cloud* is a sequence about an intimate bereavement, perhaps this way was the only way to suit the subject. Certainly, in 'Pieve di Cadore: The Lost Child', we encounter what perhaps a bold and ambitious art must always deny itself (we look for it in vain in Peter Redgrove)—that is to say, tenderness, a piercing pathos.

TWO ANALOGIES FOR POETRY

POETRY IS a special kind of verbal discourse; it is also a special kind of art. So we may approach not a definition of poetry, but at least a description of it, in at least two ways. On the one hand we may approach poetic discourse by comparing it with, and distinguishing it from, other kinds of discourse in words—the discourse of the philosopher, of the orator, of the scientist writing in his laboratory book, of the priest in prayer, of the mother murmuring to her child, and so on. On the other hand we can approach the poetic art by comparing it with, and distinguishing it from, other kinds of art or, as we say more naturally, other arts—the art of the painter, of the architect, the sculptor, the choreographer, the musician.

But in this country in the present century it is striking how much more common it has been to approach poetry in the first way, as a special kind of discourse, than in the second way, as a special kind of art. There is the ancient and honourable philosophical discipline of aesthetics which is committed to finding common ground among all the arts, and assumes that poetry is one of these; but aestheticists are not very thick upon the ground, and their speculations and conclusions are by no means common currency among students of poetry. Such 'students'—and by 'students' I mean here simply keen and curious readers—are prompt and at ease with discussions about how a poetic use of language differs from a scientific use of it; they are at a loss—so my experience tells me—with discussions about how a poet's use of his medium, language, differs from a sculptor's use of stone or a painter's use of pigment. Indeed they are not just at a loss; they are at once suspicious and resentful. In the circles I am thinking of—and they are the circles where I find the keenest and most thoughtful readers of poetry—the very word 'art' is a danger-signal. Hackles rise at the very expression 'the art of poetry'. For unsophisticated speakers of current English, 'art' is the name of only one among the arts, that of painting; for sophisticated speakers it is, commonly, a word irremediably tarnished by its association with Walter Pater and Oscar Wilde, a word so tarnished by this (for them) criminal past that they resent it as a confidence-trickster.

I have never understood why this should be so. Even if Walter Pater were such a narrowly eccentric thinker and such a corrupting influence as these people seem to believe (and surely Pater is neither of these things), this would still not account for the passions which his name arouses. But I am not concerned to vindicate Pater; and in any case I am fairly sure that the prejudice against 'art' in relation to 'poetry' is far too deeply rooted, as well as too passionate, to derive only from prejudice against Pater's aestheticism. But however it may arise, this attitude is exasperating to me personally, and this is what I should like to explain.

For some years now I have found it easiest to set my ideas in order, about the poems I write myself and the poems of others, by thinking of the poet by analogy with other kinds of artist—specifically, by analogy with the musical composer on the one hand, the sculptor on the other. I shall try to explain what this means in practice, but first I want to insist that practice is indeed the only court I appeal to. I find it useful, convenient, personally profitable, to think along these lines, using these ideas. I have no wish to make these ideas prevail, if that means denying that other ways of thinking may be more convenient for others. I do not maintain that thinking along these lines makes one see poetry more truly for what it is, than thinking in other ways about it. I would maintain only that this way of thinking brings one to *part* of the truth about poetry, and to a part which is now generally and misleadingly overlooked. For what is frustrating in my experience is that in the present climate of literary opinion thinking along these lines cannot get a hearing; literary people refuse to think in these terms at all, refuse to those of us who think in this way even the right to participate in the give-and-take of literary discussion.

To make poetry-like-music seems to have been an avowed aim of the French symbolist poets. The last of these, Paul Valéry, insisted that this was the central and distinguishing trait of the whole school; and to wrestle instead with the word 'symbol' could never bring us to the heart of what these French poets were up to. For a succinct and lively image of poetry-like-music we can go to Pasternak, at a point in *Doctor Zhivago* where he is talking about how poetic inspiration came to the poet Zhivago:

> At such moments the correlation of the forces controlling the artist is, as it were, stood on its head. The ascendancy is no longer with the artist or the state of mind which he is trying to express, but with language, his instrument of expression. Language, the home and dwelling of beauty and meaning, itself begins to think and speak for man and turns wholly into music, not in the sense of outward, audible sounds, but by virtue of the power and momentum of its inward flow. Then, like the current of a mighty river polishing stones and turning wheels by its very movement, the flow of speech creates in passing, by the force of its own laws, rhyme and rhythm and countless other forms and formations, still more important and until now undiscovered, unconsidered and unnamed.

A passage such as that is so remote from the vocabulary, or the one or two vocabularies, recognized by English criticism today that I fear, if its author were anyone less illustrious than Pasternak, it would be regarded as a mere flight of dangerous rhetoric. Our poets may know—it is to be hoped they *do* know—the state of affairs in which the creative initiative is no longer with the artist but with his medium, language; but our critics, so far as I can see, have no way of allowing for this state of affairs, of distinguishing it from variously vicious kinds of verbal intoxication and more or less 'automatic writing', or of squaring it with their demands (which are just, so far as they go) that the writer be in control of his experience and of his language. Yet the poetic work in English which by common consent is perhaps the most splendid achievement of the last twenty-five years, Mr Eliot's *Four Quartets*, advertises by its very title that it belongs with poetry-like-music. If our prejudices will not permit us even to entertain speculations about analogies between the arts, how can we appreciate the structure and the meaning of the *Four Quartets*? Indeed, I believe we have not even begun to do this.

Obviously it is meaningful to speak of both poems and pieces of music as having 'structures'. Yet to most of us it will seem, after a moment's thought, that this term can be applied to poetry and music only by drawing an analogy with another art, architecture. It is only in respect of architecture that the term 'structure' has a literal meaning; it is only there that the word is really at home. The interesting thing is that 'structure' is common currency in our literary criticism. Equally is it common form for our critics to speak of planes and levels of meaning, and also of stresses and tensions which are created, balanced, and resolved. The real home for all of these expressions is architecture.

Thus it appears that our literary criticism does proceed, after all, by drawing analogies with other arts—at least with one such art. But it does so in the most perilous way, not realizing what it is doing. When Pasternak speaks, in relation to poetic language, of 'the power and momentum of its inward flow', we cannot come to terms with what he is saying because the model which our critical vocabulary creates for us is of a poem as analogous to a building or an arch, architectural compositions which make no provision for the idea of 'flow'. A poem is necessarily a shape made out of lapsing time, out of the time the poem takes to be read; yet we seem to conceive of a poem by analogy with architectural forms, forms which occupy not time but space.

We are not necessarily wrong to do this. Though all poems are shapes cut out of lapsing time, not all poems exploit this feature of their existence. There are poems, and fine ones, which on the contrary contrive to make us forget the reading time which they occupy. I am thinking of those poems which come full circle, which return upon themselves, of which we feel, when we finish reading them, 'How well the end was foreseen in the beginning'. For these poems, it seems to me, our current vocabulary, devised on an analogy with architecture, is the most useful and illuminating vocabulary possible. On the other hand it is plain that other sorts of poems, those which exploit and emphasize the time they take between first line and last, poems which do not come sweetly home upon themselves but on the contrary are open-ended, can be discussed in our current critical vocabulary only at the price of being certainly distorted and probably undervalued.

It thus appears, first, that we cannot help drawing analogies with the other arts when we discuss poetry: we cannot help it because such analogies are in and behind the very terminology we use, since criticism of any one art necessarily takes in the washing from criticism of the others; and, secondly, precisely because this is so, there can be no question of one among the other arts being the one right analogy for poetry: we have to be prepared to draw our analogies from architecture or painting or music or sculpture, according as the poem we are to deal with lends itself to, or implicitly asks for, one of these analogies rather than the others.

There are some poems which ask for the analogy to be drawn from sculpture. If I were learned enough I dare say I could find that the idea of the poem-as-sculpture has as long a history as the idea of the poem-as-music, or the poem-as-architecture, or (the most ancient of them all) the poem-as-painting. But there is no need to go back further than to the imagist and vorticist movements of less than fifty years ago. Imagism, at least as Ezra Pound conceived of it, opposed to the symbolist ideal of the poem-as-music an ideal of the poem-as-sculpture; and his fullest statement of this position came a few years later when he was fighting under the banner of 'vorticism'. It comes, appropriately enough, in the memoir which Pound wrote for the sculptor Henri Gaudier-Brzeska—a most important document happily made available again, last year, by the Marvell Press.

The first thing to be said about sculpture in this connection is that it comprises two radically different operations: those of carving on the one hand, and of moulding, or modelling, on the other. Pound appears interested chiefly, if not exclusively, in the sculptor as carver, chisel in hand, assaulting the block. According to Michelangelo, at once great sculptor and great poet, the carver feels or persuades himself at such a moment that the form he wants is already present in the marble, and that his own function is to make what is already there reveal itself. This is as far as possible from what the moulder feels, for whom, as he begins, the whole world is infinitely malleable, literally 'like clay in his hands'. The carver's activity enforces humility as surely as the moulder's invites presumption. It is for this reason that the carver's way with his medium attracts and challenges the poet more than the moulder's way. For the moulder's way of making something out of nothing is what the poet can see already from the case of the musician. And poets, like the symbolists, who want to make poetry-like-music, are characteristically excited by the degree to which their art can cut loose from the world of nature, creating an alternative world answering only to its own laws. Poetry can never be as 'pure' in this sense, as independent of nature and answerable to its own laws, as music is; it can never equal music in this respect since its medium, language, necessarily refers to the world the poet wishes to be free from. Yet the symbolists went further towards music in this respect than one would have believed possible.

To a poet who is enamoured of the world offered to his senses in all its copious variety, who believes that his mission is not to transform, still less to annihilate, but rather to serve that world—for such poets, of whom Gerard Manley Hopkins might be one example and Ezra Pound another, the analogy with music or with sculpture-as-moulding offers a freedom they do not want, and tempts to an arrogance which they distrust. The analogy with carved sculpture is what their poems demand of the reader who wants to do them justice.

But this poetry-as-carving is divided from our students of poetry by an even wider gulf than poetry-as-music. For what this poetry has to do with is a reality which is as fully and undeniably *out there*, as certainly other than us and confronting us, as is the block of marble where it lies in the quarry before the sculptor. This reality may be physical—in which case this poetry is making a claim which our critics have for the most part abandoned, the claim to be exploring the same reality as the sciences explore, but with different categories and different instruments. Or the reality which poetry-as-carving explores may be metaphysical: in which case it is making a claim which, once again, our mostly agnostic or infidel criticism has agreed to abandon, the claim to be exploring the same reality as religion or ontology. To be sure, many symbolist poets claimed to be exploring a metaphysical reality through their poems, just as many musicians have claimed the same for their music. But in these cases sceptical or materialistic critics find it easy enough to transform the metaphysical reality allegedly *out there* into a psychological reality *in here*, inside the artist's head. The art in these cases constructs a reality independent of the natural world; and the critic need not violate or distort the art-work by taking its world as altogether inside the head of the poet in the first place, and subsequently in the head of the reader. But poetry-as-carving, which claims to have to do with no world but the world of nature, cannot be transformed in this way; the reality it deals with cannot be seen as a reality only in the poet's head.

The great advantage of taking poetry as a special kind of verbal discourse, rather than a special kind of art, is that it evades these ancient and troubling questions about the metaphysical or religious grounds of the poetic activity. To take poetry as a special kind of discourse is to make it a special kind of communication between persons; and thus, it seems, one reality which all poems explore is the social and psychological reality of how we get on together and communicate with each other. This is the reality which the most infidel reader, and the most fervently religious, can be sure that they share.

However, since all poetry is a making no less than a saying, and since some poems offer themselves, not as a way of getting or keeping in touch or practising group-therapy, but as a truthful report on a reality not social at all nor even human, it may be that we sell the pass on poetry from the start by refusing to consider any metaphysical or ontological grounds for the poetic activity. To approach poetry as a special kind of art is to make it difficult, indeed I think impossible, to evade any longer these troublesome but necessary questions.

Postscript: The points made in this piece, written when I had newly arrived at these perceptions, seem to me now, many years later, very important.

A'E GOWDEN LYRIC

'BETTER A'E gowden lyric/Than a social problem solved', wrote Hugh MacDiarmid thirty years ago; and again—'Better a'e gowden lyric/Than onything else ava!' So too, in his 'Second Hymn to Lenin':

> Sae here, twixt poetry and politics,
> There's nae doot in the en'.
> Poetry includes that and s'ud be
> The greatest poo'er amang men.
>
> —It's the greatest, *in posse* at least,
> That men ha'e discovered yet
> Tho' nae doot they're unconscious still
> O' ithers faur greater than it.

MacDiarmid alone among British socialist writers has kept the priorities thus clear. It's a great thing to have done.

On the other hand we look in vain for any reason why lyric poetry is such a tall order. We are no wiser at the end of 'One Golden Lyric' about what makes a lyric golden, what golden-ness is. Perhaps this is the critic's job, not the poet's; but the trouble is that the calling of lyrics 'golden', with no questions asked, is precisely the language of bad critics—and spelling it 'gowden' doesn't make it any better.

Still, the young MacDiarmid had better things to do. Instead of arguing the case, he proved it—by exemplifying, in one lyric after another, the golden-ness we can recognize before we can define it. 'The Frightened Bride', 'Farmer's Death', 'Wild Roses', and the Hardyesque 'Sea-Serpent'; the equally Hardyesque trio, 'God Takes a Rest', 'In the Pantry' and 'The Innumerable Christ'; 'Crowdieknowe' and 'Whip-the-World'; 'Trompe l'Oeil', 'Wheesht, Wheesht', 'Tam', 'Focherty', 'Under the Greenwood Tree', 'Scunner', 'On the Threshold', 'Supper to God', 'The Quest', 'Empty Vessel'—what a harvest!

There may indeed be others, for reading Lallans with the usual maddeningly inadequate glossary, an English reader finds many that remain locked in their foreign language. Is it the foreign language that has kept these poems almost unknown outside Scotland? I should like to think so. But I'd blame instead chiefly our squeamishness about eroticism, in particular the notion that in love tenderness and heated solemnity go together; that, and the distrustful philistinism which thinks a poem of eight lines necessarily more 'slender' than one of eighty.

What is especially astonishing is that all the poems I've listed come from the two collections, *Sangschaw* (1925) and *Penny Wheep* (1926). However, if this is the glory, it is also the sadness of MacDiarmid's *Collected Poems* (Oliver & Boyd, 1962). For where in his later work do we find poems to set by these? In *A Drunk Man Looks at the Thistle*, there is one that surpasses them all, the justly famous 'O Wha's the Bride?' And in *Stony Limits* (1934) there are the nine Shetland Lyrics, which include for instance 'Gruney'. Otherwise there is terribly much of this:

The sin against the Holy Ghost is to fetter or clog
The free impulse of life—to weaken or cloud
The glad wells of being—to apply other tests,
To say that these pure founts must be hampered, controlled,
Denied, adulterated, diluted, cowed,
The wave of omnipotence made recede, and all these lives, these lovers
Lapse into cannon-fodder, sub-humanity, the despised slum-crowd.

And at once we know what the lyric golden-ness is; it is language on the gold standard, each word ringing true and worth its weight, not needing to be supplemented, eked out, overlapped. It is 'vigil's pin-point motion': it assuredly is *not* 'to weaken *or cloud*', 'to fetter *or clog*'.

This comes from a poem, 'In the Slums of Glasgow', which neither MacDiarmid nor anyone else would describe as a lyric. But then golden-ness of this sort is what nowadays we demand of all poetry, lyrical or not. MacDiarmid however might not agree. For this demand we make, for a lyrical cleanness in the language of all poetry whatever, is almost entirely a distinctively modern thing. And MacDiarmid, though he is the least insular of British poets, is also among the most oldfashioned; at least as oldfashioned as Hardy. More indeed; for the poems of his which recall Hardy recall not the greatest Hardy but the dated and quaint, though sturdily impressive Hardy who is ironical about the cosmos. Similarly, when MacDiarmid wanted to extend his range from the lyric as traditionally conceived, the best he could do was, like Hardy, to contrive what used to be called 'a dramatic framework'. In *A Drunk Man Looks at the Thistle* this is less cumbrous than in *The Dynasts* because it is less ambitious. Instead the poetry remains in that awkward half-way house to drama, the Browningesque dramatic monologue.

Eneuch? Then here you are. Here's the haill story.
Life's connached shapes too'er up in crowns o' glory,
Perpetuatin' natheless, in their gory
Colour the endless sacrifice and pain
That to their makin's gane . . .

The ugliness of this writing is not the sometimes functional ugliness of modernism: it is something inseparable from the dramatic monologue, which fakes up by such uncouth gambols the liveliness of those dramatic exchanges it cannot provide. The speaker gets more and more embarrassed by his own garrulity, and the ugliness is how his embarrassment shows up.

A Drunk Man Looks at the Thistle is the turning-point in MacDiarmid's career. (Its date remarkably is 1926, the same as *Penny Wheep*—MacDiarmid in the twenties was very prolific.) One sees why it was necessary and even admirable for MacDiarmid to write this book, and there are fine things in it; but it makes tedious reading as a whole. The form he found for it was too much of a makeshift, and discredited before he chose it; as a result even the fine things are jammed in with poor stuff. (Compare, in 'The Light of Life', the first three stanzas with the last two.)

It would be wrong to think, though, that MacDiarmid's talent never recovered from the violence he did to it in order to write *A Drunk Man*. True, there are no more lyrics like 'The Frightened Bride' and 'Wild Roses'. But their disappearance was probably inevitable anyway. Even as one turns from *Sangschaw* to *Penny Wheep* one sees the stance growing oblique, quizzical, even knowing; and 'Scunner', for instance, is a coarsening of 'The Frightened Bride'. There would be something wrong and retarded, or too complacent, about a poet nowadays who stayed lyrical all through.

In any case the more relaxed and expansive writing that MacDiarmid has mostly done over the last thirty years is not all like 'In the Slums of Glasgow'. A poem must be permitted to set its own pace; and to ask for language to be golden all through a poem is not to demand that every word be a full sovereign, nothing of smaller denominations. There must always be room for the small change. This is seldom understood; and a poem such as 'Direadh 111' has been grossly underrated already, and will be again. It moves from a delighted but leisurely description of a particular scene 'near the summit of Sgurr Alasdair', through an extended Ruskinian simile between 'water-crowfoot leafage' and 'the Gaelic genius', into a brief sad diatribe against the modern world; then a description of a rock-pigeon recalls a line from Euripides and sparks off a comparison between the Greek spirit and the Scottish (the Chinese too—but this is gratuitous), and between MacDiarmid's service to Scotland and the Greek-inspired Hölderlin's to Germany; so back to the Gaelic genius compared now with 'quake grass'; and the poem concludes by identifying the poet's feeling for Scotland with his feeling for a loved woman. Here again it's easy to go wrong. Seeing the wayward progression, the abrupt transitions, the lines occasionally interlarded in Greek and German, the chopped-up prose of citations from academic authorities, one begins to think that this is a modernist poem like one of Pound's Cantos. And certainly there are things in common—MacDiarmid's political affiliations have become as ruinous to him as Pound's were to Pound, and they produce a more-than-Poundian silliness. But this is not really a 'modern' poem at all. The models for it are not in Pound, not even the Pound of the Pisan sequence. The poem is a meditation. To object to it that it 'rambles' is to miss the point entirely. In the rambling is all the beauty and the truth.

The precedents are in Romantic poetry. I think particularly of Wordsworth's lines, 'When to the Attractions of the Busy World', where not only is there the same pleasure in thinking 'Wherever will he go to next?' but also in Wordsworth's blank verse, as in the free verse of 'Direadh 111', the full sum is made up entirely of coins of small denominations, very prosaic language. 'Direadh 111' is prosaic where 'In the Slums of Glasgow' is prosy; there is all the difference in the world.

A poem like this, in fact, answers exactly (though on a small scale compared with the gigantic structures that MacDiarmid now envisages) to what the poet himself seems to be asking for in 'The Kind of Poetry I Want'. According to Edwin Morgan, writing very persuasively in *Hugh MacDiarmid: A Festschrift* (edited by K. R. Duval and Sydney Goodsir Smith), what MacDiarmid is demanding

> is a poetry which is highly organized in parts, but not prescriptively with regard to the whole. It is not so much an organism as a colony, a living and in one sense formless association of organisms which share a common experience. Shape and architectonics are not so important as the quick movements of the thought. . . . As zoologists may argue whether a colony is an organism, critics may hesitate to say that the kind of *poetry* MacDiarmid wants is a kind of *poem*.

Perhaps Morgan would agree that such hesitation among critics is rather pointless, since for a hundred and fifty years they've been hesitating on just these grounds about some of the open-ended poems of Wordsworth, and indeed of other Romantics.

The happiest sort of Collected Poems is the volume which makes us feel how each new phase of the poet's life, though it may be less fruitful than what went before it, yet grows out of that earlier one as if inevitably, in a living rhythm which is apparent to hindsight though never predictable. None of the fifteen contributors to the *Festschrift* find that sort of organic inevitability in MacDiarmid's career. (Do we find it for that matter in Wordsworth's?) And in fact the *Festschrift* is good just because nearly every admiring essayist has to disentangle what he admires in MacDiarmid from much that he doesn't. Though he sometimes seems to boast, MacDiarmid has never spared himself, never stopped being restless. This is why the *Collected Poems* show an account that is still open. The crown may not yet be set on this life's work. If energy and seriousness could earn it, it has been earned already, many times over.

Postscript: Most admirers of MacDiarmid think better than I do, of *A Drunk Man Looks at the Thistle*. If I were to write on MacDiarmid now, I should want to dwell admiringly on a relatively late non-lyrical poem like 'On a Raised Beach'. I recall reading for this article, and composing it in my head, in a pavement café in Leghorn—the deliciousness of such aromas!

MR ELIOT

IN 1928, introducing Pound's *Selected Poems*, Mr Eliot protested against 'those who expect that any good poet should proceed by turning out a series of masterpieces, each similar to the last, only more developed *in every way*.' On the contrary, he went on, though 'it may be only once in five or ten years that experience accumulates to form a new whole and finds its appropriate expression,' yet, to be ready for these accumulations when they come, the poet has to keep in training 'by good workmanship on a level possible for some hours' work every week of his life.' And the implication is that the poet has the right to publish some of these practice pieces. Pound has taken advantage of this right perhaps outrageously; Mr Eliot seems not to have taken advantage of it at all.

What is striking all over again, leafing through his poems (*Collected Poems, 1909-1962*, Faber), is how little he needs to enter the plea. Not that each of his poems is a masterpiece, nor that he has advanced simultaneously on every front. The second collection, *Poems 1920*, advances beyond the 'Prufrock' volume of 1917 in very few ways, and in many ways is a falling-off. 'A Cooking Egg', for instance, deserves nothing much better than the fate which has come upon it—of being the occasion for a protracted critical wrangle; and in 'Gerontion' the relation between poet and persona is far more fluctuating and frustratingly evasive than in 'The Love Song of J. Alfred Prufrock'. All the same, if we think of Mr Eliot putting in a few hours' work each week of his life, we boggle, appalled, at the sheaf on sheaf that must have been destroyed, and at the austere self-control which decided time and again what, and how little, should be preserved.

The extraordinary fact is, surely, that Mr Eliot has published between hard covers not a single poem which he now needs to blush about reprinting. This is a fantastic achievement; an achievement not of poetry (for greater poets have not proceeded like this and we don't think any worse of them), but of judgement, taste, self-knowledge, self-control. We are not prepared for this rigour of self-criticism in poets. In *Poems 1909-1935*, and again now, Mr Eliot consigns to the austere category, 'Minor Poems', such exquisite pieces as 'Cape Ann' and 'Rannoch, by Glencoe'; and one's admiration for them quails and stammers before the conclusiveness of his deprecation. And in the new collection, which gathers into the major canon only the belated Ariel poem, 'The Cultivation of Christmas Trees', I similarly want to rescue 'A Note on War Poetry' from the rubric, 'Occasional Verses', which stands over five uncollected poems of wartime and since. If, reluctantly, we set aside the poems herded into these carefully subordinated categories (one is called, explicitly, 'Five-Finger Exercises'), what we have from Mr Eliot is pretty much what he said in 1928 that we could not expect from anyone—the accumulations of five or ten years at a time, conclusively discharged in one considered poem or group of poems with no near-misses, no ranging shots, no labour-pains, no afterbirths.

What's particularly remarkable is the way in which the poems and the critical essays are sealed off from each other. The variously cock-eyed or idiosyncratic readings of cultural history which in Pound lay waste whole areas of the Cantos, which in Yeats infect past redemption a poem like 'The Statues'—these appear in Mr Eliot's essays without once spilling into his poetry. Now that many of the essays, having served their vast polemical purpose, seem dated or out-dated, the poems soar on completely undamaged. The criticism never fitted the poems anyhow. And more and more it looks as if it couldn't fit because it tried to assemble, using only English products, a reader's kit which needed, to be serviceable, many tools of foreign and especially French manufacture. From 'Prufrock' to 'Little Gidding' is a movement from Laforgue to Valéry; the body of poetic theory which illuminates and explains it is not in Mr Eliot's essays nor anywhere else in English, but in French. Comically, of recent years we've been detecting in this professed classicist, this admirer of Donne and Dryden and Johnson, elements which we call Tennysonian. Is this to find Mr Eliot out? Hardly. His is a late-Romantic sensibility, and the poems are late-Romantic poems. Written when they were, how could they be anything else? In particular, how could they have escaped the late-Romantic ambition, which according to Valéry over-rode all else in French *symbolisme*, the will to make poetry approach the condition of music? They did not escape this ambition, in the end they realized it—as the title, *Four Quartets*, triumphantly declares.

Normally literature lives in two times at once. 'I wandered lonely as a cloud' lives in the time which we take to speak it, rhythmically shaping that time as we read; but it lives also in the imagined time which Wordsworth took on the walk he is telling us about. Music on the contrary lives in only one time, the time it takes for its performance, time which it shapes as we listen. One way to make poetry into music is to collapse the two times of literature into the one time of music, by making the poem refer to no time except the time it takes in the reading; and this means making the only events in the poem be the happening of its constituent words as one by one they rise and explode on our consciousness. Thus, in 'The Love Song of J. Alfred Prufrock':

> Shall I say, I have gone at dusk through narrow streets
> And watched the smoke that rises from the pipes
> Of lonely men in shirt-sleeves, leaning out of windows? . . .

> I should have been a pair of ragged claws
> Scuttling across the floors of silent seas.

This is Prufrock's poem; everything he says before or after this in Eliot's poem isn't Prufrock's poem but only talk about it, mostly about the impossibility of writing it. This is Prufrock's poem, or as much of it as he was able to stammer out. He got even so far with it only because he took himself by surprise. 'Shall I say . . .' what? And of course in saying what he has to say, he says it. The eventfulness of language is on him before he is prepared, the future tense ('Shall I say') is overtaken by the present tense of verbal happenings, much too fast for him to control. Suddenly language is happening through him. And before he can gather his wits (which is to say, his crippling selfconsciousness), the language carries him beyond what he meant to say, into saying what he didn't know he wanted to say, didn't know he had it in him to say: 'And watched the smoke that rises from the pipes/Of lonely men in shirt-sleeves, leaning out of windows . . .'

For this moment Prufrock, as he steps cat-like but with mounting apprehension through the 'certain half-deserted streets' of the poem's own maundering development, is suddenly carried out of himself, to feel that others exist besides himself, to pity the loneliness of others even as he pities his own loneliness. This is the moment when the Ancient Mariner, seeing the sea-serpents, 'blessed them unaware'—but with this difference, that the unawareness isn't stated but takes place before us, as a verbal event. Just because, in asking, 'Shall I say such a thing?' such a thing gets said, language can take us unawares, blurting out precisely what we were wondering about perhaps not saying at all. To compare that moment in Coleridge's poem with this moment in Eliot's is to compare Romantic poetry with late-Romantic or *symboliste* poetry, poetry like music with poetry that aspires to *be* music.

An effect like this appears to correspond to what Mallarmé demanded, in translation by Symons:

> The pure work implies the elocutionary disappearance of the poet, who yields place to the words, immobilized by the shock of their inequality; they take light from mutual reflection . . . replacing the old lyrical afflatus or the enthusiastic personal direction of the phrase.

It is language which happens through the speaker, not the speaker who expresses himself through language. And this seems to have been what Mr Eliot was groping for when he talked about impersonality in his essay, 'Tradition and the Individual Talent'. If so, he made a bad botch of it, for instead of talking about impersonality as a poetic effect, a valuable illusion, he talked about the psychology of artistic creation, and has rightly been taken to task for seeming to advance the quite unbelievable proposition that the quality of an artist's products has nothing to do with the richness or poverty of the artist's emotional life at times when he isn't composing.

Yeats also knew this tag of Mallarmé and echoes it in early essays. But as soon as he decided that actor and orator were nearer to the poet than the musician could be (and this he did explicitly in his Abbey Theatre years), Yeats was committed to precisely that 'enthusiastic personal direction of the phrase' which Mallarmé condemned. And this is why, later, Donne could be a strong immediate influence on Yeats as he could not be on Mr Eliot. It means too, so far as I can see, that Yeats's connection with French *symboliste* poetry had to be altogether looser and more remote than Mr Eliot's.

It is only with *Four Quartets* that we reach the logical conclusion of this line of speculation and experiment. There, just as the only happenings in the poem are the occurrences of its own words, so the poetry talks about nothing but itself, continually gnawing its own vitals—though, language being what it is, it can be argued that poems which talk only about their own language by that token talk about everything else. How this can be we see foreshadowed in many places in *The Waste Land*. For instance:

  At the violet hour, when the eyes and back
  Turn upward from the desk, where the human engine waits
  Like a taxi throbbing waiting,
  I Tiresias, though blind, throbbing between two lives,
  Old man with wrinkled female breasts, can see
  At the violet hour, the evening hour that strives
  Homeward, and brings the sailor home from sea,
  The typist home at teatime, clears her breakfast, lights
  Her stove, and lays out food in tins.

This is a sentence, grammatically flawless, which is nevertheless designed to trap the reader more than once. 'I Tiresias . . . can see (at the violet hour, that is to say, the evening hour . . .) the typist.' But in this case, there is no subject for the next verbs, no one left to clear the breakfast, light the stove, lay out tins. So, when we get to 'clears her breakfast', we make a rapid retrospective revision, and pretend that what we read from the first was 'I Tiresias . . . can see . . . *the evening hour.*' In this way we get a subject for the later verbs because we make it the evening hour which, besides striving homeward etc., also clears breakfasts, lights stoves, lays out tins. But of course 'clears' and 'lights' follow 'the typist' too closely for us not to think that it's still she who does the clearing, the lighting, the laying out. Because in this way we have to revise our expectations continually as the sentence unfolds, the effect is that the typist is both an object of two distinct verbs (of Tiresias's seeing and the evening hour's bringing) and also the subject of 'clears her breakfast'.

  When we turn the page and come upon her pathetically squalid seduction, we see the point of all this: for she has not chosen to surrender, but has permitted time and the circumstances to make the choice for her. It is, indeed, the evening hour that has done everything, even to seducing her. And (this is the point) we are made to feel that it is in the very structure of language that this should be so. This is why the syntax has to be flawlessly correct. When we had to revise our notions of how the sentence was going, we also, and by that very token, revised our notion of how people are free agents. It is language that trapped us into our wrong notions, and it is language that makes us put them (dejectedly) right. It is language that does this, not the speaker manipulating language to his own purposes. (Tiresias helps because, being bi-sexual, he is as a speaker unimaginable.)

  In an important sense, we, the poets of now, have nothing to learn from

Mr Eliot. There is no following him down the roads he has taken because he has been right to the end of them himself, once and for all. As Dryden said of Shakespeare, he has laid waste his whole territory simply by occupying it so conclusively. We can learn from a poet so different as Yeats, and a poet so imperfect as Pound, in a way we cannot learn from Mr Eliot. The one lesson he might teach us—of inhuman accuracy and self-control in publishing only those poems we need never be sorry for— this we shall never learn because the lesson is too hard.

Postscript. I apologize for repeating here things I said a few pages back, in 'The Relation between Syntax and Music in Some Modern Poems in English'—the latter, incidentally, a paper delivered at an international conference on 'stylistics' in Warsaw.

ALAN STEPHENS—A TONE OF VOICE

QUITE SUDDENLY, looked at across the Atlantic, the current poetry of the United States begins to look homogeneous. This may be an illusion created by distance, and to those on the spot the arena doubtless seems as much of a hurly-burly as ever—the echoes reach us of altercations, challenges; and not only is the lunatic fringe as broad as ever, but there are writers set in their ways who persist in courses which they set for themselves years ago. But with all these allowances made, it still seems that the spectrum is much narrower than it was.

Poems now are very often spoken in a level tone of voice, levelly sustained. There is the voice of innocence which speaks the poems of Robert Bly, or, more convincingly, of Robert Creeley; and there is the voice of experience, the voice of Edgar Bowers or, better, Alan Stephens. But because each voice speaks levelly, often for good and ill they sound remarkably alike—at least to an ear which had learned to expect rapid, often bewildering changes of pitch and tone and inflection. Only the harried and furious voice of Robert Lowell has moved a little towards flexibility; mostly the voices now are subdued, grave and direct. Once one had to fear that the flexible voice was irresponsible, its frequently ironical inflections not responses to experience, but evasions of it; now one fears the inflexible tone which means a mind stolidly closed to whatever experience will challenge its predetermined attitudes. It's not that one asks for 'wit'; only for that uncommitted varying response which wit at its best is one version of.

The stance of the American Adam, his cleansed and innocent eye professedly open to all experience whatever—this can be a predetermined attitude also, enforcing its own inflexible tone, the tone of the *faux-naïf*. But this was never a danger for Alan Stephens. In his first collection, *The Sum* (1958), there is a longish poem called 'Viatic', which seems to be in part an act of piety towards his own western origins; and here the British immigrant who speaks (the date is 1885) expresses the dream of impossibly innocent perceptions which allegedly drew him to Colorado:

> I had thought out a place
> Blown clean of thought—the clear winds would efface
> Each scribbled trace of it; there I would drink
> Purest perceptions down, and then would think,
> While winds blew fresh each clean particular,
> Exacter, suppler, thought: no edge would blur.

The poem ends with the speaker realizing that this aspiration can never be realized. But it was a foregone conclusion anyway. It was very plainly the voice of experience, not of innocence, which riveted a rhyme on every tenth syllable. And the experience was bought on the cheap. For who that knew what pure perceptions were would speak of them as (the meaningless poeticism) 'purest'? Or who that was capable of 'drinking' such perceptions would permit himself to drink them *down*? What man who spoke this fatty language could begin to know what 'exacter, suppler thought' might be? And, although mostly the language of *The Sum* is less muffled than this, still this voice that spoke supposedly out of 1885 was not different from the voice of Stephens himself in 1958. It was a voice that knew the answers before it asked the questions. It could not register surprise; and so it was a voice which could not in truth interrogate experience at all. Once the tone of voice was set (often, as in this case, by relentless regularity of rhyme and metre), the voice then subjugated, and drained of independent reality, everything that it spoke about.

But there was one little piece in *The Sum* which explicitly discussed just this matter of tone of voice; and it exhibited, as well as spoke about, a tone which was altogether less settled and domineering:

> After he concluded that
> he did not wish to raise his
> voice when he spoke of such mat-
> ters as the collapse of the
>
> Something Empire, or of things
> the folk suffer from, he sim-
> ply set in words such meanings
> as were there, and then, when he
>
> finished the final verse, van-
> ished in the blank below it:
> he'll reappear only on
> the next page (not written yet).

It's an unimportant piece; yet here each line-break has a little surprise in store, and the voice which speaks the poem has to be alert and resilient enough to recognize and accommodate each surprise as it comes. This piece is called 'The Vanishing Act', and subtitled 'Syllabics for T. G.'. English syllabic verse, for many years a sort of metrical curiosity known only from some admiring pages of Yvor Winters on Elizabeth Daryush, has lately, since Thom Gunn began to practise the form, become a matter of concern and even controversy. I suspect it is mostly a device for poets who do not want to trust their ear alone, nevertheless to participate in the oddities and adventures of *vers libre*. Certainly it has liberated Stephens. In the third part of his new collection, syllabics release him, just as in 'The Vanishing Act' he promised himself they would, from the necessity to 'raise his voice'; he speaks in syllabics, as he might in *vers libre*, with the flexible tone of subdued conversation. The new subjects this opens up for him include trivia, for instance fugitive domesticities. But the risk was calculated, and worth taking; it is vindicated for instance in the last poem in the book, where different effects of light and air, much talked of in the earlier collection, are no longer just talked about but seem immediately present. Nor is this all that syllabics have done for Stephens: in a poem called 'My Friend the Motorcyclist', a poem which explains the title of the second collection and is a reply apparently to some poems by Gunn, the voice is raised and the tone is comparatively elevated, yet without drawing off attention from what is said to the voice that says it.

However, Stephens is still in a halfway house. In *Between Matter and Principle* (1963), the poem which corresponds to 'Viatic' is called 'A Pastoral'. Except for an unaccountable opening passage, in which the grammatical and other disarray is so total that I suspect co-operation from the printer (who may have left out a line), the rhyming iambic pentameters of 'A Pastoral' are better written than 'Viatic'. But the tone is as dead and as deadening, as inflexible, as ever—and in a way which can be pinpointed, for the voice which speaks is the voice of Yvor Winters reading 'The Journey' and 'A View of Pasadena from the Hills'. One need not have heard Winters reading the poems on disc, it is enough to have read the Winters poems for one's self, to detect the ventriloquism. And of course John Muir's diaries, which are the source of Stephens's poem, are one of Winters's sources also. (Before his poem is over, Stephens has moved beyond Winters by internalizing Muir's Sierra landscape, making it a *paysage intérieur*; but by that time the damage has been done.)

It is not simply that the syllabics come off, the accentual-syllabics fail; for 'Visitor' is a poem in accentual-syllabics which works well, whereas some syllabics 'For a Painter about to Begin My Portrait', have the old bad tone of stolid self-esteem. No. It is, it must be, behind all technical manoeuvres and expedients, a matter of the searchingness of the poet's self-knowledge, the unsparingness with which he will regard himself, the readiness with which he will risk exposing himself and looking a fool for his pains. The self-esteem one objects to is in the tone, not in what is said. For instance:

> —Friends at my gate, and men on business,
> Find intimations stirring less and less
> Through the asperity of the happiness
> In which I greet them there.

In their context at the end of a poem called 'Encounters', these lines, though what they say seems self-approving, are perhaps the most memorable, and the most to be envied by other writers, of any that appear in *Between Matter and Principle*. On the other hand, a few lines earlier:

> I knelt this afternoon beside my fence,
> A dozen steady violets cleared my sense,
> After a time I rose.

The comical pompousness of those lines is what Stephens has to work away from; the 'Friends at my gate' passage, and most of the syllabics, show what he can attain to. *Between Matter and Principle* reveals a remarkable and unpredictable breakthrough. But it is still partial, not yet assured.

YEATS, THE MASTER OF A TRADE

ON 21 APRIL 1930, Robert Bridges, the Poet Laureate, died. On 7 May, Yeats wrote a letter of condolence to Mrs Bridges. This is what he wrote:

> Dear Mrs. Bridges, May I, despite the slightness of our acquaintance, tell you how much I feel your great loss. I think I remember your husband most clearly as I saw him at some great house near you where there were some Servian delegates. He came through the undistinguished crowd, an image of mental and physical perfection, and one of the Servians turned to me in obvious excitement to ask his name. He has always seemed the only poet, whose influence has always heightened and purified the art of others, and all who write with deliberation are his debtors.
>
> My wife joins with me in sending you our sympathy.
>
> Yours,   W. B. Yeats.

It's entirely characteristic that, wanting to pay a tribute to a man he had known, Yeats should dwell upon his physical presence as something arresting or commanding in itself. For Yeats this was a matter of principle; it shows him trusting the image just as fearlessly outside the world of poetry as inside that world. This way of standing by the image through thick and thin is one of the most striking things about Yeats, and it's something that has been noticed time and again. But there's something else in the letter which is just as characteristic, though this is noticed much less often—I mean, the sentence: 'He has always seemed the only poet, whose influence has always heightened and purified the art of others, and all who write with deliberation are his debtors.' I can conceive that to someone who is not a poet or not a practising artist or craftsman of some sort, it may appear that, in saying this about Robert Bridges, Yeats is not saying very much. He's saying that Bridges was never anything but a good influence on other poets. And 'influence', we may think, is something that interests critics and commentators but doesn't interest or concern the poet himself. And so we might even suppose that Yeats is 'damning with faint praise', tactfully getting round the difficulty that he doesn't think much of Bridges's poetry in itself, by saying that all the same it was always a good influence on others. But I'm sure that this isn't at all what Yeats intended; he meant this as very high praise of Bridges indeed, almost the noblest tribute that one poet can pay to another.

For if there are indeed some kinds of 'influence' that excite commentators very much and poets hardly at all, there are other sorts of influence by which a poet sets much greater store than any of the critics do. And this sort is one that Yeats points to when he appeals to 'all who write *with deliberation*'. It's the sort of influence which we describe (not very happily) as *technical* influence; a matter of quite cold-blooded 'know-how', having to do with tricks of the trade and rules of thumb—such as a note on how it's usually better to rhyme verb with noun than verb with verb. This is the sort of practical tip which a poet has in mind when he talks about 'influence', and this is what Yeats means when he talks about the influence of Bridges. 'Tricks of the trade'—that's what I said. And in fact 'trade' is the word that Yeats uses himself: 'Irish poets, learn your trade,/Sing whatever is well made . . .' Or if it isn't trade, it's craft:

> All things can tempt me from this craft of verse:
> One time it was a woman's face, or worse—
> The seeming needs of my fool-driven land;
> Now nothing but comes readier to the hand
> Than this accustomed toil.

'Accustomed toil'—there the point is even clearer. Yeats gave himself all sorts of airs, claimed special privileges and access to special sources of wisdom—and all in the name of poetry; but equally, whenever he speaks narrowly of the act of composition, he talks of it in terms which are quite disconcertingly matter-of-fact, as a skill or a body of skills to be learned and practised, to be learned *through* practice, except (and here we come back to 'influence')—except for such skills as can be learned through following good models, inherited as it were from accomplished masters, from masters such as Bridges.

Yeats, in a word, was very thoroughly and completely a *professional* poet. And it's because of this that we know he intended his tribute in the letter about Bridges to be a very noble tribute indeed. He must have hoped that such a tribute might be paid to him after he too was dead. And so I ask if the tribute that Yeats paid Robert Bridges thirty years ago can now be paid to Yeats himself.

At first blush, it may seem that the question has only to be asked, to be answered with a resounding affirmative. Yeats, surely, is a much greater poet than Robert Bridges; and so it must follow that poets of today have far more to learn from him, that he is a far more accomplished master for them to follow. But in fact an artistic tradition doesn't work in this way, not at all. The greatest poets are hardly ever the best models to follow, the best influences on those who come after them. The tradition—the tradition in the sense of a body of transferable skills, of heritable 'know-how'—is carried far more by poets of the second rank than by the first rank. And a very little thought will show how this must be so. For it's precisely a sign of the greatest talents, that they can take risks which would be suicidal for the less abundantly gifted. This is one of the reasons for keeping, to describe such really great talents, the now unfashionable term, 'genius'. The genius is almost by definition the man who breaks the rules, the man who can get away with murder. And so, obviously, to try to follow such a model is disastrous. Even in the unlikely case that you, as a beginning poet, are yourself as great a genius as John Milton, you will still be asking for trouble in modelling yourself on Milton; because your genius, though equal to his, will be different—you will break as many rules, but they will need to be different rules. For this is the second thing about genius—that it is (not quite always, but very nearly) above all *distinctive*. What the great genius does is to twist the language to suit what he is and what he has to say. To adopt his style is to have to adopt his personality and his standpoint; and the greater he is, the more likely it is that his personality will be idiosyncratic, his standpoint highly individual. This must be so, just because the personality and the standpoint which emerge from his style are so indelibly, so magnificently *his*, and no one else's. What one wants as a model is almost the exact opposite of this—the sort of poet (so much more precious to other poets than to any one else) whose personality is expunged almost completely from what he writes, so that one has the peculiarly winning and rare effect of the language speaking through the poet as medium, not the other way round. This effect of anonymity, an extreme of impersonality in poetry, *can* be associated with truly great poets (Ben Jonson, I would say, is the unique example of this in English), but this is a very rare occurrence; it's much more common to find this, or something like it, in poets of the second rank such as Bridges. And it's from poets like these that one can learn to use the language poetically without at the same time having to adopt a false personality and a foreign standpoint. It's for these reasons (and many others like them) that there is nothing in the least paradoxical about saying that the worst disaster which befell English verse drama was Shakespeare, the worst disaster which befell the English epic was Milton.

And so you have anticipated, of course, the point which I must make: no, we *cannot* say of Yeats, what Yeats said of Bridges, that his influence 'has always heightened and purified the art of others'. We cannot say this of Yeats precisely because Yeats was a greater poet than Bridges; because Yeats was a genius, whereas Bridges wasn't.

I have laboured this point a little because in England at any rate (much more, I think, than in Ireland or the United States), there is a very general reluctance to face up to this fact about Yeats; there is a general assumption that with Yeats we can both have our cake and eat it, can declare him a great poet and yet a 'central' poet, a highly individual voice and yet a model to be generally followed. We have him proposed to us as exemplary because he expresses a twentieth-century sensibility as faithfully as his great contemporary, T. S. Eliot, yet without having to throw over as many of the traditional skills as Eliot did. What we are asked to believe in fact is that Yeats is like Ben Jonson, one of those very rare great poets whose influence is in no way vitiated by the very fact of their greatness. I do not believe this. And to justify my not believing it, I need only point to any one of the very numerous poems I seem to come across, in which it is all too clear that the authors have lately been reading Yeats. These are poems in which the master's voice quite drowns out the pupil's. I don't want to inflict poor poetry upon you, and so I'm not including any poem like this. Anyone who reads the current magazines, anthologies and slim collections will have come across such poems for himself; they are very common, and indeed you will find the reviewers noting them.

But in any case, it would surely be very strange if Yeats *were* a poet like
Ben Jonson, in this respect. It would be very strange if an Irish poet, a
poet so consciously and deliberately Irish as Yeats was, should have that
sort of centrality in the English tradition which some of Yeats's English
admirers claim for him. I will name only one feature of Yeats's poetry
which seems to me indelibly Irish; and this is its very marked *histrionic*
element. Yeats was very conscious of this, and quite deliberate about it.
He wrote:

> Every now and then, when something has stirred my imagination, I
> begin talking to myself. I speak in my own person and dramatize my-
> self, very much as I have seen a mad old woman do upon the Dublin
> quays, and sometimes detect myself speaking and moving as if I were
> still young, or walking perhaps like an old man with fumbling steps.
> Occasionally, I write out what I have said in verse, and generally for
> no better reason than because I remember that I have written no verse
> for a long time.

This catches exactly what I mean by the histrionic quality of Yeats's
imagination. And it may or may not be a naturally Irish way of composing
poems; I am sure it is not an English way. I am not aware of any English
poet who by his own account went to work in anything like this way.
Certainly I cannot conceive that Ben Jonson thus dramatized himself
in order to write his poems.

All the same, it is not for nothing that I keep coming back to Ben Jonson's name. For while I believe that Yeats's poetry as a whole isn't of the
sort that always or often has a good influence on the art of others, yet it
is true, I think, that there is one body of poetry by Yeats which comes
near to this, one phase in Yeats's career when he wrote poems which *can*
profitably be taken as models by other writers. And this phase of Yeats's
writing life is announced when the poet invokes, specifically, Ben
Jonson's name:

> While I, from that reed-throated whisperer
> Who comes at need, although not now as once
> A clear articulation in the air,
> But inwardly, surmise companions
> Beyond the fling of the dull ass's hoof
> —Ben Jonson's phrase—and find when June is come
> At Kyle-na-no under that ancient roof
> A sterner conscience and a friendlier home,
> I can forgive even that wrong of wrongs,
> Those undreamt accidents that have made me
> —Seeing that Fame has perished this long while,
> Being but a part of ancient ceremony—
> Notorious, till all my priceless things
> Are but a post the passing dogs defile.

These verses—the lines I've just quoted—are the tailpiece to a collection
which Yeats published in 1914, called *Responsibilities*. And it's generally

agreed that this collection marks an important stage in Yeats's development. In fact you still find people who believe they can pinpoint the stage at which Yeats grew from a good poet into a great one, or at least (to use their own vocabulary) the 'mature' Yeats takes over from the immature; and it's in *Responsibilities* that some of these critics claim to find this turning-point, a turning away from the use of a special literary language for poetry to the use of a common, colloquial language. For my part I believe that no such turning-points are to be found in Yeats, that on the contrary it's one of his glories to have moved so far and changed so continually, *always in an unbroken and gradual process*. All the same *Responsibilities* does announce a sort of new departure for Yeats, and I'd like to give you my sense of this.

I'd do so by pointing not after all to the explicit invocation of Ben Jonson, not to that in the first place, but to the line, 'Being but a part of ancient ceremony'. For the next few years 'ceremony' is a word that recurs constantly in Yeats's poems. I need remind you only of 'The Second Coming':

> Things fall apart; the centre cannot hold;
> Mere anarchy is loosed upon the world,
> The blood-dimmed tide is loosed, and everywhere
> The ceremony of innocence is drowned: . . .

'The ceremony of innocence . . .' And then there is the last stanza of 'A Prayer for My Daughter', the poem which follows 'The Second Coming' in the collection of 1921:

> And may her bridegroom bring her to a house
> Where all's accustomed, ceremonious;
> For arrogance and hatred are the wares
> Peddled in the thoroughfares.
> How but in custom and in ceremony
> Are innocence and beauty born?
> Ceremony's a name for the rich horn,
> And custom for the spreading laurel tree.

As those last lines in particular make clear, 'ceremony' is the word that Yeats uses for what he finds most valuable, at this stage of his life, in the aristocratic way of life. He recognized that way of life in the household of Lady Gregory at Coole; and he envisaged himself at this time as a specifically privileged retainer of such a noble house, the poet maintained by the family to serve them by his poetry just as their grooms and chambermaids served them in humbler ways. This was a relationship between poet and patron which Ben Jonson celebrated in many of his verse-epistles, and which he preferred to being patronized by the public at large, just as Yeats preferred it after his disappointment with the Abbey Theatre audiences. In fact of course, as Yeats realized, this sort of poet-patron relationship was common all over Europe at the time of the Renaissance, as much in the Italian city-state of Urbino as in Elizabethan England. And Yeats at this time in his life tries to impose this Renaissance relationship, and the valuable things in that relationship, upon the quite different and as he thinks inferior relationship between poet and reader which rises out of twentieth-century society.

Accordingly, it's at this time, when Yeats sees himself, not as an isolated individual dramatizing himself and his personal predicaments, but as a professional hired to serve a patron; when he sees himself above all as in the lineage of Ben Jonson and the poets of Renaissance Europe—it's at this time that Yeats strives for and sometimes attains that impersonality, that effect of anonymity, which alone can make a poet the best sort of model for others to follow. Consider only the last two lines of 'A Prayer for My Daughter': 'Ceremony's a name for the rich horn,/And custom for the spreading laurel tree.'

The images here—of the cornucopia, the horn of plenty, and the laurel tree—are the most hackneyed images imaginable. And that is only to say, the most traditional. These lines could have been written by any good poet writing in any western European language at any time from the sixteenth century to the present day. That at least is the effect that Yeats was striving for; and I think he attains it. This *had to be* the effect. For what the poet is saying is that 'ceremony' in the sense of time-hallowed precedent, immemorial unwritten usage, is supremely important in life; and so he's in duty bound to conform to his own prescription, and in that part of his life which is his writing to use no devices but those which are authenticated by precedent, taken out of common stock, traditional.

And this is the first lesson which a poet of today can most profitably learn from this body of Yeats's poetry: that hackneyed, conventional images are in themselves no worse, and in fact are probably better for most purposes, than unprecedented images. The young poet can learn, in fact, that all his efforts to be above all original, distinctive, himself and no one else—all these exertions are probably wasted labour.

He can learn something else. He can notice, in this last stanza of 'A Prayer for My Daughter', how many of the words are abstract words— 'arrogance', 'hatred', 'custom', 'ceremony', 'innocence', 'beauty'. To be sure, it's no accident that this cluster of abstractions comes in the last stanza out of ten: the preceding nine stanzas have given these words the meaning that the poet can now take for granted; he's earned the right to use them. All the same the 'prentice-poet can learn from this that he almost certainly has an excessive fear of abstract words; that his efforts to be always concrete, always specific, never to state a thing but always to embody it in an image—these efforts too, like his efforts to be original at all costs, are largely superfluous.

This is related, I think, to the point about how Yeats came to use common speech in his poetry, the speech of the street-corner instead of the speech of the library. By and large this is no doubt true. And by and large it is also true that the young poet has to learn this, how there is no special language for poetry, no specially poetical words as against others that are unpoetical. But Irish speech-usage differs from British and

American usage; and so British and American poets, at any rate, can model themselves in this respect more easily and surely on some of Yeats's British and American contemporaries than on Yeats himself. But there *is* one sort of speech which they can learn about from Yeats better than from any other master. This isn't the language of the street-corner; it's the language of the political hustings and the leading article in the newspaper. Padraic Colum recalled how Yeats in his younger days used to tell young poets never to use a word that a journalist might use. But John Synge said to Colum, 'Words have a cycle; when they become too worn for the journalists the poets can use them again'. And writing in 1947 Padraic Colum could see that Synge had been right, and that Yeats's own practice proved it. For by the end of Yeats's life, as Colum rightly observed, Yeats was using to superb poetic effect the words of the journalists. The instance Colum gave was the line, 'The Roman Empire stood appalled'; and there could hardly be a better example. What shows up in this, I tend to think, is the Irish tradition of oratory. At any rate it's in Yeats's use of this range of vocabulary, in what I'm inclined to call *civic* speech, that he has most to teach a young poet about poetic diction.

And I limit myself to this aspect of poetry, its *diction*, because it's here that I think Yeats's practice is most instructive for us later poets. Fifteen or twenty years ago this would not have been true. At that time it was Yeats's use of metre which was most instructive, and if this is instructive no longer it's because the lesson has been very thoroughly learned already. For nothing is more striking about poems in English over the last twenty years than the way in which poets have turned away from 'free verse', to using again the traditional metres. In fact poets today mostly adhere to these traditional forms more strictly than Yeats did; yet there seems to be no doubt that no one has been so influential as Yeats in bringing about this most marked reversion to metre. And this is a point that I should have made earlier perhaps. Yeats has already been, for good or ill, more influential than any other poet writing in English in the present century.

'For good or ill', I say. And this brings us back where we started. Yeats's influence has not been universally beneficial. His greatest poems—'Sailing to Byzantium', 'The Tower', 'Among School Children'—these poems, which come later than those I've been talking about, have tended to lead later poets astray. For these are poems in which Yeats takes liberties which hardly anyone else can afford to take; this is what makes these poems glorious, it is also what makes them dangerous. It's the slightly earlier collections—above all, *The Wild Swans at Coole* and *Michael Robartes and the Dancer*—which contain the poems which are models of poetic diction. And of these at least I believe we *can* say that their influence 'has always heightened and purified the art of others'. And it's for the sake of these poems by Yeats that all of us who write with deliberation are now his debtors.

TWO WAYS OUT OF WHITMAN

Pictures from Brueghel and Other Poems, William Carlos Williams, Mac-Gibbon & Kee.
The Far Field, Theodore Roethke, Doubleday.

THE CASE of William Carlos Williams remains the rock on which Anglo-American literary opinion splits. And ready as we may be to cry out on British taste for its confident insularity, I do not find myself sorry or indignant that British readers, by and large, hold on to their misgivings about what Williams's achievement amounts to. This is no more than Williams himself seems to have expected: he was so sure that American poetry must break free of British precedents, and applied himself so resolutely to this end, that it is no surprise if the British reader finds himself shut out from Williams's poetry. This makes it sound as if Williams were an oldfashioned cultural nationalist, parochially American all through, and the poorer for it. And for many years, especially when Williams the stay-at-home was set up against Pound the cosmopolitan, it seemed that the case was indeed as simple as that. But no one can think so any longer. Williams was not simple-minded, though it was part of his rhetorical strategy often to seem so; he was an elaborate and sophisticated theorist of poetry, though the affectations of his prose conceal the fact; and in his way he was thoroughly cosmopolitan, though his court of appeal was French rather than British, and French painting more than French poetry. And so younger Americans have been able to make a programme for themselves out of what Williams and Pound have in common. One may agree with the Black Mountain poets that this programme, or something like it, represents indeed 'the tradition' in American poetry of the present (more than, for instance, the currently fashionable poetics of exhibitionism derived from Lowell's *Life Studies*), and yet one may still believe that Williams's intrinsic achievement is altogether more precarious and perverse than such poets will admit. One may admire Williams's disciples (I think of Edward Dorn, of Robert Creeley), more than one admires Williams.

Or rather, more than one admires Williams's poems. For Williams himself was obviously an exceptionally amiable man, upright and unswerving in his vocation. He earned the windfall which undoubtedly came to him (and this is touching) at the very end of his life, in three collections all published when he was over seventy: *The Desert Music and Other Poems* (1954), *Journey to Love* (1955) and *Pictures from Brueghel* (1962). These now appear in London, in a book confusingly entitled after the last of them. They ought to be read in chronological order, which is not how they are printed.

Some of Williams's best pieces are here: in *Desert Music* 'The Descent', 'To Daphne and Virginia' and (less certainly) 'The Host'; in *Journey to Love*, 'The Ivy Crown' and (much less certainly) 'Asphodel, that Greeny Flower', as well as a slighter piece, 'Address'; and in *Pictures from Brueghel*,

'The Polar Bear', 'The Dance', 'The High Bridge above the Tagus River at Toledo', 'An Exercise' and 'The Turtle'.

The poems in *Pictures from Brueghel* are mostly slight, though deft and graceful at their best. Many pages are both self-indulgent and self-regarding, and the pretentiousness of, for instance, 'Some Simple Measures in the American Idiom and the Variable Foot' will raise the blood-pressure of all but the most committed devotees. (I agree with G. S. Fraser that British readers cannot *hear* Williams's rhythms; I often doubt if Americans can hear them either.) In this, his last collection, Williams is much of the time writing as *chef d'école*, there are many 'exercises' or examples of how-to-do-it, and the poems about Brueghel paintings, for instance, talk about 'art', and therefore about themselves, in a way which in any other writer would be stigmatized as the most constrictive sort of aestheticism. On the other hand, there is a new departure here: *Pictures from Brueghel* experiments, as the earlier poems do not, with suppression of punctuation-stops, so as to achieve syntactical ambiguities of great complexity, yet controlled.

Even in the more ambitious and impressive poems from the other collections, Williams spends a lot of time talking about what he is doing even as he does it. For example, in 'Asphodel, that Greeny Flower',

> And so
> > with fear in my heart
> > I drag it out
> and keep on talking
> > for I dare not stop.
> > Listen while I talk
> against time.

Or, later in the same poem,

> Begin again.
> > It is like Homer's
> > catalogue of ships:
> it fills up the time.
> I speak in figures,
> > well enough, the dresses
> you wear are figures also,
> > we could not meet
> > otherwise. When I speak
> of flowers
> > it is to recall
> > that at one time
> we were young.

This is a poetics of ad-libbing; the poet starts at a point very far from his subject, and talks his way nervously nearer and nearer to it. Wherever we pick up the poem we find Williams speaking with a blunt and vulnerable directness which is peculiarly his, and very appealing, but because of his doctrine of 'figures', the poem as a whole is not direct at all, but extremely oblique and circuitous in the way it approaches the subject.

Among the 'figures' which Williams uses most often are flowers. We think of him, on the basis of his earlier anthology-pieces, as remarkable particularly for finding his figures (or his 'images', as we tend more laxly to call them) in unpoetical places—in the waste lot, the rubbish heap, the suburban by-pass: and, sure enough, he seems to admire Brueghel for finding figures that are unpoetical by Italian Renaissance standards. But in these later pieces we are more often disconcerted by figures such as flowers which by our standards are very poetical indeed. Not only asphodel but daisies, mustard-flowers, jonquils and violets, even, and indeed especially, roses—flowers, or rather the names of flowers, are all over the place. The device is at its lamest in 'The Pink Locust':

> The poet himself,
>> what does he think of himself
>>> facing his world?
> It will not do to say,
>> as he is inclined to say:
>>> Not much. The poem
> would be in *that* betrayed.
>> He might as well answer—
> 'a rose is a rose
> is a rose' and let it go at that.
>> A rose *is a rose*
>>> and the poem equals it
> if it be well made.

This is something worth saying. But the way of saying it! From whatever standpoint this is surely wretched writing, ad-libbing at its most poverty-stricken. In a slightly better poem, 'Deep Religious Faith', or in one of the positively good ones, 'The Ivy Crown', flowers still have a symbolic significance which is fixed and inert, imported into the poem as a stock response, not created nor re-created in language. (The same is true of the flowers in Olson's *Maximus Poems*.) And not only flowers get this treatment. In 'The Desert Music' the music which is appealed to is as much of an inert talisman, as little created or re-created, as near to the unsupported assertion, as in many of these poems flowers are. And under the influence of this the valuable directness of utterance degenerates into something stolid and glib, as at the end of 'A Negro Woman':

> holding the flowers upright
>> as a torch
>>> so early in the morning.

To my ear the same tone sounds at the end of 'The Gift', where none of the stock 'figures' are in play:

> The very devils
>> by their flight give praise.
>>> What is death
>> beside this?

Nothing. The wise men
     came with gifts
and bowed down
     to worship
        this perfection.

One can admire the courage of this directness in confronting a subject
so awesome as Christ's Nativity, and it is perhaps our nervousness with
the subject which makes us hear as mawkish what in fact is tender. But
the flatulence of this ending is another matter. It is, I suspect, the very
note of the *faux-naïf*. And I suspect also that no American ear can register this as off-key, simply because so much of American literature from
the first has been committed to recovering Adam's innocence, a valuably
child-like *naïveté* of perception. If Williams, like other devoted Americans, lapses into the *faux-naïf*, this is the price he cannot help but pay
for what he sometimes triumphantly achieves, the tone of the true *naïf*,
piercing and unforgettable. Almost certainly the British reader values this
less than he should; we are nervous at being found so much in the open,
unprotected by any armour of wit. And so the poems we shall find it
easiest to admire are 'The Descent', where Eliot's 'Burnt Norton' in the
background (Williams triumphantly survives the comparison) gives a sort
of witty double perspective; and 'To Daphne and Virginia', where the
tone becomes momentarily, and untypically, sardonic:

We are not chickadees
     on a bare limb
          with a worm in the mouth.
The worm is in our brains.

In Theodore Roethke's posthumous collection, *The Far Field*, we have
only to turn the first page to come upon 'The rose exceeds, the rose exceeds us all', and we are back in the language of flowers all over again.
The last of a sequence of longish poems called 'North American Sequence'
is entitled 'The Rose'. It concludes:

And in this rose, this rose in the sea-wind,
Rooted in stone, keeping the whole of light,
Gathering to itself sound and silence—
Mine and the sea-wind's.

The betraying repetitions—'this rose, this rose', 'the rose exceeds, the
rose exceeds'—point up by contrast Williams's economy and elegance, the
clean spareness of his perceptions and procedures. On a later page Roethke
exclaims: 'Be with me, Whitman, maker of catalogues'. And except for
some lyrics in short-lined stanzas, mostly love poems, where the intrusive
voice is Yeats's, Whitman is indeed ubiquitous. In profound ways Williams
too is writing in a Whitmanesque tradition, but his Whitman has been
made over and made new; the influence is at a level far below similarities
of syntax and metre. But in Roethke the allegiance is plain for all to see;
syntax and metre are indeed those of the 'maker of catalogues'. And
coming to Roethke after Williams, the effect is fatty and wasteful, coarse;

the method lends itself to incantation, but its poverty shows up when it can contrive an emphasis only by rhapsodically excited repetition. As for the flowers, Roethke in a memorable early collection, *The Lost Son*, used flowers very strikingly indeed by re-creating the world of hot-houses and unnaturally thriving vegetation in which he grew up as the son of a florist. There are incidental references to this in *The Far Field*, most pleasingly in a poem called 'Otto', but they do not add up to a frame of reference for the whole. Instead, the scene most often referred to is the seashore, presumably near Roethke's last home on an island in Puget Sound, and their state of mind is what used to be called 'the oceanic feeling'. Unhelpful because hackneyed expressions like 'the immensity of nature', or even 'Wordsworthian pantheism', are what come to mind. And one can sympathize with Roethke: these experiences are real enough, and powerful, though both the reality and the power have drained away from the words we use in speaking of them. Roethke's words are not a lot better; and in fact to proceed by excited cumulative catalogue is almost to admit defeat, spattering the target instead of aiming for the bull.

Postscript: This piece has annoyed many of my American friends, for whom Roethke's last poems, and Williams's also, are precious and admirable achievements. They are at liberty to believe that what is manifest here is the inability of a British ear positively to *hear* one distinctively American sort of voice—a deafness not just to its cadences, but also its tone. At the risk of immodesty however I must say that I don't believe that is the case. At least, that isn't the whole story.

AFTER SEDLEY, AFTER POUND

All. The Collected Short Poems 1923-1958, Louis Zukofsky, W. W.
Norton & Co.

FOR THOSE who need to know that Picasso could draw a likeness if he
chose, Exhibit A is Zukofsky after Sir Charles Sedley:

> Not, Celia, that I look for rest
>> In what I do or am;
> In its own time this song addressed
>> To you is not for them:
>
> The hurrying world, our hastes have
>> No part in you like me;
> Faces stop showing what they crave
>> In my attempt to see.
>
> 'All that in woman is adored'
>> Grows my phrase, and your mind
> Sings some hundreds of years to afford
>> My cadence in kind.
>
> And if your ears hear me I store
>> It in our book *Anew*
> Where we last who make Sedley—more
>> Than he was perhaps—true.

Would he had writ thus always? Hardly. The high gloss on this elegant
pastiche obscures rather than clarifies—certainly on a first reading and
even on a second: the suavity of the phrasing conceals its compactness,
although it is the compactness that makes the poem both difficult and
rewarding. 'Like me', for instance, means both 'such as I have' and 'such
as they (our hastes) have in me'. Again, the colon after the first quatrain
explains 'them' as being 'this hurrying world' and 'our hastes'; and yet
when it turns out that these are the joint subject of another sentence, we
make a rapid retrospective adjustment, and read 'them' as the speaker's
doings and beings ('what I do or am'). And this is not to mention the
elusive sense of the faces that stop showing what they crave. This is a
language to which the norms of prose syntax are essential (hence the very
sedulous punctuation), though it breaks the norms even as it respects them.

Zukofsky respects and uses grammar because many of his poems, early
and late, are tight argumentative affairs. And this means that, although
he belongs in the Poundian tradition with which he aligns himself, he is
quite often within hailing distance of a quite distinct tradition which for
a long time was more influential among us—the wit writing of Allen Tate,
say, or William Empson. As Empson writes about cleaning his teeth into a
lake while camping out, so Zukofsky addresses his washstand and, through
elliptical allusions to designs half-glimpsed in accidental scratchings on its

marble tiles, he comes to the noble humaneness of Empson at his best:
> so my wash-stand
> in one particular breaking of the
> tile at which I have
> looked and looked
>
> has opposed to my head
> the inscription of a head
> whose coinage is the
> coinage of the poor
>
> observant in waiting
> in their getting up mornings
> and in their waiting
> going to bed
>
> carefully attentive
> to what they have
> and to what they do not
> have

The Empsonian or 'new' criticism ought to have appreciated the many poems by Zukofsky which are dense with compressed conceits in the seventeenth-century manner, or (as with a piece about barberries in snow) in the not ultimately different manner of Hopkins. But in fact that criticism ignored Zukofsky, and among his peers it was Pound and Williams who appreciated and helped.

The ties which bind him to Pound are thus in the first place personal and grateful. But he is indebted to Pound also for concepts and preoccupations, as appears from the notes which in one or two cases he appends to poems. And not only concepts but perceptions also come to him sometimes from the same source, as in a poem about a privet leaf in winter, which ends:

> it happens wind colors like glass shelter,
> as the light's aire from a vault
> which has a knob of sun.

Surely the most Poundian lines not written by Pound!

But above all what aligns Zukofsky with Pound and Williams, what removes him from the world of wit writing, is his concern, first and last, with the musical measure of verse. The poem about the washstand is in places obscure. But it is less obscure than the poem after Sedley which at first seems so straightforward. And it is less obscure because, being so much further from counting off syllables to the verse line, it can use line endings, as apparent on the printed page and to the listening ear, to compel meaningful inflections:

> carefully attentive
> to what they have

and to what they do not
have . . .

This is rudimentary. Zukofsky's more elaborated music offers itself most
frankly in the opulent orchestration of a poem to Tibor Serly, midway in
a first section headed '55 Poems 1923-1935'. (This poem is still full of
witty conceits, and excellent ones.) It is at its most elusive in the section
'Anew 1935-1944', where it most often eludes me—and for reasons
which are made clear:

The lines of this new song are nothing
But a tune making the nothing full
Stonelike become more hard than silent
The tune's image holding in the line.

In the longest poem in the collection, '4 Other Countries' from *Barely
and Widely 1956-1958*, the music, in its double aspect of submerged half
rhyme and of spaced intervals at the ends of short lines, makes for
astonishingly compact expression, and this vindicates more than one
would have thought possible that inherently unsatisfactory form, the
poem as travelogue.

SINCERITY AND POETRY

KENNETH REXROTH declares, introducing *Selected Poems of D. H. Lawrence*:

> Hardy could say to himself: 'Today I am going to be a Wiltshire yeoman, sitting on a fallen rock at Stonehenge, writing a poem to my girl on a piece of wrapping paper with the gnawed stub of a pencil,' and he could make it very convincing. But Lawrence really was the educated son of a coal miner, sitting under a tree that had once been part of Sherwood Forest, in a village that was rapidly becoming part of a world-wide disembowelled hell, writing hard, painful poems, to girls who carefully had been taught the art of unlove. It was all real. Love really was a mystery at the navel of the earth, like Stonehenge. The miner really was in contact with a monstrous, seething mystery, the black sun in the earth.

And again:

> Hardy was a major poet. Lawrence was a minor prophet. Like Blake and Yeats, his is the greater tradition. If Hardy ever had a girl in the hay, tipsy on cider, on the night of Boxing Day, he kept quiet about it. He may have thought that it had something to do with 'the stream of his life in the darkness deathward set', but he never let on, except indirectly.

This is outrageous, of course. In part, at least, it is meant to be; it is outrageously unfair to Thomas Hardy. But then, fairness is what we never find from anyone who at any time speaks up for what Rexroth is speaking for here. Are prophets fair-minded? Can we expect Jeremiah or Amos or Isaiah to be *judicious*? D. H. Lawrence was monstrously unfair; so were nineteenth-century prophets like Carlyle and Ruskin; so was William Blake unfair to Reynolds and to Wordsworth. And some of them, some of the time—perhaps all of them, most of the time—know that they are being unfair, as I think Kenneth Rexroth knows it. Fair-mindedness, Lawrence seems to say, is not his business; if judiciousness is necessary to society, it is the business of someone in society other than the prophet or the poet.

'The prophet *or* the poet.' . . . For, although I've gone along with Rexroth for the moment in accepting this distinction, I am not really convinced by it. For what *is* the distinction which Rexroth has drawn, between Hardy and Lawrence? As he presents it to us, it has nothing to do with prophecy, though he seems to think it has. The distinction is quite simply that when 'I' appears in a poem by Lawrence, the person meant is directly and immediately D. H. Lawrence, the person as historically recorded, born in such and such a place on such and such a date; whereas when 'I' appears in a poem by Hardy, the person meant need not be the historically recorded Thomas Hardy, any more than when King Lear in Shakespeare's play says 'I', the person meant is William Shakespeare.

When Rexroth introduces the notion of a tradition of *prophecy*, above all when he puts in that tradition the most histrionic of modern poets

(W. B. Yeats), he is shifting his ground abruptly and very confusingly. What he is saying to start with is simply and bluntly that Lawrence is always sincere, whereas Hardy often isn't; and Lawrence is sincere by virtue of the fact that the 'I' in his poems is always directly and immediately himself. In other words, the poetry we are asked to see as greater than Hardy's kind of poetry, though it is called 'prophetic' poetry, is more accurately described as *confessional* poetry. Confessional poetry, of its nature and necessarily, is superior to dramatic or histrionic poetry; a poem in which the 'I' stands immediately and unequivocally for the author is essentially and necessarily superior to a poem in which the 'I' stands not for the author but for a *persona* of the author's—this is what Rexroth asks us to believe.

This is, as he well knows, to fly in the face of what seemed, until a few years ago, the solidly achieved consensus of opinion about poetry and the criticism of poetry. That consensus of opinion seemed to have formed itself on the basis of insights delivered to us by the revolutionary poets of two or three generations ago. It had taken the idea of the *persona* from Ezra Pound, and the closely related idea of the *mask* from W. B. Yeats; and it had taken from T. S. Eliot the ideas that the structure of a poem was inherently a *dramatic* structure, and that the effect of poetry was an impersonal effect. It had elaborated on these hints to formulate a rule, the rule that the 'I' in a poem is *never* immediately and directly the poet; that the poet-in-his-poem is always distinct from, and must never be confounded with, the-poet-outside-his-poem, the poet as historically recorded between birthdate and date of death. To this rule there was a necessary and invaluable corollary: that the question 'Is the poet sincere?'—though it would continue to be asked by naïve readers—was always an impertinent and illegitimate question. This was the view of poetry associated with the so-called New Criticism, and (although it has been challenged from other directions than the one we are concerned with) it is still the view of poetry taught in our university classrooms. Must we now abandon it?

I think we must—or rather, that we may and must hold by it for the sake of the poetry which it illuminates; but that we can no longer hold by it as an account which does justice to *all* poetry. It illuminates nearly all the poetry that we want to remember written in England between 1550 and about 1780; but it illuminates little of the poetry in English written since 1780. For my own part, I often bitterly regret having to give it up as regards the poetry of our own time. I see too clearly the grievous consequences of doing so, of having the question of 'sincerity', which we thought to be safely scotched, once again rearing its head as a central question. Anyone can see these consequences—*see* them, not *foresee* them; because they are with us already. For the question has been settled already, off campus; and it is only in the university classrooms that anyone any longer supposes that 'Is he sincere?' is a question not to be asked of poets. Confessional poetry has come back with a vengeance; for many years now it is the poetry that has been written by the most serious and talented poets, alike in America and in Britain.

Consider only the case of Robert Lowell, probably the most influential poet of his generation. It is a very telling case indeed: trained in the very heart of New Criticism by Allen Tate, Lowell made his reputation by poems which are characteristically dramatic monologues, in which the 'I' of the poem was hardly ever to be identified with the historical Robert Lowell. Then in the mid-fifties came his collection called *Life Studies* in which the 'I' of the poems nearly always asks to be taken, quite unequivocally, as Robert Lowell himself. At about the same time, from under the shadow of Rexroth himself, came Allen Ginsberg's prophetic-confessional poem *Howl!* And ever since, confessional poems have been the order of the day, with the predictable consequences—the poem has lost all its hard-won autonomy, its independence in its own right, and has once again become merely the vehicle by which the writer acts out before his public the agony or the discomfort (American poets go for agony, British ones for discomfort) of being a writer, or of being alive in the twentieth century. Now we have once again poems in which the public life of the author as author, and his private life, are messily compounded, so that one needs the adventitious information of the gossip-columnist to take the force or even the literal meaning of what, since it is a work of literary art, is supposedly offered as public utterance. And woe betide that poet whose life, when the gossip-columnist-reviewer goes to work on it, does not reveal fornications and adulteries, drug-addictions, alcoholism and spells in mental homes. 'What?' the reviewer exclaims, 'when it appears that your poems have cost you so little, when the writing of them has apparently disorganized your life hardly at all, can you expect me to give them as much attention as the poems of Miss X here, whose vocation drove her last week to suicide?'

If this is what can happen when the question of sincerity once again becomes central to the judgement of poetry, how much we must wish that we could hold firm to those precepts of the New Criticism which ruled that question out of order. Why not? If the universities are the bulwarks of that more decorous view of poetry, what more proper than that the universities should resist with disdain the dishevelled sensationalism of the literary worlds of London and New York? And after all, aren't most of these new confessional poets very bad poets? Yes, they are; as most poets of any kind, at any given moment, are bad poets. But Robert Lowell isn't. In fact, it won't wash: the question of sincerity can never again be out of order. For as we see now, even in the heyday of the *persona* and of impersonality in poetry, there were poets writing who would not fit the doctrine and who came off badly in consequence. Ezra Pound, the very man who introduced the concept of *persona*, was one of those who came off badly. His *Pisan Cantos*, written late in his career, are

confessional poems, and they have been esteemed by many who find all
or most of the rest of Pound unreadable. Who shall say those readers are
wrong? William Carlos Williams wrote confessional poems which a criticism evolved to do justice to T. S. Eliot could get no purchase on. Thomas
Hardy, for all that Kenneth Rexroth herds him in with the poets of the
persona, in fact came off badly at the hands of a criticism which based
itself on the *persona*. And there is, indeed, D. H. Lawrence. Was Lawrence
a poet at all? The New Criticism, true to its lights, decided for the most
part that he wasn't. But he wrote, along with too much that is messy
and strident, 'River Roses' and 'Gloire de Dijon' and 'Snake', poems
which any candid and unperverted taste must applaud, poems which do
indeed (and this is the strength of Kenneth Rexroth's case) make us ex-
claim at finding the business of poetry once again so simple, so straightforward, so direct.

To be sure, Lawrence is not a confessional poet as Lowell and Ginsberg
are confessional poets. For the confessional poet comes in two sizes:
there are the Wordsworthian poets who confess to virtue (like Pasternak),
as well as the Byronic poets who confess to vice (like Baudelaire). Lawrence in this respect is of the Wordsworthian sort, and in fact he was
very hard and contemptuous towards writers such as Rozanov who con-
fessed to meanness and perversities. For myself, I find it easier today to
sympathize with the Wordsworthians that the Baudelaireans. For our
leaders of literary fashion long ago fell over backwards in their determination not to treat the Baudelaires of our day as the pundits of Paris in
the 1860s treated Baudelaire. In other words, those who demand most
insistently that our poetry be confessional, demand also that its confessions
be Baudelairean; they are so determined that the poetic vocation be
agonized and dishevelled that they are never so affronted as by the
Wordsworthian or Pasternakian poetry which confesses on the contrary,
to having found the poetic vocation stabilizing, composing, refreshing.
Robert Bly is one contemporary poet who makes this Wordsworthian
claim to have gained access through his vocation to sources of refresh-
ment and composure; and however we might differ as to the intrinsic
quality of Mr Bly's poems, we can see that it is this pretension which
has provoked some of his reviewers to fury.

But there is more than this to be said. 'Byronic' is a term we may use
lightly; 'Wordsworthian' is not, or not in my usage. If it is true, as I am
suggesting, that with those of our poets who confess to virtue we have a
recovery of the note of Wordsworth, we need to understand just what
this means. What is involved is the assumption or the contention (with
Wordsworth it was a contention) that the living of a poetic life is more
important than the writing of poems; that the poems indeed have their
value less in themselves than as pointing back to the life that they have
come out of, which they witness to. (1) This view of poetry is horribly

dangerous, especially in our age when publicity is an industry with a fear-some range of techniques for exploiting the personality, distorting it, and destroying its privacy. This view of poetry opens the door to the exhibi-tionists; to the deceivers and self-deceivers (the conscious and uncon-scious hypocrites); to the man who will plume himself on his status as a poet, and demand special privileges on the strength of it, without ever submitting to having his qualifications examined. All this is true. These are indeed the lamentable consequences of once again admitting the Ro-mantic pretension that the poetic life is more important than any of the poems which come out of it. Nevertheless these consequences must be accepted, and even gladly accepted. At those infrequent moments when, as readers or writers, we think really earnestly about what poetry is and means, we cannot regret that the question of sincerity has once again become central. On the contrary we must welcome it; we must welcome the change from poetry seen as the extant body of achieved poems, to poetry seen as a way of behaving, a habit of feeling deeply and truly and responsibly. If poetry is once again making Wordsworthian pretensions, we must be glad of this, whatever the untidy, embarrassing, and discon-certing consequences.

In the first place, we must be glad to be compelled to recognize that we are all, like it or not, post-Romantic people; that the historical develop-ments which we label 'Romanticism' were not a series of aberrations which we can and should disown, but rather a sort of landslide which permanently transformed the mental landscape which in the twentieth century we inhabit, however reluctantly. It seems to me now that this was a recognition which I came to absurdly late in life; that my teachers when I was young encouraged me to think that I could expunge Roman-ticism from my historical past by a mere act of will or stroke of the pen, and that by doing this I could climb back into the lost garden of the seventeenth century. It is not a question of what we want or like; it is what we are stuck with—post-Romantic is what we are.

But there is a more urgent reason why we should welcome 'sincerity' back into our vocabulary, and it is for this reason that I have coupled (I think justly) the name of Pasternak with that of Wordsworth. For who of us can doubt, examining the spectacle of Pasternak, that there is a case in which the witness of a poet's life lived through matters more than any of the poems which that poet wrote—poems which most of us can't judge in any case, for lack of adequate translations? It was poets, at all events writers, who brought the Hungarians into the streets of Budapest in 1956, as it was a poet, Petöfi, who in 1848 incited the Hungarians into revolt against the Austrian Empire. This is what it means to be a poet, or what it *can* mean, in societies less fortunate than ours. What these ex-treme situations put to the test is not a poem but a poet; or (more pre-cisely) it is poetry embodied in persons who have dedicated themselves to a life of sincere feelings, not poetry embodied in poems which resist all the guns of the critical seminar. Isn't this indeed what Pasternak spells out for us in his *Doctor Zhivago*, that narrative of a poetic life, which, simply by being lived through, challenges and criticizes and condemns the society about it?

To be sure it is easier to applaud in this way the Wordsworthian poetry which witnesses to virtue, than the Byronic or Baudelairean poetry which confesses to vice. The name of Baudelaire is there to show (and in some measure the name of Allen Ginsberg shows it also) that the latter sort of poetry can challenge and condemn the society it is written from. But over this Byronic sort of poetry there necessarily falls the shadow of a divided purpose: the poet confesses to discreditable sentiments or behaviour, but in doing so he demands credit for having the courage or the honesty of his shamelessness. By contrast the Wordsworthian poet is asking for credit quite unequivocally. He may be deceiving himself, he may not have earned the credit which he asks for, and we may withhold it. But at least he knows, and we know, what he is up to; and he is not wooing us, coquetting with us, glancing at us sidelong.

If the question, 'Is he sincere?' is reinstated as a legitimate question to be asked of a poet, what is the consequence of this for those of us who read and write poetry specifically *in the universities?* The most revolutionary consequence is one that is really counter-revolutionary: the biographer, who a generation ago was excluded from literary criticism, or at least demoted, must now be re-installed as a highly respectable figure. In itself this does not matter much; for in fact we have all continued drawing on the biographies of dead poets, though it's been important for some of us to pretend that we weren't doing so. In the case of our living contemporaries, however, the case is different; for until the biography of a poet is written, his place has to be taken by the retailer of gossip. Or so it may seem. In fact, however, in the case of a living contemporary poet, we rely not on biography but autobiography; the confessional poet is his own biographer, and his poems are his autobiography. Like any other autobiographer, he selects what he will reveal and suppresses much more; and in so far as the confessional poet thus presents only a trimmed and slanted image of himself, he may still be thought to be revealing to us not a personality but a *persona*. This is to use the term 'persona' in an extended but thoroughly legitimate sense. Yet it seems to me unhelpful, and even a sort of evasion. The poets we are speaking of are trying to break out of the world of rhetoric; and although we can spread the nets of rhetoric wide enough to catch them despite their struggles, in doing so we are being ungenerous and we are even being dishonest, because we are refusing to acknowledge what is so patently the impetus behind their writing. Moreover, as critics we need to ask ourselves why we should so much want to do this. Why is it so important to us as critics to seal off the world of literature from the adjacent worlds of biography and history and geography? What are we afraid of?

In any event, however, we are not required to dismantle the whole body of our current assumptions. In part at least, the measure of a poet's sincerity is, it must be, *inside his poem*. This is to say that confessional or prophetic pretensions in the poet do not absolve him from producing poems that are well written. This seems too obvious to be worth saying. But, alas! among the hoary fallacies which the new confessional poetry has brought to life among us is the notion that we know sincerity by its dishevelment; that to be elegant is to be insincere. To be sure, we must beware of supposing that the marks of good writing are few and obvious. Confessional poetry, when it is good, is characteristically limpid, thinly textured semantically. And so, for instance, ambiguity, a high incidence of words with double meanings—this, which we have thought of as a feature of all good writing, we must now recognize as a feature of only *one kind* of good writing. For rather different reasons, irony and paradox are features which we must learn to set less store by. We must learn, I dare say, to give more weight to other features, notably to the *tone* in which the poet addresses us, and to the fall and pause and run of spoken American or spoken English as the poet plays it off against his stanza-breaks and line-divisions. In short, a poet can control his poem in many more ways, or his control of it manifests itself in more ways, than until lately we were aware of. Nevertheless we were right all along to think that a poem is valuable according as the poet has control of it; now we must learn to call that control 'sincerity'. For, after all, what is the alternative? Are we to collect gossip about his private life? Are we to believe the poet sincere *because he tells us so*? Or because he shouts at us? Or (worst of all) because he writes a dishevelled poetry, because the poem and the experience behind the poem are so manifestly *out* of his control?

To be sure, 'control' is a word that may easily be misunderstood. Yet I think we need it in order to acknowledge how much of the poetic activity in the act of composition can be summed up in words like 'judgement' and 'prudence'. For I should maintain, in the teeth of Kenneth Rexroth, that, as for *prophetic* poetry (which may be, but need not be, confessional poetry also), it is necessarily an inferior poetry. My reasons I have given already. The prophet is above being fair-minded—judiciousness he leaves to someone else. But the poet will absolve himself from none of the responsibilities of being human, he will leave none of those responsibilities to 'someone else'; and being human involves the responsibility of being judicious and fair-minded. In this way the poet supports the intellectual venture of humankind, taking his place along with (though *above*, yet also along with) the scholar and the statesman and the learned divine. His poetry supports and nourishes and helps to shape *culture*; the prophet, however, is outside culture and, really, at war with it. He exists on sufferance; he is on society's expense-account, part of what society can sometimes afford. Not so the poet; he is what society cannot dispense with.

A POETRY OF PROTEST

OVER THE last ten years, the political and social history of the United States has accelerated, and left its literary history far behind. This is quite different from saying that the social and political reality of the Kennedy assassination, the Vietnam war, atrocities in Alabama and Mississippi, has got beyond the point where American writers can encompass it. On the contrary, the bitter truth that poetry in particular thrives on extreme situations has been vindicated anew where we foolishly least expected it— in America. Out of an America explosive and tormented as never before in this century has come poetry of an unprecedented kind and interest. If such detachment were not loathsome, one might say with a smirk that every bomb thrown in Alabama is a shot in the arm for American poetry. But this is not the point. The point is, rather, that to get this American poetry into our sights no amount of literary historian's knowledgeableness will serve. Trends and traditions, schools and groupings—these will get us nowhere: what we need is to know by imaginative sympathy what it feels like to live, as a devoted and feelingful citizen, in an America as divided, frustrated and self-wounding as America is now.

The latest school of American poets (probably not the latest in fact, but the latest that British reviewers have caught up with) goes by the name of 'Black Mountain', from a small college in North Carolina where in the early fifties Charles Olson, the group-leader, taught those who are now his principal lieutenants. The school has its own manifesto, Olson's pamphlet, *Projective Verse*; it has its own maddeningly inexact terminology, its own jargon, its own conventions and styles—in social behaviour as well as in writing; and it has adumbrated its own 'tradition', meaning by that simply its own heroes (notably Pound, W. C. Williams and Louis Zukofsky) among writers of a previous generation. And all of this information is totally irrelevant to getting at those poets and those poems that are worth the trouble. It is irrelevant because in the years since Olson taught at Black Mountain the United States have plunged into the maelstrom where we see them now; and the only distinction that matters for the moment is which of the Black Mountain poets know the maelstrom for what it is, which do not.

The British reviewers cannot register this, only because they are incapable of the imaginative sympathy that would tell them how it feels to live in another society than their own. For that matter, none of them has yet acknowledged how Ginsberg's *Howl!*, which they could be excused for jeering at in 1955, has been eerily vindicated since, the tone which seemed so extravagant ten years ago striking us now as thoroughly appropriate for dealing with the social reality of America, 1966. But that, we recall, was another American school, the last but one, the Beat poets; and we have left it just where we found it, Ginsberg still indiscriminately confounded with trivial or ludicrous figures like Gregory Corso and Brother Antoninus. We are dealing with the Black Mountain poets as a package-deal in just the same way.

Does it matter? It matters so long as there are poems to be isolated like
'Mourning Letter, March 29, 1963' (1):

> No hesitation
>   would stay me
> from weeping this morning
> for the miners of Hazard Kentucky.
>   The mine owners'
> extortionary skulls
> whose eyes are diamonds don't float
> down the rivers, as they should,
> of the flood
>   The miners, cold
> starved, driven from work, in
> their homes float though and float
> on the ribbed ships of their frail
> bodies,
>   Oh, go letter,
> keep my own misery close to theirs
> associate me with no other honour.

The reviewer will say perhaps: 'His sentiments do him credit, but poetry
is something else.' Is it? After all, what is the poem *for*? In the first place
it is emphatically *dated*: it isn't interested in any hall of fame, outside
historical time, where the notional reader, posterity, wanders the galleries
of an Oxford Book of American Verse among things of beauty, each a
joy for ever. Beauty is not this poem's business; but, as it says, honour. It
is not partisan; it is neither Commie nor Birchite. It is written (I take it)
so that other Americans, reading it, may feel at once more ashamed of
being American, and less ashamed: more ashamed, because of what
happened to the miners of Hazard, Kentucky; less ashamed, because
those miners were themselves Americans, and so was the man who wrote
the poem.

The reviewers might say that my tone here is 'hortatory', as the tone of
the poem is also; and this will be thought enough to damn both the poet
and me. So far are we in England from thinking of poetry as the conscience of a nation, where honour matters more than beauty. The later
Pasternak would have understood well enough, and so would his readers.

If this is the sort of poem we have, what is the point of asking whether
its lineation can be justified according to the precepts of Olson and
Williams, and Thomas Campion? Or whether it belongs to 'the Modern
Movement'? Doubtless these literary historian's questions are, as they
say, legitimate; what is certain is that they take us comfortably far away
from Hazard, Kentucky, and from 29 March 1963. It is on that dateline
that 'the tradition'—whether we take it broadly (the Modern Movement)
or narrowly (Pound and Williams and the rest)—comes to pieces in our
hands. Both Zukofsky and Williams, in poems they wrote in the thirties,
and Pound nearly all through the Cantos, tried to be the conscience of

their nation. They failed, and the enormity of Pound's failure still thunders in our ears. Zukofsky is trying still, and failing still. It seems that the tensions between society and the distinguished individual have to build up to a certain pitch before the possibility is open for the poet to constitute himself the national conscience. Thus in any society this kind of poetry is a possibility only for certain generations of poets, not for others. This is to say only that the literary history of a nation does not proceed unaffected by its social and political history—a contention which we all accept as true of all periods but our own. Only with our contemporaries do we act as if literary history were autonomous and self-contained, and all traditions traditions of style and manner.

What has surprised us, I suppose, is that the political and social pressures we are used to allowing for in, say, Russian poetry should now have turned up in America also. American must always be the foreign literature that touches us most, because it is the one written in our own language. And only a few years ago it seemed the thing one had to say about American poetry was that in the present century it had been Franco-American, at any rate more international in outlook, more 'European', than British poetry had been. Accordingly, this was the time when we sorted British poets into American-influenced internationalists like Charles Tomlinson and Christopher Middleton, and little-Englanders like Amis and Larkin. This issue is now a dead one, and its deadness shows up, I'm afraid, in for instance Middleton's latest collection. The good Black Mountaineers are still internationalists; in fact they have emancipated themselves from the post-colonial resentment that still inhibited Williams, so as to draw on English precedents (Lawrence especially) with as little fuss as on French or any other.

This internationalism is not a salient fact about their styles, as it was about Stevens's style and Eliot's, Zukofsky's and Pound's. What is un-English about these new Americans is something that goes on beneath the level of style: it's a matter of how the poet stands in relation to the national society that he speaks for, speaks out of, speaks out against. And the fact that American poets can now cast themselves as the dissident conscience of their nation, just as Russian and Polish and Hungarian poets have consistently done, ought to bring home to the English reader how remote from our current ways of thinking is any such conception of what being a poet means. As for the English poet, he may find himself wishing that the acute but muffled tensions between himself and his society might build up to the point of strain where he too might be able, without stridency or falseness, to speak for the honour of his nation.

A CONTINUITY LOST

'Anna Karenina' and Other Essays, F. R. Leavis, Chatto.

IT OUGHT to be taken for granted, by now, that F. R. Leavis is one of the important English authors of the present century. His career has had the same tenacious, and yet fluid, unremittingly exploratory character as that of any writer of our time whom he has celebrated in his essays. He is one of our *authors*, not just one of our critics, though the critical essay is the only form of literature he has practised.

His new book is enthralling. I could not put it down. The sixteen essays which make it up are not selected at random, nor placed at random; each leads into the next, one is built upon another, and a drama unfolds as we move through. The drama is a function, in the first place, of language. And even if these essays were as heterogeneous as they seem at first glance, the very idiosyncratic style would make a unity of them. By a happy chance or else by contrivance, those of them which were first delivered as public addresses are interspersed so as to forestall monotony, by their greater colloquialism. Yet the style is colloquial all through. It is the colloquialism which makes the writing as a whole, and especially the syntax, difficult. And it is the difficulty, the corrugation of the style, which gives the writing substance and savour. The author wrestles—with his subjects certainly, but no less, and by that very token, with himself. The voice (for this is English as spoken) is utterly distinctive. And that is why it is right for us to wrestle also; we wrestle with the man, not just with what the man has said.

He is thought to be, as a critic, quite brutally severe. Yet the fact is that Leavis's criticism is radically encomiastic. His essays are characteristically appreciations—of some one work. Within one essay, or (in this collection) in essays juxtaposed with that one, other works or other writers are censured, trenchantly; but this is only to prove that the central encomium is considered and judicious. The appreciation of *Anna Karenina* involves censure of James, of Arnold and of Lawrence—writers whom, in other places and for other things, Leavis will applaud. To appreciate *The Pilgrim's Progress* involves mild censure of Defoe. And so it is throughout the first eight essays, each an encomium on a particular work of prose fiction, by Tolstoy, Bunyan, George Eliot, Henry James, Conrad, Mark Twain. The second half of the book is much more tart, dealing as it does with criticism and critical scholarship; but here again, when Van Wyck Brooks is censured for not measuring up to Henry James, Harry T. Moore for travestying Lawrence, what should count with us is the generous indignation on James's behalf, and on Lawrence's.

The James and the Lawrence who are worth fighting for are 'the true James' and 'the true Lawrence': the Henry James of *The Europeans*, not of *The Golden Bowl*; the Lawrence of *The Rainbow*, not of *Lady Chatterley's Lover*. For the encomiastic intention requires that discriminations be made even within a corpus of work by one hand: hence that the appreciations be not of authors, but of one or a few works by that author. And so once again the severity is the consequence of generosity, of the generous conviction that 'the true Lawrence' is the best Lawrence. Is it presumptuous of criticism thus to try to save an author from himself? Does it prove an excessive assurance in the critic? We do not think so when it is a question of a living author, nor should we when the author is dead. It is the stringency of Leavis's standards that disconcerts us.

All the same, if we think that Leavis is intemperate alike in his approbations and his castigations, I think we are right. We are saying that his concern for literature is excessive; and so it is. He expects too much of literature. This is clearest in the penultimate essay, 'Towards Standards of Criticism', which dates from further back than any other in the volume, for it was published as long ago as 1933, as the introduction to a book of the same title:

> The fact that the other traditional continuities have so completely disintegrated makes the literary tradition correspondingly more important, since the continuity of consciousness, the conservation of the collective experience, is the more dependent on it: if the literary tradition is allowed to lapse, the gap is complete. But what gives the literary tradition its unique importance also makes it desperately precarious. Can it last, we ask, in isolation, unsupported by extra-literary sanctions, and not merely in isolation, but in a hostile environment?

Leavis's salvaging of this essay from so long ago, and his placing of it in this collection where he does, can only mean that the answer he gives to that last question is still, however wearily and desperately: 'Yes, it can.' My own answer would be: 'No, it cannot; and it has not.' To be sure, in Russia, where the environment has been so much more overtly and directly hostile than ours, a literary tradition survives, in writers like Pasternak and Sinyavsky, still apparently capable of sustaining 'the continuity of consciousness, the conservation of the collective experience'. But unless I wholly misunderstand these last expressions, it is surely clear that in the English-speaking world there survive no literary traditions—whether English or American or Anglo-American (and there are pages here which earnestly and profitably discriminate among these possibilities)—capable of carrying with them 'the conservation of the collective experience'. And surely Leavis's was the last generation in which a first-rate literary intelligence could blink this deplorable fact.

Indeed Leavis knows the fact well enough, as we see from his diagnoses of the cases of Pound and of Auden. The diagnoses are sound, the animus which informs them is that of one who goes on hoping against hope, flying in the face of the fact. It is surely quite true that Pound 'shows himself utterly unable to understand what the conditions were—what kind of things were the "culture" and the "tradition"—out of which European art and literature grew'. And it is surely quite true, as regards Auden, that 'there is no paradox about his easy exchange of allegiance and habitat'; that he could be esteemed as a major writer 'only in a "culture" in which the continuity with the past had failed'. But ours is such a culture, as Leavis never wearies of telling us. And so what does this mean except that Pound in his generation, and Auden in his, divined the breakdown before the rest of us, and that they applied themselves to creating a literature which should take the discontinuity for granted, a literature of the Imaginary Museum? It is entirely reasonable for Leavis to judge this literature a less fine thing than what is represented by the better achievements of Hawthorne and Melville, James and Twain, George Eliot and Tolstoy, Conrad and Lawrence. It is understandable that Leavis has no interest in it, and no patience with it, nor with any literature that does not carry 'the conservation of the collective experience'. And so long as George Eliot and Conrad and Lawrence represent for him 'what maturity and creative achievement are like', he must of course continue to deny either maturity or creative achievement to Pound and to Auden. But in a culture that has lost its continuity with the past, who knows what 'maturity' will look like? It may look like Auden. ('Creative achievement', on the other hand, surely need not look like Pound, need not be quite so partial nor so wilful.)

I hope I do not sound glib. The loss we talk of is incalculable. I make my point most harshly when I say that Leavis's criticism is no longer useful. It is useless because it takes its bearings from a state of society and a state of culture such as, in the English-speaking world, no reader and no writer will experience henceforward. After all, F. R. Leavis grew up before 1920. But there are values above utility. And we point to these if we insist that Leavis is an English author, rather than an English critic. His writings constitute an *oeuvre*, a brave and painful imaginative witness, as irreplaceable as if it were made up of novels or of poems rather than essays.

Postscript: It is clear that when I wrote this, I was in a mood of exasperated impatience with Ezra Pound. (I know the mood very well; it alternates with another in which I revere Pound as highly as any writer of the twentieth century.) Except for what I say about Pound, there is nothing here that I want to retract.

THE TRANSLATABILITY OF POETRY

LAST YEAR there appeared *The Penguin Book of Modern Verse Translation*. The very idea of such an anthology is a novel one, and greatly to be welcomed; and the anthology, as edited by George Steiner, is extremely interesting and challenging. In his introduction, for instance, Dr Steiner asserts roundly: 'The period from Rossetti to Robert Lowell has been an age of poetic translation rivalling that of the Tudor and Elizabethan masters.' I don't know how one starts getting to grips with a claim so sweeping and so sanguine, and I am not going to try. What interests me for the moment is that this period, for which such claims can be made, has also been a period in which the mere possibility of translating poetry has been denied—many times explicitly but also by implication.

For the explicit denial we can go to Robert Frost, who defined poetry as 'what gets left out in translation', or to Robert Graves, who has endorsed Frost's definition. For a statement of the opposite case, I find myself having to go back to Doctor Johnson. In his *Life of Denham*, Johnson comments on the four lines from Denham's 'Cooper's Hill', which, he says, 'since Dryden has commended them, almost every writer for a century past has imitated'. After he has analysed and applauded the felicities of Denham's verses, Johnson observes: 'The lines are in themselves not perfect: for most of the words, thus artfully opposed, are to be understood simply on one side of the comparison, and metaphorically on the other; and if there be any language which does not express intellectual operations by material images, into that language they cannot be translated.' Clearly, Johnson is here taking a position directly contrary to that of Robert Frost and Robert Graves. He is applauding poetry the more, according as it more nearly approaches the presumably unrealizable ideal of infinite translatability. 'Poetry', says Frost, 'is what gets left out in translation'—and we may take it he means reasonably intelligent and scrupulous and skilful translation. 'Poetry', says Dr Johnson in effect, 'is what survives all translations short of the crassly stupid, unscrupulous and incompetent.'

The battle-lines are drawn and there is no reconciling them by negotiation. Still, there is room for parleys which may limit the conflict. First of all, then, it is clear that in this difference of opinion the word 'poetry' is as usual playing a double role: in the first place it is simply descriptive, defining what is not prose; in the second place it is evaluative, a hooray word, distinguishing poetry from more or less misleading imitations, from verse or from poetastry. In this second, 'loaded' sense of poetry, what Graves and Frost are saying is that *true* poetry or *genuine* poetry or *essential* poetry is untranslatable: in other words, that poetry is better, the less translatable it is. It's as well to get this clear so as not to lose touch with common sense altogether. For the fact is that what purport to be translations of poetry continue to appear, and they continue to be read—not least by those who would most stoutly maintain with Robert Frost that poetry is untranslatable. Indeed this is one of the things that is queerest about the whole business—our habit of talking differently on this question out of the two sides of our mouths.

It will be as well to let common sense have its say a little longer. Common sense and common experience will tell us that a poem is likely to be more translatable the longer it is: since a poem of some length normally calls upon structural devices less bedded in nuances of language than those devices which compose the structure of a twenty- or thirty-line lyric. For instance, the greatest poem of Poland, the *Pan Tadeusz* of Mickiewicz, is available in Everyman's Library in the thoroughly pedestrian but thoroughly readable prose translation of G. R. Noyes; and in that form it can be enjoyed as a very good, perhaps a great, novel. So much common sense should be ready to grant. And yet, having conceded so much, has it not conceded a great deal? For, after all, the distinction between verse and prose is not an ultimate one. An epic in verse, and a prose fiction of epic sweep and scope, are alike cases of *poesis*, or making with words. And what does it mean to say that we appreciate *Pan Tadeusz* in its English dress as a very good novel if it doesn't mean that we find in it generous feeling and a scrupulous regard for truth in portraying the human spectacle and the human condition, together with all the skills of arousing and sustaining interest by the narrative logic which guides one situation into another. Now, who is to say that all these features are not features of good poems as much as of good novels?

What are we to think then of Paul Valéry, when he confesses: 'I would even go so far as to say that the more an apparently poetic work survives being put into prose and retains a certain value after this assault, the less is it the work of a poet.'

Surely we cannot help but detect, in Valéry as in Frost and Graves (however odd this grouping appears), an exponent of *la poésie pure*, one of the once so numerous and articulate tribe for whom only lyric poetry is true poetry, and poetry is magical, a bloom on the surface of words too precarious and fugitive to bear examination. We may be excused for suspecting, behind all proponents of the maxim that all poetry is untranslatable, the lineaments of this same familiar figure who, even as he offers to put transcendent value on poetry, in fact emasculates it by demanding of it a purity, from human and quotidian concerns, which it is poetry's glory never to attain.

So far I have dealt only with some people who are explicit about their belief that poetry is better the less translatable it is. But the same view can be implied by us when we are not formally considering translation at all. I will take as examples three well-known and justly applauded critical dicta from the recent past: first, Gerard Manley Hopkins esteeming Dryden for exhibiting 'the naked thew and sinew' of the English language; second, Ezra Pound condemning *Paradise Lost* because Milton in that poem treated English as if it were a fully inflected language, Latin; and third, Dr Leavis defining the distinction of Keats's 'Ode to Autumn'. My quarrel— or rather my hesitant discomfort—is not at all with the judgements in themselves, but with an assumption which seems to be implicit in the way they are expressed.

To take Dr Leavis first. He is talking about the line from Keats's Ode: 'To bend with apples the moss'd cottage-trees'. And he remarks, comparing Keats's use of English with Tennyson's: 'That "moss'd cottage-trees" represents a strength—a native English strength—lying beyond the scope of the poet who aimed to make English as like Italian as possible.' Bluntly, by 'native' in Dr Leavis's phrase about Keats ('native English strength') I understand 'untranslatable'; and I suggest that it's hard to take it any other way in view of the contrast which follows, with the allegedly Italianate Tennyson.

We can go on from this to challenge Pound and Dr Leavis alike to explain what is self-evidently reprehensible about treating English as if it were Latin (as Milton is said to have done) or (with Tennyson) as if it were Italian. I can imagine them replying that if a poet casts the language of his poetry in a different mould from the language of his conversation, he risks a perhaps damaging discontinuity between the person he is when he isn't writing poetry and the person he is when he writes it. One thing to say about this is that there is conversation and conversation: that the conversation of barristers, for instance, is quite different in the patterns it makes from the conversation of juvenile delinquents. But what is more to the point for our present purposes is to notice that this contention all but precludes the possibility that our native language should extend its grasp, so as to apprehend new sorts of experience, as those present themselves. We might remember T. S. Eliot saying that the models which at the start of his career enabled him to say what he wanted were just not available in English but only in French. If we object whenever a poet tries to use English as if it were French or Italian or Latin or Chinese, we are assuming that there are not extant in those languages any perceptions and apprehensions which have not already found embodiment in English. We are in the position of being invited to draw *ad lib* upon the treasure invested in the language we are heir to, but never of attempting to add to that precious stock. And we are declaring that it is dishonest to try to attain to apprehensions that we don't have already as our birthright.

I am suggesting that to credit a poet with 'a native strength' is something short—may be something rather far short—of the highest praise. If so, to write English as if it were Italian, or to translate Italian into English (not that these two operations are identical), is a risk some English poets need to take—for their own good, but also for the good of the native tradition.

So much for those who assert or imply that poetry is untranslatable. But this position has not gone unchallenged, even in our own day; and in fact we find at the opposite extreme some voices raised which seem to echo Dr Johnson's contention that poetry is infinitely translatable. This is an illusion, however. Really, these voices are saying something different: they are saying that poetry does not need to be translated, that it translates

156   THE TRANSLATABILITY OF POETRY

itself, automatically and somehow mystically, in the ear of a sympathetic listener. This is what the American poet Louis Zukofsky was saying in 1950 when he declared:

> And it is possible in imagination to divorce speech of all graphic elements, to let it become a movement of sounds. It is this musical horizon of poetry (which incidentally poems perhaps never reach) that permits anybody who does not know Greek to listen and get something out of the poetry of Homer: to 'tune in' to the human tradition, to its voice which has developed among the sounds of natural things, and thus escape the confines of a time and place, as one hardly ever escapes them in studying Homer's grammar. In this sense poetry is international.

And it was in this sense that poetry was taken to be international a few months ago, at the gathering called 'Poetry International '67', in the Festival Hall. Ted Hughes, who was one of the directors, declared in the broadsheet that he circulated at the time:

> However rootedly national in detail it may be, poetry is less and less the prisoner of its own language. It is beginning to represent, as an ambassador, something far greater than itself. Or perhaps it is only now being heard for what, among other things, it is—a universal language of understanding, coherent behind the many languages, in which we can all hope to meet.

The generosity and urgency of these sentiments is something that we must all want to respond to. But if we try to get at the sense of what Ted Hughes was saying, I think we have to conclude that he was asserting what Louis Zukofsky asserted—that the poetry of Homer is accessible in the original Greek to listeners who do not know Greek.

As a matter of fact it is hard to rebut this contention. Nor is it necessary to do so. Let us admit that the poem as a structure of sounds 'comes over'. Let us leave aside the surely very real possibility that a poem in Greek thus 'comes over' where a poem in Chinese wouldn't. Let us leave aside also the familiar and fascinating speculations which have their claims upon us as soon as we isolate from poetry those features like sound-patterning which it appears to share with music—the speculations, I mean, about how music is expressive, and what it expresses. Let us leave this aside, noting only that to say Homer is accessible to a listener is not to say that he is comprehensible to him or even that he is meaningful. And then let us concede for the sake of argument that *in some degree* the poetry of Homer is accessible in the original Greek to listeners who have no Greek. It then becomes precisely *a matter of degree*: and I contend that the degree to which Homer is thus accessible is inconsiderable and useless, that what 'comes over' in such a case is a tiny part of what Homer's poetry amounts to, and that Ted Hughes and Louis Zukofsky therefore are taking a tiny part for a vast whole, and inducing others to do the same.

Mr Colin MacInnes, for instance, was persuaded. When he attended

'Poetry International' he found out, so he declared, 'that language,
though vitally important, is not such a barrier as one might have thought.'
And he explained further:

> If you heard one of these poets reciting his poem in a mother tongue
> of which you didn't understand a word, you *could* understand some-
> thing of what he was saying: so much so that the subsequent transla-
> tion seemed something of an anti-climax.

Here the word is 'understand': Mr MacInnes says 'you could *understand*
something of what he was saying'. And so there once again looms in the
offing the question, for my present purposes a sterile question, whether
a listener who is affected by a piece of music, who 'enters into' that
music, can be said to understand it. But where poetry is concerned, surely common sense will serve us. And common sense and common usage
alike take understanding a poem to mean, among other things, understanding the sense of the words of which that poem is made. Now,
clearly it cannot be true that if you have no Spanish, Pablo Neruda's
presence and his voice will magically enlighten your darkness, so that
you understand the sense of each Spanish word in the Spanish poems
which he reads to you. If not, and if poems are structures not of sounds
but of sounds-plus-meanings (that is to say, of words), then it is an abuse
of language to claim that one understands, even partially, a poem composed of words whose senses you do not know.

We need not dispute that Colin MacInnes and others had an intense experience in the Festival Hall when Pablo Neruda or Giuseppe Ungaretti
was before them, reading poems. Mr MacInnes construes this experience
as (it is his own word) revelation; I believe that it was, that it has to be,
delusion. What he apprehended was not meaning, but the illusion of
meaning.

To return to my narrower concerns, on the other hand, what is particularly significant is Mr MacInnes's honest admission that 'the subsequent
translation seemed something of an anti-climax'. Precisely! If poetry
somehow translates itself, then translators are superfluous, officious and
troublesome: an annoyance. I hold myself that translating is a noble
office. For we may agree with Ted Hughes that poetry is not necessarily
the prisoner of its own language; but it is the translator alone who can
unlock the prison-door, and release poetry from one language into another. Translating is not quite impossible. But it is damnably difficult.
And that is why, as has been said by others, the good translator of poetry
is a rarer apparition even than the good poet. Poetry *is* translatable—
just, sometimes, given luck, given above all a scrupulous and gifted and
lucky (which is to say, inspired) translator.

POETRY AND THE OTHER MODERN ARTS

TO CONSIDER poetry along with the other arts in the twentieth century is not so different as it ought to be, from considering modern poetry, as such, in isolation. At first sight, it is to many of us depressingly familiar: it is the sort of thing we have to do whenever we teach a course in 'Modern Poetry'. The unspoken or sometimes explicit assumption in the minds of teacher and student alike, when they present themselves for such a course, is that the present century has seen revolutionary innovations in the practice of this ancient art, and that these innovations, the reasons for them and the consequences of them, are precisely what are to be studied. Indeed, one must go further: because the literary arts, unlike the other arts, are tied into our systems of higher education as a central thread of our studies, a lot of us try to explore the whole matter of twentieth-century innovations in the arts by way of innovations in the one art of literature.

It is open to question whether literature loses or gains by thus being, as it were, the educationist's favourite child among the arts. One very parlous danger which arises is that readers may forget how literature, like all the arts, exists in the first place for delight; that one is meant to enjoy it, not to work at it so as to pass examinations; that if literature is instructive (as it is), it is instructive only in the second place—in the first place it is meant to delight, as music is, or painting.

But that isn't my concern—which is, rather, to ask how serviceable literature is, as a way into the whole realm of artistic experiment and innovation in the present century. And I am going to declare roundly that it isn't very serviceable. On the contrary, one of the advantages of looking at poetry in the context of all the arts is that it brings home to us how much literature, or more narrowly poetry, is the odd-one-out among the arts in the present century—how it has built into it, in a way that is not true of the other arts, a principle of conservatism; how, because of the artistic medium that poetry employs, the scope for fruitful experiment in this art is, and has been shown to be, far narrower than in the arts of painting and music, of the dance, of architecture, of sculpture. If this is true, then, despite our educationists' assumptions to the contrary, a study of twentieth-century poetry is not a good way into the study of the twentieth-century arts in general—for it does not make one free of the exciting but also frightening region of new-found freedom which other arts in the present century seem to have enjoyed, or been daunted by.

But let us not seem to assert, or to deny, too much. As a matter simply of historical record, it would be wrong to maintain that poetry has persisted unaffected by the ferment of artistic ideas and activities that has seethed for the past century, especially in the United States and in Europe. It is a matter of historical record that nearly all the most serious and talented poets of this period have been aware of, and excited by, the activities of serious and talented practitioners in the other arts. What we call 'the modern movement' in the arts was something that poets were aware of, and something which they conceived themselves to be participating in. And in fact we must go further. If, as I shall maintain, the poet in our era has had far less scope for free experiment than the sculptor has had, the painter, the musician, the architect, this is not something that the poets themselves seem to have recognized at all clearly or constantly. They talk of themselves, and of what they are doing, as if their art were capable of revolutionizing itself as totally as painting was revolutionized by impressionism, post-impressionism, cubism, action-painting; as if the art of poetry in our time were capable of being transformed as utterly as the discoveries of reinforced and pre-stressed concrete have revolutionized the art of architecture. The poets, or many of them, have shared the same sense of unlimited possibilities before them as their friends, the painters, sculptors, architects, and musicians. They have experienced the same conviction of liberation, the same eagerness and access of creative energy. In large part, this was a delusion—but it was a beneficent delusion; being thus deluded, poets could find the energy to compose works as heroically large in conception as, for example, Ezra Pound's *Cantos* or Joyce's *Finnegans Wake*. Our poets have mostly lived, and for the most part we still live, in a world of seemingly boundless possibilities. The poets talk about themselves, and for the most part we still talk of them, in terms of drastic reversals, unheard-of new departures, wholly new territories to be opened up and colonized. It has been said perceptively that the arts have lived for the last century in a state of 'perpetual revolution'. And although I do not believe that the art of poetry has in fact participated in this state at all so much as the other arts, yet we habitually talk as if it had; and our talk is apocalyptic and revolutionary in feeling.

Why is this talk wide of the mark? In the first place, because poetry, of all the arts, has been least affected, or least *can* be affected, by discoveries in technology. The physical and mechanical operations involved in the composing of poems are of hair-raising simplicity—pen, ink and paper. The ball-point pen eliminates the need for ink. Contrast the cumbrousness and intricacy of the operations involved in getting an architect's conception into a physically extant architectural composition; or a sculptor's conception extant as a bronze casting. To be sure, we can get into curious metaphysical problems here! Is a piece of music composed once it is in the form of a written score, though it has never been performed? Is the sculptor's bronze 'composed' as soon as it is in the form of a plaster maquette? Is the architect's building 'composed' although it has never left his drawing board?

Almost certainly each of the arts differs from the others in this respect, and doubtless it comes back to a question of psychology, to the point in the process of composition at which the artist feels satisfied that he has rid himself of the burden of his own conception, has cut the umbilical cord between himself and it, has cast it free of himself into the public domain. But I should be surprised if for the poet the avenue from conception to execution were not shorter and more direct than in any of the other arts. Much as it matters to the poet to see himself in print, it must matter less than for the musician to have his works performed, or for the architect to have his works lived in. A scrawl on a single sheet of paper— the poet's product can be as simple as that, and deeply satisfying in that form. To speak for myself, I treasure this very feelingly: my art is in this sense the most inviolable—I can make a poem in my head and carry it about with me in that form, for years, if need be; even denying me pen and paper does not stop me. And I pity the architect, or (to take a case nearer home) the playwright, that the practice of their arts is so dependent on an accumulation of materials. The process of poetic composition is mechanically so simple that there is no point where technology can enter its wedge.

It may be objected that I am missing the point. Very well, you may say, I am showing how poetry in the act of being composed need not take account of modern technology. It *need* not take account of it. But what of the poet who sees that technology as a challenge, who *wants* to take advantage of it? Is there no way in which he can adapt his processes of composition to take advantages of technical resources, as the composer of music adapts his way of composing so as to profit from electronics? I can think of only two such adaptations open to the poet, neither of them at all so far-reaching as the musician's adaptation to take account of electronic music. They are composing on the typewriter, and composing on the tape-recorder. The first is undoubtedly important. Composing on the typewriter *feels* quite different from composing with pen and ink. And the product is different also. There is an eloquent and hard-headed acknowledgement of this in the latest document that has presented itself as a revolutionary manifesto and herald of a new dawn in Anglo-American Poetry, Charles Olson's *Projective Verse*. And Olson is undoubtedly right, in so far as several generations of critics have been unaccountably obtuse about the effects they call 'merely typographical' in the poetry of Cummings, the Cantos of Pound, and the poems of William Carlos Williams. These effects should I think be categorized not just as a variant of 'free verse', but as *typewritten* verse: genuinely a new thing, now being widely practised in the U. S. by many serious writers who work under Charles Olson's or Williams's influence. On the other hand, that the judgement 'merely typographical' should have seemed conclusive for so long, and still seems conclusive to so many readers, shows how far we students of poetry are from accepting what I think is taken for granted in other modern arts—the fact that a new technology can decisively transform an art which has recourse to it. As for composing directly on to the tape-recorder, this I understand is currently the practice of Allen Ginsberg and a few others. The effects attained by this means seem much less genuinely novel than the effects attained by the typewriter. It has yet to be shown that composition on to tape-recorder is significantly different from composition by way of sustained improvisation against the clock, which was quite a common practice a hundred and fifty years ago in the heyday of the Romantic Movement in Europe: the effect it is likely to have, as I would guess, and has had already, thanks to some of the poems by Ginsberg himself, is to re-introduce styles and effects long discredited, Shelleyan or Coleridgean styles of writing—this, rather than the inauguration of the unprecedented.

One may also think that it is incongruous for poetry composed in either of these ways to have as its ultimate objective the printed page. The logical end-state for a poem composed to the tape-recorder is not the printed page, but the tape itself or else the phonograph disc. (It is not altogether foolish to think that this is as true of some of Shelley's poems as of Allen Ginsberg's.) For the poem composed on the typewriter, on the other hand, the logical end-state is not a pattern of sounds on the air but a pattern of marks on a white sheet. To this extent, the printed page is still a valid objective for this kind of poetry; but the page of print, in order to do justice to the thoroughly typewritten poem, has itself to be transformed—as we see very clearly when we turn the printed pages of a book by Cummings or Williams or Charles Olson, or the *Rockdrill Cantos* of Pound, especially in the very beautiful first Italian printing of those late cantos. From the hands of a truly sensitive and devoted compositor, the page emerges as itself a harmonious composition of printed blocks and spaces; and accordingly the operation which we as 'readers' are required to perform on a page of Cummings's poems or a page of Pound's Canto 90 is something radically different from what we normally understand as 'reading'. It seems to have nearly as much to do with the operation we perform when we stand before an abstract painting.

Thus we may almost say that what we are confronted with in these cases is a work of art produced in collaboration between the poet on the one hand, the printer on the other. Accordingly, we now have an international movement of 'concrete poetry' or *poésie concrète*, of which one of the seminal centres seems to be Brazil; this is a sort of poetry (if we continue to call it that) to which the look of the words on the printed page is at least as important as their meanings in conjunction. I must confess that I have seen no specimen of this work worth much more than its value as a curiosity, and precious little even of that. But if the practice is uninteresting (except in the case of nondoctrinaire practitioners like Cummings and Pound, who have stumbled upon it), concrete poetry has a very interesting body of theory to appeal to—particularly in *The Gutenberg Galaxy* and other writings by Herbert Marshall McLuhan. For McLuhan argues that the predominance over the last five centuries of the solidly printed page as a medium of communication has conditioned us to think in linear terms, terms increasingly and dangerously inappropriate to the electronic age we live in, in which we need more and more to perceive 'in field' rather than in series.

At this point I am dealing no longer with processes of composition, but with processes of transmission. And here we cannot fail to be struck more forcibly than ever by the extent to which poetry is today out of step with the other arts. In painting, the perfection of colour photography and colour-reproduction have indeed revolutionized the processes of transmitting art to the widest public; and indubitably the painter's knowledge of these improved means of transmitting his product influences him in the act of composition. Similarly, in music, the discovery and perfection of the techniques of recording and reproducing sounds have genuinely revolutionized the means of transmitting the art-product, and so to some degree the art itself. But if we look at the literary arts for the technological revolution corresponding to these in the other arts, we have to go back to the invention of printing more than five hundred years ago!

If we take the force of this discrepancy of half a millennium between the historical experience of poetry and of the other arts, in this matter of techniques of transmission, we cannot help but be dismayed. For it soon appears that poetry in the present era is at a frightening disadvantage compared with other arts. André Malraux has pointed out that the recent technological advantages made in reproducing and transmitting the arts have created what he calls 'the imaginary museum' or 'the museum without walls'. What this means in fact is that the vocabularies of painting and music, sculpture, architecture and the dance—vocabularies that were always *potentially* international, are now *effectively* so. And this points up quite glaringly the fact that the vocabulary of the art of poetry has not been, is not now, and can never be, an *international* vocabulary. All the other arts nowadays release us from the prisons we were born in; but poetry forces us back inside the iron cage of being of a certain race speaking a certain language. The art of poetry imprisons, whereas all the other arts liberate. And let poets writhe and wrestle as they may, let them write a polyglot poetry as Ezra Pound does, let them explore the possibility of bizarre conjunctions and juxtapositions (as all of them do, undoubtedly in response to the imaginary museum), let them exert themselves as never before to the problems of translation (as they do, and rightly, and most fruitfully)—still, this condition of poetry is inescapable; every poem is written in some one of the languages of men, and is therefore insignificant to the vast majority of the world's inhabitants to whom the language is unknown. To be sure, we who write in English are luckier than any others, for our tongue stands a better chance than most of becoming an effective international tongue. But in fact, we are for the most part as unaware of our relative good fortune as of our absolute deprivation—we seldom notice for instance that many of the best poems of emergent Africa are being written in our language, and using our language in ways that to us are strange and may be fruitful. However that may be, can it be denied that poetry is necessarily, for good and ill, the most conservative of the arts at the present time? The most conservative, since it forces us back inside the national or ethnic, at any rate inside the linguistic, frontiers, which the other arts, true cosmopolitans, leap over?

And all this while I have been rehearsing only one of the reasons for thinking poetry a conservative art. I have been talking about how this one of the arts can be, and to a great extent *has* to be, immune from the technological changes that have wrought revolutions in the other arts. But it is immune also from other changes. A few minutes ago, I was confessing that I pitied the architect and the playwright (and I could have added painter, sculptor and musician also), because the practice of their arts required, by contrast with poetry, such an accumulation of bulky and often expensive materials. I could have gone on to say (and now I say it) that by the same token the practice of these arts depends upon the co-operation and the goodwill of other people. Not so the poet. He needs no impresario, no orchestra, no concert-hall; no director, no stage-manager, no actors and stage-hands, no theatre; no dealer and no gallery; no blacksmith, no quarryman, no foundryman, no studio; no masons, no carpenters, no plumbers, no electricians, no contractors or subcontractors, no building-site. It is not even certain that a poet needs a publisher. It is certain that he does *not* need a critic! He is his own man, all along the line, sublimely independent not only of physical materials but also of human colleagues and subordinates and instrumentalists. And so his art can be practised, as none of the others can, in almost total immunity from capital on the one hand, and the labour-force on the other. Patrons, public dignitaries, committee-members, financiers, politicians, benefactors, sponsors, middlemen of all kinds—these people, whom other artists have to cajole and coax and flatter, or else bully and tyrannize—they have next to nothing to do with the practice of poetry, except in the extreme political situations of the police-states. And so, far more than any other artist, the poet can be immune not only to technological change but to social and economic and political change also. The particular disposition and development of social, political and economic forces that characterize the twentieth century—these, no less than the disposition and development of technological resources, have no necessary or immediate connection with the poet's operations. Unless he is the citizen of an unhappy country, the poet need pay no attention to these matters.

He *need* not. But of course, as with technology, the poet *may* take note of these realms of action and may choose to act in them, to act in them not in his capacity as citizen but as poet. And in fact when he does choose to act, for instance politically, the poet's actions are far less equivocal than those of other artists—far less equivocal, therefore far more immediately influential, and far more perilous to himself. It is not altogether easy to make a political painting or a political sculpture (without, that is, betraying the artistic principles of those arts); it is next to impossible, I suppose, to compose a political symphony or to build a political house. With poems, it is quite different; indeed, it is almost impossible to write a poem that does *not* have political implications of some kind, however tenuous or remote.

And yet it is not the content of poems that I have chiefly in mind. I prefer to think still of, on the one hand, composition of poems, on the other hand, their transmission. And certainly here in modern times there is wide scope for the poet to relate his operations to mass movements in society. One example surely is the practice of Russian poets of delivering their compositions through massed microphones to a mass audience. Another is the setting of one's poems to a tune, singing them, and recording them. Yet here too, we notice, these are not genuine innovations but rather rediscoveries of very ancient ways of communicating that were forgotten through the centuries when the printed page enjoyed supreme status. And in fact, if one thinks of the peculiarly modern mass-media such as radio and TV, one is surely struck once again by how little they have to give the poet, and how little he has to give to them.

Thus I end where I began—with the stubborn and apparently ineradicable conservatism of poetry among the arts at the present day. And for the most part I am pleased and grateful that my art is the conservative art; that there cannot be abstract poetry; that there cannot be action-poetry as there is action-painting. (Either no poetry is action-poetry, or all poetry is.) Poetry cannot live in a state of perpetual revolution, even though it goes through the motions of doing so. And I am glad of that too; because a state of perpetual revolution seems to me an unhealthy and unnatural state for culture to be in.

Postscript: This piece repeats, in places almost word for word, the broadcasts on 'The Poet in the Imaginary Museum'. But my second thoughts differ from my first in several ways; in particular, where my first reflections were alarmed and despondent, on this later occasion I seem to have contrived to be sanguine, not to say *complacent*!

LANDSCAPE AS POETIC FOCUS

KARL SHAPIRO has asked, 'Is Poetry an American Art?' He finds reasons
for thinking that it isn't. For instance:

> Notice the tremendous pull toward translation in our time. Our poets,
> the best of them, Lowell especially, have turned translation, not into
> an art but into a new poetic medium. What does this point to except
> a failure of our own medium? Doesn't it mean that our poetry can no
> longer digest the contents of our life? For this kind of translation is
> not scholarly nor even culture-tradition translation—it is a life-line or a
> feeding tube from afar, a temporary supply of life to revive our sickly
> poetry. We will translate Cavafy one day, Catullus the next, Evtushen-
> ko, Lorca, or Gottfried Benn. We do this as if to reassure ourselves
> that poetry is possible in the old manner. But at the bottom we don't
> believe it. We don't believe the spatter of quotations at the close of
> *The Waste Land* or the beautiful gleaming links of Homer and Ovid
> and Cavalcanti in *The Cantos. Dove sta memoria.* But we have no me-
> mory. Memory is a luxury Americans cannot afford. (1)

But then Shapiro comes up against the case of Frost:

> The only good poet in the English tradition we have produced in our
> time is Robert Frost. I myself have never been able to see anything in
> the slightest American about Frost. Oxford and Cambridge knew this.
> He was our last Colonial, the shining light of that group of British
> poets who called themselves the Georgians. It can scarcely be said that
> he lived in America. His habitat was that mythological New England
> which, since it does not exist, might as well be Old England. We know
> very well that Frost is not read in the United States; he is studied . . .
> . . . Frost, it goes without saying, is a master. But it is no accident
> that he had to go to England for recognition and that to the end . . .
> his audience was English. (2)

Since Oxford and Cambridge are appealed to, an Englishman from Cambridge may intervene in this private quarrel—simply by pointing to Frost's
most anthologized poem, 'Stopping by Woods on a Snowy Evening', and
remarking, as mildly as possible, that in England we do not have such
woods, nor such snow either. Elsewhere in the same issue of *College
English* there is an interesting article by James Armstrong about this
poem of Frost's, endorsing John Ciardi's view that the poem is the expression of a death wish, and setting beside the most famous line in
Frost's poem ('The woods are lovely, dark and deep . . .') (3) a line from
that laureate of the death wish, the British Romantic Thomas Lovell
Beddoes: 'Our bed is lovely, dark, and sweet'. But it would surely be
wrong, it would reduce and impoverish Frost's poem quite unacceptably,
to have it said that the poem is 'about' the death wish, and not also about
New England, the landscapes of New England, and its climate. One sees
clearly enough what Shapiro means when he calls Frost's New England
'mythological', which in any event is not the same as calling it 'fictitious'
or 'false' or even 'mythical'. But in what sense can any of these words be

applied to the *landscape* of New England as New Englanders experience
it, to its flora or its weather? These—the flora, the physical configurations,
the climate—are facts, which can be presented statistically as well as
poetically.

It is only if we notice this blank indifference to landscape in Shapiro's
view of poetry that we can put our fingers on the most monstrous of
the many fallacies involved in what he says of Yeats: 'I am not trying to
be witty when I say that the average graduate student who works a little
at it can write a poem as well as Yeats. My opinion of Yeats hàs suffered
considerably from this discovery. Was Yeats a graduate student?' Keeping
our tempers as best we may, trying not to step on the coat thus broadly
trailed (however our opinion of Yeats may have 'suffered' in recent years),
let us ask only, 'What landscapes are Yeats's poems made from?' Was that
landscape, when Yeats first tried to make poems from it, as tractable to
poetry as the American landscapes out of which the graduate students
quarry their admittedly accomplished Yeatsian *pastiches*? Is it not true
that part of the wonder of Yeats's career is his having made poetry of world
significance out of a landscape so much at the edge of things, so unrepre-
sentative in the twentieth century, as the landscape of Ireland, having for
precedent nothing better than William Allingham? So far as poetry in
English is concerned, the landscape of Ireland is positively Yeats's single-
handed creation. And at times he saw his task and his achievement in just
those terms. As he wrote in *The Trembling of the Veil*, 'I, that my native
scenery might find imaginary inhabitants, half-planned a new method
and a new culture.'

Yeats's word, 'scenery', is in bad odour now. It is in even worse odour
in Britain than in America. If an American like Shapiro is indifferent to
landscape in poetry, the British poet is often positively hostile to it. And
yet I would argue unfashionably that poetry may legitimately, and often
does, originate in a response to landscape. And I am not alone in this.
The Maximus Poems of Charles Olson, the only poetic enterprise of the
present day which appears planned on a scale to challenge comparison
with Pound's *Cantos* and Williams's *Paterson*, is geographical rather than
historical in its focus; it aspires to give in language a *map*, a map of one
place, the town of Gloucester, Massachusetts. To be sure, it incorporates
also much of the history of the place it maps. But so did Herodotus, one
of the authorities Olson appeals to. As Humboldt remarks: 'In classical
antiquity the earliest historians made little attempt to separate the description of lands from the narration of events the scene of which was in
the areas described. For a long time physical geography and history appear attractively intermingled.' There is a 'disk of light over von Humboldt' in Pound's *Thrones*; and *periplus*, a crucial term for the ancient
geographers, is a crucial term and a crucial concept for the *Cantos* throughout, as has often been noticed. But more probably Olson's source is C. O.
Sauer's essay, 'The Morphology of Landscape' (4), where Sauer remarks:
'The *historia* of the Greeks, with its blurred feeling for time relations, had

a somewhat superior appreciation of areal relations and represented a far from contemptible start in geography.' For Sauer figures in Olson's 'basic reading list' in his pamphlet, *A Bibliography on America for Ed Dorn*. And Dorn responds dutifully, in the very title of the poem he has addressed to Olson, 'From Gloucester Out':

> To play areal as particulars, and out of the span
> of Man, and as this man
> does,
>   he does, he
>   walks
>   by the sea
> in my memory
> and sees all things and to him
> are presented at night
> the whispers of the most flung shores
> from Gloucester out

In John Leighly's selection from the writings of Sauer, a volume which I commend as exceptionally instructive for poets and students of twentieth-century poetry, the early essay on the morphology of landscape is supplemented by three later papers on geography as a learned discipline, and Leighly points out that the later papers withdrew from the exposed and extreme position taken up by Sauer in 1925. However this may be for professional geographers, it is the statement of 1925 which will have the readiest appeal for poets. Its tone is militant:

. . . area or landscape is the field of geography, because it is a naively given, important section of reality, not a sophisticated thesis. Geography assumes the responsibility for the study of areas because there exists a common curiosity about that subject . . .

   The subject existed long before the name was coined. The literature of geography in the sense of chorology begins with parts of the earliest sagas and myths, vivid as they are with the sense of place and of man's contest with nature.

For 'chorology', the Shorter Oxford English Dictionary gives: '1879. The scientific study of the geographical extents or limits of anything.' Sauer in 1925 was recalling geography to this ancient root, from overweening divagations to which it had lent itself in the nineteenth century:

In the nineteenth century the contest between the cosmologic and the chorologic views became acute and the situation of geography was in much doubt. Rationalism and positivism dominated the work of geographers. The milieu became a leading doctrine and this continued through the century. Divine law was transposed into natural law, and for geography Montesquieu and Buckle were prophets of major importance. Since natural law was omnipotent the slow marshaling of the phenomena of area became too tedious a task for eager adherents of the faith of causation. The areal complex was simplified by selecting certain qualities, such as climate, relief, or drainage, and examining them as cause or effect. Viewed as end products, each of these classes of facts could be referred back fairly well to the laws of physics. Viewed as agents, the physical properties of the earth, such as climate in particular with Montesquieu, became adequate principles for explaining nature and distribution of organic life. The complex reality of areal association was sacrificed in either case to a rigorous dogma of materialistic cosmology . . .

Instead, so Sauer contends, modern geography must take for its task 'the establishment of a critical system which embraces the phenomenology of landscape, in order to grasp in all of its meaning and color the varied terrestrial scene . . . It includes the works of man as an integral expression of the scene.' And, he declares, 'This position is derived from Herodotus rather than from Thales. Modern geography is the modern expression of the most ancient geography.' Plainly a geography thus conceived, finding its true place near to anthropology and even archaeology, is drawing by that token near also to sculpture, photography, painting, architecture, and literature. And indeed Sauer extends an implicit invitation to the creative arts to collaborate with geography, when he notes: 'A good deal of the meaning of area lies beyond scientific regimentation. The best geography has never disregarded the aesthetic qualities of landscape, to which we know no approach other than the subjective.' Sauer notes Humboldt's 'physiognomy' as the category made by one great geographer to accommodate subjective responses to landscape, and a parallel example from Sauer's own practice is, in Leighly's volume, his paper, 'The Personality of Mexico' (1941) (5). It is in line with this that he should include in a footnote W. H. Hudson among 'Geographers of the highest accomplishment'.

Charles Olson, though he recommends Sauer's work as a whole, specifies as of particular importance his 'Environment and Culture during the Last Deglaciation' (1948). (6) This essay applies particularly to North America and to the Mesolithic period the much disputed minority opinion, previously argued more generally by Sauer in his 'Agricultural Origins and Dispersals', (7) that the culture-hearth of agricultural man, and hence of the Neolithic, is in south-east Asia, not in south-west Asia as more generally held. And it is easy to see why this is important to Olson. For the argument for south-east rather than south-west Asia rests upon the thesis that the Neolithic breakthrough to agriculture came from a fishing rather than a hunting culture; and it is on this hypothesis alone that Olson in his *Maximus Poems* can use the geography and history of his chosen locality, Gloucester (a primarily *fishing* community) as access to, and paradigm of, human community and mythology however archaic.

This, it may be thought, is an instance of how poetry may become entangled with geography too much for its own good, an ambitious poetic enterprise perilously dependent upon a particular geographical thesis. Nor should it be supposed that, because Dorn and Olson are my examples, the use of geography as a poetic focus depends upon adopting the particular styles and methods employed by them and some of their associates in the so-called Black Mountain group. But by focusing upon human and communal relations in physical space rather than recorded time, or rather (more exactly) considering the historical relations as secondary to and conditioned by the areal relations, I am inclined to think that these poets have read the signs of our time correctly, so that other writers may learn from them.

For after all we can no longer blink the fact that the poets who wrote in English through the first half of our century have been proved, disconcertingly many of them, notably unwise about politics. In the right-wing positions which they took up in the thirties, not just Pound but Eliot and Yeats also showed themselves unwise about politics and unwise about history also. Indeed, their unwisdom in politics is for the most part the consequence of their unwisdom about history, their imperfect grasp of the reality of historical change; and what is wrong with their politics is characteristically that their politics are anachronistic. They mistook fascism for aristocracy. And if this is true, we are surely obliged to abandon the conviction for long dominant, as much in Anglo-American criticism and pedagogy as in Marxist thinking, that the wisdom which study of literature inculcates is above all wisdom about history, accurate historical perspective. I am the last to deny the educational value of the long and mostly pessimistic perspectives which literary study opens up to young students, who otherwise would be left at the mercy of the astonishingly short and facilely optimistic perspectives purveyed by technology and the social sciences. And yet it is surely time that we made up our minds about the unsound and the politically inflammable historical nostalgias peddled by Yeats, by Eliot ('the undissociated sensibility'), by Pound, by the Agrarian Southerners, by all the Anglo-American poets of the right. Pound's is the case which reveals how politically naïve and perilous these historical nostalgias are, if we take them as the central burden of the poetry, not just as part of the poem's machinery, necessary fictions—as modern versions perhaps of the literally false but poetically useful and time-honoured myth of the Golden Age. Yet in the case of Eliot and Yeats and even Lawrence students are led by their teachers, and readers are led by the critics, into taking these observations on history by the poets not as necessary fictions but as 'insights', literally and valuably true.

Would that Yeats had held firm by his own perception, that the historical perspectives he opened up were pieces of machinery, means to an end, 'that my native scenery might find imaginary inhabitants'. It begins to seem as if a focus upon scenery, upon landscape and the areal, relations in space, are a necessary check and control upon the poet's manipulation of the historical record. If this is what Olson and Dorn have discovered, all honour to them. And any poet who seeks to follow them cannot do better than to read with instructive excitement this volume of the writings of Carl Ortwin Sauer.

THE POETRY OF SAMUEL MENASHE

SAMUEL MENASHE, a man in his forties, lives alone and frugally in New York City. His sole collection of poems, *The Many Named Beloved*, appeared in London in 1961 from a publisher, Gollancz, who normally published little or no poetry at all. Thus there was something freakish about Menashe's being published in the first place; and although he seems since 1961 to have accumulated as many poems again as the eighty in that collection, his poetry is so out of any current fashion that his chance of appealing to another publisher must be remote. By the same token, though poems of his have appeared in *Encounter, The New Yorker, Commonweal* and elsewhere, they aren't designed to make their impact on us as we flip the pages of a magazine. And *The Many Named Beloved* is familiar to so few readers that this poet who has been writing for a quarter of a century might as well never have written a line, so little is he known.

One trouble is that his poems are as far from being traditional as they are from being in the fashion, or in any of the several fashions that have come and gone, whether in British or American poetry, over the last twenty-five or for that matter one hundred years. When Menashe himself is asked what tradition he thinks he is writing in, he is embarrassed and bewildered. Partly the question baffles him because the terms in which he thinks of his writing, and of writings by others, are not literary at all but as it were liturgical. And in the second place his linguistic situation is peculiar: his native tongue was Yiddish, though he was speaking English by the time he was five, and French (a language which ever since has meant much to him) by the time he was eleven. Since Yiddish is written in Hebrew characters, and Menashe never learned the Hebrew that was used by his parents, he has had no access to the literary tradition of Yiddish. And indeed his access to the tradition of English poetry seems to have been intermittent and imperfect, to say the least; for when Austin Clarke, reading some of Menashe's poems over the Irish radio, speculated that he had been influenced by Herbert, that name meant nothing to Menashe at all. On the other hand, though Menashe's attitude to poetry is thus un-literary, it is very insistently *linguistic*; his liturgical or devotional intent is directed to releasing the worshipful potentialities of *language*, most often of single words placed so as to draw out the full meaning locked in their etymologies—etymologies for which he has a very sure nose indeed, being aware through his Yiddish of the Germanic roots of many English words, and through his French of the Romance derivations and kinships in others. Accordingly he will say with politely suppressed impatience that, since English is the language he writes in, the tradition that he writes in or aspires to must be that of English. (The question of a distinctively American poetry is not one that he seems to have considered; and though in one or two poems he reminds me strikingly of Emily Dickinson, I should be surprised if that attribution meant more to him than Austin Clarke's reference to George Herbert.)

In this, Menashe is being a little less than fair. He stands and utters his poems at a linguistic and cultural crossroads; and unless the reader knows down which of four roads the poet is facing (English, French, American, Jewish), he cannot be sure what expectations to bring to the poem nor even, sometimes, whether to trust his ears that he has heard aright. The truth is that Menashe faces two ways at once: his culture (not just his inherited culture, but the one that he lives by and within) is Jewish; his language is English. And here is the wryest paradox of his situation. For the expression or exploitation of Jewishness in English is, and has been for many years, a boom-industry in American writing, not least in Menashe's own city of New York. And yet, so far from helping him, that American-Jewish boom is the worst obstacle in his way. So long as *Portnoy's Complaint* stays in the best-seller lists, and the words 'Jewish Momma' are good for a wink and a smirk at any cocktail-party, what hope is there of a fair-minded consideration for poems in which the principal human relationship celebrated (with straightforward grief and devotion) is that of the Jewish poet with his dead mother? And the cleavage goes deeper; whereas the theme or the assumption of successful Jewish-American fiction is the alienation of the Jewish American in American life, Menashe sees no alienation beyond that of the original diaspora, and contrives to be thankful for it:

> At the edge
> Of a world
> Beyond my eyes
> Beautiful
> I know Exile
> Is always
> Green with hope—
> The river
> We cannot cross
> Flows forever   (1)

The sentiment may for all I know be a commonplace in some Jewish tradition; but the reader who comes to it from English, unless he realizes that a Jew is speaking, may well relate it quite irrelevantly to unfocused yearnings for the unattainable, common in the English nineteenth century. Similarly, when Austin Clarke thought of Herbert, the poet of 'The Temple', he had in mind a poem by Menashe called 'Small Stones':

> Small stones from the Temple
> Are as the body's unseen bones—
> In their shape is the seal
> That only a true mason knows   (2)

Unless we realize that a Jew is speaking of the Temple of Jerusalem (which was indeed Herbert's temple also, but altogether more allegorically) we shall miss the conceit—which appears in other poems by Menashe—of how Jewishness is for a Jew like him sealed (stamped) in his physiognomy, in bone-structure. And yet in its reverent gravity the poem is indeed nearer to George Herbert than to the world of Bernard Malamud and Philip Roth.

The same conceit makes Menashe see a witty seriousness in an idiom like 'follow your nose'. This happens for instance in, or somewhere behind, 'Pirate's Port and Voyage':

> Like a cliff
> My brow hangs over
> The cave of my eyes
>
> My nose is the prow of a ship
> I plunder the world   (3)

And this in turn casts a specific cross-light on to 'Voyage':

> Water opens without end
> At the prow of a ship
> Rising to descend
>
> Away from it
> Days become one
> I am who I was   (4)

—where a half-pun on 'become' illustrates how the worshipfulness in a single word can be released from it, in forms so compressed as these. However, the most masterly poem along these lines is a recent one, 'The Niche':

> The niche narrows
> Hones one thin
> Until his bones
> Disclose him

For here the two chains of intertwined assonance ('niche, thin, until, his, him' spliced into 'narrows, hones, bones, disclose') only point up a surprising rhyme as it were in sense as well as sound; 'disclose', the one word in the poem whose first syllable chimes with the 'his' sequence as its second does with the 'bones', has a meaning that is itself 'disclosed' (unclosed, opened up) as the poem unfolds or flowers towards it. And of course it is all true; the meaning of a word is disclosed to us as we narrow it down. And yet of a word like 'Jewishness', and of the condition which that word denotes, it is true with a literalness which gives the truth a special intensity.

When I reviewed *The Many Named Beloved* in the *New Statesman*, I quoted two of the shortest poems in that book—first:

> Pity us
> By the sea
> On the sands
> So briefly

—and then:

> The hollow of morning
> Holds my soul still
> As water in a jar.

And I commented:

Fragments? Images without the poems that would place them? At best a costive talent? Not at all. This is the imagination risking all on a single throw, hedging no bets, leaving no way open for retreat or recouping losses, a testcase for readers and a challenge for writers. Such confidence in the naked imaginative act, disdaining all aid from rhetoric, can only come from sustained meditation about what poetry is, as distinct from any and every extant poem. Which is not to say that no poems should be longer.

And I went on to say: 'Menashe's poems, though so brief, are not epigrams. They have not been whittled down or chiselled clean of rhetoric. The rhetoric was never there. (I speak of the effect they make)...' There is nothing in this that I now want to unsay, but at one time I thought there might be; and I have been at pains to establish that Menashe has indeed had no acquaintance with the tradition of ancient epigram, neither the Latin nor the Greek, neither in Ben Jonson nor in Landor. What led me to doubt was the recurrence in the poems of the images of honing and whittling, of cutting to the bone; for these are tropes frequently used by the epigrammatist to characterize his chosen activity. However, in Menashe as we have seen they have a quite different function. And now I like to think that Menashe's personal aesthetic, his testament as to method, is in a recent poem, 'To Open':

Spokes slide
Upon a pole
Inside
The parasol.

For this imagery—of jointings, of ribs and spars—conveys the important point that Menashe is in the strictest sense a highly articulate poet; not for him that pregnant juxtaposition without copula which Pound discovered in some *haiku* (by no means in all) and brought over into English to make the imagist poem. Menashe I suspect has never read the Imagist poets, nor translations from the Japanese either. (Not that he is an ill-read man, however; I owe to him my introduction to the rewarding Portuguese novelist of the last century, Eca de Queiroz.) Menashe's verbs carry much of the thrust of his meanings, and he writes in sentences; if he suppresses punctuation, this is not to disorder or derange syntax, but simply for rapidity. He is also able to suppress punctuation precisely because his syntax is firm and clear without it; ambiguous syntax occurs at times, but sparingly, and only when the poet intends it and can control it. It is articulation, the grammatical ordering of his speech, which alone permits the poet to open himself to experience and to lay it open for us; and what that opening does for us (so Menashe's poem seems to say) is something necessary and humane like shielding, tempering, giving shade.

A negative reason why Menashe is not an epigrammatist is that he is at his weakest when he essays what is often thought to be the epigrammatist's chosen field—the massive commonplaces like *Carpe diem*. The least

memorable pieces in *The Many Named Beloved* are some in which he
addressed himself directly to the commonplace, mutability:

> In the world
> A while we go
> And soon are gone
> As last year's snow.

'Ice' and 'Small Kingdom', both from *The Many Named Beloved*, are
more elaborate attempts in the same vein, but really no better. I'm not
sure that I'm much happier with recent pieces which try to give us new-
minted a familiar commonplace about how the dreamer and the poet are
near allies; such a poem is 'Dreams':

> What wires lay bare
> For this short circuit
> Which makes filaments flare—
> Can any bulb resist
> Sockets whose threads twist
> As fast as they are spun—
> Who conducts these visits
> Swifter than an eclipse
> When the moon is overcome?

The conceit is certainly ingenious, and sustained with ingenious consistency; moreover, like 'The Niche', the poem shows a vast increase since
The Many Named Beloved in musical expertise, in using no word that is
not bewilderingly related through sound to others in the same poem. Yet
in such a poem I miss the flash of insight, the delivering of something
new. For unlike the epigrammatist (and unlike the *haiku* poet also, so
far as I understand him), what Menashe offers in the best of his short
poems is not poignant recognition, but astonishment; not confirmation,
but discovery—though we must always allow for the possibility that a
Jewish commonplace is an English novelty.

I suspect indeed that Menashe is a Jewish poet more profoundly than
he recognizes. For instance, set beside 'Promised Land', which I have
given already, a poem called 'Fastness':

> I shoulder the slope
> Which holds me
> Up to the sun
> With my heels
> Dug into dust
> Older than hills

That 'older than hills' . . . one saves it from vapid hyperbole only by setting beside it a thoroughly Jewish poem like 'My Mother's Grave':

> Bones
> Are mortar
> For your wall
>
> Jerusalem

> Dust
> Upholds
> Your street.

What precedent can the poet appeal to in English, for giving 'Jerusalem' the weight that in such poems he asks us to give? Menashe's own answer, which seems to me conclusive, is to point to the one English writer, apart from Shakespeare and the translators of the Authorized Version, who has meant much to him. This is William Blake; not the Blake of the Prophetic Books, but the poet of

> I give you the end of a golden string.
> Only wind it into a ball
> It will lead you in at Heaven's gate
> Built in Jerusalem's wall.

And indeed, for the form of Menashe's small poems we need look no further than to the aphorisms, some in verse but more in prose, which we may find in Blake. The whole theme of the mystic and yet quite literal significance of the Jewish physiognomy depends for instance on a central Blakean tenet, conveyed by Blake in aphorism: 'The body is that part of the soul perceived by the five senses.' To a Jewish child who knew his own Scriptures only in their English version, Blake's short poems were not merely the logical next step but also the talisman and guarantee that the Jewish experience of exile had been, and could be again, naturalized into English. If we continue to ignore Menashe, or allow him only the abstracted nod that we give to unclassifiable oddity, we are in effect saying that he doesn't deserve to profit by the promise that Blake made.

A poet can be damaged—even destroyed, certainly mutilated—by lack of recognition. Blake himself may be thought of as a case in point; his writing becomes more private and idiosyncratic as he advances into his Prophetic Books, with less and less hope of getting any public response and therefore writing more and more for no one's eye but his own. There is a real danger of the same thing happening with Menashe. It shows up particularly with his revisions. Short as his poems are, he revises them constantly, and always so as to abbreviate them further. For instance, one of the longest poems in *The Many Named Beloved* is called 'There is no Jerusalem but this':

> The shrine whose form within
> My physical form is limned
> Streams fire to my skin
> And I, kilned one, chant
> Canticles which flames scan
> Through me shaped as I am
>
> There is no Jerusalem but this
> Breathed in flesh by shameless love
> Built high upon the tides of blood

> I believe the Prophets and Blake
> And like David I bless myself
> With all my might

> I know many hills were holy once
> But now in the level lands to live
> Zion ground down must become marrow
> Thus in my bones I'm the King's son
> And through Death's domain I go
> Making my own procession

This has now been revised: 'terrain' comes into the penultimate line in place of 'domain' (a notable improvement), and the first stanza is only three lines long:

> The shrine whose shape I am
> Has a fringe of fire
> Flames skirt my skin

The withdrawal from public statement into private talisman is manifest in this revision, and the privacy closes around the poet impenetrably when he nowadays regards those three lines, untitled, as in themselves a complete poem. Similarly, he confesses that he has been tempted to cut down 'Small Stones' (its four lines I have given earlier) to the single ejaculation: 'Small stones for the Temple'. This was perhaps a trap laid for him from the first because he saw poetry as liturgical, as worship; for the untranslatable ejaculations 'Hosannah' and 'Hallelujah' are not poems. But if this is the trap, it is one that Menashe might have, and could still, evade, if he had some play-back from an audience, particularly a Gentile audience.

And it is time in fact to make it clear that, despite my emphasis on his Jewishness, Menashe does address a Gentile audience and has much to give to the Gentile reader. When he is writing confidently, and with hopes of being heard, he can universalize his Jewishness and thus transcend it. My example shall be one of his most astonishing and memorable poems, 'Cargo':

> Old wounds leave good hollows
> Where one who goes can hold
> Himself in ghostly embraces
> Of former powers and graces
> Whose domain no strife mars—
> I am made whole by my scars
> For whatever now displaces
> Follows all that once was
> And without loss stows
> Me into my own spaces   (5)

The fifth line is flat; the remainder—with 'hold' fulfilling its verbal and its nominal functions at once, and with the crucially meaningful submerged rhyme, 'hollows . . . follows . . . stows'—is magnificent. And what is said holds as true of Gentile and personal wounds as of historical Jewish ones.

THE BLACK MOUNTAIN POETS:
CHARLES OLSON AND EDWARD DORN

THE NAME 'Black Mountain', as it is attached to the poets I am going to discuss, derives from Black Mountain College, an institution in North Carolina, now long defunct, where several of the most prominent members of the group first came together in the early 1950s. The history of Black Mountain College is itself of great interest, though it isn't my concern at this moment. Suffice to say that it was in most ways the earliest instance of something that is now much in the public eye, which is to say, 'the anti-university'. It was founded by disaffected teachers from an American university, who despaired of effecting what they understood as 'education' in the institutionalized places of higher learning in their country, smeared and distorted as those places were by the prevailing ideology of the national society. In the last years of its brief but eventful history, Black Mountain College was directed by Charles Olson, who at the age of forty-one came from a career in politics and government service to serve as rector of the college from 1951 to 1956. Olson, who did not publish his first poem until he was thirty-five, was at that time known in literary circles chiefly as the author of a monograph on Herman Melville's *Moby Dick*, a book entitled *Call Me Ishmael* which first appeared in 1947 and is still the best introduction to his thought. But the exceptionally discerning reader of poetry might have noted also, published in a New York poetry magazine in 1950, Olson's essay-manifesto, *Projective Verse*, which has since been reprinted several times and is available most readily as a 'Statement on Poetics' in an appendix to D. M. Allen's anthology, *The New American Poetry 1945-1960*. Allen's sadly indiscriminate anthology, which came out in 1960, was the means by which the so-called Black Mountain group of poets came to be recognized as, for good or ill, a feature of the Anglo-American literary scene. And this delay in the group's establishing itself was no accident. For just as Black Mountain College repudiated the institutionalized organization of higher education in the U.S.A. (and so repudiated the normal, high-powered channels of publicity for itself), so the members of the group for many years shunned the normal channels of publication, the well-established and soundly-financed magazines, and the New York publishing houses. Their own magazines, shoddily produced in small printings and distributed privately, often for free, are now already collectors' items; as are their slender booklets and pamphlets, often produced on private printing presses. Even now, when in many cases the reputations can be said to be firmly established, the collections are brought out by small and sometimes fugitive publishing concerns; they are very seldom reviewed, and hardly ever in the expected places; and they are hard to come by except through a few booksellers, whether in New York, in San Francisco or in London.

This distinguishes the Black Mountain poets from a group which externally looks similar, with which they have had, and still maintain for the most part, friendly relations. I mean the so-called Beatnik poets centred on San Francisco in the late 1950s, of whom the most familiar names are doubtless Allen Ginsberg, Gregory Corso, Jack Kerouac, Lawrence Ferlinghetti. The Beatniks were always, and remain, very astute self-publicists, whereas the serious Black Mountaineers have shunned publicity very effectively.

So much for general information: now for the poetry. But at once I must warn you that there is a disappointment in store for you. I have chosen no specimen poems to dissect for your benefit. No, on consideration I have decided against this. For that procedure smacks altogether too strongly of precisely the milieu for poetry that the Beatniks and Black Mountaineers alike want to avoid: the graduate seminar class which spends a happy hour winkling out the symbols and the ambiguities from a dozen lines of Allen Tate or Robert Lowell or Ted Hughes. The poems of Charles Olson, of Ed Dorn and Robert Creeley, are not written for that sort of reading, any more than are the poems of Allen Ginsberg or Walt Whitman. As Olson's treatise makes clear, they are written very insistently for the speaking voice, and for the speaking voice of the poet himself; and they are composed so as to be performed, live, before a live audience, by the poet in person. It need not be the bravura performance before massed microphones of an Allen Ginsberg; on the contrary, Creeley's poems in his way, and Dorn's in his (I haven't heard Olson read) are meant to be given a very soft-voiced performance, hesitant and deliberate, intimate and personal. And equally, it does not mean with Creeley and Dorn as it seems to do with Ginsberg that the text of the poem is a slack and colourless 'score', which comes to life only in the charismatic presence of the bard. The poems have much to give to the solitary and silent reader, as I hope to show. (And the scoring for the speaking verses is in some cases, notably Creeley's and Duncan's, extremely punctilious and exact.) But they are not meant to be mulled over excitedly, and tugged this way and that, in earnest discussion. And in fact, of course, we too seldom remember how few poems ever were written with that sort of reading in mind; how very special and peculiar is this sort of treatment of poems, which we tend to regard as normal.

But there is another reason why it isn't appropriate to approach the Black Mountain poets by close reading of selected specimens. Some of their poems can be submitted to that sort of inspection, and can survive it, as can the poems of Milton or Ezra Pound. But in Olson's case and Dorn's, as in Pound's case and Milton's, such an experiment is in any event wide of the mark. With these poets it is not the case that the poem in isolation, if only you scrutinize it closely enough, will reveal to you everything you need to understand it and enjoy it. Even of T. S. Eliot and Robert Lowell, Allen Tate and Ted Hughes, this is not true; for all these poets, like all poets there ever were, expect the reader to bring something to the poem—and something more than just receptivity, sympathy and alertness. The reader is expected to bring to the poem a certain body of information, and certain assumptions. In the cases of Olson and Dorn, Milton and Pound, this is more than usually important; for the stock of information, and the body of assumptions, which you are expected to bring to the poem are not those you would normally come by as part of the equipment of a normally well-educated person. Poets like the four I've named have followed a wayward and eccentric path through the records of human experience; they have read books that aren't on the normal curriculum, and they set more store by these than by some which *are* on the curriculum; as a result, when they do encounter a monument of the curriculum, an acknowledged 'classic' (Homer, for instance) they find their way into him as it were from an unexpected angle, they are interested in things about him that are not the things usually singled out for attention, they place the emphasis in places we do not expect and are not prepared for and which, often enough, we consequently fail to recognize. As a result, with poets like these, there is a lot of spadework for us to do before ever, as it were, we open their books. They are very learned poets, who write very learned poems; and they have come by their learning in out-of-the-way places. What's more, they are not interested in making their poems self-sufficient, sailing free like so many rockets from the learning that was accumulated only as it were to assist take-off; on the contrary the poems depend on the learning, they emerge from it only to burrow back into it again, the poems depend upon—and are themselves *part of*—the lifelong addiction of the poet to the business of educating himself, i.e. the business of understanding the world that he and we are living in. The poems differ in degree but not in kind from the excited letters that the poets write to each other and to their admirers, or from the reviews and articles they write for each other's magazines. And so the poems have, quite deliberately, the sort of untidiness and hastiness that we associate with lecture-notes and reading-lists.

This is very different indeed from the fastidious impersonality that T. S. Eliot sought for and attained in his poems, or Wallace Stevens in his. And in fact what gets in the way of most of us apart from the very young, when we attempt to approach these poets at the present day, is precisely our experience of Eliot's poetry and the way we have nearly all been conditioned, more than we realize, to regard Eliot's procedures in poetry, and Eliot's sort of poetry, as the norms for poetry in English in the present century. This is the point of insisting on the name of Pound. For Olson and his followers derive from that side of Ezra Pound on which Pound is most unlike his esteemed colleague and one-time protégé, T. S. Eliot. To put it more exactly, these poets, as Americans, use Pound so as to bypass Eliot, because only by bypassing Eliot can they re-establish contact with the great American poet of the last century, Walt Whitman. (The line of descent from Pound to Olson can be traced in more detail through two other American poets—William Carlos Williams and Louis

Zukofsky.) Not only Eliot, but also the poets of the past whom Eliot taught several generations to esteem afresh (for instance John Donne and Andrew Marvell) are stumbling-blocks if we want to get into the world of Black Mountain poetry.

Far more useful, if as British readers we want a British name—far more helpful and worth remembering is the name of D. H. Lawrence, and not just Lawrence's poems either. Olson's most Lawrencian book is his *Mayan Letters*, written from Central America to Robert Creeley, when Olson was pursuing archaeological researches into the Maya civilization. And Dorn is at his most Lawrencian in *The Shoshoneans*, his prose book on the Amerindian peoples of the part of America he has made his own.

After what I have said, it will not surprise you that I think the best thing for me to do in the space that I have is to introduce you to some of the preoccupations that Dorn and Olson share. (For these are the two poets I'm really concerned with.) These preoccupations appear in—indeed, they are the substance of—many of the poems that these men write; but in order to recognize them when they appear in the poems, you need to be acquainted with them beforehand—in other words they are part of that stock of information and assumptions which you have to bring to the poems. The ones that I want to isolate turn around the notion of 'geography'. And as good a way as any of beginning to show how important this has been, and is, for Dorn and Olson, is by quoting from one of their acknowledged forerunners, William Carlos Williams, writing a manifesto in 1930: 'To what shall the mind turn for that with which to rehabilitate our thought and our lives? To the word, a meaning hardly distinguishable from that of place, in whose great virtuous and at present little realized potency we hereby manifest our belief.'

The portentousness of the phrasing here should not prevent us from recognizing that this is the sort of thing that has been said often before. The crucialness of a grasp on *locality*, the imaginative richness for poetry of a sense of *place*—this is no novel perception. We need go no further back than to the generation preceding that of Williams; to Yeats saying, 'And I, that my native scenery might find imaginary inhabitants, half-planned a new method and a new culture.' And so it should not surprise us if *The Maximus Poems* of Charles Olson, the only poetic enterprise of the present day in English which appears to be planned on a scale to challenge comparison with Williams's *Paterson* and Pound's *Cantos*, should be geographical rather than historical in its focus. *The Maximus Poems* aspire to give in language a *map*, a map of one place, the town of Gloucester, Massachusetts. This town, Olson's home-town, is otherwise known to twentieth-century literature only by way of Rudyard Kipling's *Captains Courageous*. And the Portuguese-speaking fishermen of Gloucester, embodied by Spencer Tracy in the film that was made of Kipling's story, figure repeatedly in the poems that Olson has made about his home place. For the poems do not, by concentrating on the geography of Gloucester, thereby *ignore* its history. Quite the contrary. The great geographer Alexander von Humboldt remarked that 'In classical antiquity the earliest historians made little attempt to separate the description of lands from the narration of events the scene of which was in the areas described. For a long time physical geography and history appear attractively intermingled'. And of course this is true; the ancient Herodotus is the father of geography but also the father of history, and he fathers the one by virtue of fathering the other. Crucial terms from Herodotus, as well as the name of Alexander von Humboldt himself, figure in Pound's *Cantos*. Yet it was probably not in Pound that Olson found the grounds for the veneration of Herodotus which he has repeatedly professed. A more likely source is an American geographer of the present day, Carl Ortwin Sauer, whose name figures in a pamphlet that Olson published some years ago, called *A Bibliography on America for Ed Dorn*.

(The slangy in-group flavour of that title, incidentally, as of much of the excited telegraphese prose which it introduces, is something that you may well find tiresome; but it is inevitable, given a movement which defines itself as all that organized society is not. Such a movement is an open conspiracy, which is only another word for a coterie, though an unusually ambitious and serious one. The same set of social circumstances produces the equally tiresome and not dissimilar telegraphese idiom of Ezra Pound's letters.)

At any rate Sauer's essay of 1925, 'The Morphology of Landscape', makes the same point about the ancient geography of Herodotus that we have just seen Alexander von Humboldt making: 'The *historia* of the Greeks, with its blurred feeling for time relations, had a somewhat superior appreciation of areal relations and represented a far from contemptible start in geography.' Dorn dutifully learned his lesson, from Olson's reading-list, and uses the very word 'areal', in the poem he has addressed to Olson, called 'From Gloucester Out':

> To play areal as particulars, and out of the span
> of Man, and as this man
> does,
>   he does, he
>   walks
>   by the sea
> in my memory
> and sees all things and to him
> are presented at night
> the whispers of the most flung shores
> from Gloucester out.

The same emphasis—on the home-base, on the local terrain as needing to be securely grasped by the imagination before it can afford to look further abroad—is in Dorn's similarly entitled poem 'Idaho Out', in his third collection with the significant programmatic title, *Geography*. (The poem

is now available in a booklet by itself.) These poems by Dorn, like many
of *The Maximus Poems* by Olson which they emulate, may be regarded
as investigations of just what it means to have 'a standpoint'—the place
on which you stand, the place which necessarily conditions everything
which you see when you stand on that place and look from it.

Olson recommends the geographer Sauer's writings as a whole. But he
specifies as particularly important an essay by Sauer called 'Environment
and Culture during the Last Deglaciation'. And it's easy to see why Olson
does this. For this particular essay by Sauer takes up, and applies to
North America particularly, a thesis which Sauer argued in another
paper called 'Agricultural Origins and Dispersals'. Both these essays argue
that the culture-hearth of agricultural man, which is to say of Neolithic
man, is not, as is still most generally supposed, in south-west Asia, but in
south-east Asia; and this for the reason that (so Sauer maintains) the
breakthrough to agriculture made by Neolithic man came from a fishing
culture rather than a hunting culture. Only if this precarious and disputed
thesis is true can Olson in his *Maximus Poems* use his chosen standpoint,
Gloucester (which is primarily a *fishing* community), in the way he wants
to do—as a vantage-point for surveying and understanding human society
however various, and human mythology however archaic.

This, it may well be thought, is an instance of how poetry may become
entangled with geography too much for its own good, an ambitious
poetic enterprise perilously dependent upon a particular disputed geographer's thesis. But the point is important, because otherwise we might
think that Olson chose to concentrate on Gloucester simply because it
happened to be the poet's home-town, out of some familiar Romantic
notion of mystical properties available for a man in his native origin, his
'roots'. This is not the case; Olson *chose* to make Gloucester his standpoint, there was no mystical compulsion upon him to do so. This is where
it's instructive to remember his essay on Melville, with its title 'Call Me
Ishmael'. Ishmael—the archetypal nomad and wanderer. And in fact
Olson's argument about Melville's *Moby Dick* shows once again with
what desperate seriousness he takes the matter of geographical location;
for his argument is that the greatest character in Melville's great and
strange romance is the Pacific Ocean, that the book as a whole celebrates
the imaginative discovery and appropriation by Western man, specifically
by American man, of that great waste of waters in the West, the Pacific—
one more territory which the pioneers could light out into when they
had crossed the entire continent and found themselves faced by the sea.
The standpoint which Olson, and more consistently Dorn, are concerned
to investigate is not characteristically a fixed point, the place where roots
are sunk; it is a moving point, the continually changing standpoint of a
man who is on the move across continents and oceans. Thom Gunn ex-
horts us to be 'on the move', but Dorn's poem 'Idaho Out', *gives us* this
man moving, and moving by automobile, from Idaho into Montana and
back again, his standpoint changing as he moves, yet conditioned by the

terrain it moves through and over, as much as by the consciousness which occupies the moving point. One might compare the novels of a prose-writer, Douglas Woolf, who has published in the same magazines with Olson and Dorn; in particular his wittily entitled *Wall to Wall*, the fictional narrative of a trans-continental journey by car from the Pacific Ocean to the Atlantic.

But one could compare equally a much earlier poem by a quite different kind of poet, Yvor Winters's 'The Journey', which is like Dorn's poem in nothing except in being a very Western poem about the experience of moving over the vast distances of the American West. The America of these poems has nothing whatever in common with the Atlantic seaboard America of Robert Lowell, or indeed Charles Olson. (For Olson's slim little volume, *West*, is an exception for him, and to my mind not distinguished.)

Edward Dorn and Yvor Winters, neither of them Westerners by birth, choose to live in the West and to celebrate it in their poems, not at all because they had chosen to sink their roots there (as Wordsworth chose to root himself in the English Lake District), but because the history of the Western States—both the brief recorded history, and the much longer unrecorded history of the indigenous Indian peoples—is a history of human *movement*; and the still largely empty landscapes of those territories are images of nomadic life, an arena for human life to which the imaginative response is still (as it always has been) to *move*, to *keep moving*. Moreover, because the human history of those territories is so short and scant, and because they are still so empty, the spectacle of them—like the spectacle of the oceans when one travels on them—teases the imagination into conceiving that human migrations across these spaces are only the last chapter of a history of non-human migrations, a history which is read out of geology and climatology. This is what Olson says in a recent poem:

> in successive waves basically NW
> as in fact the earth's crust once—and mantle or at least
> the depth of the asthenosphere broke
> apart and went
> itself mid-
>   north north West
>   150,000,000 years ago to that,
>   definitely now established by
>   J. Tuzo Wilson as well as other
> oceanographers and geographers who have paid
>   attention to the
>   fit of the Earth's continental shelfs
>   on either shore of each
>   ocean—including runs right down the middle
>   such as when
> India ground a path for herself traveling

              from an original place as African about where
                                         Mozambique
              and sometime about 150,000,000 years ago
              went off to where she now is, attaching herself to
              Eurasia—as if Tethys went under Ocean to
                 maka the love with him
                    a love with

                                      near Crete
                 on the water's
                    surface at or about
                 Gortyna

                                   migrations
                 turn out to be
                 as large as
              bodies of earth and of
                 stories

                                   and primaries
              of order which later is taken for granted are
              such as the Atlantic migration which filled America.   (1)

And this same area of human learning—where geography and geology,
oceanography and climatology, anthropology and archaeology and pre-
history meet—is the area which Dorn's imagination explores: not didac-
tically like Olson (who in this respect is much nearer to Pound), but
more freely and provisionally, as a sort of serious make-believe. Dorn is
not committed to this field for imaginative speculation, as Olson is. On
the dustjacket of his latest collection, he says for instance: 'In *The North
Atlantic Turbine*, the poems since *Geography*, I have tried to locate
another hemisphere. And I want this collection to be the last necessity
to work out such locations.'

That is to say, his explorations of geographical space are now over; as
he says elsewhere in the same blurb: 'That non-spacial dimension, intensity, is one of the few singular things which interest me now.'

The element of make-believe, of merely *provisional* belief in the pri-
macy of geography, shows up in Dorn's humour, which is much more in
evidence and also more various and shifting than in Olson. Olson's jokes
(like 'maka the love with him') are hearty, but bluff and simple-minded.
Dorn's humour is much harder to pin down, and also much harder to
take—particularly in *The North Atlantic Turbine*, the latest collection,
where it seems to be often raucous and sick, a sort of snarl. This is particularly hard for the British reader to take, because *The North Atlantic
Turbine*, Dorn's fourth collection, consists of the poems he has written in
England since he came here, to the University of Essex, in 1965; and the
image he gives of England, often in this languid snarling tone, is decidedly
unflattering. He is no more flattering to his own country, the United
States. But then . . . he refuses to take nation-states (the U.K. vs. the
U.S.) seriously. That indeed is the meaning of his title. His subject is the

North Atlantic, as Herman Melville's (so Olson argued) is the Pacific. The tide of human migration long ago crossed the North Atlantic, and left it behind; and so the only movement left in it is rotation, a 'bind' or circular swirl; it is now to all intents and purposes a landlocked ocean, and the swirl around it (imaged as the pulse from a dynamo at its centre) locks together and makes virtually identical, in one pointless round of activity, all countries that have a North Atlantic seaboard—the U.K., the U.S., Canada, France, Spain.

The North Atlantic Turbine contains a long poem in six parts on 'Oxford'. The most immediately accessible and engaging of these is Part II, in which we see Oxford through an eye which refuses to be daunted by the historical patina on that or any other city of the Old World, insisting instead on 'locating' it for the imagination in a way which is natural for territories like Idaho, Montana or the Dakotas—by way, that is, of the geological structure of the land mass which supports it:

> The sands of the Cotswolds
>   line the streets, the stone portals
> a light of light brown brilliance
> when the suns of May
>   cast a black swatch
> by Radcliffe Camera
>   solitary as
>   any Baptistry encrusted
>   or a product
>   of the sea.
>   However the streams of thin
>   elegance come down past the town
>   it is the linear strip
>   of the beautiful Jurassic lias
> running from Flixborough in Lincolnshire
> hanging from there
>   this liana falls, lier
> as the most springing joint
>   of England
>   to Bristol

But more challenging, and less palatable, is for instance 'Oxford Part V':

> England beware
>   the cliff of 1945
> turns a natural insularity
> into a late, and out of joint
> naturalism of inbred
> industrial indecision. The hesitation
> to hard sell small arms
> to backward countries and
> 'if we must, can't the man
> be more civilized' of a man

who only knows his business
be it selling washing machines
or machine guns: un 'produit
de l'industrie moderne'.
                    White Sunday,
the day of the Big White Sale.
We speak of payments as
                    balanced
Oxford, the dull if sometimes
                    remote
      façade
      is balanced in limestone, the
Bodleian has as a copyright
every book,
           Lincoln College
      has high on the wall
           in the first court
      a small bust of John Wesley, fellow
there is in Merton an Elizabethan
stretch of building and beyond
that, under a passage
the treed lawn where only fellows
and there is the garden where Hopkins
as at Cambridge the tower
where Byron's Bear near
      the rooms of Coleridge
   or Shelley's notebook in the
case at the Bodleian, the Lock
of His Hair, his glove, in a case.
not two gloves as he must
have had two hands to cover
but that hip thing
one glove you can do something
                    with
in terms of those and these brown spectacular
times, two
of course are a boring reminder
we are the animals we are
a lovely glove admittedly
but not so lovely as Shelley.

I walked back from Merton
with two lads who spoke of the police
and their perilous adventures
in Oxford's streets of explanations
'I shall climb up a drain pipe—

'But won't that disturb the authorities?
'it shall disturb them more
'if you wake them to report me
and thus we walked along—
there were more great names
than you'd care to hear
But at one point one of them said
it's impossible to write of it
every substantive fit
to name and celebrate has been spoken
and named. Then there was
a turning, we entered another street which
I'm more used to a grid,
swore to myself I'd never reenter,
but once I loved the idea of such narrow places.
And the easy talk of obscure things
I must admit I envied
       those children
because I love the dazzle of learning
and I am only concerned
when I think the strings
have gone loose.
    if I weren't an intelligent man
I'd share the attitude
    of my president
'Education is a wonderful thing.'

          But I said *everything*?
has been talked about
around Oxford. I was assured
it had been. I didn't *say* while walking
but I thought well then make up!
something! Because baby if you don't
they's gonna take all your wine away
they's gonna turn you into a state
institootion and you'll all be working
for the state just like in America
and you'll have to *prove*
you're useful, the most *useless*
sort of proof you'll ever have to make
....   Thus those children
could start by naming themselves and the rocks
in a larger than
national way and then more intimately,
if only for a more hopeful world

say what hope this 'rock
from which the language springs'
can be in the world. Can't
you tell yourselves it is time
Oxford stopped having a place
in English life as sanctuary,
World War II was *not* ended
in Europe because you failed
to take up the language
—not *the* language
oh you still have *that*, you
are stuck with that, that's
all you have,
because you so desired
to be the English Race
you so much wanted the courses
to come in their proper order
'where's the fish' you said
you were so impatient
and now
all you have is a few people you consider
problems anyway who won't even bother to speak
your language
and all they want to do is beat
your unemployment schemes, the best
of them have gone off
to Katmandu, the best of them
aren't even interested, except Tom
   Pickard
  who still makes his own sense
     in Newcastle, but he's a northerner.
  and will steal and resell
every book Calder and Boyars prints
God bless him.

Part IV is introduced by 'An Epistolary Comment: knowing none of it
accurately, the world can be surveyed'. And this ought to tell us the sort
of poem we are dealing with: a poem in which concern for locality and
for 'locating', so far from leading to localism or regionalism, lends itself
on the contrary to vast and rapid panoramas. This poetry sets up the
tourist as hero, and would persuade us that the only trustworthy eye is
the travelling eye, casual and disengaged. In this *The North Atlantic Turbine* is like eighteenth-century poems such as Goldsmith's *The Traveller*,
or Thomas Gray's *Education and Government*, or the prose-poetry of
Burke's speech 'On Conciliation with the Colonies'. For those eighteenth-
century works were similarly inspired by geography, indeed by a geographer
—the French thinker, Montesquieu. The difference is that Montesquieu's

bird's-eye view nourished a buoyant sense of diversity and plenitude. He argued that differences of climate and terrain made for different national temperaments, and hence that the form of government evolved by one people would not be appropriate for another differently located. Some of this buoyancy and eagerness appears in Olson. But Edward Dorn's space-capsule eye reports on the contrary that none of the differences matters, that one 'turbine', pumping out trade-cycles of production and consumption, governs and defines us all—the Communist East set on the same objectives as the Capitalist West, the Negro American indeed different from the white American in (alas) no more than the pigment of his skin. The only valid and total alternative is the *Red* American.

POSTSCRIPT
In his latest work, *Gunslinger*, Dorn has reached the 'spiritual address' which he announced he was setting out for after *The North Atlantic Turbine*. Departing from geography and moving across 'that non-spacial dimension, intensity' (its colouring that of the American southwest, but not literally located anywhere), Dorn has beautifully recovered his good humour. Of the verbal horse-play which carries the surreal narrative on a steady ripple of comedy ('horseplay' is exact—a talking horse occasions much of it), a broad and therefore quotable example is when in Book II we notice, as do the more-than-human travellers in the poem, that the first person has disappeared from the narration. Lil, archetypal madam of a western brothel (but of much else—she practised two thousand years ago in Smyrna) is first to notice: 'What happened to I she asked/his eyes dont seem right.' The Poet, another of the company, reports, 'I is dead', and is reproved: 'That aint grammatical, Poet'. Lil responds:

> Oh. Well I'll be . . .
> We never knew anything much
> about him did we. I
> was the name he answered to,
> and that was what he had
> wanderin around inside him
> askin so many questions
> his eyes had already answered . . .

Gunslinger himself, archetypal westerner but also Greek, sun-worshipper and solar deity like Alexander the Great, explains:

>   Life and Death
> are attributes of the soul
> not of things. The Ego
> is costumed as the road manager
> of the soul, every time
> the soul plays a date in another town
> I goes ahead to set up
> the bleechers, or book the hall
> as they now have it,

the phenomenon is reported by the phrase
I got there ahead of myself
I got there ahead of my I
is the fact
which not a few anxious mortals
misread as intuition . . .

Since among the areas of language drawn upon for ambiguities is the dia-
lect of drug-takers ('acid', for instance, and 'grass'), this questioning of
personal identity is serious and comical at the same time. At once comic
and profound, narrative and piercingly lyrical, the form and idiom of
Gunslinger transcend completely the programmes of Black Mountain,
just as they transcend (dare one say?) any programme so far promulgated
or put into practice in Anglo-American poetry of the present century.

Postscript: The verbatim repetition here of so much of the article
'Landscape as Poetic Focus' is unfortunate, perhaps inexcusable. Here the
same material is made to point in a different direction—towards a body
of American poetry which, in this lecture under the auspices of London
University, I was trying to introduce not so much to a British public as
into the world of British discourse *about* poetry. In fact an uninstructed
enthusiasm for Olson's and Dorn's poetry was a feature of the youthfully
dissident and 'cop-out' England of the 1960s; and this poetry is now
often regarded as just one of the characteristic fashions of that time, now
happily superseded. It deserves much better than that. Though my concluding claim for Dorn's *Gunslinger* is probably overstated, yet England
of the 1970s is impoverished if (as I suspect) it cannot respond to poetry
such as his and Charles Olson's.

POUND AND ELIOT: A DISTINCTION

REVIEWING YEATS'S *Responsibilities* in *Poetry* for May 1914, Pound envisaged a reader who asked, 'Is Mr Yeats an Imagiste?' And Pound replied: 'No, Mr Yeats is a symbolist, but he has written *des Images* as have many good poets before him . . .' Later in the review, after quoting the first five lines of 'The Magi', Pound remarked: 'Of course a passage like that, a passage of *imagisme*, may occur in a poem not otherwise *imagiste*, in the same way that a lyrical passage may occur in a narrative, or in some poem not otherwise lyrical.' (1)

It is hard for us to recover the state of literary opinion in which the first, most urgent question to be asked about Yeats is 'Is he an Imagiste?' The literary historian can be called upon to show, by appeal to the historical record, that this state of opinion once existed. It might be thought that to the literary critic, however, these echoes of battles long ago are of no consequence; and, indeed, this is how our critics have proceeded, using for instance 'Imagism' and 'Symbolism' as interchangeable terms. I am sure that this is wrong: for Imagism as Pound promulgated it, or as he later elaborated it into 'Vorticism', is not a variant upon Symbolism but an alternative to it; and this forking of the ways confronts the poet hardly less challengingly in 1970 than it did in 1914.

This is not to say, however, that Pound was in the right of it, that fifty years ago he had laid hold of a distinction which we have since lost sight of, much to our disadvantage. He was right to think that there was a distinction, and a crucial one, but he surely failed to trace the line of cleavage accurately. Except very intermittently, and then in a highly idiosyncratic way, Yeats was surely not a symbolist poet, even though Edmund Wilson in *Axel's Castle* and many another commentator have, like Pound, asserted that he was. Similarly, Pound never to my knowledge asked whether Eliot was an Imagist or a Symbolist. And yet, I maintain, it is in relation to Eliot, not Yeats, that the question is a momentous one. Depending on the answer we give to it, we shall either succeed or fail in uncovering the structure of the Eliotic poem. For as I read Eliot he is the one poet writing in English who is centrally in the *symboliste* tradition. What Eliot puts into his poems is determined preponderantly by his being an American; how he structures his poems is determined preponderantly by his sitting at the feet of the French, in the first place (as is generally acknowledged, and as he testified himself) at the feet of Jules Laforgue. Four decades of commentary and explication have been largely wasted, because of the refusal of commentators to explore either the American or the French backgrounds. Instead, the attempt has been made over and over again to come to terms with Eliot without going outside the narrowly English tradition. In this endeavour, Tennyson and Beddoes have lately supplanted Webster and Donne as the most appropriate and useful points of reference; and this is a gain, but a necessarily limited one. The urgent question to ask is: 'Was the late Mr Eliot an Imagiste?' And the right answer is the answer which Pound gave, wrongly, when the question was asked about Yeats: 'No, the late Mr Eliot was a symbolist, though he has written *des Images* as have many good poets before him.'

In this section of my essay I take the relatively obvious and easy case of the late poems.

It is notable that, as Eliot got older, he could be seen in his critical writings to give steadily more attention to symbolist poetry, narrowly considered. The crucial name is that of Valéry. Eliot's long and important introduction to what is called *The Art of Poetry*, a volume out of the scheduled complete translation of Valéry's prose into English, was only the last of several considerations, always absorbed and respectful, of what Valéry stands for in the landscape of twentieth-century poetry. If Laforgue was the presiding genius of Eliot's earlier poems, no figure presided more insistently over the later ones than Valéry, deliberately Mallarmé's disciple, and like his master as much high-priest of symbolist theory as a writer of symbolist poems.

We cannot but suppose, therefore, that it is Valéry, bringing with him the whole symbolist endeavour to make poetry approximate to music, who stands behind the title—*Four Quartets*—by which Eliot explicitly indicates a musical analogy for the work which crowns his maturity. And we shall not be surprised to find that 'Burnt Norton', the first of the Quartets, is a poem very much à la Valéry—a poem in the first place about itself and about the writing of poetry, even (more narrowly) about poetry and music and the specifically close relation between these two arts among the others.

Just as 'The Love Song of J. Alfred Prufrock' and 'A Cooking Egg' are generally considered (wrongly) as stories told in verse with some of the chapters left out, just as 'Mr Eliot's Sunday Morning Service' has been considered (wrongly) as the setting of a scene with certain items of description left out (and impaired by others that bulge out of the frame), just as *The Waste Land* has been misconceived by Cleanth Brooks and numberless others as a cryptic allegory with some of the links in the argument deliberately omitted, so *Four Quartets* is generally misread as a philosophical disquisition or a treatise of Christian apologetics with, again, large and deliberate lacunae. But, if the musical analogy is taken seriously at all, just as the structure of 'A Cooking Egg' cannot be narrative structure (however much disguised and fiddled with), just as the structure of 'Mr Eliot's Sunday Morning Service' cannot be scenic, and just as the structure of *The Waste Land* (at least up to the last two sections, where the poet perhaps loses his way) cannot be allegorical, so the structure of *Four Quartets* cannot be logical, discursive. We should not come to *Four Quartets* with those expectations, we should not give it that sort of attention, we should not try to understand it in that way. And, since it is 'in that way' that we nowadays conceive of what understanding is, it becomes almost true to say that we should not try to 'understand' these poems at all. Consider:

> What might have been is an abstraction
> Remaining a perpetual possibility
> Only in a world of speculation.
> What might have been and what has been
> Point to one end, which is always present.
> Footfalls echo in the memory
> Down the passage which we did not take
> Towards the door we never opened
> Into the rose-garden. My words echo
> Thus, in your mind . . .

'Thus'! Thus? How? What is the connection, the resemblance, thus confidently asserted? Words spoken one by one are like footsteps—well, yes; the argumentative mind can see that in certain circumstances the comparison might be just. But it turns out that the footsteps never happened, for they are footsteps in a direction which was never taken. So it appears that the poet's words dropping into the silence are like, not any actual footsteps, but only his thoughts of those footsteps. To be sure it isn't the sound of the words that is like the sounds of footsteps, but the words themselves (sounds plus meanings) that are like footsteps, perhaps figurative ones like footsteps in an argument. But then, that argument, it seems, was never embarked upon. It is easy enough—we are too ready perhaps—to see words spoken as identical with stages in an argument: we say the right word and thereby we advance one stage in the argument. But words that are specifically not stages in an argument, but only like such stages—this is harder to conceive of. Yet we can corroborate it readily enough from experience—'It all sounds very fine,' we say, 'but in fact when you look at what he's saying, it doesn't hang together at all.' This is something that we might want to say in fact about what might have been and what has been pointing to one end, which is always present. 'It sounds very fine but . . .' And, if that was what we may have wanted to say, suddenly it turns out that we were right: we ought to have said it. For the poet himself is pointing out that that is just the effect he was after and attained. Anyone who sits down and tries to worry out what these lines mean, as a proposition in a treatise, is flying in the face of just what the poet tells him a few lines later: that his labour is wasted, that meaning of that sort isn't there. Yet the warning goes unheeded; the devout exegeses continue.

It would be just as wrong to fly to the other extreme, and to suppose that because we can't understand 'What might have been and what has been/Point to one end, which is always present' these lines are meaningless. They add up to something, they amount to something; as we know from the very fact that the something they amount to can be talked about. We can say, for instance, as the poet says for us, that this something is like remembering how we didn't go down a passage to a rose garden. At the very least we can say that the experience of not understanding them is more like the experience of not understanding a book of mystical theology than it is like the experience of not understanding the drunken confidence of a stranger met in a bar.

'Burnt Norton' opens in precisely the same way as 'The Love Song of J. Alfred Prufrock'. There, 'something' ('Oh, do not ask, "What is it?" ') was, we remember, like going 'through certain half-deserted streets,/The murmuring retreats/Of restless nights in one-night cheap hotels/And saw-dust restaurants with oyster shells . . .' This is different from going or not going down a passage to a rose-garden, if only in this respect—that an encounter with a garrulous drunk is much more of a possibility. In both poems, we have hardly begun reading before we find the poem talking about itself, appealing to the reader with the question: 'So far as you've gone the experience of reading this poem is rather like this, isn't it?'

Put like this, the procedure seems to be no more than a gimmick. And of course that is all it is, in itself. But it can be made to work. In the present case for instance, after six lines of the poem we accept it as self-evidently true that 'What might have been is an abstraction/Remaining a perpetual possibility/Only in a world of speculation'. But nine lines later we ought to have changed our minds. For 'what might have been' (we might have been reading a treatise of mystical theology instead of a poem) has now been presented to us not as an abstract possibility in a world of speculation, but—extraordinary though this seems—as a manifested actuality in a world of lived experience, the experience of language.

These are vistas to set the clearest head spinning. The same possibilities are opened up, but in a more manageable way, by a passage later in the poem:

> Words move, music moves
> Only in time; but that which is only living
> Can only die. Words, after speech, reach
> Into the silence. Only by the form, the pattern,
> Can words or music reach
> The stillness, as a Chinese jar still
> Moves perpetually in its stillness.
> Not the stillness of the violin, while the note lasts,
> Not that only, but the co-existence,
> Or say that the end precedes the beginning,
> And the end and the beginning were always there
> Before the beginning and after the end.
> And all is always now. Words strain,
> Crack and sometimes break, under the burden,
> Under the tension, slip, slide, perish,
> Decay with imprecision, will not stay in place,
> Will not stay still. Shrieking voices
> Scolding, mocking, or merely chattering,
> Always assail them. The Word in the desert
> Is most attacked by voices of temptation,
> The crying shadow in the funeral dance,
> The loud lament of the disconsolate chimera.

Helen Gardner comments on this, intelligently enough: 'The word itself, like the note in music, has meaning only in relation to other words. It exists in time and in usage; and since contexts and usages change, the life of a word is a continual death.' (2) Certainly the semantic history of word-usages is being alluded to here, though less memorably than in a related passage from 'East Coker'. But the emphasis surely falls much less on the historical time, in which contexts and usages alter, than on the time which a musical composition takes to be performed or a literary composition to be read. And though Miss Gardner acknowledges this she hardly makes it salient enough. For the perceptions at work in these lines are those which lie at the heart of symbolist poetic theory. In Eliot's verse as in Valéry's prose, the first thing to be said about poetry is that it works, it unfolds, only in duration, in lapsing time: 'Words move, music moves/Only in time . . .' Unlike 'What might have been and what has been/Point to one end, which is always present', the statement 'Words move, music moves/Only in time' does not just sound as if it made sense; it makes sense. Yet we must still beware of supposing that this passage therefore, unlike that first one, is consecutive argument. For all the primness of punctuation and the earnest dryness of the vocabulary, this passage too *is* what it talks about: its structure is musical, not logical. Consider, for instance, the force of 'but' in what follows—'but that which is only living/Can only die'. This means, first, 'Words which live in time as we do, must die as we do'; *but* also 'We on the other hand, because we are living as words aren't, must die as they needn't.' At the point where the semi-colon comes, something has been left out which in normal prose discourse would limit what follows to one or other of these meanings. The poet, wanting to have both meanings at once, constructs around the semi-colon a meaningful silence, a blank place on the paper, where the clause that would have settled the question is felt by us as present, as a 'might-have-been'. And the next sentence makes room for yet another meaning.

> but that which is only living
> Can only die. Words, after speech, reach
> Into the silence.

Wondering, as the rhythm carries us over the full-stop, what cluster of mutually incompatible logical links lies concealed in the silent space which that punctuation creates (it could be 'And so', it could be 'And yet'), we realize, as 'Words, after speech, reach' (we reach also, for the next line) another sense in which words can be said to die, the sense in which they may compose a dying fall, a cadence which prolongs itself into the silence after the voice has stopped. This is an effect which poetry shares with music: 'the stillness of the violin, while the note lasts . . .' The fiddle and the bow are motionless, while the note which their movements created still sounds in the air about them.

It's just as well to insist on this because otherwise it will seem as if the poem here (and elsewhere) is discontented with its own medium, language,

because that medium, like the musical medium, by locking it into the dimension of time, makes it incapable of rising to the simultaneity, the
stillness, of the plastic art which produces the Chinese jar. And indeed
many interpretations of *Four Quartets* as a whole, especially those con-
ducted from the standpoint of Christian piety, invite us to see the poems
as yearning always for some impossible stasis, 'the timeless moment'.
Certainly the poet, by introducing quotations from St John of the Cross
and other mystics, invites us to set over against the 'time' which he talks
of so constantly the concept of 'eternity'. And so the terminology of
mysticism is undoubtedly useful for coming to grips with the poem. Still,
in this very poem, it is said, 'Only through time time is conquered.' And
for readers of other temperaments and interests it may be useful to see
not time as opposed to eternity, but musical time as opposed to pictorial
or sculptural space; (3) and to think, when they read, for instance, 'And
all is always now', not of the mystic's contemplative trance, but of the
perpetual present tense which is the tense of a symbolist poem, where
words do not stand for events but *are* those events. Because the very first
page of 'Burnt Norton' established it as a poem in the symbolist tradition,
a poem which describes and discusses itself, this sort of meaning for
'time' and 'present' and 'now' should be, while certainly not the one
meaning they will bear, at least the first meaning to be brought to them.

'Burnt Norton', which stands last in *Collected Poems 1909-1935*, employs just the same devices as the poem which stands first, 'The Love
Song of J. Alfred Prufrock'. Like 'The Love Song', 'Burnt Norton' continually feeds upon itself, gnaws its own vitals, postures before its own
glass. As in 'The Love Song', in 'Burnt Norton' much that is most crucial
and affecting is 'between the lines'; in both poems the syntax of what is
said serves to hint at what is unsaid, to frame the meaningful silences
which may be gaps between blocks of lines but may equally well, in both
poems, be the pregnant stillnesses around colons or semi-colons or full-
stops.* And there are other resemblances. In 'The Love Song', there is a
point where the syntax ceases to be that of written prose or studied
conversation and becomes, with a sudden access of earnestness and
anxiety, the dishevelled syntax of speech: 'It is impossible to say just
what I mean!/But as if a magic lantern threw the nerves in patterns on a
screen.' The same thing occurs in *Four Quartets*, as here:

> Only by the form, the pattern,
> Can words or music reach
> The stillness, as a Chinese jar still
> Moves perpetually in its stillness.
> Not the stillness of the violin, while the note lasts,
> Not that only, but the co-existence,
> Or say that the end precedes the beginning,

---

* cf. Mallarmé: 'L'armature intellectuelle du poème se dissimule et tient—a lieu—
dans l'espace qui isole les strophes et parmi le blanc du papier: significatif silence
qu'il n'est pas moins beau de composer que les vers.'

> And the end and the beginning were always there
> Before the beginning and after the end.
> And all is always now.

One looks with impatience, among all the exegeses, for a little literary criticism, which would examine, for instance, the points at which, and purposes for which, Eliot switches from written to spoken syntax, a criticism which would note how in the sentence about the Chinese jar there is the inversion—'Only by the form . . . Can . . .'—so as to point up its written quality, precisely so that the spoken syntax which follows can come with all the greater desperation. And again, what of 'J. Alfred Prufrock' himself, those syllables which have no reference at all except the phantasmal one which they conjure up for themselves? This, too, occurs in *Four Quartets*. When we read in 'East Coker', 'On the edge of a grimpen, where is no secure foothold', we all know what a grimpen is, yet we shall look in vain for any dictionary to confirm us in our knowledge. For 'Grimpen' occurs elsewhere only once, as a place-name in Arthur Conan Doyle's *Hound of the Baskervilles*. It may not be so clear that much the same thing happens here, in 'Burnt Norton'. Yet:

> The Word in the desert
> Is most attacked by voices of temptation,
> The crying shadow in the funeral dance,
> The loud lament of the disconsolate chimera.

And, if we ignore the capital letter on 'Word', then it must seem that the temptations to which the word is exposed, the vices of language, are not so much described as exemplified, in that last opalescent couplet where the shell of Augustan antithetical balance, as it might be in Dryden, holds no kernel of sense but only the vast suggestiveness of a most un-Augustan sonority.

Still, 'Word' does get its capital letter; and very important it is. It permits us, and obliges us, to face up to a restive objection which I dare say we have had more and more difficulty in suppressing, the further we have penetrated through the looking-glass: the exasperated protest that poetry which has for its subject only itself cannot be other than trivial, the narrowness of its scope and focus a damning indictment of the men who write it. What have we been saying, if not that there are no real typists in Eliot's Waste Land, no real flowers and birds in his Burnt Norton, but only the names of these things? If it may be objected to Yeats that in his poems swans are not really swans but stand-ins ('Another emblem there!'), how much more heavily must not the same charge be levelled at Eliot? The ancient and arcane doctrine of the Logos—'In the beginning was the Word, and the Word was with God, and the Word was God'—provides Eliot, as it sometimes provided Mallarmé himself, with an answer to this comprehensive indictment.

The non-Christian reader, while he may acknowledge that this doctrine, so central as it is to twenty centuries of European thought, somehow carries more weight than the more eccentric ideas of Yeats, may yet feel that the doctrine of the Logos is no less remote than the Yeatsian doctrines from his own lived experience. He may object, though respectfully, perhaps regretfully, that however far the poet may have been from seeing in this no more than a pun it is impossible for him, the reader, to take it as other than a pun or a historical curiosity. Yet in fact the doctrine of the Logos—or at least some aspects of it—can be readily translated into secular quite unmystical terms which no one can afford to ignore. Meta-linguistics seems to have established, by thoroughly verifiable methods, that the language we speak determines not only how we communicate to others our sense of the truth, but how we communicate to ourselves; the categories which we find in nature or impose on nature, in order to under-stand it, are (it now appears) linguistic categories. The speaker of English and the speaker of Chinese will not merely arrange nature differently in order to speak of it, but will arrange it differently in order even to think about it. The syntax of our language determines all our ways of seeing the world and of coming to terms with it. To a personality like Pound's, convinced above all of the plenitude, the variety and multiplicity of ex-perience, this realization will carry the implication, as it did for Pico della Mirandola, that a poem is in duty bound to deal with experience in terms of as many linguistic moulds as possible. But it is equally possible to be-lieve that all the languages move towards the same point by different me-thods, that the language anyone speaks provides the method, the form or mould, precisely fitted for him to explore reality. This is to believe that the secret answers are concealed in the very structure of the language one uses. This is one way of understanding that 'the Word was with God, and the Word was God'; and on this showing a poem which examines only the structure of its own language by that very token examines everything else, everything there is to examine. And so when Eliot goes on in 'Burnt Nor-ton', from talking about the poem as a form like a Chinese jar and yet as a process, a sequence of events in time, to talking of Love as 'itself un-moving' yet issuing in Desire which moves continually, he is not 'changing the subject'; he is not even making a witty or fanciful analogy (Poem as achieved form=Love; poem as process=Desire), but simply changing the one discussion into other terms and a new key.

Metaphysicians appear to have pursued the same logic. After retiring in confusion before critics who pointed out that the questions they discussed could not be asked in languages with a different structure from their own, who accused them therefore of being tricked by language into dilemmas which were merely verbal, they now take heart and ask why 'verbal' must be '*merely* verbal' and whether, if language tricks them, it does not trick them for their own good and to some purpose. Once the structure of lan-guage is taken to be the structure of reality, then merely verbal dilemmas are seen to be the most real of all dilemmas; and the hoary topics of metaphysics, having suffered a sea-change, present themselves as no less worthy of attention than they ever were. Let God be called 'Reality'; and then meta-linguists and metaphysicians alike appear to agree that 'the

Word was with God, and the Word was God.'

Some French theorists have divided all men, in their dealings with language, into 'terrorists' and 'rhetoricians'. The terms when translated into English are misleading. The French mean by 'terrorist' the man who is suspicious of language, who takes it for granted that language is always trying to trap us into saying what we don't mean, that every word we use must therefore be scrutinized with a sort of baleful resentment. England in the present century has been full of 'terrorists' of this sort, and our poetry reflects the pressures they have brought to bear. It is only lately, and even so very grudgingly and fearfully, that English poets and philosophers and theorists of language have come to see the strength of the alternative position, that of the 'rhetorician' who trusts language to do his thinking for him, who casts himself trustingly into the sea of language, confident that its currents will carry him to better purpose than if he insisted on swimming against them. If we had not resisted and evaded for so long the challenge of symbolist theory and practice—particular phases of that resistance are signalized by the names of I. A. Richards and F. R. Leavis—we might not have needed to learn the hard way. Eliot to be sure is not to be herded conclusively into either camp; he seems to believe that in the act of successful composition the poet's dealings with language somehow comprehend both attitudes, both suspicious vigilance and trustful surrender. But, as compared with Pound, Eliot presents himself as pre-eminently a rhetorician, a man who serves language, who waits for language to present him with its revelations; Pound by contrast would master language, instead of serving language he would make it serve—it must serve the shining and sounding world which continually throws up new forms which language must strain itself to register. Either all the forms of reality are hidden in language and will be revealed by language if we only trust it sufficiently; or else nature is inexhaustibly prodigal of new forms, for ever outrunning language, which must be repeatedly constrained to keep in the chase.

II

In what remains of this essay, I shall attempt to show how the principles which operate in *Four Quartets* operate also in earlier poems by Eliot. In particular I shall try to justify my coat-trailing about two of those earlier poems: 'A Cooking Egg' and 'Mr Eliot's Sunday Morning Service'.

Reading some famous lines in which Prufrock compares the activities of a fog to the activities of a cat, sturdy common sense, whose voice, alas, is so seldom heard in Eliot-land, would protest: 'It isn't so. I am not convinced. He can talk for as long as he likes, but he doesn't persuade me that a fog behaves as a cat behaves.' Similarly, even earlier in the poem, reading, 'When the evening is spread out against the sky/Like a patient etherised upon a table', common sense will retort, once again and quite simply, 'I don't believe it.' Instead of the voice of common sense, the voice of the critic (in this case F. O. Matthiessen) protests that the comparison of the evening with the etherized patient is 'too intellectually manipulated, not sufficiently felt'. (4) And this is the very reverse of the truth. For common sense is right: the comparison has no substance at all for intellection to worry out of it, no justification at all in terms of logic and/or sense-perception. To the normal mind, fogs and cats, evening skies and operating-tables have nothing in common whatever. And this is just the point of these comparisons; it is precisely because to a normal mind they are absurd, that we are led or forced to conceive of the abnormal mind, or the abnormal state of mind, to which these comparisons are not absurd but exact. The truth is the opposite of what Matthiessen says: if the comparison has any validity at all, it is in terms of feeling—of the feeling of the observer, projected so intensely upon these disparate objects as to deceive him into thinking them similar; the comparison has no 'intellectual' substance whatever.

The moral is so obvious that I blush to draw it. On all sides we have been told, and are still told, that in Eliot's early poetry the influences of French Symbolists and of English 'metaphysicals' intersect. The case of F. O. Matthiessen shows that if the two traditions *do* intersect, if they *can* intersect (and Rosemond Tuve will tell us that they can't), the point of intersection is easy to mistake. A reader who comes to Prufrock from Webster and Donne, will, like Matthiessen, read these comparisons as if they were conceits, and the poem will fall to pieces in his hands before he has got through the first three lines of it.

When Donne compares lovers with compasses he presents two images (that is to say, two human experiences—of love and of mathematics) which are normally regarded as belonging to widely different kinds or orders of human experience as a whole. We may say, then, that to begin with there is a wide gap between them. And the poem exerts itself to close this gap. But when Eliot compares a fog with a cat, or an evening sky with an etherized patient, the object of the exercise, for him, is to leave the gap wide open. Only in this way can he incite the reader to close the gap for himself, by deducing from the two terms given the third term which is missing, the state of mind of the observer, Prufrock, who sees a similarity where none exists.* The poetry isn't a riddle: why are fogs like cats? It is a puzzle: puzzle—find Prufrock. There is left between the images a gap which the reader has to fill for himself; sometimes the gap, the meaningful silence of Mallarmé, exists as a space of blank white paper on the printed page, whereas in the cases we are considering the gap is papered over by what looks like normal syntax. But of course it isn't normal syntax, but the symbolist syntax which is working upon us in ways which have nothing to do with the perception of logical patterns.

This is the view of symbolist procedure which was expressed by one critic

---

* It is true, of course, that if the reading of Eliot has been distorted by a gravitational pull in the reader's mind towards Donne, the reading of Donne has been distorted by the presence of Eliot. We are asked to read Donne's poems as if the interest in them were the mind we deduce from them.

when he said that in poems in the symbolist tradition 'images or symbols are ranged about, and the meaning flowers out of the space between them'. But as it turns out this formulation does not get us very far, for it seems to leave the reader free to fill in the gaps with whatever materials he pleases, according to whatever may be the idiosyncratic bent of his own interests. This emerged very clearly from a discussion a few years ago of Eliot's poem, 'A Cooking Egg', from his second collection, *Poems 1920*. This rather trivial poem does not deserve all the attention that has been lavished on it; and indeed in most ways Eliot's second collection as a whole cannot measure up to the first. (This is true, I think, even of the most ambitious poem, which stands first in the collection, the famous 'Gerontion'; for Eliot seems to identify himself with this *persona*, unwittingly, far more than he did with Prufrock.) But this only means that 'A Cooking Egg' perhaps deserves nothing much better than the fate which has come upon it—to be the occasion of a sustained critical wrangle. The discussion will be found in the quarterly *Essays in Criticism* for July 1953 and January 1954. The spectacle it affords, of several distinguished critics falling out about what the poem means, is instructive and rather shocking, and unfortunately, at the time, it gave a handle to the philistines to pluck up heart and exult, 'I told you so; it's nothing but gibberish.' However the discussion was not so pointless as has been made out. Real progress had been made when at the end of it I. A. Richards could ask, 'perhaps it is a current conception of interpretation which is out of focus, at least for such a poem?' (5)

However, the most instructive contribution was F. W. Bateson's. For he began by quoting the formulation already offered—'Images or symbols are ranged about, and the meaning flowers out of the space between them.' (6) But the problem then became, for Mr Bateson, how the reader was to supply the links which the poet left out; and he supplied them by making up a story about a love-affair between Pipit, the central figure in the poem, and the narrator. That is to say, he treated the poem not after all as a symbolist poem or a poem in the symbolist tradition, but as if it were a narrative with every other chapter left out. The critics found themselves solemnly debating whether Pipit was a little girl or a grown up or (agreeable lunacy!) perhaps the poet's nannie. And they posed each other such unanswerable conundrums as: did the narrator when he was an undergraduate buy for his old nannie, *Views of Oxford Colleges*? This, of course, is a question on a par with 'How many children had Lady Macbeth?'—and even less relevant to Eliot's poem than the question of the children is to Shakespeare's. The whole procedure is ludicrous. For what spaces are left in the poem, for meanings to flower in, when Mr Bateson has busily paved the whole area with fictions of his own devising? The poet leaves spaces, and he wants them left. If the riddles could be solved, why didn't the poet solve them, for himself and for us? A range of possible answers can be found, and a vast range of other answers can be ruled out as impossible. But if there were one clear and conclusive answer,

one key which, when found, broke the poet's code, the whole poetic procedure would lose its justification and its point. It's just here, in fact, that
we make room for what at first may look like the most disreputable
feature of symbolist poetic theory—the value it places upon a deliberate
vagueness, and upon the suggestive hint rather than the plain statement.
What it amounts to, on this showing, is the never treating any issue as
entirely closed.

We narrow the range of possible answers, and close the gap so far as is
proper, not by constructing impressive fictions of our own, but by
attending to the developing shape of the whole poem, and above all by
noticing in particular the tone of voice where it leaves off before the gap
and where it picks up again afterwards. In 'A Cooking Egg' tone is determined above all by rhyme and by verse-movement:

> Pipit sate upright in her chair
>> Some distance from where I was sitting;
> *Views of Oxford Colleges*
>> Lay on the table, with the knitting.

The silly archaism 'sate', and the rhyme on 'sitting'/'knitting' (worthy of
Mr Cyril Fletcher) define the tone as detached and a trifle sourly amused,
and rule out at once the shame and disgust that some of the contributors
to *Essays in Criticism* wanted to impart to the lines. Similarly,

> I shall not want Honour in Heaven
>> For I shall meet Sir Philip Sidney
> And have talk with Coriolanus
> And other heroes of that kidney.

> I shall not want Capital in Heaven
>> For I shall meet Sir Alfred Mond.
> We two shall lie together, lapt
>> In a five per cent Exchequer Bond.

It is the fatuous rhyme of 'Sidney' with 'kidney', and of 'Mond' with
'Bond', together with the very heterogeneity of the proper names, which
makes it certain that the unspoken refrain in the space between these
stanzas is something of the nature of ('I shall meet Sir Philip Sidney'),
'Like Hell I shall', or else (the poet's voice placing perhaps the anonymous speaker), 'Like Hell you will'.

The poem is in three sections marked off by rows of dots, and I. A.
Richards, who alone among the contributors to the discussion was sensitive to tone, rightly perceived that verse-movement dictates a wholly new
tone in the last section:

> But where is the penny world I bought
>> To eat with Pipit behind the screen?
> The red-eyed scavengers are creeping
>> From Kentish Town and Golder's Green;

> Where are the eagles and the trumpets?

> Buried beneath some snow-deep Alps.
> Over buttered scones and crumpets
> Weeping, weeping multitudes
> Droop in a hundred A.B.C.'s.

In the first quatrain, as the verse-movement changes, the tone becomes, for the first and last time, serious and engaged. A real loss is being really lamented. And this holds over to the line printed by itself. The trumpet echoes through the blank space which follows like the horn of Roland carrying from Roncesvaux the last signal of a noble order doomed. But a trumpet after all is not a horn (the horn sounding through the forest—stock image of European romance)and if we have forgotten—as up to this point we are meant to do, meant to make fools of ourselves—that a trumpet is brassy at best and may be a child's toy, we are made unavoidably aware of it, and of our own stoop to self-indulgent folly, with the conclusively deflating rhyme, 'crumpets'. This changes the tone again, so that when we look back at the space after 'the eagles and the trumpets', a space so lately brimming with our own romantic melancholia, we now hear a voice saying mockingly into the silence, 'It's a shame, so it is.' In fact, that whole line about the eagles and the trumpets forces home the recognition that every word and every poetic line has two contexts, what leads up to it and what leads away from it, and that the second context may spring (here by a cruelly delayed-action mechanism) a trap laid for us by the first. This is language as music, exploiting to the full, as music does, the lapse of time in which it has its being and its operation.

Yet it's essential to realize, even as we begin to recognize how nicely in these ways the range of possible readings can be narrowed, that the range is never narrowed so far as to provide only one right reading. One of the possible readings of 'A Cooking Egg' would begin by dwelling on the title. An egg once fresh now stale; hence (perhaps) a hope once entertained now abandoned. It would read out of the first two stanzas, noting their tone as defined by rhyme and archaism, English upper-class security, continuity and assurance. Oxford (if we remember the date) and Pipit (the excruciating coyness of the name) define class; 'Oxford' means English; 'grandfather and great great aunts' means continuity; sitting upright ('Pipit sate upright') means assurance, even dignity; *Invitation to the Dance* means sentimental philistinism in the arts. And so much for the first section. The middle section shows (through a speaker who either mocks himself or is mocked from the wings by the poet) a ruling class no longer assured of its right to various good things, no longer assured that its own monumental figures (Sir Alfred Mond, Madame Blavatsky) are equal to the great figures of other cultures, like Sidney, the Borgias or Coriolanus; or else, in so far as the class does retain this assurance, its claims are laughed out of court. We may permit ourselves the self-righteous reflection that, in so far as this assurance was insufferable complacency, it is good to see it go. But, says the last section in effect, the loss of security is another matter from the loss of assurance, a real loss and one which may be mourned—which may be mourned, but only a little; for, try to inflate it to a tragedy, and the rhyme on 'crumpets' brings out all the brassiness of the trumpet and the inadequacy of the occasion for the tears being spilled about it. This reading of the poem may seem all the more plausible if we remember that the author was at this time in close alliance with Ezra Pound, another American poet who at just this time was writing a similar mocking threnody on the British imperial twilight, in his *Homage to Sextus Propertius*.

At the bottom of the symbolist method, it has been said, is the discovery that words may have meanings though they have no referents. And most of the misreadings of Eliot derive from a failure, less frequently from a refusal, to recognize this fact about the way language works: 'But where is the penny world I bought/To eat with Pipit behind the screen?' The mind that thinks that looking for a word's meaning is looking for its referent will ask: What is a 'penny world'? And gravely observing that worlds cannot be eaten, it decides that 'penny world' cannot mean what it says, and that 'world' must be a fanciful way of referring to something else, something that is edible, perhaps a bun. 'Penny world' thus revised to become 'penny bun', it asks what sort of a person penny buns may be eaten with, and so comes up with the answer that Pipit must be a nursery playmate, or else a nannie. Its next question is: In what conditions are penny buns eaten, with or without dear little girls or dear old nannies, *behind a screen*? And with that little poser before him, this dogged reader may be abandoned. For enough has been said to show that in symbolist poetry a word always means what it says—always, because what it says is always only itself. 'Art is as realistic as activity and as symbolic as fact', declared Pasternak. In the world of symbolist poetry worlds can be bought for a penny, and they can be eaten. 'Penny' and 'world' are verbal events occurring rapidly one after the other, the cheapness and littleness of 'penny' crammed up against the vastness of 'world'. The penny, the world, the eating, and the screen are here brought into an arrangement which need not correspond to any possible or likely arrangement of these items in the life which we observe about us. This arrangement of them is possible in language and therefore in the mind of the speaker and thereafter, if the poem is successful, in the mind of the reader. The penny and the world and the screen are in just the same case as the fog and the cat, or the evening sky and the etherized patient, in 'Prufrock'. In every case what seems to be asserted is a relationship between items which is impossible or highly unlikely in the world we observe; and in every case, as a result, we have to realize that the items are arranged thus, not in the world observed but in the mind of the observer. For of course there are dreams and other mental phenomena to tell us that the laws of space and time, which operate outside the mind, do not obtain inside it.

In a brilliant and momentous essay, H. M. McLuhan has traced, over the past two centuries of poetic effort, the logic which led the poets to this startling discovery, that they had been observing, in the stories and pictures

they created, laws of temporal and spatial arrangement which in fact did
not bear upon their activities at all. In this article, called 'Tennyson and
Picturesque Poetry' (*Essays in Criticism*, vol. I, no. 3), McLuhan credits
James Thomson, author of *The Seasons*, with the original discovery: that
there could be maintained in poetry a constant relationship between external events or appearances described, and the state of the mind which
first observed and then described them. Thomson is described in the Literary Histories as the poet who first made description of 'nature' (i.e.
for the most part, of landscape and weather) self-sufficient matter for
poems. It seems an unexciting, a dubiously useful innovation. Thomson
is a much more startling innovator if, as McLuhan suggests, what he discovered was not verse-description as such, but verse-description of such a
kind that, in offering and seeming to describe the landscape and weather
of the observable world, it described equally the landscape of the observer's mind, the weather in the observer's soul. Whether this claim for
Thomson can be allowed, is not here the question; in any case it must be
allowed that the discovery was repeatedly made, if not originally by
Thomson, certainly by his successors in this mode, Cowper, Wordsworth
occasionally, Keats and Tennyson certainly. Who can doubt—who has
ever doubted—that Keats's 'Ode to Autumn', offering to describe a season
of the year, describes at least equally a season in the spiritual life of the
poet, a landscape or climate of the human mind? By Keats's time, the
psychological fact of this possible correspondence between inner and
outer was already almost a commonplace, and built into the poetic
theories of, for instance, William Hazlitt and Arthur Hallam. Are we saying, then, that the 'Ode to Autumn' is already a symbolist poem? Not at
all. For Keats and Tennyson are still, like Wordsworth, Cowper and
Thomson before them, dependent upon nature to present them with the
landscape and the weather that will, because they correspond to a state
of mind, permit them to express that state. The symbolist poet, on the
other hand, has realized that he can do better than wait patiently upon
nature until she provides what he wants. Knowing the state of mind he
wants to express, he can construct the landscape he wants, so as to make
it correspond. And with that recognition comes another: being thus free
of nature's caprice, the poet when he creates a landscape is under no obli-
gation to make it observe all the laws which govern nature's landscapes.
In Mr McLuhan's words:

> The romantic and picturesque artists had to take advantage of acci-
> dents. After Baudelaire there is no need for such accidents. The pic-
> turesque artists saw the wider range of experience that could be
> managed by discontinuity and planned irregularity, but they kept to
> the picturelike single perspective. The interior landscape, however,
> moves naturally towards the principle of multiple perspectives as in
> the first two lines of *The Waste Land* where the Christian Chaucer,
> Sir James Frazer and Jessie Weston are simultaneously present. This is
> 'cubist perspective' which renders, at once, a diversity of views with

the spectator always in the centre of the picture, whereas in picturesque art the spectator is always outside. The cubist perspective of
interior landscape typically permits an immediacy, a variety and soli-
dity of experience denied to the picturesque and to Tennyson. (7)
The change, I suspect, was hardly such sheer gain all round as Mr McLuhan
suggests; the intent and patient waiting upon nature which is the constant discipline of a Coleridge, a Ruskin, a Turner or a Hopkins (and I
would add, a Pound)—this may induce a religious apprehension of the
spiritual in nature, which it is not worth losing just for the sake of a more
streamlined poetic method. Nevertheless, McLuhan sufficiently explains
the fatuity of asking, about those lines in 'A Cooking Egg': When, in
what sort of room, under what circumstances, does one eat behind a
screen? To attempt to visualize the scene like this is as woefully wide of
the mark as to object to Picasso that he disregards the laws of perspective
as conceived by Raphael. Yet this is a not uncommon way of misreading
Eliot: having taken from *Essays in Criticism* one example of how-not-to-
do-it, I will go there for another, Ernest Schanzer's reading (in the issue
for April 1955) of the poem called 'Mr Eliot's Sunday Morning Service'.
   Another exegesis would be tedious. 'The poem's setting', Mr Schanzer
begins, 'is indicated by its title', and in this setting the narrative (which,
like Mr Bateson, Mr Schanzer assumes to exist, waiting for him to recon-
struct it) 'is supplied by the wandering eye and mind of Mr Eliot'. (8) If,
because of the title, we are led to imagine the speaker at a church-service
such as we know from observation, we shall start wondering, as early as
stanza three, what sort of church Mr Eliot can attend that has an Umbrian
easel-painting inside it. Mr Schanzer becomes indignant when the last
stanza presents Sweeney in his bath. For even his imagination cannot
accommodate in his mental image of Eliot's church an Umbrian easel-
painting and an inhabited bathtub. It is hard not to sympathize: Mr
Schanzer wants to know if he is in a church or in a bathroom, and all we
can tell him is that he is in a poem. The structure of the poem is neither
pictorial nor narrative, though Mr Schanzer assumes it is both; it is sustained on the two axes of reference presented in the epigraph ('Look,
look, master, here comes two religious caterpillars') by the last phrase,
'religious caterpillars'. The caterpillars announce the flies of the first
stanza, and the bees of the sixth, while 'religious' looks forward to the
church fathers of stanza two, to the Umbrian painting, and the presbyters.
Throughout, these two sets of images interact, particularly in terms of
sexual fertility, sometimes very plainly as in 'epicene' (stanza seven),
sometimes subtly as in the half-echo, 'pustular'/'pistillate'; but the interaction is not at all so reducible to the one right and clear reading as
would be 'the satiric focus' which Mr Schanzer asks for and thinks he
half finds. One begins to misread the poem in Mr Schanzer's way, as soon
as one assumes, for instance, that the window-panes of the third line are
window-panes which Mr Eliot can see from his pew. In these poems the
images are ranged about not according to the laws of space nor (in the

case of narrative images, actions and events) according to the laws of time, but simply as they are ranged about in the poet's head.

The plain directive to the reader was given once and for all in the poem which stands first in the *Collected Poems*: 'It is impossible to say just what I mean!/But as if a magic lantern threw the nerves in patterns on a screen.' The magic lantern is somewhere at the back of the poet's skull. Throwing its beams forward through the meshes of the poet's sensibility, it illumines at last the world which faces him; but he is interested, and his readers should be interested, not in that world itself at all, but only in that world as a screen, on to which are projected 'the nerves in patterns', that is to say, the shape and character of the observer's sensibility.

Postscript: This essay, I am aware, is not easy reading. And I sympathize with the reader who should protest that the reading of poetry ought not to be such a strenuous activity. One way of answering him is to say that, however it may be with other poetry, with T. S. Eliot's the challenge thrown down is indeed as exacting as I make it seem. But a better answer is that this essay presents a model not of 'how to read', but rather (a very different matter) of how to understand what happens to us *as* we read.

EMINENT TALENT

Landor's Poetry, Robert Pinsky, University of Chicago Press.

MR PINSKY'S elegantly compact and well-written monograph—astonishingly, the first on its important and difficult subject—has been justly praised in other places. It has a special claim on my esteem and my interest because Mr Pinsky does me the honour of getting a focus on Landor's poetry by attending to some of my writings on Landor, and setting me in this respect over against no less a figure than Pound. I am pleased and flattered; and may be forgiven, I hope, if I consider Mr Pinsky's thesis by defending my own position against his—the more so, since what is involved, as Mr Pinsky realizes, is an attitude towards poetry in general, not just Landor's.

Following Mr Pinsky through the close and scrupulous argument of his first chapter I learn something about myself. I recognize for instance more clearly than ever before that he is entirely accurate when he says: 'Davie's criticism . . . suggests that "how to write" which was a starting point for Pound and Landor, is for him a search—and that this search points in at least some ways from Pound (*qua* anti-Romantic) and toward Wordsworth'. Mr Pinsky is talking about the style, or the successive styles, which I seek for in order to go on writing my own poems. And if I do think along these lines, I conceive that I have the authority of Eliot who in many places spoke of his own search for style in just this way—notably in a passage of *Four Quartets*, where he speaks of having repeatedly mastered a style only for what he no longer wished to say. In this, I think, Eliot is very un-American. For Pound's and Mr Pinsky's contrary notion, that 'how to write' is what one starts from, surely smacks of—indeed, is part of—the distinctively American bent for 'know-how': the poet, it suggests, masters the techniques—assembles as it were, his stylistic kit—and thereafter is free to *apply* his techniques to any subject whatever. One of the puzzles about this is what the beginning poet uses for subjects during his long and arduous apprenticeship; and indeed whether subjects are ever, at any stage, available to be 'used' in quite that cold-blooded way. As a matter of fact I am far from thinking that there is no virtue and no truth in Pound's way of thinking about style; otherwise I should not (as I do) teach creative writing. But in the long run my experience very markedly corroborates, rather than Pound's assumption, Eliot's—the assumption, that is, not only that there are or may be as many respectable styles as there are poets, but that there are as many styles as there are poets *and subjects* (or occasions). Doubtless this seems dangerously near to a lax eclecticism and to the ideology of each man 'doing his own thing'; but these are risks that have to be run, and in practice they can be guarded against. At any rate, I feel more confident about diagnosing a specifically American aberration on this point when I notice the role that Yvor Winters plays in Mr Pinsky's criticism. It is a major role. For not only are Mr Pinsky's own poems, to judge from the few I have seen, much more like Winters's than they are like Pound's, but also Mr Pinsky's criticism in many of its aspects has recognizably Wintersian virtues, notably in a rare capacity for accurate and sensitive scansion of metrically regular verse. No two American poets or critics could be much less alike than Winters and Pound; and yet they have at least two things in common—first, an esteem for Landor (though Landor apparently dropped out of Winters's canon before the end); and, second the assumption that 'how to write' is what one starts from. If Americans so different as Winters and Pound can agree on this notion, no wonder if, as an American, Mr Pinsky is disconcerted to find me rejecting it.

For that matter, of course, there are British poets who endorse the American position. I suspect that Robert Graves does. And certainly Landor did. Working from that assumption Landor achieved certain effects outside Wordsworth's range. And the reverse is also true. On this Mr Pinsky and I agree. My contention is that Wordsworth's range (and I speak of the short poem only) is more important than Landor's. Since mine is on this point the conventionally accepted view (though accepted without enthusiasm I think—an enthusiast for Wordsworth's lyrics is nowadays hard to find), it is enough for me to record it, and to recommend the several pages in which Mr Pinsky challenges it by way of formal comparison between poems by Landor and poems by Wordsworth. It is certainly good to have the challenge thrown down and sustained in critical commentary with spirit and resourcefulness.

But from this initial difference of attitude and opinion, there flow certain others. And Mr Pinsky is aware of them. Since the Landorian, or Wintersian, aspiration is to make a style that shall be timeless, such writers cannot afford to take spoken usage into account as any sort of check or control. For spoken English at all times, and of all ages, is too fluid and changeable for their purposes. This is a crucial matter for Mr Pinsky, because (and here he is valuably original) he wants to claim that Landor's achievement is a valuable urbanity, achieved and sustained 'by tone'. This means that, still civilly arguing with me, he has to contest not my assessment of Wordsworth in relation to Landor, but my assessment of Shelley. Here, to be frank, I am a good deal less comfortable. For not only would I rather reread Landor than Shelley, but I firmly prefer what happens to English at Landor's hands to what it has to suffer from Shelley. In fact my case for Shelley as an urbane poet rests on certain poems which by the devout Shelleyans (who still exist, alas) are thought of as more or less minor writing, off-centre. However, though the test-case is thus one that I would not have chosen, I will uphold the principle—which is that urbanity presupposes an *urbs*, a civil society idealized indeed from any society of which we have historical record, yet within recognizable reach of some one such society; and that its level of civility is measured by the conversation which it fostered or provided for. Against this contention of mine, and against a passage from 'The Sensitive Plant' by which I sought to support it, Mr Pinsky posits an urbanity that is different: 'Landor's urbanity is literary, not conversational: it consists in restoring life to the conventional language of letters, not to the conversational cliché'. And to prove the possibility of such an urbanity from outside Landor, he shrewdly quotes a quatrain by, of all people, David Garrick:

> The gentle reader loves the gentle muse
> That little dares, and little means,
> Who humbly sips her learning from Reviews
> And flutters in the Magazines.

Mr Pinsky comments that in these lines 'Garrick has made a very important achievement. His lines show a coherent, undated attitude toward an aspect of civilisation which has persisted from the birth of a certain kind of literary culture to yesterday'. And the tradition that these lines exemplify is, he says, Landor's tradition. The point is, so Mr Pinsky's argument goes, that a timeless style such as Landor sometimes attained conveys an urbanity which is similarly timeless, related to an *urbs* which is *wholly* ideal, peopled only by the cultivated writers of all ages: 'His voice was meant to suggest the voice of a certain, historical vertical civilisation, modified by the voice of W. S. Landor, not the voice of an age or place'.

Rather than point to the oddity of 'voice' in that sentence (seeming to appeal to a spoken usage which in fact it spurns), and rather than quarrel with the assumption that the language of Garrick's quatrain has no contact with the spoken usage of Garrick and his circle (Goldsmith's 'Retaliation' might suggest otherwise), I will confess myself ready to kiss the rod, though not very abjectly. For if it is an American aberration to see style too readily as 'timeless', the corresponding British vice is to see it as altogether too time-conditioned. Many British readers need to be told— and Mr Pinsky comes near to telling them—that it was not 'the eighteenth century' nor 'Augustan civilization' that wrote 'Retaliation', but Oliver Goldsmith; in other words, that in the eighteenth as in any other century (though not always to the same degree) memorable English is produced by distinguished individuals—a Goldsmith or a Garrick—rising above, and contending with, the slack linguistic habits of their society. And so, to complete my concession to Mr Pinsky, the non-conversational urbanity which he speaks of does indeed exist; and Landor sometimes exemplifies it. Only (and here's the sting in the tail of my concession) it is rather unimportant—for reasons that may appear.

This is the place to interpose the only consideration that I shall have space for, of a specific poem by Landor. This is the 'Faesulan Idyll', which is relevant to the issue of spoken as against written language because like other poems by Landor, it includes an exchange which is proferred as spoken language written down.

> I said: *you find the largest.*
> This indeed,
> Cried she, *is large and sweet.*

Mr Pinsky, who has looked at my discussion of these lines, does not take account of a footnote which records a relevant though instructively inconclusive difference of opinion between Mr Bateson and myself, about whether 'You find the largest' is to be understood as imperative or indicative. Instead, in a piece of brilliant special pleading, Mr Pinsky comments: '. . . the chaste and artificial simplicity of two italicized statements are translations, fictionally, of the more earthy simplicity of idiomatic Italian. The resultant language (Hemingway's mock-Spanish is a similar device) nicely solves a stylistic problem . . .' The invocation of Hemingway is masterly; but it is quite implausible, resting as it does on an assumption which the poem gives no warrant for—that the poet's companion in the poem is a Tuscan peasant-girl, not his wife, his daughter, his mistress, or a well-born visitor.

An art that seeks to be timeless disdains historical contingency. The voice that it speaks with is 'not the voice of an age or place'. Those who doubt the feasibility of such an achievement, or who think it of limited value if and when achieved, are likely to be, in Mr Pinsky's words, 'those who consider Pound (or Eliot) to be . . . greater than Wallace Stevens because Stevens does not "contain history" '. I am of their company, as Mr Pinsky doubtless suspected. But Landor, so furiously partisan in the politics of his lifetime? Surely it is distinctly odd to range him with those, like Wallace Stevens, who disdain history, or at least largely ignore it? Landor repeatedly plunged or lunged into the political history of his own times, and got into hot water in consequence, as when his praise of tyrannicide as a virtue was linked in the English press (after all, not unjustly) with Orsini's attempt on the life of Napoleon III which killed several innocent people. There is a real difficulty here for Mr Pinsky, and he confronts it frankly:

. . . as to nineteenth-century society, my impression is that on the whole Landor (apart from his radical politics) found it slightly less worthy of his serious attention than the several other societies with which he was familiar. But this question is complicated, and Landor was a violently complex man.

A reader of R. H. Super's fine biography may feel like saying roundly that Landor never noticed that the nineteenth century had happened or was happening. Born to the eighteenth-century squirearchy, he seems to have survived till 1864 still expecting, at home and abroad, the privileged treatment that an English squire in the eighteenth century might have received (if he was lucky). To the end of his days bewildered and outraged when such treatment was not forthcoming, Landor walks through Super's pages as a living anachronism; and this, if it brought him many bruises in what was after all a very unhappy life, brought him also, as a gloriously genuine eccentric, the affection of Dickens and, as a no less genuine innocent, the extraordinarily patient fostercare of Browning and surprisingly many others. And thus Mr Pinsky's parenthesis, 'apart from his radical politics', which provokes to begin with a rash of exclamation-marks in the margin, is in fact, for all its audacity, quite reasonable. For Landor's anti-democratic republicanism (if only he had been Russian, he could have been a Decembrist) is as anachronistic as everything else about him; however arguable or even admirable in the abstract, it was not remotely relevant to any of the nineteenth-century societies that Landor lived in and tried to influence. And yet we can hardly be as indulgent to him, now that he's been dead for a century, as Dickens and Browning were to him when he was alive. Surely Landor deserves censure for continually inciting political action, and usually violent action at that, in societies which he knew so little that he could never see that they were different from the society he was born to. Mr Pinsky allows, in a startling aside, that Landor was 'self-indulgent all his life'. And perhaps he would agree that Landor's politics were part of this self-indulgence. And yet he invites us to embrace a view of poetry in which such habitual self-indulgence and self-ignorance on the part of the poet has no damaging effect on his poetry. I cannot swallow this: the insanely or childishly headstrong arrogance which characterizes Landor's life (however 'innocently') seems to me abundantly manifest and damaging in his poetry. With the greatest respect, therefore, I have to say that Mr Pinsky has not persuaded me. According to R. H. Super, Elizabeth Barrett, meeting Landor for the first time, at a dinner where Wordsworth was present also, 'was struck by the contrast between the brilliance of Landor who dominated the conversation and the simplicity of Wordsworth; she felt, rather than saw, the difference between eminent talent and great genius'. Just so!

Postscript: Rereading this, as also several other pieces in this collection, I am forced to realize how I take William Wordsworth's genius to be self-evident whereas many people, I suspect—whether they have read Yvor Winters or Pound or some other—believe Wordsworth's reputation to be suspect. Could it be that Wordsworth's is the voice from our past that nowadays most needs to be attended to, though in fact it goes for the most part unheard?

PUSHKIN, AND OTHER POETS

Pushkin: A Comparative Commentary, John Bayley, Cambridge.
Pushkin on Literature, edited and translated by Tatiana Wolff, Methuen.

PUSHKIN THE untranslatable: the notion has been in the air ever since
the first rumours of a great Russian poet reached early Victorian England.
When, of late, Edmund Wilson and Vladimir Nabokov joined issue about
it, the famous talking-point was engaging two livelier minds than ever before. And Nabokov's four volumes devoted to *Evgeny Onegin*—supposedly a translation with commentary, but really a sustained demonstration
that the translation was impossible—are a comic masterpiece by one of
the greatest comic imaginations of our time. If the translations are not
getting any better (though in fact Walter Arndt's *Evgeny Onegin* is more
serviceable than any of its predecessors), at least critical discussion of
this poet has been moving on to an altogether higher level of awareness
and discrimination. And now John Bayley's 'comparative commentary'
sets the seal on this development. With Bayley's help English readers
capable of responding to a poet so sophisticated as Pushkin, whose procedures are so much at odds with our current assumptions, can—even if
they lack Russian—construct for themselves an image of this poet more
accurate, more faceted, more intriguing and challenging, than they could
construct from any extant translations—or from any translations we are
likely to get. A critical commentary as good as this, focused so severely,
so resolutely refusing to be distracted by side-issues, makes translation
for most purposes unnecessary.

   And yet I cannot think that John Bayley will succeed in creating an
intelligent enthusiasm for Pushkin in England, any more than D. S.
Mirsky did nearly fifty years ago. The times, as I read them, could hardly
be less propitious for a recognition among us of the radiant paradox that
Pushkin embodies: the union of impregnable impersonality and reserve as
an artist with eager and vulnerable frankness as a person. If Mr Robert
Conquest's charming talent were multiplied a hundredfold, we might
have a British Pushkin: and we'd be mightily disconcerted by it. For all
our thinking about poetry and its idioms seems to be dominated still
by a simple-minded either/or, according to which 'impersonal' means
'aestheticist', and 'personal' means 'dishevelled'. Ted Hughes, for instance,
says, with becoming hesitancy:

> I think it's true that formal patterning of the actual movement of
> verse somehow includes a mathematical and a musically deeper world
> than free verse can easily hope to enter. It's a mystery why it should
> do so. But it only works of course if the language is totally alive and
> pure and if the writer has a perfectly pure grasp of his real feeling ...
> and the very sound of metre calls up the ghosts of the past and it is
> difficult to sing one's own tune against that choir. It is easier to speak
> a language that raises no ghosts.

Easier it may be. Pushkin seems to have thought it was too easy to be worth doing. As John Bayley shows on page after page, Pushkin's method was always to call up ghosts into his language, knowing very precisely just which ghost he was summoning at any given point; and indeed Pushkin's 'perfectly pure grasp of his real feeling' seems to have been indistinguishable for him from knowing what ghost to summon, how long to entertain him, and when to exorcize him so as to entertain another. But then, Pushkin had no worries about a duty 'to sing one's own tune': as Bayley says, 'in *Evgeny Onegin*, then, the style is not the man but a complex instrument manipulated by him.' And yet Pushkin is no olympian aesthete, imperturbably detached and paring his fingernails, as Nabokov would have us believe: his use of delicate parody has more to do with Chaucer than with Max Beerbohm. John Bayley, who points this out, reflects discouragingly that what Chaucer and Pushkin share is 'an artifice that can probably only be achieved in a poetic language at an early stage of its development, when freedom and formality are allies who can bring out the best in each other.' I hope this isn't true, and I don't believe it is. If we go for coarser effects, it's because we are lazy and lack conviction, and our public lacks taste.

Seeking for English analogues like Chaucer is what Bayley commits himself to when he calls his commentary 'comparative'. But it's inescapable in any case, because Pushkin advertises his own traffic with certain English authors—particularly Shakespeare (in his verse-dramas), Scott (in his prose fiction) and Byron. Byron is the case that is hardest to handle. As Tatiana Wolff says of Pushkin in her massive and well-ordered volume of selections, *Pushkin on Literature*:

> With the rise of interest in comparative literature a new niche was found for him: 'Russia's Byron'. Had this been said at the beginning of the nineteenth century, when Byron blazed like a sun in European eyes, it would have been understandable; but it was said when Byron himself had been allotted a modest position in the English poetic hierarchy, only just holding his own as a major poet.

I hope that other eyebrows than those of Professor Wilson Knight will be raised at the information that Byron's status as a major poet is in doubt; and in fact I believe that the formula 'Russia's Byron' goes back further than Mrs Wolff allows for. However that may be, it certainly seems impossible to write about Pushkin without being unfair to Byron, for Pushkin so obviously modelled himself on Byron that it becomes imperative to show that he surpassed him. John Bayley does better than most in giving Byron his due, but misses an opportunity when he applauds Pushkin's bold and sparse epithets in his lyrics to the sea, yet fails to acknowledge the same feature in Byron. 'Roll on, thou deep and dark blue Ocean—roll' is a verse that deserves to be rescued from a passing gibe by Henry James.

How good Bayley can be with his comparisons (and yet how demanding, how scornful of readers who will see in this procedure only name-dropping in an echo-chamber) comes out in a passage like this:

Wordsworth's finest poetry puts on loftiness or a penetrating simplicity under the impulse of the poet's desire to communicate, so that incongruity seems almost like a needful aspect of the very urgency of communication. Wordsworth seems to blow his blasts as if absent-mindedly: his argument is too intensely scrutinized to justify a change of diction which in a more formal poet would signify the discarding of a sufficiently handled commonplace and the taking up of another. Keats's finest poems depend equally on a seemingly uncontrolled mixture of the sublime and the banal; and when, in *Hyperion*, he seeks to confine his utterance to an artificially sublime diction, it rises like that of *The Excursion* into an inflexible monotony.

By reason of its very uncertainty, its absorption in the feel of its experience rather than in any attention to appropriateness of diction, romantic poetry can generalise and philosophise in a way that is not available to Pushkin. When Keats speaks of 'the feel of not to feel it', or Wordsworth of 'blank misgivings of a creature moving about in worlds not realised', they make a break-through in the verbal exploration of human experience. Such things can be implied by Pushkin in the drama of narrative—Keats's phrase might describe the impression Tatyana gives in her Petersburg salon—but Pushkin's styles have no power to give the thing in itself. His generalisations are the weakest things in *Evgeny Onegin* and redeem their weakness only by not taking themselves too seriously: their elegance seems good-humouredly to patronise an emptiness for which it is itself largely responsible.

Bayley goes on to speculate that Pushkin lacks 'the ability of the English romantic poets to be clumsy with point and power' because 'in terms of a literary tradition Pushkin has only the eighteenth century behind him'. One sees what he means, of course. Yet to commiserate with a poet for lacking the ability to be clumsy (however powerfully) seems to be a reach of refinement which would have raised a laugh from either Pushkin or Keats, who each had, as Bayley points out, a 'briskly straightforward and unpretending personality'. And then again, of course, one wonders whether 'literary tradition', in isolation from other traditions that might be called 'socio-political' or 'ideological', can do quite so much as John Bayley suggests, whether in liberating a poet or constricting him. Bayley permits himself one comment of a socio-political kind which is venomous:

Like all great artists he is the product of his age, and a more liberal social and political environment would not have made him a better one. The very negativism of tzarist tyranny was a liberating factor. The censorship that really deadens and kills is the positive one of a secularized state culture, with its apparatus of arts councils and writers' unions, a culture that decrees the proper style and function of literature.

Is it indeed this sort of set-up which gives us our undoubted ability to be clumsy, and our conviction that by being so—pointedly or not, with power or without it—we are at all events being sincere, being 'ourselves'?

Thinking of the aristocratic robustness of Pushkin's attitude to his vocation (for a vocation it was, not a mere accomplishment), and of what John Bayley calls 'the heroic commonplace of Pushkin's own nature', it seems as if that might indeed be what is wrong with us.

THE ADVENTURES OF A CULTURAL ORPHAN

Discretions, Mary de Rachewiltz, Faber.

WHEN EZRA POUND'S daughter alludes by her very title to her father's *Indiscretions*, the ironies are manifold: and none of them are lost on Mary de Rachewiltz. She herself, born out of wedlock, was a scandalous indiscretion on her parents' part; and the consequences were less than disastrous for the professional career of her musician mother chiefly because those who were in the know behaved with discreet and unappealing correctness for twenty years. At the end of the war in Europe, when Pound paid for his massive indiscretions over Rome radio by being arraigned as a traitor to his country, it was taken to be all the more important, so as not to further inflame American opinion against him, that Mary and her mother should retreat even further into the shadows, unacknowledged. Thus, discreet is what she has been, perforce, throughout her life, chiefly because her father has been so much the reverse. It strikes one as a story out of the nineteenth century rather than the twentieth. And yet in the end it is some of our twentieth-century suppositions that are made to look silly. For according to our apprehensive tendermindedness towards our children and their 'rights', this child, farmed out to foster-parents and repeatedly made to feel that her existence was an encumbrance and an embarrassment, should have grown up emotionally crippled, maladjusted and thwarted, incapable of fidelity or trust or good humour. In fact, however, the Tyrolean peasant couple who were her foster-parents were kind and wise and good; she was radiantly happy in her life with them, and is still in her memories of them; and Mary de Rachewiltz herself emerges from her own pages as exceptionally serene and strong with an emotional and domestic life of firm ties and secure satisfactions. It is a happy outcome, though the happiness has been earned and paid for, time and again, at a very high price. And it looks as if the best the child-psychologists will be able to do is regard it as the exception that proves their rule!

When in 1920 Pound, prompted by A. R. Orage, called upon his memories for the weekly instalments in *The New Age* which were subsequently collected as *Indiscretions*, he found in his personal and familial past nothing to hide, therefore nothing to reveal. How to be indiscreet about what, as it disconcertingly turned out, was blamelessly respectable? His daughter, by contrast, has plenty to hide if she chooses; plenty to reveal if she can manage it without cheapness. In fact she hides very little, so far as we can judge. And yet her title is not wholly ironical: for it is in revelation, not in suppression, that she has most need of tact and good taste, of 'discretion'. She has to avoid, and does, any vulgar hint of 'the inside story', of 'now it can be told'. Because her story has cost her dear, she does not sell it cheaply to us, but supplies it for the most part obliquely and allusively, especially through allusions (neatly indexed for us) to her father's writings and the *Cantos* in particular. This makes her book different from classics or near-classics of a similar kind, such as Stanislaus Joyce's *My Brother's Keeper* or, more remotely, *The Life of George Crabbe by His Son*. And in this respect too Mary de Rachewiltz is following Pound's precedent: for the style of his *Indiscretions* alludes throughout, in distinctly unsubtle fashion, to Henry James. At times his daughter deliberately but more subtly strikes the same note, as when she tells of her foster-mother ('Mamme') bringing her as a little girl to visit her parents staying briefly in the nearest town:

> And from now on whenever the scrupulous biographer will report a concert in Budapest, a performance in Vienna, a trip to Frankfurt, Wörgl, Salzburg, it may be assumed that the journey was interrupted, for a few hours or for a few days, in Bruneck . . .
> On a balcony on the Hotel Post, the Herr and the Frau, enthroned on wicker chairs. I pastured a flock of thin caoutchouc flatbellied geese precariously floating in a bowl of water at their feet. And I wanted to stroke the shoes dangling in front of my eyes, so smooth and shiny. '*Net!*' Mamme warned watching over me from the doorway. *Net*. I must not touch the Lord and the Lady's shoes and I must call them Tattile and Mamile.

Pound's subtitle to *Indiscretions—Une Revue de Deux Mondes*—shows the point of his allusions to James: he sees the story of his early life as a contribution to that typically Jamesian fable, 'the international theme'. It is the fact of the *deux mondes*, of the Old World in tiers of boxes along one side of the stage and the New World equally cognizant of the spectacle from the other side, which gives to the items of his family history a representative or symptomatic or even clinical interest such as they certainly do not have in themselves, for their own sake, nor for the most part by virtue of any raciness or pungency in the language that is found for them. Mary de Rachewiltz respects and endorses her father's sense of himself as the heir to the earliest expatriate generation of James and Berenson and others, as 'the last American living the tragedy of Europe'. Thus she writes of the *Pisan Canto* 81 ('Pull down thy vanity'):

> And the cry of 'AOI' is an outburst more personal than any other in the *Cantos* and expresses the stress of almost two years when he was pent up with two women who loved him, whom he loved, and who coldly hated each other. Whatever the civilised appearances, the polite behaviour and the façade in front of the world, their hatred and tension had permeated the house.
>   *Les larmes que j'ai créés m'inondent*
>   *Tard, très tard je t'ai connue, la Tristesse,*
>   I have been hard as youth sixty years.
> Until then the attitude toward personal feelings had been somewhat Henry Jamesian: feelings are things other people have. One never spoke of them or showed them.

There are sides to Pound which are not accounted for in this image of decorous over-refinement. It may be felt that there is in the father a vulgar streak which the daughter has not noticed: she was wounded and bewildered, for instance, when she visited him in St Elizabeth's in 1953, by his amused tolerance for the rabble-rousing roughnecks who visited him there. All the same, a Jamesian hauteur, or a fastidious unease about seeming to 'make a scene', does indeed seem a good reason why intense and confessional utterances like these (another example: *J'ai eu pitié des autres. Pas assez*) get themselves said in French. Pound chooses for the expression of intense feeling the decent obscurity, if not of a learned language, at least of a foreign one.

What we have in Eliot's and Pound's lives, more than in their writings, is the touching drama of the New World come back to experience (and not vicariously—not in Pound's case, nor in Eliot's, nor in James's before them) the agonies of the Old. Eliot and Pound acknowledged in effect that, since they had got sustenance from European springs, it devolved upon them as a duty to declare their allegiance when the European centre fell apart. When we think what it meant to make such declarations (what it meant for Pound, and what it cost him), the question whether they chose right is less significant than the fact that they chose at all. What Pound chose to invest in the Old World was nothing less than a child. (Eliot never risked so much.) In Mary de Rachewiltz's book we have that child's testimony: and it is, in the end, to the effect that she endorses the investment that her father made of her. From whatever place on the political spectrum we observe this gesture being made, it is in any case, on its own account, poignant in the extreme. Her devotion to her father is evident, and it is touching. For if she had resented him, and what he let her in for, this would have been entirely understandable. Because of him she found herself, time and again, on the wrong side. Between the wars the Pustertal, where she grew up, was Italian territory: but it was wholly Austrian in feeling, and accordingly the Italians were much disliked there—the child, schooled by her distant parents to feel pro-Italian, and required by them to observe Fascist youth disciplines as none of her Tyrolean associates did, was impaled on divided loyalties long before the war came. When towards the end of the war she worked in a German military hospital, she found herself on the wrong side of another cultural and political divide, apprehensive lest her having thus worked for the Germans should be used to strengthen the American case against her father. Pound called his *Indiscretions* a *revue de deux mondes: Discretions* gives us the adventures of a cultural orphan in and out of three or four worlds, not just two. Because Mary de Rachewiltz is so clear-sighted about the successive plights that she found herself in, her loyalty to her father is the more remarkable, and the more moving. (For all that, on a second reading one notices her asking more than once why, in instance after instance, it is her father who gets the benefit of the doubt, her mother who has to take the rap.)

Pound, most pedagogical of poets, was as much of a demanding school-master towards his child as the most securely established Victorian father could have been. And what he demanded, year after year, was a vocational allegiance not merely declared but acted upon. For this writer's child turned out to be herself a writer, hypersensitive towards language—as indeed she could hardly fail to be, having to master, on top of the Austrian patois she spoke with her foster-parents, first the Italian language, then the English (in which she is not quite infallible even today). It seems now, with hindsight, as if she could not have saved herself except by being a writer, an artist in language. At any rate, what the expatriate American father demanded of his Austro-Italian daughter was, in whatever circumstances and at whatever cost, the literary conscience—exact fidelity in language to the recognizable contours and spatial dispositions of the physical world, due allowance made for the emotional disposition or compulsions of herself as disciplined but also involved spectator. It is a requirement that few fathers of our day, browbeaten as we have been and morally blackmailed with the guilt of having conceived any son or daughter whatever, will dare to enunciate, let alone to enforce. So much the worse for us; for our sons and our daughters! What Mary de Rachewiltz made of the cruel assignment is enough to make her father not just satisfied but proud. Not for nothing did he insist that she learn, at one and the same time (and out of the same text, Hardy's *Under the Greenwood Tree*), both the English language and the principles of imagistically scrupulous writing in that language. The payoff is here, in this book. It is a unique witness, as beautiful as it is brave.

HARDY'S VIRGILIAN PURPLES

AMONG HARDY'S 'Poems 1912-13', there is 'Beeny Cliff', with below
that title the dates, 'March 1870-March 1913':

i.

O the opal and the sapphire of that wandering western sea,
And the woman riding high above with bright hair flapping free—
The woman whom I loved so, and who loyally loved me.

ii.

The pale mews plained below us, and the waves seemed far away
In a nether sky, engrossed in saying their ceaseless babbling say,
As we laughed light-heartedly aloft on that clear-sunned March day.

iii.

A little cloud then cloaked us, and there flew an irised rain,
And the Atlantic dyed its levels with a dull misfeatured stain,
And then the sun burst out again, and purples prinked the main.

iv.

—Still in all its chasmal beauty bulks old Beeny to the sky,
And shall she and I not go there once again now March is nigh,
And the sweet things said in that March say anew there by and by?

v.

What if still in chasmal beauty looms that wild weird western shore,
The woman now is—elsewhere—whom the ambling pony bore,
And nor knows nor cares for Beeny, and will laugh there nevermore.

The poem has many features that are disconcerting to current taste—notably the unabashed *bravura* of alliteration, and the elaborately cunning
metre. (The poem is in septenaries, but they are very artfully masked, especially near the start.) However, for present purposes, a single phrase in
the poem will give us quite enough trouble to be going on with, and quite
enough entertainment. I mean the five words in the third stanza, 'and
purples prinked the main.' It is characteristic audacity: from the imperial
splendour of 'purples' we are required, with 'prinks', to sidle through a
boudoir or an aviary on our way to the no less imperial vastness of 'the
main'. Such strenuousness is typical of Hardy. But not all his audacities
are successful, he is not always strenuous to some purpose. And if we
look for his purpose here, we are led far afield.

 J. O. Bailey says, 'Hardy's description in the poem is accurate.' (1) And
those who have visited Beeny will agree. In particular the rendering of the
shifting tones as the little rain-squall passes over is recognizably from the
same hand as scrupulously registered appearances in a notebook in 1872:
'August: At Beeny Cliff . . . green towards the land, blue-black towards
the sea. Every ledge has a little, starved, green grass upon it: all vertical
parts bare. Seaward, a dark-grey ocean beneath a pale green sky, upon

which lie branches of red cloud . . .' And so we ask: could a slate-blue cliff under certain rainbow conditions cast a shadow so as to colour the sea at its foot in various shades of purple? Straining more than a little, we can just envisage how this might be so, can just about summon up the sense-impression which 'purples' seems to register. But in that case 'prink' confronts us just as startlingly as ever; and 'the main' necessarily invokes not the patch of the sea at a cliff's base but on the contrary, very insistently, the oceanic expanse of the Atlantic stretching to the horizon. And thus it is not enough merely to cite the Preface (1895) to *A Pair of Blue Eyes*, where Hardy evokes the same area, Beeny Cliff and its Cornish vicinity: 'The place is pre-eminently (for one person at least) the region of dream and mystery. The ghostly birds, the pall-like sea, the frothy wind, the eternal soliloquy of the waters, the bloom of dark purple cast, that seems to exhale from the shoreward precipices, in themselves lend to the scene an atmosphere like the twilight of a night vision.' If we are still looking for accurate register of sense-impressions, the 'bloom of dark purple cast', in this crepuscular scene where the sea is 'pall-like', does not help us at all with what the sea looked like on a clear-sunned day in March; and in any case this purple is not a shadow cast by the cliff but a bloom that seemed to exhale from it. The longer we look at this piece of prose, the more we realize that it is further from straightforward description than the verse is.

And yet the answer to the riddle is indeed in *A Pair of Blue Eyes*. For we read in chapter XXI of that novel another account of Beeny: 'What gave an added terror to its height was its blackness. And upon this dark face the beating of ten thousand west winds had formed a kind of bloom, which had a visual effect not unlike that of a Hambro' grape. Moreover it seemed to float off into the atmosphere, and inspire terror through the lungs.' This makes it plain that the purple of Beeny Cliff is on the one hand 'a visual effect' (the cliff-face *is* purple or purplish—as indeed it is), but on the other hand, in terms of what Beeny does to its ambience of sea and sky and land and the people who move there, the purple is not a visual effect at all (in, for instance, any shadow which the cliff casts upon the sea), but is spiritual—a seeming, a floating off, an exhalation; something which may at times inspire terror, at other times the quite different feelings that go along with 'prink'. And what those feelings might be we learn from chapter IV of the novel, where Hardy describes the effect made on a young man (such as Hardy was when he first met Emma Gifford, and in Beeny's vicinity) by Elfride, the heroine, who is physically very like Emma, as Hardy himself pointed out: (2) 'She looked so intensely *living* and full of movement as she came into the old silent place, that young Smith's world began to be lit by "the purplish light" in all its definiteness.' This clinches it: the purples which prink the main as seen from Beeny Cliff are the spiritual light of sexual love—as indeed we should have guessed, for what but sexual passion is so likely to terrify and irradiate alternately or at the one time?

However, this is only the beginning. For the purple light which begins to irradiate the world of Stephen Smith is offered to us inside quotation-marks. Where is it quoted from? It is not hard to guess if we consider *A Pair of Blue Eyes* as a whole; if we note for instance, in chapter IX, that 'perhaps Stephen's manners, like the feats of Euryalus, owed their attractiveness in her eyes rather to the attractiveness of his person than to their own excellence'; or observe, in chapter XII, how the fingers of Elfride's step-mother 'were literally stiff with rings, *signis auroque rigentes*, like Helen's robe'; (3) or if we envisage, in chapter XIV, 'Elfride, who like Aeneas at Carthage, was full of admiration for the brilliant scene'. This early novel is interlarded profusely with allusions to Virgil's *Aeneid*. And sure enough that is where the purple light comes from, from *Aeneid*, vi. 641: 'largior hic campos aether et lumine vestit/purpureo, solemque suum, sua sidera norunt'. Virgil's *purpureus* there is glossed by William Smith in his Latin-English Dictionary (19th ed., 1888) as 'brilliant, beau-tiful'. In fact, it is the 'purple' of Pope's *Pastorals* ('Spring', l. 28): 'And lavish Nature paints the Purple Year', on which Warburton notes in his edition (1751) '. . . used in the Latin sense, of the brightest, most vivid colouring in general, not of that peculiar tint so called.'

This is Hardy's 'purple', not just in *A Pair of Blue Eyes* and 'Beeny Cliff', but consistently. It is for instant the purple of 'The Revisitation', first published in August, 1904:

As I lay awake at night-time
In an ancient country barracks known to ancient cannoneers
And recalled the hopes that heralded each seeming brave and bright time
Of my primal purple years . . .;

as also of 'The Change', dated 'Jan.-Feb. 1913':

Out of the past there rises a week—
Who shall read the years O!—
Out of the past there rises a week
Enringed with a purple zone.

And we realize that it was not any cartographer's colouring that Hardy had in mind, when he wrote in 'The Place on the Map', published 1913:

I look upon the map that hangs by me—
Its shires and towns and rivers lined in varnished artistry—
And I mark a jutting height
Coloured purple, with a margin of blue sea.

(The 'height' is either Beeny, if the poem is about Emma, or Portland, if it is about Tryphena.) So too in *The Woodlanders* (chapter XXIV), a woman reflects: 'But what an attenuation this cold pride was of the dream of her youth, in which she had pictured herself walking in state towards the altar, flushed by the purple light and bloom of her own passion . . .' (4) All these purples, we now realize, are Virgilian.

Which ought to remind us, if we hark back to where we started from, that 'Beeny Cliff' belongs in a sequence of poems that bears a Virgilian epigraph. We have been unaccountably reluctant to inquire what Hardy meant by this, and what bearing the epigraph has upon the poems which, as it were, it sponsors. Of recent commentators J. Hillis Miller has come nearest to grasping the nettle, and yet all he says is this:

> The epigraph for the whole group of poems is *Veteris vestigia flammae*: 'ashes of an old fire'. The phrase comes from *The Aeneid* (iv. 23), where it is part of Dido's statement that the love she once felt for her now dead husband is about to renew itself for Aeneas. Her love for Aeneas is of course doomed to end in separation and leads to her suicide. There is a complex relation between Hardy's poems about his dead wife and Virgil's story of Dido's betrayal by Aeneas. The analogy involves not only Dido's feelings for her dead husband, Sychaeus, but also the relation of Aeneas to Dido after her death. As Aeneas confronts in Book vi of *The Aeneid* the mute unforgiving ghost of Dido, so Hardy in the poems glimpses the voiceless ('After a Journey', *CP*, 328) ghost of his dead wife.

This raises many more questions than it answers. For instance if in 'After a Journey' the ghost is voiceless, in 'The Haunter' she is a chatterbox, and in 'The Voice' she is 'calling'. Again, if we recall that Hardy in 1913 was presumably already attached to Florence Emily Dugdale, whom he was to take as his second wife in the next year, the 'complex relation' would work out: Hardy equals Dido; Emma equals Sychaeus; Florence Emily equals Aeneas. (We have already seen the sexes thus switched when Elfride in *A Pair of Blue Eyes* was said to be 'like Aeneas at Carthage'.) One thing certainly the epigraph supplies—an understanding of sexual passion as one undifferentiated energy running wild, fastening itself seemingly at random on this person or that one, and switching itself from one to another in a way that makes nonsense of all human vows of constancy. This is the classical and terrible conception which Racine recovered for later ages when he made Phèdre cry out, in appalled awareness of her own condition. 'C'est Vénus tout entière à sa proie attachée'. And it is Hardy's conception also, as we can see from poem after poem and story after story. We must stop thinking of his classicism as no more than skin-deep, or as (worse still) the pathetic pretentiousness of the self-educated. J. Hillis Miller hurries us into *Aeneid* Book vi, but the striking thing is that Hardy goes for his epigraph not to Book vi (nor to Book ii, where Aeneas meets the ghost of his first wife, Creusa) (5) but to the altogether more ambivalent and disturbing passage in Book iv. And this I shall return to.

As we have seen, however, it is indeed in Book vi that we find 'the purple light'. It comes more than a hundred and fifty lines later than Dido's celebrated silence when she turns from Aeneas towards the shade of Sychaeus. Aeneas has now penetrated the underworld as far as the abode of the blest, where he is to encounter the shade that he came to seek, his father Anchises:

> devenere locos laetos et amoena virecta
> fortunatorum nemorum sedesque beatas.

largior hic campos aether et lumine vestit
purpureo, solemque suum, sua sidera norunt.
William Morris in 1876 had rendered the lines:
  They came into a joyous land, and greensward fair and sweet
  Amid the happiness of groves, the blessed dwelling-place.
  Therein a more abundant heaven clothes all the meadows' face
  With purple light, and their own sun and their own moon they have.
Dryden gives, in that translation which Hardy's remarkable mother gave
to her son when he was eight years old:
  These holy rites performed, they took their way,
  Where long extended plains of pleasure lay.
  The verdant fields with those of heaven may vie,
  With ether vested, and a purple sky—
  The blissful seats of happy souls below:
  Stars of their own, and their own suns, they know.
But it is Robert Bridges's version which, grotesque though it is in both
diction and metre, rams home the fact that what Virgil is speaking of here
is not anything that can be dismissed as fanciful hyperbole:
  They came out on a lonely pleasance, that dream'd-of oasis,
  Fortunat isle, the abode o' the blest, their fair Happy Woodland.
  Here is an ampler sky, those meads ar' azur'd by a gentler
  Sun than th' Earth, an' a new starworld their darkness adorneth.   (6)
Virgil's *purpureus* describes a light that is not any terrestrial light, however
preternaturally radiant and keen; it is preternatural through and through,
the light of an alternative cosmos, lit by another sun by day and other stars
by night. And it is this light, no other, that Hardy, agnostic and scientific
humanist, claimed to see from Beeny Cliff when 'purples prinked the main'.
  The unavoidable question is whether we can dismiss the matter as hyperbole any more in Hardy's poem than we can in Virgil's. To put it
another way (a way that incidentally makes hyperbole more of a life-
and-death matter than we normally take it to be), do those 'purples'
exist in a psychological reality, or a metaphysical one? I am prepared to
suggest that this is the question that Hardy asks himself, and wrestles
with, all through 'Poems of 1912-13'.
  For consider: *veteris vestigia flammae*, sounding out of Virgil, had
awakened other echoes in the poetry of Europe before the sound carried
to Thomas Hardy. In Canto XXX of the *Purgatorio* the pilgrim at last
sees Beatrice, the lode-star of all his pilgrimage. Overwhelmed, he turns
to share his transport, and with whom but Virgil, who has so far instructed
and protected him at every stage?
    volsimi alla sinistra col rispitto
      col quale il fantolin corre alla mamma
      quando ha paura o quando elli è afflitto,
    per dicere a Virgilio: 'Men che dramma
      di sangue m'è rimaso che non tremi:
      conosco i segni dell' antica fiamma;

The moment is superbly managed and poignant. For not only does the pilgrim find that Virgil, embodiment of pious and prudent reason, has at this moment withdrawn from him, ceding to the divinely inspired reason that is Beatrice; but the words which the pilgrim addresses to Virgil are Virgil's own, as the commentators do not fail to notice—*i segni dell' antica fiamma* is Dante's translation of *veteris vestigia flammae*. And so when Hardy meets the dead Emma in 'After a Journey', in the shadows which they cast not only does Aeneas meet the dead Dido but Dante meets the dead and transfigured Beatrice.

Because Hardy is as secretive and devious about his reading-habits as about his other habits and activities, there is I think no firm evidence that he ever read the *Purgatorio*. And yet it is inconceivable that he didn't. (After all, the reviewers had jeered at him for letting Tess Durbeyfield cite the *Inferno*.) And if Hardy knew the *Purgatorio* at least in Cary's translation, if he knew *i segni dell' antica fiamma* no less than *veteris vestigia flammae*, this vindicates us all over again in refusing to take the apparitions of the dead wife as no more than hyperbole, conventional machinery. The status of Emma's *being*, now that she is dead— more than ever this metaphysical question seems to be the question that the poems ask, and ask about.

Indeed, if we scan the pages that Erich Auerbach devotes to 'Dante's Early Poetry', one passage after another must strike us as applicable to Hardy's 'Poems of 1912-13' no less than to the poems of Dante. For instance:

> From the motif: my spirit often dwells with my dead beloved—a poet like Guinizelli would scarcely have made more than two lines; in order to write more, he would have had to move away from his point of departure, that is, from himself, and introduce something else, a related but new motif, perhaps a description of the condition of the departed, a message from her, in short an assortment of different elements. But when Dante's spirit wanders aloft, his vision of the event is all of a piece; there is nothing metaphoric about it; it is as though he were registering a real event in slow motion; the whole poem is a record of his spirit's ascent and return. (7)

Or again:

> Dante's whole striving is to intensify his feeling to the utmost by raising it above the sphere of subjectivity to which feeling is ordinarily confined . . . Even today we feel the power of this will, and the poem with all its unevenness still breathes the same magic. It is the magic exerted by Dante's passion for unity, by his striving to involve the whole cosmos in his own experience. The direction of his feeling is so definite that it cannot be deflected by the awkward rational order of the poem but operates, in the parts and in the whole, as a radiation of power, as a fiery enchantment.

Or:

> he insists on being followed into the extreme particularity of the real

situation that he conjures up. It would be inaccurate and perhaps unjust to say that his experience was stronger and more immediate than that of the earlier poets of the Middle Ages; and there is in his verses a considerable element of strain and exaggeration, which springs not from the prevailing taste but from his desire to express himself at any price. The truth is rather that the earlier poets tend to branch outward from their experience, to adduce, through association or logical connections, everything that is in any way related to the experience or likely to explain or ornament it metaphorically, whereas Dante holds firmly to his concrete point of departure and excludes everything else, whether alien, related, or similar. He never spreads himself thin but digs down.

And finally:

the composition of most of the poems has a cohesion and unity that may have seemed both bare and pedantic to the older generation. Seldom does one of the customary poetic ornaments appear; and when it does, it is not introduced with taste and charm, but is so immoderately exaggerated, so earnestly transposed into the realm of reality as to frighten and repel Dante's older contemporaries. By its insistence on the concrete, unique situation, by its unabashed disclosure of personal feeling, the poem takes on such an intensity that those who were not prepared to commit themselves with passion felt wounded and alarmed.

By 'one of the customary poetic ornaments ... immoderately exaggerated', may we not understand that feature of 'Beeny Cliff' which we began by noting in a tone at once 'wounded and alarmed'—its *bravura* of alliteration?

However that may be, there is undoubtedly one respect in which Hardy stands closer to Dante than to Virgil. This is in his concern for locality and topography. The geography of Virgil's afterworld and otherworld is vague (though it is true that his sense of the geography of southern Italy is not). On the other hand, Dante's afterworld—and particularly the mountain of Purgatory—is structured geographically very exactly indeed. As Auerbach says of *The Divine Comedy*,

In the eschatological sphere physics and ethics, or as we should say today, the natural and humane sciences, are no longer separate; here nature, too, is ordered by an ethical stand: and, the measure of its participation in divine Being, *every natural site has the ethical rank of the rational beings who dwell in it*. With that the meaning of landscape is defined. The vivid descriptions of landscape in which the great poem abounds are never autonomous or purely lyrical; true, they appeal directly to the reader's emotions, they arouse delight or horror; but the feelings awakened by the landscape are not allowed to seep away like vague romantic dreams, but forcefully recapitulated, for the landscape is nothing other than the appropriate scene or metaphorical symbol of human destiny.   (8)

Whether we think of the landscape of the successive terraces on the purgatorial mount, or of the particular earthly terrains and catchment-areas which the dwellers on the terraces recall as soon as they are engaged in conversation, this is equally true—all the figures in Dante's poem tend to identify themselves by the landscapes which they inhabit now or have inhabited in their earthly past.

And so, if we say that the landscapes presented so insistently in 'Poems of 1912-13' are so many stations in a personal purgatory, we can mean something quite precise: we mean that each locality—and there are three of them, Dorset around Max Gate, Plymouth, and north Cornwall around Boscastle—is presented as the location, the haunt and habitat, of some one particular moral proclivity or principle. Max Gate is the landscape of treason, Boscastle (Beeny Cliff, St Juliot) is the landscape of loyalty and love. (When Hardy says, in 'At Castle Boterel', that he will 'traverse old love's domain/Never again', he doesn't mean that he won't ever fall in love again, but that he won't come to Boscastle any more.) The half-way house of Plymouth is the questionable, the problematic location; but of that more in a moment. What is crucial is to realize that the Dantesque focus—by which 'every natural site has the ethical rank of the rational beings who dwell in it'—precludes not just the psychological analysis so brilliant in Meredith's *Modern Love*, but also any moral discrimination, any apportioning of blame between the two partners to a marriage that had gone disastrously wrong. Max Gate is simply the landscape of treason; thereabouts he will betray her, she will betray him. North Cornwall is a landscape of loyalty; thereabouts he will be true to her, she will be true to him. The use of landscape is as starkly emblematic as that. The 'Poems of 1912-13' are sometimes said to be poems of remorse; through most of the sequence the chilling achievement is on the contrary that remorse is excluded from them. For remorse, and reproach also, are from the poet's point of view irrelevances; they only distract from and serve to obscure, the practice of Venus *à sa proie attachée*. Passion happens, Venus acts; and the ambivalence of her actions can be controlled only by locating the malevolence of her action in one place (Dorset) and its benevolence in another (Cornwall).

As for Plymouth, the problematical halfway house (where Emma grew up, where he promised to go visiting with her, but never did), Hardy does not take us there until late in the sequence, and then only that once. What J. Hillis Miller calls the 'wavelike pulsation of recovery and loss' through the sequence will no doubt be charted a little differently by each reader. To this one, the first sixteen poems rise very slowly from the desolation in which they start, at and around Max Gate. It is in the fifth poem, 'I found her out there', that the Cornish landscape first appears; and sure enough, it brings with it the first 'lift', the first movement towards recovery. This is in the 'maybe' of the last stanza:

> Yet her shade, maybe,
> Will creep underground
> Till it catch the sound
> Of that western sea

> As it swells and sobs
> Where she once domiciled,
> And joy in its throbs
> With the heart of a child.

(The grotesque literalness which sees, not Emma's spirit flitting to Corn-wall, but her dead body as it were *burrowing* thither, may strike us as genuinely Dantesque. For Hardy, resurrection must be of the body; as it would have to be for any one who took location, in all its physicality, as seriously as Hardy did.) There follows a slump back. But the trough of renewed desolation ('Without Ceremony' and 'Lament') is quite soon over. 'The Haunter', in which the dead Emma assures the widower that she attends and listens, expresses a conviction that the first poems of the sequence had denied. In the next poem, 'The Voice' (which Bailey, on the strength of the 'air-blue gown', locates in Boscastle), the dead woman has found a voice which can carry to him—she is calling. But for a second time the flickers of hope are quenched, blasted by the landscape of Max Gate in 'His Visitor' and 'A Circular'. At this point, however, the pace quickens, through 'A Dream or No' to 'After a Journey', as this Aeneas plans and then undertakes his journey into the underworld. 'After a Journey' is a high point; though the ghost is voiceless, the man appre-hends her meaning well enough, and the poem ends in an unprecedented serenity—naturally enough, for both are now firmly in the Cornish land-scape of reciprocal loyalty, as Dido was when she turned to Sychaeus. Two poems later he has, with 'Beeny Cliff', penetrated the underworld or other-world as far as the abodes of the blest, as we have seen. The assurance and controlled excitement continue to mount, and 'At Castle Boterel' sees the poet making a measured affirmation: love triumphs over time. Only at this point, after five poems all set firmly in Cornwall, does the poet dare to try carrying his consoling revelation back into the upper air—outside of Cornwall, to Plymouth. The poem is called 'Places':

> Nobody says: Ah, that is the place
> Where chanced, in the hollow of years ago,
> What none of the Three Towns cared to know—
> The birth of a little girl of grace—
> The sweetest the house saw, first or last;
>   Yet it was so
>   On that day long past.
>
> Nobody thinks: There, there she lay
> In the room by the Hoe, like the bud of a flower.
> And listened, just after the bedtime hour,
> To the stammering chimes that used to play
> The quaint Old Hundred-and-Thirteenth tune
>   In St Andrew's tower
>   Night, morn, and noon.

Nobody calls to mind that here
Upon Boterel Hill, where the wagoners skid,
With cheeks whose airy flush outbid
Fresh fruit in bloom, and free of fear,
She cantered down, as if she must fall
    (Though she never did),
    To the charm of all.

Nay: one there is to whom these things,
That nobody else's mind calls back,
Have a savour that scenes in being lack,
And a presence more than the actual brings;
To whom today is beneaped and stale,
    And its urgent clack
    But a vapid tale.

The writing here, it must be admitted, is well short of masterly. Yet in
the sequence this poem is irreplaceable; it is indeed the fulcrum on which
the whole series turns. This appears, however, only if we append to it, as
Hardy did, the firm dateline: 'Plymouth, March 1913'. On the one hand
this makes it clear that the poem belongs on the way back from the pilgrimage. But it has a more crucial function: for it forces upon our attention (if we are attentive, as apparently most readers aren't) how, though
the poem is thus insistently placed in Plymouth, the Plymouth places are
continually called 'there', whereas it is the Cornish place, Boterel Hill,
that is said to be 'here'. The superior reality of the domain of love and
loyalty, over the domains of indifference and cold hatred, could hardly
be asserted more pointedly; Cornwall is 'here' even when he is outside
it, and somewhere else. This is a reach of spiritual conviction beyond any
that he has reached earlier. As the next poem, 'The Phantom Horsewoman', declares, driving the point home:

    Not only there
    Does he see this sight,
    But everywhere
    In his brain—day, night,
    As if on the air
    It were drawn rose-bright—
    Yea, far from that shore
Does he carry this vision of heretofore:

A ghost-girl-rider. And though, toil-tried,
    He withers daily,
    Time touches her not,
    But she still rides gaily
    In his rapt thought
    On that shagged and shaly
    Atlantic spot,

                            And as when first eyed
                    Draws rein and sings to the swing of the tide.

And in this poem, which J. I. M. Stewart has called with entire justice
'a splendid taunt hurled at oblivion by the imagination', the execution is
equal to the conception—witness the internal rhyme and sudden ripple of
elated anapaests which make the last line so buoyant. The poem ends on
a note of sublime assurance, of exultation even. And in its original form,
in *Satires of Circumstance*, this was where the entire sequence ended—at
the joyous tip of a long and climbing curve of spiritual apprehensions.

II

Leave Dante out of it. Hardy's contact with the *Purgatorio* is unproven.
But his Virgilianism is another matter; he forces it on our attention. Why
then have we never acknowledged it? (For Virgil rates not a single entry
in the index to Bailey's *Handbook and Commentary*, all seven hundred
pages of it.)

The answer I fear is too plain: we are determined to condescend to
Hardy, to see in him what Yvor Winters saw—'a *naif*'. Even when we mean
to praise, we patronize; when Hardy's 'sincerity' is offered as a simple
and straightforward value by F. R. Leavis and Douglas Brown and those
who think with them, the implication is very plain that to Hardy—sturdily simple soul that he was—sincerity came more naturally than it did to
his more sophisticated peers, or than it does (of course) to us. The great
value of the biographical researches that have uncovered Tryphena Sparks
and others is, quite apart from the illumination of certain poems otherwise obscure, that the biographers have exploded all notions of sturdy
simplicity. What they have shown past any shadow of doubt is that
Hardy on the contrary was a remarkably devious and tortuous man—just
the sort of man who would at once convey and cloak his meanings with
the allusive deviousness that I have been trying to demonstrate.

Even so, it is almost comically disconcerting that the past master we
discern behind Hardy should turn out to be, of all people, Virgil. The idea
of a Virgilian Hardy will not be readily or willingly entertained; it crosses
too many wires, muddles too many of the alignments and counter-
alignments that nowadays the studious reader clings to, in order to orient
himself in the landscape of his reading. What! Hardy a Virgilian, he who
was an admired eminence for two of our most redoubtable and influential deriders of Virgil's pretensions, Robert Graves and Ezra Pound?
Hardy, who was singled out for untypically ferocious dismissal by Eliot,
Virgil's eloquent champion? And any way, isn't Tennyson, by common
consent and for good or ill, the English Virgil *par excellence*? And isn't
Hardy's Victorian allegiance quite conspicuously *not* to Tennyson, but
to Browning?

So we could go on. But the case, all the same, is clear. From Ford's
account of Hardy quoting at him from *Aeneid* Book ii, through the characteristically laconic but repeated references to Virgil in the ghosted

autobiography (Florence Emily's *Life*), there is sufficient evidence to support what the writings themselves prove—that Virgil was one writer from the past who was never far out of Hardy's mind. Improbably, it is the Public Orator of the University of Oxford who is in some sort vindicated. For the Orator in 1920, A. D. Godley, when presenting Hardy for an honorary degree, suggested: *Scilicet ut Virgilio nostro sic huic quoque 'molle atque facetum adnuerunt gaudentes rure Comenae'*. Perhaps what is most telling about this is that the author of the *Life*, that is to say Hardy himself in disguise, opens his chapter XXVI by quoting this, and obligingly provides a translation: 'Surely as with Virgil, so with him, have the Muses that rejoice in the countryside approved his smoothness and elegance.' If we balk at attributing smoothness and (of all things) elegance to Hardy, it may be because we have a too impoverished conception of elegance. More certainly, we have a drastically impoverished idea of Virgil if we think *his* elegance lies wholly within the compass of Tennyson.

Moreover, if for a moment we stop thinking about style, and lean back from the open page so as to think of Virgil as a whole, of Hardy as a whole, of the two personalities, their patterns of interest and allegiance, we can easily find so much in common between them that it becomes natural—it becomes, indeed, almost inevitable—that the modern poet should have responded intimately and keenly to the ancient one. To begin with, the Mantuan Virgil was, as everyone knows, profoundly a countryman and a provincial—as Hardy was. Bonstetten was the first to demonstrate that Virgil was moreover, in the late books of the *Aeneid*, a very scrupulous topographer—as was, of course, the writer who mapped 'Wessex'. Again, Virgil was in his time a devoted antiquarian and folklorist, almost indeed an anthropologist. G. M. Young remarked that, 'if you had asked a Roman what struck him most in Virgil he might have replied, "His profound knowledge of Italian antiquity".' (Italian, as against Roman.) And is that not what an Englishman of Hardy's day might have noticed first, about a writer who thought it no ignominious motive for either poem or story that it should commemorate a custom still remembered though no longer practised, or an episode only orally recorded? To abstract still further, to the point where one can talk of the cast of a temperament, who does not know that the cast of Virgil's temperament was melancholy? And what a difference it would make if, instead of arguing whether or not Hardy was 'pessimistic', we could agree that he was congenitally melancholy! (Some of Hardy's own exasperated impatience with the label 'pessimist' seems to point this way.) Finally, G. M. Young sees Virgil as 'too philosophic to believe in the gods and too Italian to do without them'; (9) and does this not correspond to Hardy's position, non-Christian since the 1870s but throughout (as he testified himself, and as many a poem like 'The Oxen' is there to show) indelibly 'churchy'? All in all, there is quite enough of a 'rhyme in history' between Virgil's situation and Hardy's for the one to have served as paradigm for the other.

III

My story has an unhappy ending. For Hardy could not leave alone the 'Poems of 1912-13' as he had them in *Satires of Circumstance*. For the *Collected Poems* of 1919 he pulled in to the end of the sequence three additional poems; and this sequence of twenty-one poems, not the original eighteen, is what we now understand as 'Poems of 1912-13'. Henry Gifford has remarked that this extension of the sequence 'destroys the remarkable unity of Hardy's earlier design'. It certainly does. The first of the added poems, 'The Spell of the Rose', introduces the note of remorse that had been excluded, for good and necessary reason, from the original sequence. The second, 'St Launce's Revisited', recalls the Cornish landscape of constancy, only to deny it with a snarl:

> Why waste thought,
> When I know them vanished
> Under earth; yea, banished
> Ever into nought!

And with the third and last, 'Where the Picnic Was', the best we can do is take some melancholy satisfaction in having J. O. Bailey show us that its landscape is not, as Carl Weber thought, Cornwall, but—appropriately enough for the spiritual inertness with which it brings the extended sequence to a close—the landscape of betrayal and cold distrust, in Dorset.

It is from the perspective of 'Where the Picnic Was' that J. Hillis Miller is able to detect

> the poet's gradual recognition, recorded explicitly in 'At Castle Boterel' and 'The Phantom Horsewoman', that Emma exists not as an objective ghost which any man might see, but in the poet's mind. Though the 'primeval rocks' by a certain roadside record in their color and shape the fact that he and his lady passed there one March night long ago, this imprint of the transitory on the permanent is visible only 'to one mind', the mind of the poet in whose vision 'one phantom figure/ Remains on the slope', though time, 'in mindless rote', has long since obliterated the reality. (10)

As should be clear from some of my earlier comments, I repudiate such a reading totally, and with a sort of fury. What is more to the point is that the poem itself repudiates the parody thus foisted upon it:

> It filled but a minute. But was there ever
> A time of such quality, since or before,
> In that hill's story? To one mind never,
> Though it has been climbed, foot-swift, foot-sore,
> By thousands more.

> Primaeval rocks form the road's steep border,
> And much have they faced there, first and last,
> Of the transitory in Earth's long order;
> But what they record in colour and cast
> Is—that we two passed.

And to me, though Time's unflinching rigour,
   In mindless rote, has ruled from sight
The substance now, one phantom figure
   Remains on the slope, as when that night
      Saw us alight.

I look and see it there, shrinking, shrinking,
   I look back at it amid the rain
For the very last time; my sand is sinking,
   And I shall traverse old love's domain
      Never again.

The crucial word is 'quality'—'a time of such *quality*'. For the qualitative
has no existence outside of a mind that registers it. And quality is therefore invulnerable to time, since the 'rote' by which Time works is mindless. (All that time can destroy is 'substance'—a philosophical word to set
against the other philosophical word, 'quality'.) Miller with bland audacity writes a minus for every plus in the poem, and a plus for every minus.
When he speaks of 'this imprint of the transitory on the permanent', he
takes as self-evidently transitory what the poem declares is permanent—
that is, quality; and he takes as permanent what the poem thinks of as
comparatively transient—that is to say, the primeval rocks, long-lasting
though they are. 'Well, but' (I hear the protests) 'what happens to the
quality when the one mind has gone, in which alone it had existence?
What happens to it when Hardy is dead?' Who shall say? It's at this point
that everything hinges on whether the reality that Hardy explores is psychological merely, or metaphysical. If Hardy is concerned only with
psychological reality, as Miller and most other readers assume, then he is
saying only that he will remember Emma, and the quality of this moment
he shared with her, until the day he dies. Which is touching; but hardly
worth saying at such length. But if the 'time of such quality' persists indestructible in a metaphysical reality, then it is *truly* indestructible—
because a man's mind survives the death of his body, or because quality
exists as perceived by a Divine Mind, or . . . The poet does not have to
decide these matters; he does not have to decide the mode in which the
quality will persist after his death, it is enough for him to affirm his
conviction that persist it will. And here, as I read the poem ('The Phantom Horsewoman' also), Hardy makes that affirmation. My reading of
'At Castle Boterel' makes it a much more Virgilian poem, and a much
greater one.

   The pity is that Hardy, by adding on 'The Spell of the Rose' and 'St
Launce's Revisited' and 'Where the Picnic Was', himself psychologizes his
own metaphysical insights, and so invites the sort of reading that Miller
gives to 'At Castle Boterel'. It is as if, in the interim between *Satires of
Circumstance* and *Collected Poems*, Hardy had remembered that he did
not traffic in spiritual or metaphysical realities because he did not believe in them. That means that he did not believe in them *even though he*

had experienced them; and that he pulled in the three extra poems so as to deny his own experience, to persuade himself and others that the experience had not happened.

This is an ugly imputation. (I must confess to finding it much uglier than the imputations of imperial time-serving that are cast at Virgil by Robert Graves and others.) But Hardy did not always live up to his vocation and his gifts; amid the deviousness of this devious man there was at times a capacity for selling short, for reneguing and defensive small-mindedness. In such a case we have the duty to save the works in which he lives up to his genius from the others in which he does not. 'At Castle Boterel' seems to me one of many works by Hardy that have this claim upon us; 'Beeny Cliff' is another.

Postscript: One thing that excited me in this investigation was the proof it seemed to give, that Hardy at his best proceeded in a way not wholly different from Pound's way, or Joyce's, or (I could have added) Eliot's. But in the years since, the sudden spate of books and essays about Hardy's poetry seems for the most part still impelled by a wish to prove that Hardy provides a viable insular alternative to the international 'modern movement'. I am quite out of sympathy with that sort of endeavour.

THE CANTOS: TOWARDS A PEDESTRIAN READING

POUND APPEARS the most crucial case, at least among poets writing in English, of those whose poetry—for those who value it—has to survive a self-evidently and perilously wrong understanding of history, and hence of politics. And yet, as may be seen from the cardinal importance he attaches to a Herodotean term like the *periplus*, Pound can be invoked by poets for whom the natural subject-matter is topographical rather than historical, or at any rate historical only so far as history is checked against, and embodied in, and qualified by, topography. This indeed is the burden of Pound's own poem, 'Near Perigord', which argues that the puzzle of a particular poem by Bertrand de Born—a historian's puzzle about the reasons for certain historically recorded events—is to be solved only by realizing the strategic implications of the location of Born's own fortress of Hautefort. At a time when Pound was principally a student of Provençal poetry, he appears to have been as good as his word, and to have travelled on foot over the terrain in question. This seems to have been, at least in part, the motive behind a walking-tour which Pound took in 1911, of which we learn in chapter 16 of his *Guide to Kulchur*, written twenty years later: (1)

> If a man can't afford to go by automobile, and if he is content with eating and architecture, the world's best (as I have known it) is afoot from Poitiers, from Brives, from Perigord or Limoges. In every town a romanesque church or chateau. No place to stay for any time, but food every ten miles or fifteen or twenty. When I say food, I mean food. So, at any rate, was it. With fit track to walk on.

This experience is referred to many times in the Cantos:

> The valley is thick with leaves, with leaves, the trees,
> The sunlight glitters, glitters a-top,
> Like a fish-scale roof,
> > Like the church roof in Poictiers
> If it were gold.   (4/14:18)

And a quarter-century later, in the Pisan cantos, when the poet is imprisoned in the American Army detention-camp at Pisa, these are among the memories which come back to him most poignantly. In Canto 74 for instance, there are lines which allude to the Magdalenian cave-paintings discovered at Lascaux and elsewhere in this region of Perigord and Limousin:

> and at Limoges the young salesman
> bowed with such french politeness 'No that is impossible'
> I have forgotten which city
> But the caverns are less enchanting to the unskilled explorer
> > than the Urochs as shown on the postals,
> we will see those old roads again, question,
> > > possibly
> but nothing appears much less likely   (74/428:455)

And in Canto 76, altogether more plangently:

But to set here the roads of France,
   of Cahors, of Chalus,
  the inn low by the river's edge,
the poplars; to set here the roads of France
Aubeterre, the quarried stone beyond Poitiers (76/455:482)

It seems to have been this last line which caused the editors of the *Anno-tated Index to the Cantos of Ezra Pound* to provide one of the few pieces of misinformation in that admirable work. For they give, against 'Aube-terre', 'A church just outside Poitiers, France'. (2) In fact the Aubeterre that Pound means is Aubeterre-sur-Dronne, not in Poitou at all but south-ward, in Perigord. The proof is in the very beautiful early poem, 'Provincia Deserta':

At Chalais
 is a pleached arbour;
Old pensioners and old protected women
Have a right there—
  it is charity.
I have crept over old rafters,
  peering down
Over the Dronne,
  over a stream full of lilies.
Eastward the road lies,
 Aubeterre is eastward,
With a garrulous old man at the inn.
I know the roads in that place:
Mareuil to the north-east,
 La Tour,
There are three keeps near Mareuil,
And an old woman,
  glad to hear Arnaut,
Glad to lend one dry clothing.

Anyone who opens before him Carte Michelin No. 75, can see the places named, related just as Pound says: Chalais, on the main line from Paris to Bordeaux; Aubeterre in the valley of the Dronne, twelve kilometres to the east; then thirty kilometres north-eastward a little place called La Tour Blanche; and perhaps fifteen kilometres further, just on the edge of the map, Vieux-Mareuil. The Michelin guide to Perigord will reveal a castle either preserved or in ruins at each of these places, though one would need to go off the map to Mareuil-sur-Belle, as well as Vieux-Mareuil, to identify all the three donjons which Pound speaks of in that vicinity. Equally, one needs to have walked these roads one's self if one is to locate 'the inn low by the river's edge'. That inn is what Pound always remembers of Aubeterre, for instance in Canto 80:

and at Ventadour and at Aubeterre
or where they set tables down by small rivers,
and the stream's edge is lost in grass. (80/509:544)

And yet that inn, the Hotel de Perigord, being set down by the Dronne, is on the outskirts of Aubeterre. For Aubeterre is a hill-town, set on a chalky cliff above the river (whence the name—Aubeterre, Alba Terra). I suspect that Pound never went further into Aubeterre than this inn, and one needs to have walked in his footsteps from Chalais to Aubeterre to see how he could well have done this, skirting the hill, stopping for perhaps a mid-day meal in the inn, and then pushing on at once for La Tour Blanche. If he did this, Pound missed a great deal, for Aubeterre is one of the most beautiful and delightfully peaceful places in the whole of old Aquitaine. (In the days of Bertrand de Born, Aquitaine of course was a province of the English crown; Eleanor of Aquitaine, the princess whose marriage to an English King brought this about, is one of the *femmes fatales* of the Cantos; and Richard Coeur de Lion, trying to make good his claim to all this part of France, was killed at Chalus—a place in this area to which the Cantos refer repeatedly in connection with the King's death.)

If Pound in this way did bypass Aubeterre, he missed something after his own heart. For one of the curiosities of Aubeterre is a church in the form of an artificial cave hewn in the face of the chalk cliff. The Michelin Guide to the *Côte de l'Atlantique* says that this eerie and impressive cavern, which communicates by a passage through the cliff to the château on the summit, was probably made in the twelfth century to shelter relics of the Holy Sepulchre at Jerusalem brought back from a Crusade by Pierre II of Castillon, who at that time held the château. Now Pound has interested himself a great deal in the order of the Templars, to which Pierre of Castillon belonged. In fact it is the Templars, some of whose ritual survives in the practices of modern Freemasonry, who account for Pound's interest in Poitiers, one of their principal centres. In the thirteenth century the king of France, abetted by a weak Pope, very brutally suppressed the Order of Templars and appropriated their enormous wealth. The Grandmaster of the Order at this time was Jacques de Molay. And that name, Jacques de Molay, is evoked by Yeats in section VII of his 'Meditations in Time of Civil War':

'Vengeance upon the murderers', the cry goes up,
'Vengeance for Jacques Molay'. In cloud-pale rags, or in lace,
The rage-driven, rage-tormented, and rage-hungry troop,
Trooper belabouring trooper, biting at arm or at face,
Plunges towards nothing, arms and fingers spreading wide
For the embrace of nothing; and I, my wits astray
Because of all that senseless tumult, all but cried
For vengeance on the murderers of Jacques Molay.

Yeats learned about Jacques de Molay in Thomas Wright's *Narratives of Sorcery and Magic* (1851). Pound's source on the other hand was almost certainly chapter 6 of *The Law of Civilization and Decay* (1896) by Brooks Adams, Henry Adams's brother. In Canto 90 we read:

to the room in Poitiers where one can stand
casting no shadow,

> That is Sagetrieb,
>> that is tradition.
> Builders had kept the proportion,
>> did Jacques de Molay
>>> know these proportions?
> and was Erigena ours?

Mr Noel Stock, who speaks as one who had Pound's confidence in recent years and was in daily contact with him, explains that this passage derives from a hint thrown out by Jessie L. Weston in her *From Ritual to Romance*, to the effect that the charges of heresy brought against the Templars were not wholly unfounded, since some of the practices of the Eleusinian mystery-cults from the Pagan Near East survived in the heart of Christendom in the rituals of the Templars, a survival to be traced in literature in the stories and poems about the quest of the holy grail. (3) *From Ritual to Romance* came out in 1920, and was a new book when T. S. Eliot borrowed from it for *The Waste Land*, thus making it permanently famous; Pound could not have known of it in 1911, but if he had then visited the Templars' cavern-church in Aubeterre he could hardly have failed to remember it in the light of Jessie Weston's argument. Certainly, in recent years Pound's interest in the mystery-cults has been more than antiquarian; in 'was Erigena ours?' he asks whether the philosopher Scotus Erigena was one of the Eleusinian brotherhood, and 'ours' can be given full weight—Noel Stock goes so far as to claim (op. cit. p. 22) that some of the obscurity of these later Cantos is deliberate and arcane—'he writes about them as an initiate in words that are both "published and not published" . . .'

Fascinating as this is, it is surely with relief that we return from thus checking printed source against printed source, cross-referring and tentatively identifying, to the open air of 'the roads of France'. And indeed I would insist on this: the first requirement for a study of Pound is a set of maps (preferably ½" to the mile) of at any rate certain regions of France, Italy and England; the second requirement is a set of Michelin Green Guides for France and Italy, and (if one is American) similar guides to the South of England. In this, the case of Pound is no different from other writers, or it is different only in degree. Yet, oddly, the only authors for whom we are ready to make this provision nowadays are the Irish ones, Joyce and Yeats. Everyone knows that a Street Directory of Dublin is essential to the reading of Joyce. There would be general agreement that maps of County Sligo and County Galway are essential aids to the study of Yeats. And perhaps most people qualified to judge would concede that there comes a time early in any study of Joyce where the student has to beat the Dublin streets on foot. Similarly no one who has attended the Yeats Summer School in Sligo will deny that the seminars and lectures are less profitable than driving to Glencar, or Gort, and walking in those places, or wandering in the demesne of Lissadell and under the shoulder of Ben Bulben. And yet we are shamefaced about this.

It smacks of the Dickensian Society making pilgrimages to Rochester and Dover and Yarmouth; or of 'poetry-lovers' haunting Grasmere and Coniston Water. Perhaps it does. But I incline to think that our grandfathers and grandmothers were in the right of it, and that no one can claim to understand Wordsworth who has not been to Hawkshead and Ambleside. The reason why we are embarrassed to admit this is that we have lived in an age when the self-sufficiency, the autonomy of poems has been elevated into dogma. Poems *can* be self-sufficient, leaning on no reality outside themselves other than the history and usage of the words out of which they are made. But in every age there have been poets who were uninterested in thus cutting their poems free of any but a linguistic reality, poets who are 'realistic' and 'mimetic' in the most straightforward senses of those two complicated words. In our age Pound, far more than Eliot or Yeats, is such a poet. And yet we have seen that the topography of Sligo (to which one should add the topography of at least one part of London, Bedford Park) is illuminating for the reader of Yeats. And who is to say that the topography of the village of East Coker is unimportant to a reading of Eliot's *Four Quartets*? And yet how few of us have made that pilgrimage!

Chalais and Aubeterre figure at least once in the Cantos that Pound has written more recently. In Canto 101, which was published in the volume *Thrones* (1960), we read:

> Finding scarcely anyone save Monsieur de Rémusat
>   who could understand him
> (junipers, south side) M. Talleyrand
>   spruce and fir take the North
> Chalais, Aubeterre
>   snow-flakes at a hand's breadth, and rain.
> Trees line the banks, mostly willows.   (101/723:75)

Here only the place-names refer to France; the junipers, the spruce and fir, and the falling snow are taken over by Pound from a landscape at the other side of the world. So are 'the willows'. (4) What is amusing and significant about this latest reference to 'the roads of France' is the name of Talleyrand. For Charles Maurice de Talleyrand-Perigord, Bonaparte's grand chamberlain, is one of several new heroes who have appeared in the Cantos written since 1945. He appears once or twice in earlier cantos, but not flatteringly; whereas in Canto 105 for instance we are told, by no means persuasively:

>   Talleyrand saved Europe for a century
> France betrayed Talleyrand;
>   Germany, Bismarck.
> And Muss saved, rem salvavit,
>   in Spain
>   il salvabile.   (105/746:98)

('Muss' is Mussolini.) Now, the Talleyrand-Perigords have, as their name implies, been mighty lords in Perigord since the early Middle Ages, and in the early poem 'Near Perigord' Talleyrand is one of the powerful and menacing neighbours whom Bertrand de Born has to play off one against another, thus earning (so Pound's poem suggests) the title which Dante gives him in the *Inferno*, 'sower of strife'. The château of Chalais has been a stronghold of the Talleyrands from that day to this, and when Pound in recent years read about Napoleon's grand chamberlain, notably in the memoirs of Madame de Rémusat (a principal source for Canto 101), (5) this new association with Chalais re-activated his memories of that place, which accordingly is named afresh, bringing 'Aubeterre' with it, but in a quite different tone and spirit from 'to set here the roads of France'. The trees that 'line the banks, mostly willows' are still there, and there are places in the town of Chalais crouched underneath its château, where Pound might still creep over old rafters in search of 'a stream full of lilies'. Pound seems to have misremembered however, for at Chalais the river is not the Dronne but a smaller stream, the Tude. And although the Tude has plants in its waters, I am reluctant to believe that any of them are lilies; for Chalais has suffered from the twentieth century as Aubeterre has not, and the Tude is polluted whereas the Dronne runs clear.

Already in 1915 Pound was making this mistake about the rivers, for in 'Near Perigord', which he published in that year, he declares:

> Chalais is high, a-level with the poplars.
> Its lowest stones just meet the valley tips
> Where the low Dronne is filled with water-lilies.

A map could have put Pound right, as it can put us right. But no map, nor guide book either, can vindicate for us, 'Chalais is high, a-level with the poplars'. To confirm this we have to pause and look back from the road to Aubeterre as it climbs the eastern slope of the valley of the Tude, just as Pound must have paused in 1911; and then we see that, whereas the modern town of Chalais is in the river bottom, old Chalais, a mano-rial village grouped round the gate of the château, does indeed stand on the ridge behind, so that the tops of the tallest poplars by the river wave just below the walls of the château.

Some poetry is 'true' in just this literal fashion. And in the case of a poet like Pound, who presses upon us as 'truths' so many readings of history which in fact are dangerous errors, truths like these are precious. To take one last example, when we read in Canto 101 (and many other places) about 'Mont Ségur', the gloss we need is in the Michelin Guide to the Pyrenees, where we learn that the Château of Mont Ségur saw the last stand of the Cathars or Albigensians, another heretical movement of the Middle Ages which is mysteriously connected with the quest of the grail. But I feel sure that only by going to St Bertrand de Comminges (another name that crops up in the Cantos), and from there to Mont Ségur, shall we see the point of: 'at Mont Ségur the chief's cell/you can enter it sideways only' (101/725:77). Place and the spirit of place is the inspiration of more poetry than we nowadays like to admit; and to do that poetry justice the critic needs to turn himself into a tourist.

THE RHETORIC OF EMOTION

SOMEWHERE, PERHAPS in many places, a distinction has been drawn between 'emotion' and 'feeling'. Certainly a distinction there is, and no very fine one. I find in myself, when I think of the verbal arts, a disposition to talk of 'feeling'. Who does not prefer 'feel' to the appalling verb, 'emote'? Not only is feeling anchored in the immediacy of sensuous apprehension, tactile in the first place; but also, because it can mean 'groping', it fits those artifacts that we want to applaud as 'sensitive', as (precisely) *tactful*. Either way, 'feeling', far more than 'emotion', reminds us that art is a matter of response, and of response not to etiolated 'stimuli' but to something as substantial, as intact in its own always surprising contours, as the pebble that a blind man's hand has picked up from the beach, and now explores in order to know. Just so, surely, does a good poem or story explore, respectfully and patiently, the somehow foreign body which has provoked it.

And so, if we turn now to 'emotion', we have to start by scotching some of the misapprehensions which the less satisfactory word brings with it. The first of these comes about because of the lack, in 'emotion', of that tentative exploratory character that we have just applauded in 'feeling'. Because of this lack there arises the misapprehension that, other things being equal, a poem or story will be better if the emotion which it embodies or controls or conveys is strong, is powerful, is intense, is overmastering (for the reader, if not for the writer). 'Feeling' shows, or it ought to show, that this is not true; and this misapprehension darkens counsel and indeed experience to the point where we cannot distinguish between disturbed and alerted emotion on the one hand, and jangled nerves on the other. 'Emotion', unlike 'feeling', provides no safeguards against sensationalism—against, that is, the intense though mostly shallow experiences which, outside of art, make us vomit or put us in a state of shock. And sure enough, do we not commonly hear pieces of literature applauded because, so it is said, the emotions which they convey are 'visceral'?

Another misapprehension we have come across already; the reader who thinks about literature by way of emotion rather than feeling is likely to deny or ignore the fact that the provocation for a poem or a story comes to the artist always 'from outside'. At least in some cases, such a reader will argue, the artefact is self-generated out of some need or impulse in the consciousness of its creator. If we want to deny this, we do not have to espouse some literary equivalent of representationalism; we do not have to assert that every poem or story has 'a subject', though of course most of them do. 'Subject' is not the point. For in literature one element is *always* foreign to the writer when he begins writing, as to the reader when he begins reading or the listener who begins listening; it is language, the medium itself. There are very many bad poems and stories, and a few very good ones, in which the emotion expressed or conveyed is predominantly or even exclusively provoked by and responsive to the medium itself, sounds and meanings and their interactions. The possibility of this is allowed for when we speak of 'feeling', but only distractingly and with difficulty when we speak of 'emotion'.

This thinning-out of the artistic medium, to the point where as an independent entity in the artistic transaction it virtually evaporates from the reader's mind, is a danger whenever we approach art with expectations of 'emotion'; but it becomes all but inevitable when we couple emotion with rhetoric as I have done in my title. For 'rhetoric', though it has other more recondite meanings, is centrally and normally apprehended in literary theory as a set of coded signals sent by speaker to auditor, hence by writer to reader, to cue the hearer or the reader into . . . into what? In the strictest theories of rhetoric the hearer was to be *persuaded*; that is, he was to be induced or compelled to a conviction, and ideally into a conviction that would issue in a course of action. But conviction is different from assent, just as rhetoric is different from logic. Conviction is assent plus emotion, and the emotion is provoked in the hearers by the speaker, who inflames for instance their indignation so as to set their feet running and their fists clenching as they rush away into action, snatching up stones as they go.

Thus the orator works by provoking and inflaming emotion. But the signals which he makes are cues not to emotion but to action. The emotion is the means to that active end; and for the transaction to be most effective, the auditor should be aware of being impelled to a conviction which must issue in action, not at all of being inflamed into a state of emotion. In rhetorical art on the other hand, though the theory often maintains the pretence (for instance, in theories of satire) that action is the end, in practice the emotional inflammation is the end aimed at by poet and reader alike. Thus in rhetorical literature the signals are cues not to action but emotion; and since the audience, if it is at all sophisticated, recognizes these as the terms of the contract, there is an unpleasant flavour of masturbation about the whole transaction. 'Oh', says the compliant reader, 'he wants me to feel indignant, does he? Very well, I think I can manage that.' And he duly manipulates himself into the state required of him. Getting the cues and responding to them is what such a reader understands as experiencing literature; and he finds it enjoyable, since he is getting something for nothing. He experiences emotion without having to suffer its occasion or act upon its prompting.

Whether from distaste at this or for other reasons, responsible English writers both in theory and practice abandoned this rhetorical art a long time ago. For the poets it was relatively easy to do so, and they made the renunciation early; certainly the young Wordsworth is already a poet of feeling, not a rhetorical manipulator of readers' emotions. For storytellers, for a Dickens or a Thackeray, so much more hopeful of and dependent upon a large public, it was harder—and in both these writers, as is generally conceded, pages of feeling and pages of rhetoric lie side by side. In English verse however it might be maintained that Thomas Gray was the last serious and greatly gifted poet to practise a rhetorical art. (And it needs to be said that rhetorical art can be great art—for the 'Elegy' is rhetorical in its own way no less than Gray's Pindaric Odes.)

Yet the readers of English poets of today—our critics and also, most plainly and damagingly, our educators—still act as if poetry were a rhetorical art, and approach Roy Fisher as if he were Thomas Gray. Our schoolchildren are trained to read poems as if they were coded signals giving them cues about what and how to feel. The reader looks at the poem published yesterday to see what signals the poet is sending him, whereas the poet if he is any good is not flying any signals at all but feeling his way into or around a fragment of life. The reader may listen in if he wants to, but he is not being addressed. Of course if he attends closely he in effect enlists in the exploring expedition, and can partake of the discovery that is made. For instance: 'The wan moon is setting behind the white wave,/And Time is setting with me, oh.' If Burns in these lines is flying rhetorical signals, he is using a code which has been cracked too many times for the addressee of 1972 to trust it; unless he is unsophisticated, that reader will be unwilling, if not indeed unable, to comply with what seems to be the directive thus signalled, unable to drum up in himself the passionate wistfulness that seems to be asked for. But suppose there is no addressee? Yeats supposed there was not, saying of these lines:

> Take from them the whiteness of the moon and of the wave, whose relation to the setting of Time is too subtle for the intellect, and you take from them their beauty. But, when all are together, moon and wave and whiteness and setting Time and the last melancholy cry, they evoke an emotion which cannot be evoked by any other arrangement of colours and sounds and forms.

An emotion, Yeats acknowledges, is evoked—but not to the end that members of Burns's public shall eat their emotions' cake and have it, but to the end that a certain pattern of relationships may be explored and known, a pattern which, since it is 'too subtle for the intellect', can be explored only through emotion and known only *as* emotion.

Thus what looked like an all too recognizable signal, that 'oh' which Yeats called a 'melancholy cry', is not a signal to the reader at all. The same threadbare flag may have been flown as a signal by poorer and more vulgar writers than Burns, but when Burns hoists it, it signals nothing but itself. And so its being threadbare does not matter.

Many complications remain. For it may indeed be true that it is two hundred years since a poem in English could be both rhetorical and great. But throughout that period inferior poems have been rhetorical, or they have been nothing. Mostly they have been nothing, of no account one way or the other. But some of Swinburne, much of Kipling, most of Rupert Brooke—this is poetry which has flown its rhetorical signals very clearly and vividly; and the signals have been read and complied with, eagerly, by thousands on thousands. Why not? I call such poetry inferior—

inferior in kind; but certainly not shameful, not (in any sense that matters) depraved or depraving. Poetry comes in kinds, and some kinds are inferior to others.

The trouble is—and how often one has heard it said!—that the bad drives out the good, the inferior shoulders aside the better. And this too may be misunderstood. One does not mean that thousands have been reading Kipling when they ought to have read Hardy, Rupert Brooke when they ought to have read Edward Thomas. What happens is more complicated. Because, as we saw with the distich of Burns, rhetorical and non-rhetorical poems fly the same flags (words and arrangements of words), non-rhetorical poets can be, and most often are, read as if they were rhetoricians. They can be made to seem to be sending signals when they are doing nothing of the sort. A kind of directive, even, can be decoded from them—though not of course anything like so clear and ringing a directive as those of the rhetoricians; and so Hardy's 'Channel Firing' might be read, and doubtless has been, as a creditable but muffled attempt at what the war-poems of Kipling did better.

And so, through one generation after another in the present century, serious poets can be seen going to very great lengths indeed to advertise that they are not rhetoricians, and for their pains either finding themselves unread or else transformed by the public into rhetoricians after all. T. S. Eliot insisted time and again that *The Waste Land* was not a directive to the reader to feel thus and thus about the twentieth century. (Pound's *Cantos* in large part was; but Pound broke the other half of the rhetorical artist's contract by insisting that the feelings 'drive through to action'.) Hardy in baffled fury insisted time and again that his poetry was not a directive to feel thus and thus (rancorously, bitterly) about the Universe. It was all to no avail. And yet the poets' remonstrances were not merely in what they said about their poems, they were *inside* the poems. For the grotesque corrugations of Hardy's diction, the discontinuities of Eliot, were surely intended to advertise: 'No signals are being sent.' It was all no use; signals were somehow received and read, and in the end in many quarters cherished all the more for having been so hard to decode and misconstrue. The public had to treat these poems as signals in code, because that was the only way that the public knew, or was ever told, about how to treat any poetry at all.

So insecure is a man's sense of himself, so threatened does he feel if he is overlooked or merely tolerated rather than directly addressed, that many or most of us will twist and turn with unflagging energy and resourcefulness, rather than admit to having been present at certain transactions to which our presence or absence was a matter of indifference. Nothing else can explain our tenacity when we seek to transform the transactions of art into transactions of rhetoric. The same logic operates not only *in* Freudian thought, but behind it and beneath it: 'If she abuses me to my face, that shows she cares about me . . .'; 'He so conspicuously takes no notice of me that he must be acutely aware of me . . .'

Just as hate thus becomes the mirror-image of love, unconcern of concern, so an addiction to rhetoric creates, or at least welcomes and eagerly
accommodates, anti-rhetoric. The haughtier the artist, the more we love
him, the more eagerly do we apply ourselves to show that his hauteur
towards us is only the mirror-image of his needing us. I do not know how
else to explain what is surely one of the most extraordinary manifestations
of Anglo-American culture over the last fifty years—the way in which
Joyce and Pound and Yeats, the artists who with most conspicuous hauteur rejected our culture, have become its darlings, instituted as such aca-
demically. Somewhere surely, in someone's breast, there is a triumph of
revenge: 'Ah, so you thought you'd got away, did you? On the contrary
every struggle you make to escape our nets only limes you in them more
securely!'

Of course this is only a particular instance of a general phenomenon:
the effectiveness with which the packaging industries have taken over and
familiarized, from the literary arts as from others, stylistic dispositions
that were meant to preclude any packaging at all. For some years now,
for instance, some British poets have been practising an anti-rhetoric of
pregnant terseness. But this will not save them; Leonard Cohen has been
writing *haiku* for years. Turn and twist as he may, nowadays the serious
artist feels the rhetorician's breath hot at his heels, more pressingly than
ever before. And this is a creeping disease: not only has the writer failed
up to now to find an anti-rhetoric that is really prophylactic, one that
cannot be construed as the mirror-image of rhetoric, but the attempt to
find it has sapped and deflected the energies that should be directed in-
tently on his proper business. The search for devices that will *not* cue the
reader into having emotions is more exhausting and distracting than the
search for devices that *will*. And the energy that goes into such a search
is in the end inescapably rhetorical energy, rather than poetic. For an
anti-rhetoric *is* a rhetoric; the would-be transparent envelope is a specially sophisticated sort of packaging.

This throws a new and topical light, for instance, on Pound's celebrated
remark about free verse—that 'no verse is really free for the man who
wants to do a good job'. This can still mean what Pound intended to convey—that a writer who casts free of the crutch of metre has to be that
much more attentive to the rhythms that he can summon up to sound in
his inner ear. But in the understanding of the public, one of the things
that free verse claimed to be free from was rhetoric; from that point of
view, free verse was an anti-rhetoric in itself. And now that there is no
excuse for not realizing that anti-rhetoric is rhetoric in mirrored reverse,
free verse has to be seen to be a convention as constricting (though also
as liberating) as the iambic pentameter it was once intended to supplant.
Poets will continue to practise free verse, but there is no excuse for their
doing so in the spirit of D. H. Lawrence, who thought that by doing so he
had escaped all the fowlers' nets of rhetoric.

What seems more likely, however, and more promising, is a rediscovery by poets of the usefulness of the iambic pentameter and other metrical forms—not in the casually loosened versions that have been practised for years by Philip Larkin and others, but in all their traditional rigour. For the prophylactic against rhetoric which promises most nowadays is likely to be not avant garde but quite the reverse. There is for instance Thom Gunn's, in 'Moly':

> Oh a man's flesh already is in mine.
> Hand and foot poised for risk. Buried in swine,
>
> I root and root, you think that it is greed.
> It is, but I seek out a plant I need.
>
> Direct me gods, whose changes are all holy,
> To where it flickers deep in grass, the moly.

Far more than any avant-garde tersenesses or discontinuities, Gunn's metre and his rhymes, so determined to draw attention to themselves, deter the reader who wants poetry to cue him how to feel. And the cries of injured frustration which greeted the collection, *Moly*, show that in the short run Gunn has succeeded. 'Without exception', declared one reviewer, 'the Moly poems are dead'—dead, that is (so we may infer) to the presence of this reader, who was waiting to be 'moved'. Trying again, the reviewer (it was Michael Fried) expostulated: 'Their failure is not essentially a feature of tone. They do not *smell*.' Did Sidney's poetry 'smell'? Did Shakespeare's, in those scenes of *A Midsummer Night's Dream*, where the rhymes are as clangingly obtrusive as Gunn's on 'holy' and 'moly'? The art that refuses to conceal itself runs an insurmountable wire fence between itself and the reader; the reader may look through the wire mesh, but he cannot join in, except by the exercise of a sympathetic imagination. He cannot smell what is going on; he can only see it. And that is an affront that the reader finds too gross to stomach, if he has been schooled in a rhetorical theory of literature so as to think that the writer's prime duty is to him, the reader, rather than to his own experience, his own subject.

Thom Gunn gives peculiar offence because the subjects that he treats with this aggravating coolness are precisely those which the modern reader supposes he has a special right to feel tempestuously or intensely about. All of *Moly* is concerned, in one way or another, with drug-taking. And when Gunn in another poem in *Moly* presents the spiel of a San Francisco drug-pusher in a form strikingly reminiscent of Herrick's 'Cherry Ripe' or Dowland's 'Fine Knacks for Ladies', what can he be implying, if not that this traffic, which has called up so much agitated emotion for and against, is no more sensational than the trade that was plied by many a Jacobean Autolycus? On grounds of private morality, of personal hygiene and civic order, we may or may not agree with him; but that is another question. By purely formal means, in particular by highly conscious use of one of those ready-made forms which vulgar modernism declared to be illegitimate and exploded, Gunn has presented for cool contemplation one 'burning topic' and one possible attitude towards it. And in doing so, *in order to do so*, he has avoided both rhetoric and the anti-rhetoric that is merely rhetoric inverted. We are not to 'feel'; we are, for a change, to think.

In Gunn's own development this represents—for him, and for us if we choose to follow him—a penetration behind the ambiguous and magnetic figure of John Donne, into the Renaissance poetic out of which Donne sprang, and from which he diverged. In particular it represents a creative penetration of Shakespeare. Does Shakespeare cue the playgoer how to feel about the spectacles he presents in *A Midsummer Night's Dream*, in *As You Like It*, in *Much Ado About Nothing*? Surely, after all that the commentators have pretended to the contrary, the very titles—together with many internal features—show that Shakespeare did no such thing; that with a smiling arrogance he refused to cue our emotions, and threw his refusal in the playgoers' faces. Dr Johnson, who preferred Shakespeare's comedies to his tragedies, did not feel affronted; but it seems that we do. And indeed our fussiness about 'tone' (most baleful and most insular of all I. A. Richards's bequests to us) reveals us as more locked into a rhetorical theory of literature than ever Dr Johnson was.

AN AMBITION BEYOND POETRY

Laura Riding, *Selected Poems: in Five Sets*, Faber.
Laura (Riding) Jackson, *The Telling*, Athlone Press.

CERTAIN THINGS poetry will not do for us. In every age before our own, including the heyday of the Romantic movement, only a minority, even among poets, have claimed that poetry could deliver us the certitudes and consolations of religion. The records of the Christian centuries are full of poets who put away poetry-making, along with other worldly vain-glories, when they turned their thoughts towards eternity and salvation.

Throughout those centuries it was taken for granted that poem-making, though a noble activity by the human scale, was still an activity of the fallen man; and hence that poetry's union of beauty with truth was, like everything else in fallen Nature, precarious and dissoluble. However, once Keats had declared 'Beauty is Truth, Truth Beauty', seeming to affirm an *indissoluble* unity, it was inevitable that sooner or later there would appear a poet who, having believed in Keats's assurance, would find that it didn't square with experience, and would be honest enough to say so. Laura Riding was that poet. She let it be known, in the years after her *Collected Poems* of 1938, that on these grounds she had abandoned poetry as inadequate to her ambitions and her hungers; and because she reached this decision in the midst of our present irreligious century, it seemed, to the few who cared, something unaccountable and bizarre.

If this poet was thus exceptionally brave and honest, she was also—it must appear—surprisingly ignorant, in the sense that her perspective on history was drastically foreshortened. For now that after more than thirty years she has allowed some of her poems to be reprinted, it seems that she believes herself to have taken a step quite literally unprecedented: 'No poet before me has gone to the very breaking-point: there is nothing in the poetic corpus to suggest the pertinence to poetry of a higher standard of scrupulosity than that observed in its historic best.' On the contrary, of course; the Chaucers and the Shakespeares and the George Herberts whom she seems to think she has outdistanced are repeatedly aware that poetry even at its best only gropes uncertainly for the truths which Scripture announces securely and boldly, which Christ and the saints embody in their merest gesture more compellingly than poetry can. It would be odd not to find the same or a similar attitude among the poets of Islam. And for her to make such a bald and seemingly groundless claim in the preface to her *Selected Poems* can only raise new difficulties for the reader of poems that are difficult enough anyhow.

However, an article by Michael Kirkham (in *The Cambridge Quarterly*, spring 1971) will be found helpful. Mr Kirkham's point, that 'the most striking quality of her poems is their treatment of reality in its general rather than its particular forms', ought to be set against her own testi-mony in the *TLS* (3 November 1972) that she objected to Norman Cameron's early poems, because in them 'the general was abstract, the

actual was instances which he tended to let go by without sense of any
general coherence of connexion between them'. Nevertheless Mr Kirkham seems right when he remarks 'there are no objects for their own sake
in her poetry, no specific occasions not raised to a general status'. He observes further that she 'has made little use . . . of the idioms and tones of
casual, everyday speech'; that this means that 'current fashions are
against her'; but that, on the other hand, 'though thought is concentrated,
diction is always plain'. Lastly—it is the finest of Mr Kirkham's formulations—'wit everywhere in her poetry is the extra-shine of lucidity as
thought is brought to a fine point of definition'.

If anyone thinks these are things one wants to say about any poet one
admires, he should think again. They point rather to poetry deliberately
written against the grain of the literary taste that has consolidated itself
in Anglo-American letters since the Imagist movement of sixty years ago;
such poetry, for instance, as that of the late Yvor Winters, champion of
'the plain style', whose career as rogue-elephant on the literary scene was
not wholly unlike Laura Riding's, though it is not apparent that either
of them ever noticed the other. Winters, too, an unbeliever pained by his
non-belief but firm in it, seemed at times to ask of poetry more certi-
tude than it is in the nature of poetry to give. Laura Riding comes near
to Winters in, for example, the fine second half of 'Death as Death':

> Like nothing—a similarity
> Without resemblance. The prophetic eye,
> Closing upon difficulty,
> Opens upon comparison,
> Halving the actuality
> As a gift too plain, for which
> Gratitude has no language,
> Foresight no vision.

But here, if on the one hand the idea of death as something to be joyously grateful for seems to be out of Winters's range (a sentiment not alien
to Christian understanding, which in Laura Riding's thought has great
importance—and poignancy also, for it seems to have been the death of
her husband five years ago which impelled her to break silence), on the
other hand her prosody here is typically unambitious and roomy, as for
Winters, schooled on Renaissance poetry, it never could be.

Mr Kirkham discusses the poem 'Afternoon':

> The fever of afternoon
> Is called afternoon,
> Old sleep uptorn,
> Not yet time for night-time,
> No other name, for no names
> In the afternoon but afternoon.
>
> Love tries to speak but sounds
> So close in its own ear.

The clock-ticks hear
The clock-ticks ticking back.
The fever fills where throats show,
But nothing in these horrors moves to swallow
While thirst trails afternoon
To husky sunset.

Evening appears with mouths
When afternoon can talk.
Supper and bed open and close
And love makes thinking dark.
More afternoons divide the night,
New sleep uptorn,
Wakeful suspension between dream and dream—
We never knew how long.
The sun is late by hours of soon and soon—
Then comes the quick fever, called day.
But the slow fever is called afternoon.

Mr Kirkham explains:

The concern with the possibilities of naming, speaking and thinking is central to the poem. The framing of a language expressive of life brought to finality would signify the speaker's presence to goodness; living within the fever of time, however, impedes speaking with such conclusiveness . . . A distinction is drawn between speaking and talking. 'Love tries to speak' the single speech of general truth, but cannot because its words' meanings in their range of reference do not break the boundaries of self. To 'talk' . . . is to 'speak mingled', to speak in the separateness of individuality, and not with the singleness of truth; thus, here, it is the plurality of 'mouths' that converts speech into talk and renders talking powerless to prevent the recurrence of time's fever.

But this, illuminating though it is, does not account for

The fever fills where throats show,
But nothing in these horrors moves to swallow
While thirst trails afternoon . . .

What are the horrors so confidently pointed to as 'these'? And what does it mean for 'throats' to 'show'? Do they, by croaking, or gasping, 'show' the thirst that they feel (presumably for 'the single speech of general truth')? Or do they 'show', as when scarves or mufflers are cast aside from them? In the second case the lines link up with nothing else in the poem (for unwinding a muffler can hardly stand for undressing before love-making). But if the first reading was intended, surely the *plain*, the unambiguous word would have been 'utter'. And in that case, why is 'show' there at all, if not for the ghostly rhyme with the unstressed syllable of 'swallow'? Once we look at the rhyming, which is sparse and irregular but needed to prepare for the fine full close (where the rhyme of the poem's last word with the 'soon and soon' of the pentameter has the effect of making the last line into a poignantly disturbed but recognizable pentameter also), we may ponder 'uptorn', making its half-rhyme with 'afternoon'. Is 'uptorn', rather than 'split across' or a dozen other possibilities, really the *plain* word for what happens when sleep is dispelled, whether by daybreak, by insomnia or by a lover's importunity? This is not to deride either the poem or Mr Kirkham's admiration of it. But it is to suggest that the poet needs to be a very sure craftsman before he can disdain mere craftsmanship as Mrs Jackson does. And indeed, admire the poems as one may and does (for instance, the splendid and serious and centrally important 'Auspice of Jewels') what can one do but carp when the poet herself introduces them with, 'I think poetry obstructs general attainment to something better in our linguistic way-of-life than we have'? When all Shakespeare and Dante are thus set at risk, we inevitably take offence at the presumption, and find ourselves asking the poet to meet standards such as no one should have to meet. She has raised the stakes so high that she has to lose.

Thus the preface to *Selected Poems* seems ill-advised, to say the least. And one must, in simple fairness, put the poems in the wider and more considered context of the volume called *The Telling*. This is not to be embarked upon lightly. At its most abstruse, *The Telling* is like this:

> In our various-being, one-being mounts to emergence from the ordeal of Difference called 'the universe'; and this now begins to be visible to us, though but faintly. And as a One of ourselves counters, in tremulous appearance, the ubiquitous one and one of oneselves, and the vision ghostlike bars the individual thought-way of each, our minds hark back, or will hark back, to the sheer one-being in which by our bodies' measure we were as not but in which by our minds' measure we have, or shall have, a mirror-presence.

More typical, however, and in happy contrast to the tone of the preface, is a disarming earnestness:

> That the subject of the creation should be so treated, without leave from the theologies or sciences or philosophies, and bare of the benefit of narrative symbolism and the decoration of known names, and the protection of a Name of names, may seem a rash simplicity to you who read here. However, I am not endeavouring to excite belief, or regale the reading imagination, only to tell what I find to see where my thought takes me.

Demanding as the writing is, indeed in large part just because it is so demanding, one comes to accept this protestation without question. Though Mrs Jackson can still say, 'my thought differs in the whole from that of any other contributor to the record of human thinking', the presence in and behind *The Telling* is not oracular, sybilline, but rather of one who pleads to be heard, asking, 'Please, is it not so with you also?' And many may find that from a firm if respectful, 'No, it is not', they come to say, 'Well, perhaps it is.'

For the volume is very winningly constructed. At first it seems to be a rag-bag: 'The Telling' proper, as it appeared first in the New York magazine *Chelsea* in 1967, consists of sixty-two numbered paragraphs; it is followed by a twenty-three-page 'Preface for a Second Reading'; and that in turn by sundry appendixes, including an essay, 'The Idea of Rebeginnings', 'Extracts from Communications', and 'Some Notes . . .' Only as we near the end of the book do names begin to appear—Plotinus, Teilhard de Chardin, Nietzsche, Spinoza, Eliot, Coleridge and Keats, Freud and Jung; and along with these come mostly tart comments on such topical matters as rock-music, faddish enthusiasms for Zen and Hinduism and 'myth', Black Power, theatrical 'happenings', and the surrender of pedagogical authority in American colleges. Thus instead of critique followed by 'constructive' alternative, we get the gospel first and instances of its application second. And this is as it should be. To reverse the order, so as to fall in with our expectations, would have excited resistance just as the unfortunate preface does; and it would have made of 'The Telling' itself precisely a theory or a system—not what it is, a gospel, a story that is told with no backing but personal testimony.

Because the testimony is personal, no circumstance of the person who tells it is irrelevant to it—certainly not the circumstance that the teller is a woman. It is there, in her being a woman, that Mrs Jackson locates her inability to embrace any instituted religion, despite the respectful tenderness that she has for the religious frame of mind. Her style, which seems nearer to Carlyle's or at times to Ruskin's than to any more recent writer's, rises to a moving eloquence when she considers what has been woman's attitude to the instituted religions, all of them cast too plainly (as she sees them) in a masculine mould. Her solid good sense is nowhere more evident than in thus holding fast to the heart of truth in the ideology of women's liberation, while disdaining Women's Liberation as a 'movement'.

Because it is a story that is told, not a theory that is expounded, there can be no question of summarizing it. If it were a theory one would describe it as 'Humanist'—the capital letter serving to distinguish it not just from atheism, but from the vulgar humanism that may be called 'humanitarian'. In the latter (not that Mrs Jackson thus names it) she sees 'a collective human self-understanding to which has been given the name "compassion".' It is, she says,

> a cruel elevation of pitiableness to admirableness, in which we hope for less, less, for one-another-all, to a degree of hopefulness so close to hopelessness that we do not hope—we have 'compassion' . . . The people fete upon banquets of commiseration with their 'condition' (of being human—as pure, essentially unalterable injustice), and ask for more, more.

For her the condition of being human is on the contrary astringent and strenuous—it is rich with possibility, since only in the human, nowhere else, can Being fulfil itself. This is traditional, most strikingly in that for her, as a student of language, the distinguishing badge of the human over the animal creation is the faculty of *speech*.

Yet here, still, one suspects a foreshortened perspective on human history. Does she know just *how* traditional she is? The noble and strenuous Humanism of the Renaissance (which is what she seems to have won through to) could live happily in and with the Christian dispensation. The Fall was not just accommodated by Renaissance Humanism, but essential to it. And, most interestingly, it is essential to Mrs Jackson too: 'The division became overt. How could this be! A flaw in Being? Yes, I think: . . . the flaw that it had not been tried in any test of it! . . . no other. Even perfection has need of truth—bears within it a need to prove itself to itself'. This seems to be the equivalent in her thought to what Christian philosophy understands by 'the Fall', and not the more natural human deficiency to which she later tries to apply the name. And it is what, later again, she describes as 'a comprehensive event of the order of division—a religious event, not an ethical one'. And thus, whereas in the preface she seems to despair of the poet for not being that impossibility, an unfallen creature, in 'The Telling' she allows that the poet, no less than the rest of humankind, is 'fallen'—a condition which does not, however (and here she is surely most right and timely), give him any excuse for lethargy or self-commiseration or making paltry demands of himself.

BRAVERIES ESCHEWED

George Oppen, *Seascape: Needle's Eye*, Sumac Press.

FOR US to come to terms with Oppen, the time has long gone by—if it ever existed—when it was useful to start plotting his place in a scheme of alternative or successive poetic 'schools' or 'traditions'. Imagism, objectivism, constructivism, objectism: if there was ever any point in shoving these counters about, that time is long gone by. At present, that sort of categorizing only ducks the challenge that the poems throw down: the way of living, and of thinking about living, which they propose to us.

Oppen is not at all a representative American poet. Not only is he in earnest as few poets are, but the nature of his earnestness is not of a sort we think of as 'American'. In his background and his past there is a good deal of Marxism, and so his attempts to understand the moment in which he writes are a historian's attempts, not (as with most American poets of comparable seriousness) psychological and/or mythopoeic. Not for him, for instance, the naive pastoralism, the harking back to a pre-industrial economy, which is the stock-in-trade of the American poets currently most popular with the American public. And so it is ironical that when Charles Olson responded to Oppen's review of him he should have protested, 'I wanted to open Mr Oppen to history'; being open to history is one thing, being open to the recorded and unrecorded past is something else. And one may stay closed to that past not because of ignorance or limited imagination, but as an act of willed choice. This is the choice that Oppen seems to make in a recent poem called 'The Taste':

> Old ships are preserved
> For their queer silence of obedient seas
> Their cutwaters floating in the still water
> With their cozy black iron work
> And Swedish seamen dead   the cabins
> Hold the spaces of their deaths
> And the hammered nails of necessity
> Carried thru the oceans
> Where the moon rises grandly
> In the grandeur of cause
> We have a taste for bedrock
> Beneath this spectacle
> To gawk at
> Something is wrong with the antiques, a black fluid
> Has covered them, a black splintering
> Under the eyes of young wives
> People talk wildly, we are beginning to talk wildly, the wind
> At every summit
> Our overcoats trip us
> Running for the bus
> Our arms stretched out
> In a wind from what were sand dunes

Those who know San Francisco know that wind, they know also the ships
that Oppen means, and they will share his sense that in the Californian
scene such attempts at historical *pietas* have an air of idle connoisseur-
ship. The poem comes in fact in a sequence with the deceptively modest
title, 'Some San Francisco Poems'. But then . . . Oppen is a San Francis-
can, once again voluntarily, by choice. He moves about the city and its
hinterland seeing it through eyes that have been conditioned elsewhere.
It is an Atlantic eye that looks out over the edge of a continent and a
cultural epoch, at the Pacific. The beautiful and precarious shallowness
of coastal California, treacherously gummed on to the continent across
the San Andreas fault, is caught by him as by no native or thoroughly
assimilated Californian. He is as much a foreigner there as we might be,
and therefore as incredulous, as dubious, above all as apprehensive.

It is possible to think that poetry should be responsible for giving to
Californian youth that ballast which we feel that it so perilously lacks—
'You were *not* born yesterday!' That was the response of a thoroughly
assimilated Californian, Yvor Winters, in poems like 'California Oaks'.
Oppen will have none of it. For him on the contrary sanity is in holding
on to

> 'the picturesque
> common lot'   the unwarranted light
> Where everyone has been   ('Anniversary Poem')

And so 'the courageous and precarious children', as he calls them, are to
be—have to be—trusted, with whatever misgivings. The past will not help
them; and perhaps we only thought that it helped us.

That goes also for the past of Art, of poetic art for instance:

> O withering seas
> Of the doorstep and local winds unveil
>
> The face of art
>
> *Carpenter, plunge and drip in the sea*   Art's face
> We know that face
>
> More blinding than the sea   a haunted house   a limited
>
> Consensus unwinding
>
> Its powers
> Towards the thread's end
>
> In the record of great blows   shocks
> Ravishment   devastation   the wood splintered
>
> The keyboard gone in the rank grass swept her hand
> Over the strings and the thing rang out

> Over the rocks and the ocean
> Not my poem   Mr Steinway's
>
> Poem   Not mine   A 'marvelous' object
> Is not the marvel of things
>
>   twisting the new
> `   Mouth   forcing the new
>   Tongue   But it rang

We have heard something like this before, from William Carlos Williams.
This resemblance is real, and Oppen no doubt would acknowledge it.
But the differences are striking too. Williams after all was a mythopoeic
poet (*Paterson*) and a historian only so far as he could turn history into
myth. He was even a systematizer, and in his last years a master or a prophet looking for (and thinking he found) disciples. Oppen has no such
hopes or intentions; his tone is ruminative, intimate, domestic. There is
no writer to whom a tag like 'American expansiveness' is less appropriate.
And indeed this goes beyond 'tone'; in a very unAmerican way Oppen
seems to offer us, as Hardy did, only 'disconnected observations'. The
claims he makes on us, for himself and his art, are disarmingly modest.
  All the same, and in fact even less avoidably than with Williams, the
challenge is thrown down to us: the past is irrelevant, a dangerous dis-
traction. Well, *is* it? For instance, the past of our art . . . Much as we may
agree that 'a "marvelous" object/Is not the marvel of things', or that the
commonplace is fruitfully mysterious in ways that only this sort of
poetry can make us see, still, are we Marxist enough, historical determi-
nists enough, to agree that the time is gone for so many of the traditional
splendours and clarities as this poetry wants us to dispense with? Outside
of the San Francisco sequence there is a poem called (and the title is
important) 'West':

> Elephant, say, scraping its dry side
> In a narrow place as he passes says yes
>
> This is true
>
> So one knows?   and the forms unfurling   leaves
>
> In the wind
>
> . . . sea   from which . . .
>
> 'We address the future?'
>
> Unsure of the times
> Unsure I can answer
>
> To myself   We have been ignited
> Blazing

In wrath we await

The rare poetic
Of veracity that huge art whose geometric
Light seems not its own in that most dense world West and East
Have denied have hated have wandered in   *precariousness*

(I break off at mid-point.) 'Splendours'—is that the word for what an oldfashioned reader would feel the lack of, in these verses? Hardly; that elephant, so abruptly huge and patient before us, is himself a splendour. 'Clarities', then? Well, yes; the suppression of so much punctuation certainly makes for obscurity (though the most obscure poem is one called 'The Occurrences', which has no punctuation stops at all). But the right word, to point for instance to the melodiousness which it seems plain we must not look for in this writing, is still to seek. I suggest: *braveries*. This writing denies itself certain traditional braveries (rhyme, assonance, determinable auditory rhythm) precisely because they would testify in the poet to a bravery (in the other sense) about his vocation and the art he practises, a bravery that we cannot afford once we have acknowledged that our condition, obscured from us by western and eastern cultures alike, is above all 'precarious'.

Can we agree? I submit that we cannot. For what we are faced with is a sort of illusionism after all. The poem *has* its own splendours, its own clarities, certainly its own audacities. (Consider only the imperious rapidity of the transitions it manages.) It has all the braveries; even the melody it seems to lack may have been merely lost in the passage from a Jewish-American mouth to my British ear. The object, willy-nilly, *is* 'marvelous'. It has to be; since it is an articulation in and of the marvel that is human language. The lack-lustre phrase is certainly a shabby rabbit out of any conjurer's hat. But the shabbiness is appropriate as the response to a shabby argument. If we truly want or need to cut loose from our inherited past, then we should discard not just poetic figurations of language but any figurations whatever, including those which make it possible to communicate at all, except by grunts and yelps. Rhetoric is inseparable from language, including language at its most demotically 'spoken'. And thus, let language be never so fractured and disjointed in order that the saving commonplaceness of common things shine through it, all that is happening is that a new rhetoric is being preferred before an old one. To put it another way, no Mr Steinway manufactured the instrument, language, on which Oppen performs. And, like it or not, a performance is what each of his poems is—as certainly as a sonnet by Philip Sidney.

This is not in the first place an argument with Oppen or with Oppen's poems. It is a quarrel with those of his admirers—I have met some among 'the courageous and precarious children'—who would explain their admiration by appeal to the untenable positions that Williams's obtuseness trapped him into (from which he later tried to extricate himself by such manifest absurdities as his 'variable foot'). Granted that Oppen does not discard rhetoric for non-rhetoric (which last is an impossibility), but rejects an old rhetoric for a newer one, we have to admire what the new rhetoric permits him to do. In the first place it opens up for him, as it sometimes did for Williams, an extraordinary directness and gentleness in intimacy, as at the end of 'Anniversary Poem':

To find now depth, not time, since we cannot, but depth

To come out safe,   to end well

We have begun to say good bye
To each other
And cannot say it.

Indeed, in the world that Oppen charts about him as he thinks of approaching his end, so hedged about as it is with apprehension and misgivings, this particular tone embodies so much of what he can still feel grateful for and sanguine about, that the newer rhetoric justifies itself on this count alone. And it is quite true that the older rhetoric cannot compass this tone of voice. It speaks again on the last page of this slim but substantial collection, in a poem called 'Exodus':

Miracle of the children   the brilliant
Children   the word
Liquid as woodlands   Children?

When she was a child I read Exodus
To my daughter   'The children of Israel . . .'

Pillar of fire
Pillar of cloud

We stared at the end
Into each other's eyes   Where
She said hushed

Were the adults   We dreamed to each other
Miracle of the children
The brilliant children   Miracle

Of their brilliance   Miracle
of

I would call that (though the word may give offence) elegant as well as touching. And I would say indeed that the elegance and the touchingness depend upon each other.

ROBERT LOWELL

Robert Lowell, *History*, Farrar, Straus & Giroux.
Robert Lowell, *The Dolphin*, Farrar, Straus & Giroux.
Robert Lowell, *For Lizzie and Harriet*, Farrar, Straus & Giroux.

ELIZABETH BISHOP was quoted triumphantly on the dust jacket of the 1969 *Notebook*: 'Somehow or other, by fair means or foul, and in the middle of our worst century so far, we have produced a magnificent poet.' I feel no need to demur, though strictly I've no right to an opinion, being British and so no part of that 'we', that 'our'. Plenty of people must have felt, though, as the original *Notebook* of May 1969 was already changed in July of that year and radically changed as well as expanded for the London edition of 1970, that the Lowell verse-machine was not just overheating but also throwing up ever more sludge and waste. In a poem at the end of one of his new books, *History*, Lowell quotes somebody, perhaps himself, on his own career:

> surviving to dissipate *Lord Weary's Castle*
> and nine subsequent useful poems
> in the seedy grandiloquence of *Notebook*.

But the fact that the poet has anticipated an objection shouldn't stop us from raising it, if we think it just. And in fact something of the kind is unavoidable once we realize that of the three new books, two once again announce themselves as quarried out of *Notebook*. What sort of game is this poet playing with his public—apart, of course, from making money out of us? How resist the suspicion that *Notebook*, at least in its first version, if not indeed in its second and third, was just an unconsidered emptying out on to the page of every scribble and doodle that Lowell had perpetrated over several years? Of *History* Lowell says:

> About 80 of the poems . . . are new, the rest are taken from my last published poem, *Notebook* . . . All the poems have been changed, some heavily. I have plotted. My old title, *Notebook*, was more accurate than I wished; i.e., my composition was jumbled. I hope this jumble or jungle is cleared—that I have cut the waste marble from the figure.

Fair enough. But 'plot' was already being claimed for *Notebook* in its first version: 'My plot rolls with the seasons,' he said then. And when we discover that the three hundred and seventy poems of *History* are mostly arranged in the simple chronological order of the dates at which their overt subjects (Alexander, Caligula, Mary Stuart, Lincoln, etc.) appeared on the stage of history, we cannot but think that the Michelangelesque metaphor about the waste marble being cut away from the figure is indeed grandiloquent, and that it promises a lot more than is performed. Can we call it plotting, let alone 'sculpture', when all the poet has done is sort his poems into loose categories merely by subject matter?

However, this is unfair. There is indeed sculpturesque energy of a very imperious and exciting sort when we find three sonnets (out of four) in

Notebook under the heading 'Searchings', compressed into one called 'Statue of Liberty':

> I like you like trees . . . you make me lift my eyes—
> the treasonable bulge behind your iron toga,
> the thrilling, chilling silver of your laugh,
> the hysterical digging of your accursed spur,
> Amazon, gazing on me, pop-eyed, cool,
> ageless, not holding back your war-whoop—no chicken
> still game for swimming bare-ass with the boys.
> You catch the frenetic spotlight we sling about
> your lighthouse promontory, flights an inch
> from combustion and the drab of ash . . .
> While youth lasts your flesh is never fallen—
> high above our perishable flesh,
> the icy foam rubber waterfall stands firm
> metal pear-pointing to eternity.

The first line is from one sonnet, lines 3 to 7 are from another, lines 8 and 9, and also lines 10 to 14, (adapted), from yet another. Moreover, the original poems all belonged to private life, whereas the new poem is public (though with valuable private resonances—the statue is American womanhood as well as Liberty). Also, we pick up a thread of plot, since 'Statue of Liberty' follows a sonnet, much revised from a quite different place in *Notebook*, about walking in pinching shoes in Buenos Aires:

> the Republican martyrs lie in Roman temples;
> marble goddesses calm each Liberal hero
> still pale from the great kiss of Liberty . . .
> All night till my shoes were bloody—I found rest
> cupping my soft palm to her stone breast.

Though the strain of the adaptation shows through, for instance in the musical shapelessness of line 6, still this is an impressive example of the merely anecdotal purged and lifted to a new power. The anecdotal should not have been published in the first place; but let that pass. (What happened, by the way, to the practice of indexing books of poems alphabetically by titles and first lines? Neither Faber nor Farrar, Straus do us this courtesy, though these books cry out for it urgently.)

In any case, each edition of *Notebook* carried a clear warning that in Lowell's usage, 'plot' was an unusually capacious notion: 'Single poems and sections are opportunist and inspired by impulse. Accident threw up subjects, and the plot swallowed them—famished for human chances.' And a sonnet for Berryman that survives through both *Notebooks* into *History* makes the same point:

> John, we used the language as if we made it.
> Luck threw up the coin, and the plot swallowed,
> monster yawning for its mess of pottage.

Which enables us, leaving all sorts of questions unanswered, at least to begin answering one question we've posed already: what sort of game

Lowell is playing with us. We can begin by saying that it's an exceptionally *intimate* game: we are to be with him, we *have* to be with him, as he runs a distracted hand through his hair, leafing through his old files and trying to see what his recent writing amounts to; where and how, if at all, it 'adds up'. As much with *History* as with any of the *Notebooks* we are really left to do the adding up for ourselves—*if we can*, the poet himself having virtually admitted that for his part he can't. And so, for 'intimate' in this sense we might as well read 'democratic'. From that demotic idiom which has become, since Williams, ever more *de rigueur* for American poets, Lowell is excluded because of his early schooling in the drumming decasyllable, 'the mighty line'; his coquettish habits of publishing are his way of achieving by other means a sort of unbuttoned welcome of the reader in the workshop, something that other American poets have achieved through a low-key idiom that he's debarred from.

All the same, 'coquettish' is an abusive word, and it has to be. For as readers we just don't know where we are, or what is expected of us. For instance, if from one point of view these procedures are democratic, in another light they are just the opposite, for the poems seem to come to us under the lordly rubric, 'Never apologize, never explain'. The whole collection, *For Lizzie and Harriet*, appears to assume that we know about Lowell's marital arrangements and how they've changed lately. If we don't know about this, we don't know where to go for information; and we feel like people absentmindedly invited to a party where everyone else is in the know and knows everyone else. The least we might expect is to be introduced to at least one other person in the room; and in his 'Afterthought' to the 1970 London *Notebook*, Lowell did that much, explaining the poem that stood first in *Notebook* and now stands first in *For Lizzie and Harriet*:

> Half a year, then a year and a half, then
> ten and a half—the pathos of a child's fractions, turn-
> ing up each summer. God a seaslug, God a queen
> with forty servants, God . . . she gave up—things whirl
> in the chainsaw bite of whatever squares
> the universe by name and number. For
> the hundredth time, I slice through fog, and round
> the village with my headlights on the ground,
> as if I were the first philosopher,
> as if I were trying to pick up a car
> key . . . It can't be here, and so it must be there
> behind the next crook in the road or growth
> of fog—there blinded by our feeble beams,
> a face, clock-white, still friendly to the earth.

Of these lines, which he said were 'as hermetic as any in the book', Lowell wrote in 1970: 'The "fractions" mean that my daughter, born in January, is each July, a precision important to a child, something and a half years old. The "Seaslug etc." are her declining conceptions of God.'

With this note to help, we can admire the order of ideas and images
through the poem, in particular the propriety by which the moon,
measure of time, in the end escapes 'name and number' by being pointed
to only in a riddling circumlocution. But in *For Lizzie and Harriet*, there
is no note and all we are given instead is the child's birthdate: 'January 4,
1957'. Moreover, the new version gives, for lines 9-11:

> Like the first philosopher Thales who thought all things water,
> and fell in a well . . . trying to find a car
> key . . . It can't be here, and so it must be there

—which switches the whole thing on to a track of frigidly playful pedantry.

What I've been saying smacks fustily of those rightly suspect arguments,
once so common in America and still to be heard in England, which begin:
'The reader has his rights also . . .' The trouble with this is that it presupposes certain assumptions, shared by the poet and his public, about what
poetry is or what it does. And the truth is, on the contrary, that even less
than his readers is the poet nowadays (a poet such as Lowell) clear about
what he is doing, and why. In those circumstances, it might be said, the
only honest thing for him to do is to let it come, let it tumble out, pell-
mell—in hopes that someone, somewhere, will discern the design and the
purpose that escape him. If he still talks incongruously about cutting
away the waste marble, we need only suppose that he's less good at
writing blurbs than at writing poems. However, this doesn't explain how
he can still revise. For if he doesn't know what he is doing, or why, how
can he decide that one set of words suits his purpose better than another?
And in any case, such decisions crop up at every moment in composition
as in revision: the puerile enjambment, 'turn-/ing'—why did Lowell per-
petrate it in the first place, and then adhere to it when he came to revise? He must have had *some* reason; can we believe it was the sort of
thing that dazzles the freshman writing seminar, a disposition of line-
endings so as to (get it?) *enact* the turning that it talks about? Such odds
and ends of reach-me-down 'technique' are quite worthless in the absence
of any conviction about the point of the poetic enterprise as a whole.
One takes the point easily enough that he's sick of the well-made poem,
the expensive art object, as an end in itself; but if that is thrown out the
door, along with it have to go related fantasies about 'enactment'. And
no amount of coquettish publishing can mask, or make up for, direction-
less composing.

However, for the poet who has lost direction (or deliberately abjured it,
as Lowell for honourable reasons seems to have abjured the prophetic
and denunciatory direction of *Near the Ocean*, for instance), another
option is open: he can bring it about that the life he lives brings him into
situations at once extreme and typical, in such a way that poems skimmed
off that life, though they have in themselves no more direction than
entries in a journal, feed upon and take over the direction that the life
has. And this seems to be the case with *The Dolphin*, much the best of
these three collections and the one that owes next to nothing to *Notebook*.

One extreme and typical situation here is that of exile, the self-sought exile of Lowell in England which naturally and inevitably becomes for him the paradigm of exile in general:

> Is it honorable for a Jew to die as a Jew?
> Even the German officials encouraged Freud
> to go to Paris where at least he was known;
> but what does it matter to have a following,
> if no one, not even the concierge, says *good day*?
> He took a house in London's amused humdrum
> to prove that Moses must have been Egyptian—
> 'What is more monstrous than outliving your body?'
> What do we care for the great man of culture—
> Freud's relations were liquidated at Belsen,
> Moses Cohn who had nothing to offer culture
> was liquidated at Belsen. Must we die,
> living in places we have learned to live in,
> completing the only work we're trained to do?

'London's amused humdrum' is brilliantly just and caustic, to characterize the peculiarly English brand of philistinism; and it may serve, as well as any of dozens of equally quotable throw-aways, to show how the marmoreal conclusiveness of the mighty line survives into Lowell's most recent writing, even now when pentameter and sonnet alike are consistently violated and, as it were, disembowelled. In fact, part of the superiority of *The Dolphin* to *For Lizzie and Harriet* can be seen in the readiness of the later poem to stay with the iambic pentameter quite comfortably for several lines at a time; the compulsion to disrupt it, at whatever cost in arbitrary ugliness, seems to be something that Lowell has for the moment worked out of his system.

All the same, *The Dolphin* stays within the framework of *Notebook* and the poems that came out of *Notebook*, to the extent that 'Lizzie' and 'Caroline' and 'Harriet' are characters in a drama we're supposed to know about. And in fact *The Dolphin* pushes intimacy to a new extreme; of poems like 'In the Mail' or 'Exorcism' or 'Foxfur' the first thing to say is that they are acutely embarrassing. Or so anyone will feel who remembers, perhaps wistfully, the proprieties that went without saying up to twenty years ago. It was Lowell's own *Life Studies* that put an end to such automatic reticences; and the course which he then adopted, of making public what had been thought to be inviolably private, is the course that he sails on still. The privacies which he betrays are for the most part not those of the bedroom, but of the living room, the telephone booth, the mailbox. To my mind this makes them no less shocking, for I agree with George Steiner that fornication and buggery on stage and screen are alarming not because they expose sexuality, but because they expose *privacy*. The right to privacy for one's self, and the right not to look when the privacies of others are exposed, are rights that are now derided, if not yet explicitly denied. And for this surely baleful development, Lowell has to take some of the blame.

And yet there's no reason to think him a compulsive exhibitionist. He could have come to this practice by a line of argument which does him credit. For indeed everything I've noticed so far—Lowell's ways of publishing no less than his ways of writing (style as well as subject)—make sense only if we see them as one more desperate phase in the struggle, waged ever since the Romantics, to cut poetry clear of rhetoric. According to the Romantics' logic, as soon as the poet looks outside the circle of his intimates, and thinks of his public (of an anonymous third party—to be interested and intrigued, in short, to be *persuaded*), he is operating no longer as poet but as rhetorician. And Lowell, because he has been famous for so long, has to go to desperate lengths so as not to write with his avidly interested public in mind. He can do this (so I guess) only by writing much and writing fast—by, as it were, jumping himself into each poem; also by cramming into the poem things that will be meaningful only to his intimates; also by refusing to distinguish between the private and the public. It is a real bind for him; and his struggles in it, from *Notebook* onward, are heroic. But of course the facts of his situation, if he can suppress them from his mind as he writes, catch up with him unavoidably when he publishes. At that point it becomes impossible to pretend any longer that the faceless public doesn't exist. Writing poems may or may not be a rhetorical operation (I believe it is, in part, and has to be), but certainly publishing them is. And so long as Lowell continues to publish, his struggles not to be a rhetorician, though they may be heroic, are certainly in the last analysis fatuous.

Fortunately, by the time he finished *The Dolphin*—perhaps before he started it, certainly by the time he passed it for publication—Lowell had reached these conclusions for himself. He has had the grace to allow that the poems which present themselves as literal transcripts of letters and phone calls may be nothing of the kind (I am devoutly glad to hear it, and over-ready to believe him). He has by implication taken the side of the arch-rhetorician Yeats. And he has 'plotted' the book in an acceptable public sense, by way of a cluster of dominant images signalized by the title—images of fishnets, stirred mud, eels, salmon-trout. When he says,

> After fifty so much joy has come,
> I hardly want to hide my nakedness—
> the shine and stiffness of a new suit, a feeling,
> not wholly happy, of being reborn,

he seems to be referring in the first place to his new marriage and his new child; but his public, which is interested in *public* meanings, comes across enough evidence that the new life is a new life for his art also, a shucking off at last of the self-contradictions that snarled him in *Notebook* and the collections that came out of *Notebook*. In this new dispensation, if it's still true that 'Everything is real until it's published'—why, that's just the name of the game, the shadow of the rhetorician's dishonesty that necessarily falls on all of us who 'go on typing to go on living'.

TRAGEDY AND GAIETY

Mandelstam, Clarence Brown, Cambridge.
Selected Poems, Osip Mandelstam, translated David McDuff, Rivers Press.
Selected Poems, Osip Mandelstam, translated Clarence Brown and W. S. Merwin, Oxford.
Chapter 42, Nadezhda Mandelstam; with *The Goldfinch*, Osip Mandel-stam, introduced and translated by Donald Rayfield, Menard Press.

CLARENCE BROWN'S long-awaited study of Mandelstam deserves its place in the same series or at least under the same imprint as John Bay-ley's incomparable *Pushkin*. Among innumerable arresting and instructive things one wants to quote, there is Brown's comment on Mandelstam's poems of 1913: 'The humour is often explicit, but more often it springs from an intangible sense of elation, a gaiety of language, *that would never be absent from his poems again.*' The italics are mine. But they seem called for, since what we mostly know is the harrowing story of Mandelstam's last years told by his indomitable widow Nadezhda, in her memoir of 1970, *Hope Against Hope*. A tragic destiny; but the poems at the heart of it are *gay*. It was Mandelstam's glory that, this linguistic hilarity once discovered, he refused, even in his blackest years when his overt themes were most sombre, to do without it; as it was his calamity that even when he wanted to exclude it (as presumably in his abortive and pathetic 'Ode to Stalin'), he couldn't. We may think by contrast how the author of 'Sweeney Agonistes' gave up more and more of the game-someness, positively the *gaminess*, of poetic language, so as to become the author of *Four Quartets*. And yet in that development wasn't Eliot merely acknowledging that the spirit of the age had switched irreversibly away from the high-spirited audacity of the international avant-garde in its heyday? Mandelstam, especially in poems about Leningrad, acknow-ledged the change but couldn't or wouldn't reconcile himself to it.

In this way Mandelstam is very remote from us. He is so 'modern' that he makes us feel 'post-modern'. All the same, he has lessons for us. For instance how 'literary' he is! How insistently he experiences life 'at one remove'! And how conclusively the spectacle of his career knocks all the frail props from underneath such common and vulgar objections to a poetry that concerns itself, explicitly and shamelessly, with 'culture'!

However, we can learn from him only when we have a secure grasp of him and his poetry. Nowadays he can be introduced into a literary con-versation without seeming to up-stage anyone. But it's only in the per-spective of martyrology that we know him, not at all in the perspective of poetry. And in fact we haven't got him right even as a martyr. We get him right only when we see him as one angle of a quadrilateral: Mandel-stam, Akhmatova, Tsvetayeva, Pasternak. This constellation is hard for us to discern, if only because for so many years, first in Russian and then in Anglo-American opinion, Mayakovsky was promoted so as to overshadow and eclipse his peers. And indeed one urgent need we have is for one of our dependable Russianists to assess for us how far Mayakovsky stands up, now that these contemporaries of his begin to emerge from the shadows. But in any case they have as yet hardly emerged at all, the shadows still cling murkily about each of them. I haven't primarily in mind, what Clarence Brown rightly insists on, the extent to which official suppression and falsification still obscure the actual canon, and anything like a definitive text, of Mandelstam's work. I'm thinking more of our own sins of omission and commission, and particularly of our performance as translators. All of these poets have been mutilated (oh with the best will in the world!) by grossly insensitive translations that still circulate along with one or two that are respectable. Is Mandelstam going to have better luck than the other three?

Not, I'm afraid, if David McDuff is typical. To see how little he can be trusted, compare his number 59 ('I see a lake, standing sheer . . .') with Clarence Brown's discussion of what is admittedly a fiendishly difficult poem. Other spot-checks, and comparisons with W. S. Merwin's versions, are no more reassuring. One notes resignedly that it's McDuff's version that will get about in cheap paperback. Merwin reads much better. No wonder; he's a practised professional, and has Clarence Brown for collaborator. He alone, not always but often, makes *poems* (American ones, naturally); by which one means, quite simply, that his versions mostly make sense—perhaps not always the right sense and certainly not the complete sense, but at all events *sense*. Donald Rayfield's mostly don't; not surprisingly, since making sense is what his commentary does, very interestingly too. But with Rayfield the commentator taking this responsibility, what is there left for Rayfield the translator to do? Answer (in part): try to keep Mandelstam's rhymes—which is nearly always a mistake. Rayfield is indispensable however, for what he does is to give us a chapter omitted from *Hope Against Hope*, together with the poems that that chapter discusses. This is excellent; the Menard Press is to be congratulated, and so is Rayfield for doing a thankless and necessary job. (For Clarence Brown's discussions, it should be noted, don't extend to these late pieces.)

In the quadrilateral of names the classic polarity between St Petersburg and Moscow is represented with a symmetry that is positively disconcerting: Akhmatova and Mandelstam are Leningrad poets, Pasternak and Tsvetayeva are Muscovites. Let no one think this is accidental or trivial. If from the Olympian standpoint of Russian culture as a whole the Muscovite and the Petersburg emphases are doubtless complementary, to those actually caught up in the Russian literary scene the opposing alignment (Slavophil versus Westerner, rural versus urban, pious versus sceptical, vegetative versus lapidary—the polarity shows up in many forms in each generation) necessarily figures as competing, if not antagonistic. The undercurrent of hostility to Pasternak among some of Mandelstam's admirers is at least partly to be explained this way, as are Mandelstam's seemingly gratuitous attacks on Tsvetayeva in the twenties (ten years after he'd been in love with her).

But this polarity is crossed with another which has more to do with the martyrology than the poetry and yet has its bearing on the poetry too: on each side of the divide stood one who was intransigent, and another who strove so far as honour would permit to be accommodating. Here it is Tsvetayeva who lines up with Mandelstam, Akhmatova with Pasternak. All four were martyred before the end; but it was Mandelstam and Tsvetayeva who *looked* for trouble. On this issue we must be careful not to take sides; for if one of the four angles yawns apart, all the others are forced out of true. Mandelstam and Tsvetayeva, it seems clear, were outrageous. Impossible persons, both of them. It's one of the manifold virtues of Nadezhda's furiously honest memoir that it doesn't blink this fact. One sees it most clearly perhaps in their prose. I've had Mandelstam's 'Conversation on Dante' presented to me as a model of what criticism should be. Heaven forbid! It is a work of genius; it is even, I believe, irreplaceable as a series of insights into Dante. But I can think of nothing worse as a model of critical procedure, so joyously idiosyncratic as it is, and so discontinuous. Likewise in public life Mandelstam seems to have been so wayward that even a society much less bureaucratically rigid and cruel than Soviet society would have found him unemployable and in a profound sense unassimilable. Which is not to diminish by a hair's breadth one's loathing and contempt for what Soviet society did to him. (And the society did it, not just the State—that's another of the searing truths that Nadezhda's memoir drives home.)

This is a good place from which to force an entry into the poetry. For Mandelstam was all of a piece (whereas Pasternak, it seems, could be, in no dishonourable sense, prudent and shrewd outside poetry, as in poetry he wasn't). Roy Fuller in an Oxford lecture has decided: 'poetry seems to stand, even thrive on, outrageous imaginative collage, provided the poet remains in formal control'. It's not what we're used to hearing from Professor Fuller; at least that anxious provision for 'formal control' seems more characteristic than what precedes it. (And Mandelstam incidentally answers to the stipulation, though his satisfyingly clear and symmetrical forms are nearly always subverted, as it were, from inside.) Anyhow Fuller comes by his perception honestly. And there are precedents: Baudelaire for instance, deciding that the beautiful in poetry must partake of the bizarre. And certainly a quality of the bizarre, the outrageous, seems to be what elevates the young Acmeist Mandelstam above his pre-Acmeist self, as also above the appealing and talented doomed Acmeist leader Gumilyev, just as it is what raises the young Imagist Pound over his pre-Imagist self, and over a gifted and attractive fellow-Imagist like H.D.

The comparison isn't gratuitous. Ever since, twenty-five years ago, one first heard of Mandelstam from D. S. Mirsky, one has fidgeted and fumbled with the notion that between the Acmeist school in Russia and the exactly contemporaneous Imagist school in London there were analogies so many and so exact that one gasped to see the *Zeitgeist* so flagrantly in action. One is gratified but also a little deflated to find that the analogy is now a critic's commonplace. It should *not* be a commonplace, I think, given how striking a conjunction it is. And indeed for a Poundian of sorts like myself there is every temptation to let the extraordinary analogy run away with the rest of the review. Heroically resisting temptation, let's say only that for English-speakers the way into the Acmeist Mandelstam (and Clarence Brown believes that 'acmeist' he remained in some sense to the end) seems to be inescapably by way of the Imagist Pound. This ought to be a big help; but probably won't be, because England has certainly seen what Akhmatova protested at in Russia: the deprecating of Acmeism in the one case, Imagism in the other, as no more than a late by-blow or variant of Symbolism (to which in fact both movements were opposed).

Clarence Brown intelligently gets a lot of mileage out of the Acmeist/ Imagist analogy. Thus, when he endorses and adopts Gumilyev's pin-pointing of just where the Acmeist takes over in Mandelstam's first collection, *Stone* (1913; and only ponder the Poundian implications of *that* title!), he quotes T. E. Hulme's Imagist 'Autumn':

> A touch of cold in the Autumn night—
> I walked abroad,
> And saw the ruddy moon lean over a hedge
> Like a red-faced farmer.
> I did not stop to speak, but nodded,
> And round about were the wistful stars
> With white faces like town children.

And there is certainly a neat fit between this and Mandelstam's poem:

> No, not the moon, a luminous clock-face
> shines down on me, and how can I be blamed
> if the weak stars I register only as 'milky'?
>
> Batyushkov's hauteur also I don't care for;
> who, when they asked what time it was, returned
> compendiously, 'Eternity!' for answer.

But the fit is really too neat to be convincing, especially since the common element is thematic (moon and stars), and Mandelstam was at pains to relegate the thematic component of poetry to no more than parity with other elements. What's missing from Hulme is precisely the bizarreness of the conjunction, the audacity of the imaginative leap from Mandelstam's first tercet to his second; and for this we look in vain to any Imagist save Pound himself.

It's good that Batyushkov's name crops up here. For Batyushkov (1787-1855), Pushkin's contemporary, figures large in Mandelstam's thinking. And very properly too, since he is perhaps the most illustrious example before Mandelstam of a rare but recurrent and precious bent that the Russian imagination may take: quite directly towards the Mediterranean, by way of remembering the Greek city-states on the Black Sea, and Ovid's exile in what is now Rumania. (Mandelstam's second collection was given with brilliant appropriateness—though it wasn't he that chose it —the Ovidian title, *Tristia*.) A Petersburg poet, yes; therefore a Westerner, just so. But the Westerner in Mandelstam can draw on vast imaginative and cultural resources because, instead of looking through Peter the Great's 'window on the west' out to the Baltic and across to Scandinavia, Holland or England, he looks instead south-westward, along a tunnel through the centuries which leads his eye directly past the Crimea to the Aegean and beyond, even (and indeed especially) to Italy.

Batyushkov and Pushkin had sighted along that telescope before him; Mandelstam looks through it long and steadily, with yearning yet without the disabling nostalgia of the internal émigré he was said to be, but was not. Something of this we knew already from his widow's memoir; now we can see it in such poems as 'Batyushkov' and 'Ariosto', both of them in Brown-Merwin versions lucid, graceful and affecting. And this might seem the point at which to recall that the poet's origins were Polish and Jewish; but Mandelstam, as I read him, would have violently repudiated any such gloss—this direct access to Mediterranean humanism is an avenue open to the *Russian* imagination, opened up through *Russian* language.

Postscript: Recent verse-translations of Mandelstam by James Greene, who I think is better than Merwin (and his sensibility as European as Merwin's is American) have altered my focus on Mandelstam. I should now put less stress on the bizarre in his poetry and more on the *roundedness* of the forms that he favours, both in nature and in art. This would be to emphasize not just his 'formal control', but the extremely traditional nature of his formality. And his yearning towards the Mediterranean would then come to seem, in a quite precise sense, *classical*.

AN APPEAL TO DRYDEN

In the Trojan Ditch: Collected Poems and Selected Translations, C. H.
Sisson, Carcanet, 1974.

C. H. SISSON WAS a late starter in poetry. It was in 1943, when he was
nearly thirty, that he wrote his first poem and his first translations. The
translations were of Heine, and he made them while a soldier in India.
'The Heine who was the Sword and the Flame of the German revolutionary struggles of the first half of the nineteenth century became the
companion of the British Other-Rank in his oppressive situation in the
last decade of the British Raj.' (Sisson is an extremely reticent writer
whether in verse or prose, and we should profit by this intimation that
he ponders the era he is living through—it is easy to miss the poems of his
that may be called patriotic and political: 'Vienna' is one of these, so is
'Maurras, Young and Old', so is his splendid imitation of Horace's *Car-
men Saeculare*.)

In the late 1940s, when it was still not clear to Sisson that verse was his
vocation, what he was after, above all, was *plainness*. And this led him to
translate Catullus: 'The exercise in plainness was what I wanted when I
did the Catullus.' How this worked out in practice can be seen in the Catullus versions here reprinted, and the curious whose Latin is shaky (as mine is)
may compare Sisson's versions with the similarly post-Poundian and very
inventive translations by Peter Whigham. If we compare Whigham's

> Plunging towards Phrygia over violent water
> shot on the wood-slung Berecynthian coast
> Attis with urgent feet treads the opaque ground
> of the Goddess, his wits fuddled, stung with phrenetic
> itch, slices his testicles off with a razor . . .

with Sisson's

> Carried in a fast ship over profound seas,
> Attis, eager and hurried, reached the Phrygian grove,
> The goddess's dark places, crowned with woodland,
> And there, exalted by amorous rage, his mind gone,
> He cut off his testicles with a sharp flint . . .,

we may well feel that Sisson's plainness is excessive, or else that Catullus's
style is not always and everywhere so plain as it certainly is for the most part.
And this I'll come back to. Meanwhile Sisson was writing 'Nude Studies':

> They are separate as to arms and legs
> Though occasionally joined in one place.
> As to what identity that gives
> You may question the opacity of the face.
>
> Either man is made in the image of God
> Or there is no such creature, only a cluster of cells.
> Which of these improbabilities is the less
> You cannot, by the study of nudity, tell.

The man who wrote with this impressive plainness had, we may well think, learned to do so by translating Catullus:

Ameana, the worn-out bitch,
Is asking for a whole ten thousand,
That girl with the flattened nose
That used to go with the Formian bankrupt.

Her family, or whoever looks after the girl,
Had better call in her friends and doctors:
The girl is mad, she has never enquired
What a mirror would have to say about her.

And Sisson (see his 'A Letter to John Donne') was not the first modern poet to realize that on the features of Catullus, *this* Catullus, could be superimposed those of the famous Jacobean divine, whose concerns—with Christian revealed truth, and carnality, and the relation between them—were more urgent to the modern poet than were the ancient Roman's preoccupations.

It is not Donne, however, whom Sisson appeals to as an English precedent and master: not Donne, but (insistently) Dryden. This is our warrant for taking his translations, unusually but very properly, as of equal importance with his poems. After Heine and Catullus, it was Virgil who engaged Sisson's energies. And in undertaking, of all unlikely things, a complete version of Virgil's Eclogues, he was keenly aware of Dryden's versions as a standard he could not measure up to: 'Dryden wrote in the superb verse he was master of in his "great climacteric". For the Eclogues I wrote what I could manage at the age of 53 . . .' It is wonderful to hear, in the second half of the twentieth century, this proudly humble voice of the honest artificer: it is the voice of Dryden himself. But it speaks all too true. Dryden's version of the Eclogues is so good that it's hard to see any reason for making, or publishing, another; and Sisson's version is a wooden curiosity. Far more startling and intriguing is his reduction of much of *Aeneid* VI to a sort of stenographic summary. But in any case he knew what he was up to, with Virgil:

> There is a certain elaboration, very unfashionable in our time and perhaps of little use for contemporary literary purposes. There is also something which we ought to value. This is a deep movement of feeling, below the surface of our exacerbated daily life, and which has greater significance than any 'frankness' for those who want to understand the human brute.

In other words, the plain style just will not encompass what Virgil has to offer; and if at times Sisson's versions make this quite woefully evident, none the less the Virgilian alternative was by this process established in his mind, to bear wonderful fruit long after. For lately, disenchanted with plainness, he has written a long and mysteriously beautiful poem, 'In Insula Avalonia', where his patriotic and religious concerns come together in the legend of Arthur sleeping through the centuries in the Isle of Avalon near Glastonbury, and they are woven together in a verse which, as it were, goes nowhere and says nothing, which is Shakespearean and at times Eliotic to just the degree that it is Virgilian—a style as far from plainness as it is possible to conceive.

In between had come some lovely and quiet poems of Christian devotion ('In Kent', 'Knole', 'Easter'), others equally quiet honouring more local pieties ('On the Coast', 'Ightham Woods', 'Mortalia'), and still others of a raucously self-disgusted sexuality which predictably have attracted more attention. In between had come also, more ominously, 'The Discarnation', a logic-chopping discourse in three parts and a hundred stanzas, each of them mechanically and exactly tooled to a predetermined pattern:

> We are the heirs of an emptiness
> Of which we are extremely proud;
> The crowd
> Soothed as it never was, a less
> Extreme
> Nightmare, and a less hopeful dream.
>
> And artifacts less regarded
> Than ever before, because made
> For trade
> And not for use, and by the dead
> Hand of
> Number instead of by our love.

Is it not 'the dead hand of number' which, in a way the poet didn't intend, marshalled these stanzas so magisterially into their syllable-counting members? And is this not an example of how little salutary check the plain style can exert, once it has been mastered to facility, on a predominantly conceptualizing imagination?

It is writing of this sort, also perhaps the strutting randiness of 'The Queen of Lydia' and some similar pieces, that I take to be in Sisson's mind when he starts a recent poem with:

> Such a fool as I am you had better ignore
> Tongue twist, malevolent, fat mouthed
> I have no language but that other one
> His the Devil's . . .

and goes on, in angry self-reproach:

> Where in all this
> Is calm, measure,
> Exactness,
> The Lord's peace?

This is from 'The Usk', which I take to be one of the great poems of our time, though published only a matter of months ago (in the first issue of *Poetry Nation*). Elsewhere in this poem—it is only sixty lines long—he reveals that what he had hoped for was a style limpid enough to bear comparison with the clear running of the river Usk; but what he achieved,

he goes on to say, was not the hoped-for limpidity, but something else—
plainness:

> I speak too plain
> Yet not so plain as to be understood
> It is confusion and a madman's tongue . . .

'The Usk' is an extraordinary triumph of the plain style in poetry precisely because, even as it deploys that style, it convicts it of dishonesty.
The style rises to its greatest intensity at a point where the poet, through
tormented puns on the Eucharist, vows himself to silence and, by so
doing, out of the depths of his self-accusation earns the right to figure as
himself the Christ-figure—*Ecce homo*.

> Lies on my tongue. Get up and bolt the door
> For I am coming not to be believed
> The messenger of anything I say.
> So I am come, stand in the cold tonight
> The servant of the grain upon my tongue,
> Beware, I am the man, and let me in.

'The Usk' ends, as do many of Sisson's recent poems, with the poet
vowing himself, not just to silence, but to sleep and dream. And so it
heralds and announces the even later poem, 'In Insula Avalonia', where
the millennial sleep of Arthur calls for a style not plain at all but Virgilian.

A modern Dryden? Not really. If I read Sisson aright, he would be the
first to protest that there not only is not, but cannot be, in our time any
real analogue to that master of three centuries ago. How wonderful,
though, that not just in matters of translation nourishing composition
but in the situation of the devout Christian constantly battling his own
instructed scepticism, we should have—in this bad time—a poet who
can be mentioned in the same breath with Dryden, who can sustain the
comparison at least for a while! It is years since there appeared a book of
poems to equal this one for seriousness and accomplishment, and the
unadvertised drama that is acted out on its pages.

SLOGGING FOR THE ABSOLUTE

The Avenue Bearing the Initial of Christ into the New World: Poems 1946-64, Galway Kinnell, Houghton Mifflin.

GALWAY KINNELL is a man who hungers for the spiritual, who has no special capacity for spiritual apprehensions, who has been culturally conditioned moreover to resist the very disciplines that might have opened him up to the spiritual apprehensions he hungers for. By writing poems which thrash in and out of the impasse thus created, Kinnell has made a great reputation—which suggests that there are many readers who are walled up in the same bind, and ask nothing better than to churn and agonize within it. And Kinnell isn't alone; the same or a similar pattern shows up in other poetic careers which like his span the last twenty years. The effect has been to disperse and dissipate the artistic and intellectual riches accumulated by the great decades of American poetry earlier in this century. More specifically the effect has been to take American poetry back out of the twentieth century into the nineteenth, from the astringent and sophisticated world of Allen Tate or Yvor Winters back into the world of Emerson and Whitman. For the impasse that we are talking of—a spiritual hunger which refuses to take the steps necessary to appease itself—is not a modern impasse at all, but is really no more than the tediously familiar dilemma of those late-Victorians who vociferously 'lost their faith'.

This is not the commonly accepted notion about what has happened to American poetry in the last twenty years. For the received opinion, we can go to Ralph J. Mills, Jr, in *The Iowa Review* in 1970: 'Galway Kinnell's first collection, *What a Kingdom It Was* (1960), can be viewed in retrospect now as one of those volumes signalling decisive changes in the mood and character of American poetry as it departed from the witty, pseudo-mythic verse, apparently written to critical prescription, of the 1950s to arrive at the more authentic, liberated work of the 1960s.' Similarly 'liberated' (from what, is as yet unclear) were also 'Theodore Roethke, Kenneth Patchen, John Berryman, Robert Lowell, James Wright, Anne Sexton, James Dickey, W. S. Merwin, and . . . Sylvia Plath', as also, swarming on to the field before Mills's essay is half over, 'Robert Bly, Louis Simpson, . . . Frank O'Hara, Donald Hall, . . . John Ashbery'. (What a cornucopia of talent! One recalls the extraordinary scenario of Richard Howard's *Alone With America*, wherein America, a whore with a full engagement-book, gets to have forty-one living poets alone with her, one after another.) It's to be hoped that some of these poets would resent the company they are made to keep to satisfy Ralph Mills's anxious programme of safety in numbers. But there is plenty of evidence that a lot of them have invested heavily in Mills's reading of recent history, and are ready to come to one another's assistance. There will be rather fierce resistance, therefore, to any attempt to reopen a question so comfortably closed. Yet Kinnell himself, with an earnest candour that is characteristic,

now forces us to reopen the question, by presenting us with the poems
that *he* was writing in the 1950s, from in fact as long ago as 1946. We
can't do anything else, faced with this instructive and fascinating collection, than ask how far 'witty', 'pseudo-mythic' and 'written to critical
prescription' are indeed acceptable labels for American poetry of the
1950s, how far and in what sense 'authentic' and 'liberated' are the
words for the 1960s.

It turns out that *What a Kingdom It Was* is not, as Ralph Mills thought,
Kinnell's first collection. It had been preceded by *First Poems 1946-
1954*, which came out in a limited edition; and these are the poems reprinted in the first thirty-eight pages of this new book. I will say at once
that one or two of them seem to me as valuable as any of the more pretentious pieces that Kinnell was to write later. Charles G. Bell, the poet
who was Kinnell's mentor (as he touchingly acknowledges), some years
ago saluted two of these early poems: 'Island of Night', and 'A Walk in
the Country'. Just as good, to my mind, is 'The Feast':

> Juniper and cedar in the sand,
> The lake beyond, here deer-flesh smoking
> On the driftwood fire. And we two
> Touching each other by the wash of the blue
> On the warm sand together lying
> As careless as the water on the land.
>
> Now across the water the sunset blooms.
> A few pebbles wearing each other
> Back into sand speak in the silence;
> Or else under the cliff the surf begins,
> Telling of another evening, and another,
> Beside lapping waters and the small, lapped stones.
>
> The sand turns cold—or the body warms.
> If love had not smiled we would never grieve.
> But on every earthly place its turning crown
> Flashes and fades. We will feast on love again
> In the purple light, and rise again and leave
> Our two shapes dying in each other's arms.

Witty? Pseudo-mythic? Written to critical prescription? Of course there
was a distinctive kind of bad poem written in the 1950s, and some of us
who were writing them then are the first to laugh at them now; the two
longest pieces among Kinnell's juvenilia, 'Conversation at Tea' and 'Meditation among the Tombs', are touchingly incompetent poems which accordingly display the vices characteristic of the period, notably a lot of
unassimilated Yeats. But the extraordinary limpidity of 'The Feast', the
unemphatic tact with which the metaphor, the lovers wearing each other
into sand as the pebbles do, is divulged by a stroke here and a stroke
there, not 'built up' nor having the poem laboriously built about it—this

has nothing to do with the New Criticism, nor with wit, nor with 'myth'. It is exquisitely beautiful; it is also exquisitely civilized and mannerly. And we shall look a long way to find such good manners in much that Kinnell was to write later.

One exception, however, is the poem that stood first in *What a Kingdom It Was*. For as Charles Bell noticed, this poem, 'First Song', goes along with 'Island of Night' and 'A Walk in the Country' and 'The Feast'. And accordingly Ralph Mills is considerably flustered by 'First Song' when he encounters it at the start of his appreciation of the later Kinnell who traffics in 'stringent realities': in 'First Song', Mills concedes with some agitation, these realities 'are softened, almost sentimentalized, by pleasant details'; moreover, 'pleasurable nostalgia fills the poem'; and passages in it are unfortunately 'muted'. But of course it is possible, and not self-evidently wrong, to admire the poem for just those things in it which worry a reader like Mills:

> Then it was dusk in Illinois, the small boy
> After an afternoon of carting dung
> Hung on the rail fence, a sapped thing
> Weary to crying. Dark was growing tall
> And he began to hear the pond frogs all
> Calling on his ear with what seemed their joy.
>
> Soon their sound was pleasant for a boy
> Listening in the smoky dusk and the nightfall
> Of Illinois, and from the fields two small
> Boys came bearing cornstalk violins
> And they rubbed the cornstalk bows with resins
> And the three sat there scraping of their joy.
>
> It was now fine music the frogs and the boys
> Did in the towering Illinois twilight make
> And into dark in spite of a shoulder's ache
> A boy's hunched body loved out of a stalk
> The first song of his happiness, and the song woke
> His heart to the darkness and into the sadness of joy.

We can certainly agree with Ralph Mills that it's a matter of general interest and public concern how a poet who could write with this tenderness and delicacy should be writing ten or twelve years later (in *Body Rags*, 1968):

> The light goes out. In the darkness
> a letter for the blind
> arrives in my stunned hands.
>
> Did I come all this way only for this, only
> to feel out the world-braille of my complicity,
> only to choke down these last poison wafers?

For Galway alone.
I send you my mortality.
Which leans out from itself, to spit on itself.
Which you would not touch.
All you have known.

In between had come the Vietnam War? Yes, indeed. And does such strident writing, or the blood-boltered primitivism of 'The Bear', show poetry
resisting the brutalizing of war, or surrendering to it?

Charles Bell, who recognized the beauty of some early Kinnell—and
even, it appears, preserved early manuscripts which the poet himself had
lost—nevertheless does not differ from Ralph Mills about the shape of
Kinnell's career to date. For him too it is a story of 'upward and onward'.
In Bell's note on Kinnell in *Contemporary Poets of the English Language*
(edited by Rosalie Murphy, 1970), we learn that already when Kinnell
was putting together *What a Kingdom It Was*, 'his matter was the reaffir-
mation of the Promethean and pioneer daring of America, to which I
also, after the neo-Augustinian resignations of the war, was committed.'
This is enough to make one weep. Did it not occur to Bell, nor to Kinnell
even as he composed his brave and effective poems protesting the war,
that it was precisely 'the Promethean and pioneer daring of America' that
was drowning Vietnamese hamlets in a sea of fire? Prometheus the fire-
bringer in literal fact! And yet Richard Howard, who notes the pyroma-
niac imagery of later Kinnell, seems not to be troubled by it nor to
notice any moral ambiguity.

Bell insists that Kinnell's vision was Promethean from the start: 'What
distinguishes that vision from anything else on the contemporary scene is
its continuation of the titanism of the last century'. The last century—
well, precisely! The later Kinnell, like much American poetry of the
1960s, is an anachronism. The very vocabulary in which it is extolled by
its admirers—'the basic urge for transcendence', 'a primal level of being
which is associated with the earth' (both these gems from Ralph Mills)—
comes with an unmistakable whiff of some late Victorian critic like Stop-
ford Brooke. It is not to the point that the American titan who comes
first to mind should bear the sacred name of Walt Whitman. In the nineteenth century the U.S.A. had no monopoly of titans. Private Prometheans were
the order of the day. And should we think better of French poetry since
1945 if French poets had found a way to sound like Victor Hugo or
Claudel, of Italian poetry if it were once again sounding like Carducci
and D'Annunzio, of English poetry if it had recovered the strenuous
thrustingness of Robert Browning, of German poetry if it sounded
like Wagner and Nietzsche? Is it not the case on the contrary that two
World Wars and sundry other enormities have proved to the sensitive and
humane man of our times that the confident affirmations of the last
century, however understandable and even admirable in that age of innocence, are unthinkable for us? And why should the American be an
exception? If he makes himself the exception, does this not prove that he

has *still* not taken the true murderous imprint of the times that we are living in?

None of this is irrelevant to the case of Galway Kinnell, nor will Kinnell fail to understand what I am talking about. The proof is in another early poem now reprinted. It is called 'Primer for the Last Judgment'', and it is ill-written, yet an honest declaration of attitude towards very trouble-some matters, and one moreover which throws its shadow forward over much that Kinnell has written since:

> When Jesus bruised his toe on stone
> Men crowned him—all of them,
> The pure and the impure—punctured him
> Finger and toe, and pinned him there,
> And coughed less from conscience than phlegm;
> Then called for traditional values, unaware
> They were asking their own liquidation.
> 'The end is at hand', said Paul.
> But it did not arrive, that looked-for day
> Of devastation, except at its own slow gait.
> Daily the spent heart came home to find
> A space with the dimensions of home
> Ambiguously empty like the three-days' tomb.
>
> And now with us: only a few
> Years back, at war's close, the sun
> Touching the Pacific found
> Two cities crumbled. And men
> World over asked, 'Has the end begun?'
> Maybe it has; maybe it shall come
> Exploding flesh off the innocent bones,
> Mechanized, official, and at once.
> Or maybe it has crueler ways—
> Dread of the body, the passion to subdue—
> Not to be announced until it is done,
> Which is each day from this day
> Until the last tomb clutches the last bone.

From all of us who were writing in the early 1950s the incineration of Hiroshima and Nagasaki seemed to demand a moral stock-taking, as it demands it of Kinnell here. We should respect him for rising to the challenge. Yet one cannot help but note that his speculation about the form which the gradual Last Judgement will take—'Dread of the body, the passion to subdue'—is the merest guess. It would have been equally plausible then, and is equally plausible now, to guess that the judgement on humankind would take the form of an excessive trust in the body, an ever more feverish carnality, and a passion not to subdue others but to wash one's hands of them, by copping out and leaving the realm of public affairs to others more callous. Obviously, if the second alternatives had

seemed more likely than the first, the subsequent career of the poet, as a
moral agent and a responsible artist, would have been very different. It
would, for instance, have been less Promethean.

Clearly, for the proper understanding of the decisive turn that Kinnell
took at the end of the 1950s, a great deal turns on the matter of the
poet's openness. Ralph Mills is very sure about this, and eloquent about it:
  This kind of openness—a sensitive receptivity in which the poet, to
  borrow a phrase of Heidegger's about Hölderlin, 'is exposed to the divine lightnings' that can easily exact their toll on nerves and emotional
  balance—extends, in many instances, beyond matters of social and political experience to naked metaphysical confrontation: with the universe, the identity of the self, the possibilities of an absent or present
  God, or the prospect of a vast, overwhelming nothingness. In such
  poets as Theodore Roethke, Kenneth Patchen, John Berryman, Robert
  Lowell, James Wright, Anne Sexton, James Dickey, W. S. Merwin, and
  the late Sylvia Plath, for example, with all differences aside, the pursuit
  of personal vision often leads toward a precipitous, dizzying boundary
  where the self stands alone, unaided but for its own resources, before
  the seemingly tangible earth at hand with its bewildering multiplicity
  of life, the remoteness of space, the endless rhythms of nature, the
  turns of night and day, and within, the elusive images of memory
  and dream, the irrationality and uncertainty of human behavior, the
  griefs and ecstasies that living accumulates. Here the poet—and Galway
  Kinnell is certainly of this company—is thrown back upon his own
  perceptions; his art must be the authoritative testimony to a man's
  own experience, or it is meaningless; its basic validity rests upon that
  premise.
This is heady stuff, in a mode we have grown inured to: the reformula-
tion for our times of the nineteenth-century myth of the artist as sacri-
ficial Promethean scapegoat. It is of course necessarily blasphemous, since
it involves denying the Christian contention that we have indeed known
one such scapegoat, just one, unique and unrepeatable, whose name was
Jesus. And that is a name that Kinnell has always made great play with,
as in the poem just quoted or in the well-known Whitmanesque poem
which gives its name to this volume. It is very hard to see what 'Jesus' or
'Christ' signifies for Kinnell. So far as I can make out, it means in his
mouth roughly what it means in the mouth of a Unitarian. But it really
would be nice to know. And until we _do_ know, his making so free with
it cannot help but seem—and not just in the eyes of Christians—an unpardonable vulgarity. It is in any case very nearly related to what we mean if
we counter Mills's praise of his 'openness', by accusing Kinnell of having
resisted 'the very disciplines that might have opened him up to the spiritual apprehensions he hungers for'. Those disciplines are the disciplines
of Christian worship; and Kinnell's resistance to them, his inability even
to stand still long enough to understand them, is documented in three

poems early in *What a Kingdom It Was*: 'First Communion', 'To Christ Our Lord' and 'Easter'.

No poet can be blamed for his inability to make the act of Christian faith. But what one can ask of any such poet is, first, that the impediments to faith be real, substantial, and such as to command respect; second, that having declared his incapacity for the sacramental and incarnational act of the imagination in the forms inherited from his own culture, he should be wary of pretending to make those acts in the terms presented by cultures that are not his at all; and, thirdly, that he should not, having turned his back on the Christian dispensation, continue to trade surreptitiously in scraps torn arbitrarily from the body of doctrine he has renounced. On all three counts, whereas an honest atheist like Hardy is in the clear, Kinnell stands convicted. For in the first place, in both the poems which most explicitly deny the validity of the Christian Incarnation (in 'Easter' its invalidity is already taken for granted), the case is argued through the experience of a child; and in at least one of those cases, 'First Communion', the objections are appropriately puerile, a misplaced matter-of-factness, materialistic and indeed mercenary. The claims of Christianity are nowhere in Kinnell brought to the bar of an adult intelligence. On the third count, we have seen how Kinnell continues to import a religiose fervour by tossing the name of Jesus around. But it's on the second count that the case against him is most flagrant and most far-reaching, since it's something he shares with many other poets of his generation.

For what has been more common in recent decades than to find poets who reject Christianity (often, it seems, without thinking about it) embracing more or less seriously various forms of hinduism, buddhism, shamanism? And, while we must not rule out the possibility that some of these professions of exotic faith are genuine, yet is it not in the highest degree unlikely that a man who cannot profess the traditional faith of his own culture should be able to profess, in all seriousness, the faith of a culture in which, try as he may, he cannot be other than an outsider, a spiritual tourist? Here once again we perceive the lonely titan making his anachronistic reappearance out of the nineteenth century where he belongs, the Byronic or Faustian world-wanderer who disdains to consider his untameable mind as in any way conditioned by the times he was born to, the culture or the nation he was raised in. In Kinnell's case, the clearest and most guileless expression of this is probably his essay, 'The Poetics of the Physical World' (in *The Iowa Review*, summer 1971), where, having tossed off some predictably cheap gibes about rhyme and metre ('Had Whitman been more clever, conceivably he could have turned out to be as good a poet as Whittier or Longfellow'), he proceeds to declare himself unable to sympathize with the treatment of death by Tennyson in *In Memoriam* or Milton in *Paradise Lost*, at the same time as he can enter fervently into treatments of the same theme by a Bathurst Islander, an Australian aborigine, and a Tamil from two thousand years ago. And

this is of course the claim implicitly made by his already famous and profoundly regressive poem, 'The Bear'. At this point in Kinnell's career (and
we encounter the same thing in many of his contemporaries) the titan
who makes his reappearance comes to us not from the last century but
from the century before that, from the Rousseauistic heyday of 'the
noble savage'.

It is not really surprising that in this essay Kinnell should present us
with the Bathurst Islander's poem and the Tamil poem, as well as poems
by Lorca and Yesenin, as if they were available to us on just the same
basis as poems composed in English. Translator though he is himself,
Kinnell makes no allowances for what is lost and distorted in even the
most sensitive translation. Thus he tells the reader: 'One of the greatest
of all death poems is Lorca's lament for Ignacio Sanchez Mejias'. And the
poem is then quoted in English, quite as if we could take the force of it
in isolation both from the particular Spanish words in which it is written,
and from the entire context of Andalusian life out of which it emerges.
Instead, 'The courage of this poem is awesome. Pain, rage, torn love,
mingle undiluted, unconsoled.' We are in a world where poems are written
by courage, pain, rage and love quite immediately, not as screened and
filtered and diffracted through the fabric of any one of the tongues of
men. And Kinnell's admirers have dutifully applied the same vocabulary
to him. 'Courage' and 'rage' and 'pain', 'torn', 'undiluted and 'unconsoled'
—these are the terms in which they offer us for admiration such late
Kinnell poems as 'The Porcupine' or 'The Bear'; any more manageable
and less emotive language would bring down the poem to a level which
they would call, doubtless, *'merely* verbal'. Accordingly, it would be
foolish to look in *Body Rags* for any of the self-effacing and feelingful
dexterities that we applaud in the best of Kinnell's poems of the late
1950s, or for that matter in *Flower Herding on Mount Monadnock*. If we
are still uncertain about this, we should ponder what Kinnell says about
the revisions he has made in that collection and in *What a Kingdom It
Was*: 'Most of these changes were made while I was reading the poems to
audiences. Standing at the podium, just about to say a line, I would feel
come over me a definite reluctance to say it as written. Gradually I learned
to trust this reluctance. I would either drop the line altogether . . . or else
invent on the spot a revision of it.' I think we are meant to admire the
bold trustingness of this procedure, how 'existential' it is. But may we
not reflect instead how approximate the wording must have been in the
first place, how 'optional' the expressions must have been, if they could
be changed on an impulse thus lightheartedly? We need not deny that
improvements can come in this way; 'Spindrift' for instance has profited
from losing its last three lines. But it's obvious that poetry composed
for or at 'the podium' must be, as compared with poetry for the solitary reader, loose in weave and coarse in texture. So it is for instance in
'The Avenue Bearing the Initial of Christ into the New World'. Certainly
the poem is powerful, certainly it is inventive, yes it *is* keenly observed;

but inevitably for the solitary reader it telegraphs its punches, as when, needing to allude to the Nazi extermination-camps, it can do so only by printing in full a blank form announcing death over the signature of a Camp Commandant.

Kinnell may mistake this point, and his admirers certainly will. We are not asking for more beauty and less power, or for feelings that are tenuous and fugitive rather than those that are vehement; we are asking for feelings that shall be tracked with scrupulous and sinuous fidelity, rather than a general area of feeling expansively gestured at.

The best of Kinnell's collections to date is surely *Flower Herding on Mount Monadnock*. It represents a notable recovery from the much coarser writing of *What a Kingdom It Was*, and it is good to have it back in print. Many pages here can be read with very keen pleasure. But in these poems no more than any others has Kinnell escaped the self-contradiction that snarled him almost from the start. He still wants to experience the transcendent without paying the entrance-fee, for instance in the currency of humility. It is all very well to say, as by 1964 he had said many times already, that man's 'lech for transcendence' is unappeasable, because directed towards what is an illusion, an illusion that he must learn to do without. But in that case let him indeed do without it, and settle for the perceivable and perishing world of the creatures as being all the good he will find, and as much as he has any right to. In *Flower Herding on Mount Monadnock* Kinnell repeatedly approaches this position, yet always in the end he shies away from it or tries to go beyond it. In a rare moment of (almost) ironical self-knowledge, he speaks of himself, in 'Spindrift', as 'slogging for the absolute':

> Across gull tracks
> And wind ripples in the sand
> The wind seethes. My footprints
> Slogging for the absolute
> Already begin vanishing.

Even as he declares that the perceivable is all there is, he continually runs his head against the limits of the perceivable as if to bash his way through by main force into the transcendent, the 'absolute'. It is not hard to recognize the same phenomenon in the late poems of Roethke. And many readers of both poets apparently find the spectacle both touching and heroic; but equally, as we go through the same foredoomed motions over and over again, we may come to think them simply unintelligent and boring.

What is certain is that a poet who thus thrashes about in a manifest self-contradiction cannot help but do damage to the language that he bends to his purposes. In *Flower Herding on Mount Monadnock*, 'old' is one word made to carry more weight than it will bear, and 'amazed' is another. But the most flagrant case is that familiar tell-tale, 'mystic' (or 'mystical'). A cab-driver in Calcutta regards the poet through his rear-view mirror 'with black, mystical eyes'; Robert Frost is spoken of as 'a

man who was cursed/Neither with the mystical all-lovingness of Walt
Whitman/Nor with Melville's anguish to know and to suffer' (Kinnell of
course is with Melville and Whitman); and in 'Spindrift', we are presented
with 'the soft, mystical shine the wind/Blows over the dunes as they
creep', and also with a swan who 'dips her head/And peers at the mystic/
In-life of the sea'. In none of these cases does 'mystic' or 'mystical' bear
the tautly defined meaning which saints and theologians have honed fine
and sharp through centuries, the meaning which a responsible poet like
Eliot was at pains to master before he wrote *Four Quartets*. In Kinnell's
lines the words have more to do with 'misty' or 'mysterious' than with
St John of the Cross. And how could it be otherwise, since the word
gestures towards a realm of which by his own confession the poet has no
experience? This is what Hulme pungently and truthfully called poetry as
'spilt religion'. And the spilling, the slopping and spattering, is there in
what happens to a word and its meaning; whereas a poet, one supposes,
should use words more responsibly than other people, here we see him
deliberately fuzzing and blurring, like any adman or politician. And perhaps indeed that is why many readers find such a use of words in poetry
natural and acceptable. Hulme, it will be remembered, spoke of 'spilt religion' as a vice of nineteenth-century poetry, something which his and
Pound's exertions had made disreputable. But we can see that he spoke
too soon.

Kinnell, we must suppose, is more intelligent than his admirers. When he
hears Ralph Mills talking of a poet who 'is thrown back upon his own
perceptions', practising an art that 'must be the authoritative testimony
to a man's own experience', of which the 'basic validity rests upon that
premise', perhaps Kinnell points out to him gently that this is a description of all worthwhile poetry whatever, not of some novel kind of poetry
discovered in the U.S. about 1960. I should like to think so. For I should
like to believe also (though I know it is unlikely) that when Galway
Kinnell agreed to collect and reprint these poems of his youth, he was
asking in effect whether there was any way back for him into the twentieth century from the blowsy nineteenth-century titanism in which he
has snared himself. For a poet of such talent and such earnestness, the
answer of course is: Yes! And what after all is the alternative? In a poem
like 'The Bear' the poet, determined to reach the absolute one way if
not another, and unable to leap above his humanity into the divine,
chooses to sink beneath it into the bestial. It is a sort of transcendence
certainly. But what a fearsome responsibility for the poet, to lead his
readers into bestiality . . . A challenge worthy of a titan! So Charles
Manson may have thought. Will Galway Kinnell choose to be a titan, or a
human being?

ENGLISH AND AMERICAN IN *BRIGGFLATTS*

ANGLO-AMERICAN poetry . . . if we need such a category at all, and whatever we might mean by it, Basil Bunting's poetry seems to belong there. His sensibility is profoundly English—not British but *English*, and Northumbrian English at that; and yet his techniques, his acknowledged masters and peers in the present century, are all of them American. This makes him a difficult poet. For the American reader he is difficult because the voice that speaks in his poems (and in his case 'voice' must be understood very literally), no less than the range of his allusions, especially topographical ones (and in *Briggflatts* topography is crucial), utter insistently an alien, a non-American, experience and attitude. For the English reader he is difficult because, line by line and page by page, his words come at us according to a system of juxtapositions and disjunctions which, because we can find no precedent for it among English poets, strikes us as not systematic at all but random and arbitrary. But plainly, on this showing, the English reader is better placed than the American: whereas one hardly knows where to tell an American reader to start in order to come to terms with Bunting, the English reader has only to acquaint himself with the body of arguments and assumptions about poetry that Bunting in his youth worked out in alliance with certain American contemporaries. We study his American associations only so that we may subsequently discount them. And we may well think that in the future we shall have to do the same with other English poets besides Bunting. *Technically*, surely, Anglo-American is what our poetry will be henceforth, but at levels more profound than technique—to which however only technique gives us access—the English poet will remain as English as ever, the American as American.

In 1966 the American poet and declared 'Objectivist', George Oppen, was explaining himself to his French translator: (1) 'Several dozen commentators and reviewers have by now written on the assumption that the word 'Objectivist' indicated the contributors' objective attitude to reality. It meant, of course, the poets' recognition of the necessity of form, the objectification of the poem.' With that 'of course' Oppen is too sanguine, as he is again when he goes on to say: 'The point may seem rather obvious today . . .' The point is so far from obvious that what is meant, or might be meant, by 'the objectification of the poem' is a question not even debated, let alone resolved. As Hugh Kenner has said, (2) '*That* history is still unwritten'. History in the first place, not theory . . . For Oppen in 1966 was a veteran harking back nearly forty years to the initial formulation of a conviction that had governed his writing over the years since. Thus when he speaks of 'the contributors', he means the contributors to *An 'Objectivists' Anthology*, which appeared in 1932, edited by Louis Zukofsky and published by Oppen and his wife on a small press of their own in a French provincial town. The anthology is dedicated to Ezra Pound, and it includes two poems by Pound, but the contributors that Oppen has in mind are Basil Bunting, Robert McAlmon, Carl Rakosi, Kenneth Rexroth,

Charles Reznikoff, William Carlos Williams, Louis Zukofsky. This group had good reason to be grateful to Pound because a year before he had donated to them space allotted to him in the magazine *Poetry* (Chicago). And the interesting and affecting thing is that in 1966 Oppen still aligns himself with these men: '. . . it remains my opinion that Reznikoff, Rakosi, Zukofsky, Bunting of Briggflats [*sic*] are the most considerable poets of my own generation.' How wide of the truth it is, to say that the point these poets were making 'may seem rather obvious today', is apparent in the fact that most of these names are still unknown or go largely unregarded—the most flagrant case being that of Zukofsky, originally the spokesman and theorist for the entire group.

For our purposes, the intriguing feature is that all these names are American, save one—Basil Bunting, a name that figures along with Zukofsky's and Oppen's in Pound's own *Active Anthology* of 1933. But in the first place it's precisely Pound's patronage of this group that may cause misunderstandings. There is a general notion abroad that as it were the Poundian scriptures were promulgated, the tablets of the Poundian law were handed down, once and for all in the period of Imagism and Vorticism, and that thereafter Pound would patronize only poets who hewed very close to the line thus laid down. This is quite untrue. Some years before 1930, in his ill-advised campaign on behalf of Ralph Cheever Dunning, Pound had irritably exclaimed against those who took statements appropriate to the particular circumstances of 1914 as if they were injunctions binding upon all poets at all times; and in a few years' time he was to be forced to the same exasperated protest when he wanted to applaud Binyon's translation of Dante. And so it should come as less of a surprise, to find Oppen beginning his case for Objectivism by attacking a central Imagist document:

We could say—surely *I* would say—: The image for the sake of the poet, not for the sake of the reader. The image as a test of sincerity, as against (tho I may quote inaccurately here): 'The sun rose like a red-faced farmer leaning over a fence', which last is a 'picture' intended for the delectation of the reader who may be imagined to admire the quaintness and ingenuity of the poet, but can scarcely have been part of the poet's attempt to find himself in the world—unless perhaps to find himself as a charming conversationalist.

Of course Oppen *does* misquote. What he has in mind is T.E.Hulme's 'Autumn', the first of five poems which Pound printed provocatively (as 'The Complete Poetical Works of T.E.Hulme') at the end of his *Ripostes* in 1912.

> A touch of cold in the Autumn night—
> I walked abroad,
> And saw the ruddy moon lean over a hedge
> Like a red-faced farmer.
> I did not stop to speak, but nodded,
> And round about were the wistful stars
> With white faces like town children.

Yet Oppen's misremembering does not destroy the point he is making. For it is surely quite true that in Hulme's piece there is indeed a great deal of self-regarding and yet cajoling whimsy, which does indeed point quite away from what Oppen goes on to call 'the strength of Imagism', 'its demand that one actually *look*.' And thus, however aptly Hulme may have come to Pound's hand in 1912, when Pound wanted to assert that 'As for the future, *Les Imagistes* . . . have that in their keeping', none the less, by elevating this trivial and dubious piece to the status of a central Imagist exhibit (for this is what it has since become), Pound opened the way to whimsical trivia as well as to the 'demand that one actually *look*.' Zukofsky and Oppen were right in 1932 to want to purge the Imagist inheritance of this weakness, and Pound by giving them his blessing virtually admitted as much.

It can still be said of course that the purge 'went too far'. Readers of Oppen's own poems—exhilaratingly sparse and 'purged' as they are—may well feel so. And those who remember and endorse Wordsworth's definition of the poet as 'a man speaking to men' may well feel that Oppen's sneer at the 'charming conversationalist' is not quite so conclusive as he means it to be. When Basil Bunting says, 'Pound has had a great influence on me of course but Wordsworth has had a steady, solid one all my life on everything', (3) he declares an allegiance that none of his American associates, not excluding Pound, would subscribe to. And it is somewhere here that one starts differentiating this English 'objectivist' from the Americans, and envisaging the possibility of a distinctively English version of this otherwise all-American movement. But first it must be emphasized that 'objectivist' is certainly what Bunting is, that he undoubtedly endorses all the positions taken up by Zukofsky and Oppen more than forty years ago. And this is something that his English readers have not taken account of. They know him as a Poundian poet—as one has been in the habit of saying, 'the only card-carrying English Poundian'. But in the preface to his *Loquitur* (1965) Bunting acknowledged 'a continual debt to the two greatest poets of our age, Ezra Pound *and Louis Zukofsky*.' The italics are mine; and in what follows I shall enquire what Bunting meant by those italicized words—not principally so as to get Bunting into perspective, but rather, as an English poet addressing other English poets, to see where English poetry has got to, and where it may go to next (at our hands, if we so choose).

And so we must go back to 'the necessity of form, the objectification of the poem'—'as against', so Oppen goes on to say, 'the liquidation of poetry into the sentimentalism of the American socalled Imagists of the late twenties and early nineteen-thirties'. (Who *they* were, we need not now enquire, we need only note once again that Objectivism defines itself as what Imagism—at any rate, one sort of Imagism—is not.) William Carlos Williams in 1944 was talking about 'the necessity of form, the objectification of the poem', when he defined a poem as 'a small (or large) machine made of words'. And twenty years later Bunting is saying the same

thing when he declares: 'A work of art is something constructed, something made in the same way that a potter makes a bowl. A bowl may be
useful but it may be there only because the potter liked that shape—and
it's a beautiful thing. The attempt to find any meaning in it would be
manifestly absurd.' (4) For most readers, I dare say, Williams's 'machine'
will seem to point one way—towards *agitprop*, perhaps, and Bunting's
pot will point almost the opposite way—back towards the nineties and
Oscar Wilde. But the perception of the poem as artifact rather than
communiqué is not a monopoly of aestheticism; any more than 'form' is
a monopoly of those who write triolets and villanelles, or verses that can
be scanned:

> The lines of this new song are nothing
> But a tune making the nothing full
> Stonelike become more hard than silent
> The tune's image holding in the line.

That is Zukofsky's way of putting it, and exemplifying it too. And those
for whom the analogy with the musician comes easier than the analogy
with the potter may set beside Zukofsky's lines Bunting's from *Briggflatts:*

> It is time to consider how Domenico Scarlatti
> condensed so much music into so few bars
> with never a crabbed turn or congested cadence,
> never a boast or a see-here; and stars and lakes
> echo him and the copse drums out his measure . . .

Bunting's 'never a boast or a see-here' corresponds, at least in part, to
Oppen castigating Hulme's 'Autumn' for 'the falsity of ingenuity, of the
posed tableau, in which the poet also, by implication, poses.'

   And yet 'It is time to consider . . .' Wouldn't Oppen have to object to
that? Wouldn't he think that it established the poet merely as 'a . . . conversationalist'? Perhaps not. But it does strike a note that we seldom find
in the American objectivists: a note that is social and public, where
theirs is characteristically intimate and private. In their poems the addressee is usually in the singular: the poet is a man who speaks not to
men but to *a man*. Or, to a woman—as Oppen does, touchingly:

> To find now depth, not time, since we cannot, but depth
>
> To come out safe,   to end well
>
> We have begun to say goodbye
> To each other
> And cannot say it

This is from Oppen's *Seascape: Needle's Eye* (1972), in which the only
punctuation stops that appear—and those sparsely—are comma, dash, and
inverted comma. The punctuation is as sparse or sparser in *North Central*
(1968) by Lorine Niedecker, who was for Bunting at that time 'the best
living poetess'. (Though she never published with the Objectivists, Mrs
Niedecker, an exquisite poet since dead, was as surely of their company

as, *avant la lettre*, Marianne Moore was.) And throughout the ten poems of Williams's sequence 'Pictures from Brueghel', in his *Selected Poems* (1969), there is not a single punctuation stop. On the other hand, merely to turn the pages of Bunting's volumes is to see the full range of punctuation stops sown at least as thickly as in normal prose; and a closer inspection will show that for the most part they have the same function as in prose, clarifying the articulate structure of sentences. This points to an acknowledgement by Bunting of the social and public institution that grammar is—an acknowledgement that his American peers (though not, incidentally, Zukofsky) mostly, or often, refuse to make.

It will be clear what these comments are tending to—to the suggestion that for the English poet the writing of poems is a public and social activity, as for his American peers it isn't. Considering that until the publication of *Briggflatts* in 1966, when the poet himself was 66, Bunting had been ignored by the British public as totally as Oppen and Zukofsky and Niedecker had been by the American, this contrast is very striking. And I'm prepared to argue that this is, and should continue to be, a distinctive feature of English poetry of our time, as against American.

But this, though it is true, is something one must beware of saying at all loudly or at all often, to the English reading-public. For the sad fact is that English readers of contemporary poetry—few as they are, and perhaps just *because* they are so few—have got used to being cajoled and coaxed, at all events sedulously *attended to*, by their poets. Teachers in English classrooms have for decades now persuaded school-children and students to conceive of the reading of a poem as a matter of responding to nudges that the poet, on this showing debased into a rhetorician, is supposedly at every point administering to them. And accordingly English readers have taken to their bosoms a poet like the late John Berryman who, though an American and at times a very affecting writer indeed, does indeed nudge and cajole and coax his readers, in a way that one can be sure Americans such as Oppen and Zukofsky are offended and incensed by. Oppen flies to the other extreme when he declares, 'The image for the sake of the poet, not for the sake of the reader'; and so does Bunting when he declares, of his poem like a pot, 'The attempt to find any meaning in it would be manifestly absurd.' Neither of these declarations is worded with care, and neither is defensible as it stands. But behind them both is a conviction that is wholesome, which the English reader needs to hear about even more than the American does: the conviction that a poem is a transaction between the poet and his subject more than it is a transaction between the poet and his readers. This is to make the poet once again more than a rhetorician; and on this showing the reader, though the poet cannot be oblivious of his presence, nevertheless is merely 'sitting in on' or 'listening in to' a transaction which he is not a party to. That Bunting is more social, more public, than Oppen—this is true and significant and important; but what is more salutary for the English reader is to realize that Bunting none the less shares the Objectivists' determination to cut the reader down to size, by making him realize that he is only as it were a bystander.

The same lesson, incidentally, can be read out of Hardy. As John Bayley has said, (5) though 'his need for praise was as great or greater than that of other artists', yet 'Hardy's anthropomorphic imagination is a substitute for . . . the direct intercourse of writer and reader', and accordingly, 'the way to appreciate Hardy best in his poems is to resign oneself to being cut off from him'. Because of this the current vogue for Hardy's poetry in England, though it certainly has its unfortunate sides—as when it nourishes Little Englandism, or contrives to be at once idolatrous of Hardy and condescending to him— none the less is welcome. What needs to be said—what one wishes John Bayley had said—is that in this respect Hardy is not an odd man out: that 'being cut off from' the poet one is reading is a normal experience; that it is Berryman's intimacy with his reader that is exceptional.

How intransigently Bunting holds to the poem as artifact, as verbal machine, appears in an interview he gave about *Briggflatts*. This is a very out-of-the-way document (6)—which is a great pity, since it is indispensable for penetrating that poem, however much the author might want to pretend otherwise. Here Bunting insists that his poem came to him in the shape of a schematic diagram, which he proceeds to draw for his interviewers. They cannot believe their eyes: 'Well . . . when you started, or say at this stage, this piece of paper, this outline, did you know that it was Briggflatts, that that was the title, that the village was the . . .' And Bunting interrupts: no, he knew nothing of that, the poem was there before him in its schematic blueprint 'before there was a line written or thought of'. The actual wording of the poem, it seems, actually and quite literally its *content*, was merely the filling in of the outline thus determined in advance. And yet the writing that 'fills in' is—in cadence and orchestration of sound, no less than in the associations of images—as far from aestheticism as this:

Cobweb hair on the morning,
a puff would blow it away.
Rime is crisp on the bent,
ruts stone-hard, frost spangles fleece.
What breeze will fill that sleeve limp on the line?
A boy's jet steams from the wall, time from the year,
care from deed and undoing.
Shamble, cold, content with beer and pickles,
towards a taciturn lodging amongst strangers.

I will show my hand without more equivocation, and assert that it is writing of this quality—so compact, having no syllables to spare for nudges or tipping the wink—that English poetry needs to assimilate and build on. Only when we have done that shall we be able to deny Oppen's and Kenner's contention that the whole Objectivist endeavour is 'an American movement'. Why should we want to do that? For our own good, I think. And, heaven knows, the matter that Bunting packs into *Briggflatts*, the content of it, the experience that it re-creates and cele-brates, is indelibly and specifically English enough to satisfy anybody. He has shown us that the achievement is abundantly possible, if only we choose to emulate it. To emulate him does not mean abandoning metre; it does not mean, in his Poundian fashion, peppering our pages with the names of Catullus and Firdausi, Dante and Villon; least of all does it mean taking over his maddening habit of supplying notes that only tease. But it does mean writing like this, about autumn twilight over an ancient battlefield in the Yorkshire dales:

> Grass caught in willow tells the flood's height that has subsided;
> overfalls sketch a ledge to be bared tomorrow.
> No angler homes with empty creel though mist dims day.
> I hear Aneurin number the dead, his nipped voice.
> Slight moon limps after the sun. A closing door
> stirs smoke's flow above the grate. Jangle
> to skald, battle, journey; to priest Latin is bland.
> Rats have left no potatoes fit to roast, the gamey tang
> recalls ibex guts steaming under a cold ridge,
> tomcat stink of a leopard dying while I stood
> easing the bolt to dwell on a round's shining rim.
> I hear Aneurin number the dead and rejoice,
> being adult male of a merciless species.
> Today's posts are piles to drive into the quaggy past
> on which impermanent palaces balance.
> I see Aneurin's pectoral muscle swell under his shirt,
> pacing between the game Ida left to rat and raven,
> young men, tall yesterday, with cabled thighs.
> Red deer move less warily since their bows dropped.
> Girls in Teesdale and Wensleydale wake discontent.
> Clear Cymric voices carry well this autumn night,
> Aneurin and Taliesin, cruel owls
> for whom it is never altogether dark, crying
> before the rules made poetry a pedant's game.

That this passage about killing comes from a poem named after a Quaker meeting-house, written by a Quaker poet who went to prison for his pacifism in the First World War, is, as they say, relevant. But this is information that we may or may not bring to the poem; it is not *in* the poem, nor necessary to it. For this poet eschews the sort of intimate relation with us in which consideration of his personal history would be to the point. Instead he aims for and achieves the hieratic tone of epic and lament, in which his own voice is indistinguishable from that of the ancient Cymric poet, Aneurin. We are as little aware of the historical identity of Basil Bunting as we are of that of Thomas Gray, the vale-tudinarian Cambridge don, when Gray makes over the same Cymric poem (the *Gododdin*) into eighteenth-century heroic idiom:

> To Cattraeth's vale in glittering row
> Twice two hundred warriors go;
> Every warrior's manly neck
> Chains of regal honour deck,
> Wreath'd in many a golden link:
> From the golden cup they drink
> Nectar, that the bees produce,
> Or the grape's ecstatic juice.
> Flush'd with mirth and hope they burn:
> But none from Cattraeth's vale return,
> Save Aeron brave, and Conan strong,
> (Bursting thro' the bloody throng)
> And I, the meanest of them all,
> That live to weep, and sing their fall.

Bunting's achievement is greater than Gray's, because he achieves the hieratic tone not by archaic diction but by ramming his words so hard, one on the heel of the other (object on verb on subject), that no interstices are left through which his eye on the thing to be said can be deflected towards the reader, the person he is saying it to. Though it is unthinkable that George Oppen could, or would ever want to, address himself to this subject, yet this writing answers to his stringent prescriptions for Objectivist poetry; and we have seen Oppen admit as much. Elevated though it is, this passage is all poetry, there is no point at which it strays into the rhetorician's persuasive wooing of an audience. This is where English poetry has got to, it is what English poets must assimilate and go on from.

NOTES

p. 11. 'Essential Gaudiness': The Poems of Wallace Stevens
1. Wallace Stevens, *Selected Poems*, Faber. Wallace Stevens, *Selected Poems*, chosen with a foreword by Dennis Williamson, Fortune Press.
2. Marius Bewley, *The Complex Fate.*
3. William Van O'Connor, *The Shaping Spirit: A Study of Wallace Stevens*, Chicago: Henry Regnery, 1950.

p. 25. Poetry, or Poems?
1. R. P. Blackmur, *Language as Gesture: Essays in the Craft and Elucidation of Modern Poetry*, Allen & Unwin.

p. 32. T. S. Eliot: The End of an Era
1. One traces it as far afield as Berenson, in his remarks on Umbrian space-composition and 'the religious emotion'.

p. 57. An Alternative to Pound?
1. Yvor Winters, *The Function of Criticism: Problems and Exercises*, Denver: Alan Swallow, pp. 59, 60.

p. 81. Ezra Pound's *Hugh Selwyn Mauberley*
1. *The Letters of Ezra Pound, 1907-1941*, ed. D. D. Paige, London, 1951, p. 248.
2. Hugh Kenner, *The Poetry of Ezra Pound*, London, 1951, pp. 170-1.
3. See Thomas E. Connolly, in *Accent*, winter 1956.
4. See Yvor Winters, *In Defense of Reason*, p. 68.

p. 93. The Relation between Syntax and Music in Some Modern Poems in English
1. Avant-propos to *Connaissance de la Déesse*, translated by D. Folliot in [588].
2. *Variations sur les Bucoliques*, 1944, translated by D. Folliot as *Variations on the Eclogues*, in [588, pp. 295-8].
3. *Poésie et pensée abstraite*, the Basil Zaharoff lecture at Oxford, 1939 [588, p. 57].

p. 140. Sincerity and Poetry
1. It may be indeed that 'poetry of witness' would be a better name for what I have called 'confessional poetry'. 'Witness', for instance, fits Dr Williams's poems better than 'confession'. And 'witness', as we hear it used from the pulpit ('a Christian witness'), explains better than 'confession' why such poetry is often 'prophetic' into the bargain.

p. 147. A Poetry of Protest
1. *Geography*, Edward Dorn, London: Fulcrum.

p. 165. Landscape as Poetic Focus

1. *College English*, XXV (March 1964), p. 403.

2. ibid., p. 401.

3. ibid., p. 445.

4. *Land and Life: A Selection from the Writings of Carl Ortwin Sauer*, ed. John Leighley, Berkeley: University of California Press.

5. ibid., pp. 104-118.

6. ibid., pp. 246-270.

7. The American Geographical Society, New York, 1952.

p. 170. The Poetry of Samuel Menashe

1. 'Promised Land', from *The Many Named Beloved*. All the poems I quote are given in their entirety.

2. *The Many Named Beloved*.

3. ibid.

4. ibid.

5. ibid.

p. 177. The Black Mountain Poets: Charles Olson and Edward Dorn

1. Charles Olson, 'An Essay on Queen Tiy', *Wivenhoe Park Review*, 2 (1967), pp. 38-9.

p. 191. Pound and Eliot: A Distinction

1. See 'The Later Yeats', in *Literary Essays of Ezra Pound*, ed. T. S. Eliot, 1954, pp. 378-81.

2. Helen Gardner, *The Art of T. S. Eliot*, 1949, p. 7.

3. Pound, in the review which I have quoted from, distinguishes between 'the sort of poetry which seems to be music just forcing itself into articulate speech, and secondly, that sort of poetry which seems as if sculpture or painting were just forced or forcing itself into words'. In *Gaudier-Brzeska: A Memoir* (1917), Pound made the same distinction in almost identical words (see Marvell Press reprint [1960] p. 82). In the Memoir, Pound is fairly plainly vowing himself to poetry of the second sort: imagist or vorticist poetry which works by analogy with sculpture. Symbolist poetry on the other hand works by analogy with the art of music. And according to Valéry this analogy is more important to Symbolism than whatever may be gathered from worrying over what is meant by 'symbol'.

4. F. O. Matthiessen, *The Achievement of T. S. Eliot*, 3rd ed., 1958, p. 30.

5. *Essays in Criticism*, IV, p. 104.

6. ibid., IV, p. 106.

7. ibid., I, pp. 281-2.

8. ibid., V, p. 153.

p. 221. Hardy's Virgilian Purples

1. J. O. Bailey, *The Poetry of Thomas Hardy: A Handbook and Commentary*, 1970, p. 302.

2. ibid., p. 303.

3. *Aeneid*, I, 648.

4. I owe this example, and some of the others, to Mrs Drew Cox.

5. See especially, with 'After a Journey' in mind, *Aeneid*, II, 793-4.

ter frustra comprensa manus effugit imago,
par levibus ventis volucrique simillima somno.

In Dryden:

And thrice about her neck my arms I flung,
And thrice deceived, on vain embraces hung;
Or as a blast of wind, she rushed away.

6. Robert Bridges, *Ibant Obscuri*, Oxford, 1916.

7. Erich Auerbach, *Dante als Dichter der iridschen Welt* (Berlin and Leipzig, 1929), translated by Ralph Manheim as *Dante, Poet of the Secular World* (Chicago and London, 1961) pp. 41-2. Subsequent quotations from this volume are from pp. 43-4, 44, 45.

8. Auerbach, *op. cit. p. 95*. (Italics mine, for reasons that appear later.)

9. G. M. Young, in *Today and Yesterday*, 1948. My earlier quotation from Young is also from this source.

10. J. Hillis Miller, *Thomas Hardy: Distance and Desire*, 1970, p. 251.

p. 236. The Cantos: Towards a Pedestrian Reading

1. But see also Dorothy Shakespear Pound, *Etruscan Gate*, Exeter, 1971, p. 20: 'After the first world war we escaped from London to the S. of France . . . took two walking tours centred on Brives'.

2. Misinformation repeated by K. K. Ruthven, *Guide to Ezra Pound's Personae (1926)*, Berkeley and Los Angeles, 1969.

3. Noel Stock, *Poet in Exile*, Manchester, 1964. See *From Ritual to Romance*, Doubleday Anchor Books, 1957, p. 187.

4. See J. F. Rock, *The Ancient Na-Khi Kingdom of Southwest China*, 1947, vol. I, p. 270; vol. II, pp. 281, 298.

5. *Memoirs of Mme de Rémusat*, translated by Mrs Cashel Hoey and John Lillie, 2 vols., London, 1880.

p. 285. English and American in *Briggflatts*

1. See Serge Fauchereau, 'Three Oppen Letters with a Note', *Ironwood* 5, Tucson, Arizona (1975), pp. 78-85.

2. Hugh Kenner, *The Pound Era*, 1971, p. 406.

3. *Multi: Basil Bunting from the British Press*, Octaroon Book. A flyer distributed at Bunting's San Francisco reading, 1976.

4. Bunting, loc. cit.

5. 'Separation and Non-communication as Features of Hardy's Poetry', *Agenda* XIV, 3 (autumn 1976), pp. 45-62.

6. *Georgia Straight* (Vancouver, British Columbia). Writing Supplement 6.

BIBLIOGRAPHY

A. SEPARATE PUBLICATIONS

A1. *Purity of Diction in English Verse*, London: Chatto & Windus, 1952; New York: Oxford University Press, 1953; (2nd ed. with 'A Postscript, 1966') London: Routledge & Kegan Paul, 1967; New York: Schocken, 1967.

A2. *Fantasy Poets No. 19*, Oxford: Fantasy Press, 1954.

A3. *Brides of Reason*, Oxford: Fantasy Press, 1955.

A4. *Articulate Energy: An Enquiry into the Syntax of English Poetry*, London: Routledge & Kegan Paul, 1955; New York: Harcourt Brace, 1958; London: Routledge & Kegan Paul, 1966.

A5. *A Winter Talent and Other Poems*, London: Routledge & Kegan Paul, 1957.

A6. *The Late Augustans: Longer Poems of the Eighteenth Century*, London: Heinemann, 1958; New York: Macmillan, 1958; London: Heinemann, 1963. Editor.

A7. *The Forests of Lithuania*, Hessle, Yorkshire: Marvell Press, 1959.

A8. *Poems: Poetry Supplement*, London: Poetry Book Society, 1960. Editor.

A9. *The Heyday of Sir Walter Scott*, London: Routledge & Kegan Paul, 1961; New York: Barnes & Noble, 1961.

A10. *The Poetry of Sir Walter Scott*, London: Oxford, 1961.

A11. *A Sequence for Francis Parkman*, Hessle, Yorkshire: Marvell Press, 1961.

A12. *New and Selected Poems*, Middletown, Conn.: Wesleyan University Press, 1961.

A13. *Selected Poems of William Wordsworth*, London: G. G. Harrap, 1962. Editor.

A14. *The Language of Science and the Language of Literature, 1700-1740*, London & New York: Sheed & Ward, 1963.

A15. *Ezra Pound: Poet as Sculptor*, New York: Oxford, 1964; London: Routledge & Kegan Paul, 1965.

A16. *Events and Wisdoms: Poems 1957-1963*, London: Routledge & Kegan Paul, 1964; Middletown, Conn.: Wesleyan, 1965.

A17. *The Poems of Dr Zhivago*, Manchester: Manchester University Press, 1965; New York: Barnes & Noble, 1965. Translator and commentator.

A18. *Russian Literature and Modern British Fiction: A Collection of Critical Essays*, Chicago: University of Chicago Press, 1965; Toronto: University of Toronto Press, 1965. Editor.

A19. *Essex Poems: 1963-1967*, London: Routledge & Kegan Paul, 1969.

A20. *Poems*, London: Turret Books, 1969.

A21. *Pasternak: Modern Judgements*, London: Macmillan, 1969; Nashville: Aurora, 1970. Editor (with Angela Livingstone) and verse translator.

A22. *Six Epistles to Eva Hesse*, London: London Magazine Editions, 1970.
A23. *Collected Poems 1950-1970*, London: Routledge & Kegan Paul, 1972; New York: Oxford, 1972.
A24. *Thomas Hardy and British Poetry*, New York: Oxford, 1972; London: Routledge & Kegan Paul, 1973.
A25. *Augustan Lyric*, London: Heinemann, 1974. Editor.
A26. *The Shires*, London: Routledge & Kegan Paul, 1974.
A27. *In the Stopping Train and Other Poems*, Manchester: Carcanet New Press, 1977.

B. CONTRIBUTIONS TO BOOKS (first appearances only)
(Note: Articles from B and C reprinted in this volume are asterisked.)

B1. [Five Poems], *Poetry from Cambridge in Wartime*, ed. Geoffrey Moore, London: Fortune Press, 1946. Contents: 'A Pelican', 'A Song for These Crusaders', 'Glaphira III', 'Kites', 'Duplicity in Prayer'.
B2. [Introduction], *The Necklace* by Charles Tomlinson, Oxford: Fantasy Press, 1955, pp. 1-7.
B3. [Essay on William Cullen Bryant's 'To a Waterfowl'], *Interpretations: Essays on Twelve English Poems*, ed. John Wain, London: Routledge & Kegan Paul, 1955, pp. 130-137.
B4. [Translations from *Pan Tadeusz*], *Adam Mickiewicz 1798-1855: Selected Poems*, ed. Clark Mills, New York: Noonday, 1956, pp. 87-91, 96-8. Contents: 'House and Context', 'On Courteous Friendship', 'Day Breaks on Lithuania', 'Zosia in the Kitchen Garden', 'The Year 1812'.
B5. '*Pan Tadeusz* in English Verse', *Adam Mickiewicz in World Literature*, ed. Waclaw Lednicki, Berkeley & Los Angeles: University of California Press, 1956, pp. 319-30.
B6. [Translations], *Adam Mickiewicz: New Selected Poems*, ed. Clark Mills, New York: Voyages Press, 1957, pp. 45-7, 53-60, 68-70, 72-3. Contents: 'In the Greek Salon', 'Death of a Conversation', 'Zosia as a Nursemaid', 'Disenchantment', 'Mushrooms', 'Italophils', 'The Agitator', 'The Hamlet', 'Sunrise in Fair Weather'.
B7. 'The Young Yeats', *The Shaping of Modern Ireland*, ed. Conor Cruise O'Brien, London: Routledge & Kegan Paul, 1960, pp. 140-51.
B8. 'Syntax and Music in *Paradise Lost*', *The Living Milton*, ed. Frank Kermode, London: Routledge & Kegan Paul, 1960, pp. 70-84.
B9. *'Ezra Pound's *Hugh Selwyn Mauberley*', *The Modern Age*, ed. Boris Ford, Harmondsworth, Middlesex: Penguin, 1961, pp. 315-29.
B10. *'The Relation between Syntax and Music in Some Modern Poems in English', *Poetics*, The Hague: Mouton, 1961, pp. 203-14.
B11. [Comment on 'Corrib. An Emblem'], *Poet's Choice*, ed. Paul Engle and Joseph Langland, New York: Dial Press, 1962, pp. 197-8.

B12. 'Turgenev in England, 1850-1950', *Studies in Russian and Polish Literature in Honour of Waclaw Lednicki*, ed. Zbigniew Folejewski, The Hague: Mouton, 1962, pp. 168-84.

B13. 'Berkeley and the Style of Dialogue', *The English Mind: Essays Presented to Basil Willey*, ed. H. S. Davies and G. Watson, Cambridge: University Press, 1964, pp. 90-106.

B14. *'Yeats, the Master of a Trade', *The Integrity of Yeats*, ed. Denis Donoghue, Cork: Mercier Press, 1964, pp. 59-70.

B15. 'Tolstoy, Lermontov, and Others', *Russian Literature and Modern English Fiction: A Collection of Critical Essays*, ed. Donald Davie, Chicago: University of Chicago Press, 1965, pp. 164-99.

B16. 'Michael Robartes and the Dancer', *An Honoured Guest: New Essays on W. B. Yeats*, ed. Denis Donoghue and J. R. Mulryne, London: Edward Arnold, 1965, pp. 73-87.

B17. [Essay on Samuel Johnson's 'The Vanity of Human Wishes'], *Master Poems of the English Language*, ed. Oscar Williams, New York: Trident Press, 1966, pp. 300-3.

B18. 'Politics and Literature: John Adams and Doctor Johnson', *Politics and Experience: Essays Presented to Professor Michael Oakeshott on the Occasion of his Retirement*, ed. Preston King and B. C. Parekh, London: Cambridge University Press, 1968, pp. 395-408.

B19. 'Winter Landscape', *Eight Poets*, ed. Ian Hamilton, London: Poetry Book Society, 1968, [1 p.].

B20. 'Dionysus in *Lyrical Ballads*', *Wordsworth's Mind and Art*, ed. A. W. Thomson, Edinburgh: Oliver & Boyd, 1969, pp. 110-39.

B21. [Introduction], *Aspley Guise* by Peter Clothier, San Francisco: Red Hill Press, 1970, [5 pp.].

B22. 'To Helen Keller', *Years of Triumph: Helen Keller 1880-1968*, Los Angeles: University of Southern California Friends of the Libraries, 1970, pp. 11-12.

B23. *'The Black Mountain Poets: Charles Olson and Edward Dorn', *The Survival of Poetry*, ed. Martin Dodsworth, London: Faber & Faber, 1970, pp. 216-34.

B24. *'Pound and Eliot: A Distinction', *Eliot in Perspective*, ed. Graham Martin, London: Macmillan, 1970, pp. 62-82.

C. CONTRIBUTIONS TO PERIODICALS

C1. 'Towards a New Poetic Diction', *Prospect*, II, 11 (summer 1949), pp. 4-8.

C2. [Two Poems], *Poetry London*, IV, 16 (Sept. 1949), pp. 16-17. Contents: 'Landfall Among Friends', 'Condolence'.

C3. 'Letter to the Editor', *Scrutiny*, XVI, 3 (Sept. 1949), pp. 234-6.

C4. 'Christmas Week, 1948', *Poetry London*, V, 19 (Aug. 1950), p. 10. Poem.

C5. *'The Spoken Word', *Poetry London*, V, 20 (Nov. 1950), pp. 26-9.

Review of *Poems for Speaking: An Anthology with an Essay on Reading Aloud* by Richard Church and *Poets of the Pacific, Second Series* ed. Yvor Winters.

C6.   'Berkeley's Style in *Siris*', *Cambridge Journal*, IV, 7 (April 1951), pp. 427-33.

C7.   [Two Poems] , *Poetry London*, VI, 22 (summer 1951), pp. 13-15. Contents: 'Protesilaus and Laodamia', 'Four Moral Discoveries'.

C8.   'Hopkins, the Decadent Critic', *Cambridge Journal*, IV, 12 (Sept. 1951), pp. 725-39.

C9.   'The Shorter Poems of Walter Savage Landor', *Essays in Criticism*, I, 4 (Oct. 1951), pp. 345-55.

C10. ' "Strength" and "Ease" in Seventeenth-Century Criticism', *Hermathena*, 78 (Nov. 1951), pp. 3-11.

C11. *'The Poetic Diction of John M. Synge', *Dublin Magazine*, ns. XXVII, 1 (Jan.-March 1952), pp. 32-8.

C12. 'Poem as Abstract', *New Statesman*, XLIII, 1096 (8 March 1952), p. 278. Poem.

C13. 'Landor and Poetic Diction', *Essays in Criticism*, II, 2 (April 1952), pp. 218-9. Letter printed in Critical Forum.

C14. 'The Cyclists', *New Statesman*, XLIII, 1106 (17 May 1952), p. 589. Poem.

C15. 'Dramatic Poetry: Dryden's Conversation Piece', *Cambridge Journal*, V, 9 (June 1952), pp. 553-61.

C16. 'Transatlantic Drama', *Nine*, III, 4 (summer-autumn 1952), pp. 377-8. Review of *Beyond the Mountains* by Kenneth Rexroth.

C17. 'Evening on the Boyne', *New Statesman*, XLIV, 1118 (9 Aug. 1952), p. 164. Poem.

C18. 'Irony and Conciseness in Berkeley and in Swift', *Dublin Magazine*, ns. XXVII, 4 (Oct.-Dec. 1952), pp. 20-9.

C19. 'Thyestes', *New Statesman*, XLIV, 1129 (25 Oct. 1952), p. 482. Poem.

C20. 'Giving a Lift', *New Statesman*, XLIV, 1136 (13 Dec. 1952), p. 723. Poem.

C21. 'Machineries of Shame', *New Statesman*, XLV, 1143 (31 Jan. 1953), p. 124. Poem.

C22. 'Syntax in Poetry and Music', *Twentieth Century*, CLIII, 912 (Feb. 1953), pp. 128-34.

C23. 'Gerald Griffin's *The Collegians*', *Dublin Magazine*, ns. XXIX, 2 (April-June 1953), pp. 23-30.

C24. 'Herbert Read's Romanticism', *Twentieth Century*, CLIII, 914 (April 1953), pp. 295-301.

C25. 'View Halloo!', *New Statesman*, XLV, 1155 (25 April 1953), p. 494. Review of *The Wake of the Bounty* by C. S. Wilkinson.

C26. *' "Essential Gaudiness": The Poems of Wallace Stevens', *Twentieth Century*, CLIII, 916 (June 1953), pp. 455-62.

C27. 'Lucidity at a Price', *New Statesman*, XLV, 1162 (13 June 1953),

p. 710. Review of *Images of Tomorrow: An Anthology of Recent Poetry*, ed. John Heath-Stubbs and *New Poems, 1953: A P.E.N. Anthology* ed. Robert Conquest, Michael Hamburger, Howard Sergeant.

C28. 'The Garden Party', *New Statesman*, XLV, 1163 (20 June 1953), p. 738. Poem.

C29. 'Landor as Poet', *Shenandoah*, IV, 2-3 (summer-autumn 1953), pp. 93-105.

C30. 'Remembering the Thirties', *Spectator*, CXC, 6522 (26 June 1953), p. 827. Poem.

C31. 'Nothing New on the Augustans', *New Statesman*, XLV, 1164 (27 June 1953), p. 782. Review of *English Literature of the Eighteenth Century* by R. C. Churchill.

C32. 'Cat Beside the Shoe-Box', *Spectator*, CXCI, 6524 (10 July 1953), p. 57. Poem.

C33. 'Limited Achievement (Piranesi, *Prisons*, Plate VI)', *Spectator*, CXCI, 6527 (31 July 1953), p. 122. Poem.

C34. 'The Owl Minerva', *Spectator*, CXCI, 6529 (14 Aug. 1953), p. 184. Poem.

C35. 'How to Review', *New Statesman*, XLVI, 1171 (15 Aug. 1953), p. 186. Review of *Contemporary Reviews of Romantic Poetry* ed. John Wain.

C36. 'The Garage in the Headlamps', *New Statesman*, XLVI, 1173 (29 Aug. 1953), p. 237. Poem.

C37. 'Academicism and Jonathan Swift', *Twentieth Century*, CLIV, 919 (Sept. 1953), pp. 217-24.

C38. 'Translation Absolute', *New Statesman*, XLVI, 1174 (5 Sept. 1953), pp. 262, 264. Review of *Translations* by Ezra Pound.

C39. 'The Reader Vanishes', *Spectator*, CXCI, 6533 (11 Sept. 1953), pp. 274-5. Review of *The Modern Writer and His World* by G. S. Fraser.

C40. 'Modernist Precursors', *New Statesman*, XLVI, 1178 (3 Oct. 1953), p. 382. Review of *The Faber Book of Twentieth Century Verse* ed. John Heath-Stubbs and David Wright.

C41. 'The Evangelist', *New Statesman*, XLVI, 1179 (10 Oct. 1953), p. 425. Poem.

C42. 'Shakespeare's Tragi-Comedy', *New Statesman*, XLVI, 1181 (24 Oct. 1953), p. 496. Review of *Shakespeare's Measure for Measure* by Mary Lascelles.

C43. 'The Earnest and the Smart: Provincialism in Letters', *Twentieth Century*, CLIV, 921 (Nov. 1953), pp. 387-94.

C44. 'Surrogate and Substitute', *New Statesman*, XLVI, 1183 (7 Nov. 1953), pp. 575-6. Review of *Hound and Quarry* by Harold H. Watts.

C45. 'In the discussion that followed Dr Donald Davie said', *Hermathena*, 82 (19 Nov. 1953), pp. 72-5. Comment on Berkeley as a man of letters.

C46. 'The Critical Principles of William Cowper', *Cambridge Journal*,

VII, 3 (Dec. 1953), pp. 182-8.

C47. 'On Reading Soviet Writers', *New Statesman*, XLVI, 1187 (5 Dec. 1953), p. 722.

C48. 'Rococo Statuesque', *Spectator*, CXCI, 6547 (18 Dec. 1953), p. 727. Poem.

C49. 'Surprised by Joy. Dr Johnson at Ranelagh', *Essays in Criticism*, IV, 1 (Jan. 1954), pp. 85-6. Poem.

C50. 'Twilight in the Waste Lands', *Spectator*, CXCII, 6549 (1 Jan. 1954), p. 11. Poem.

C51. 'From the Blockhouse', *New Statesman*, XLVII, 1191 (2 Jan. 1954), p. 22. Review of *Literature and Criticism* by H. Coombes.

C52. 'Vehicle and Tenor', *Irish Times*, 9 Jan. 1954. Poem.

C53. 'A Winter Talent', *New Statesman*, XLVII, 1193 (16 Jan. 1954), p. 72. Poem.

C54. 'Pushkin: A Didactic Poem', *The Bell*, XIX, 3 (Feb. 1954), pp. 9-11.

C55. 'Russian Writing Since Chekhov', *New Statesman*, XLVII, 1199 (27 Feb. 1954), p. 266. Review of *Modern Russian Literature* by Marc Slonim.

C56. *'Professor Heller and the Boots', *The Bell*, XIX, 4 (March 1954), pp. 10-18.

C57. 'Scientist, Philosopher, Poet', *Twentieth Century*, CLV, 925 (March 1954), pp. 270-80.

C58. 'Chrysanthemums', *Spectator*, CXCII, 6559 (12 March 1954), p. 288. Poem.

C59. 'Method', *New Statesman*, XLVII, 1202 (20 March 1954), p. 374. Poem.

C60. 'Instigations to Procedures', *New Statesman*, XLVII, 1203 (27 March 1954), pp. 410, 412. Review of *The Literary Essays of Ezra Pound* ed. T. S. Eliot.

C61. 'When There's No One About in the Quad', *Encounter*, II, 4 (April 1954), pp. 86-8. Review of *The Unconscious Origin of Berkeley's Philosophy* by J. O. Wisdom.

C62. 'Sixteenth-Century Poetry and the Common Reader: The Case of Thomas Sackville', *Essays in Criticism*, IV, 2 (April 1954), pp. 117-27.

C63. [Review of *A Bibliography of James Joyce* by J. J. Slocum and Herbert Calhoun], *New Statesman*, XLVII, 1205 (10 April 1954), p. 473.

C64. 'Cherry Ripe', *New Statesman*, XLVII, 1212 (29 May 1954), p. 704. Poem.

C65. 'Is There a London Literary Racket?', *Twentieth Century*, CLV, 928 (June 1954), pp. 540-6.

C66. [Three Poems], *Listen*, I, 2 (summer 1954), pp. 6-9. Contents: 'Rejoinder to a Publisher's Reader', 'Zip', 'A Gathered Church'.

C67. [Review of *Life Arboreal* by Ewart Milne], *Listen*, I, 2 (summer 1954), pp. 27-8.

C68. 'Piranesi's Vues De Pesto', *The Bell*, XIX, 8 (July 1954), pp. 46-8. Poem.

C69. '*The Daltons*, A Neglected Novel by Lever', *Dublin Magazine*, ns. XXX, 3 (July-Sept. 1954), pp. 41-50.

C70. 'Broken Cisterns or Living Waters?' *New Statesman*, XLVIII, 1218 (10 July 1954), pp. 50-1. Review of *The Broken Cistern* by Bonamy Dobrée.

C71. 'Marcher Lords', *New Statesman*, XLVIII, 1219 (17 July 1954), p. 83. Review of *Russia, Poland and the West* by Waclaw Lednicki.

C72. ' "The Deserted Village": Poem as Virtual History', *Twentieth Century*, CLVI, 930 (Aug. 1954), pp. 161-74.

C73. 'A Masterpiece', *New Statesman*, XLVIII, 1222 (7 Aug. 1954), p. 162. Review of *The Cantos* by Ezra Pound.

C74. 'Looking for Trouble', *New Statesman*, XLVIII, 1227 (11 Sept. 1954), p. 298. Poem.

C75. 'The Auroras of Autumn', *Perspective*, VII, 3 (autumn 1954), pp. 125-36.

C76. 'The Critical Forum: Sixteenth-century Poetry and the Common Reader', *Essays in Criticism*, IV, 4 (Oct. 1954), pp. 426-8. Reply to J. B. Broadbent.

C77. 'The Fountain', *Spectator*, CXCIII, 6588 (1 Oct. 1954), p. 400. Poem.

C78. 'Eight Years After', *Encounter*, III, 5 (Nov. 1954), p. 4. Poem.

C79. 'Miss Edgeworth and Miss Austen: The Absentee', *Irish Writing*, 29 (Dec. 1954), pp. 50-6.

C80. 'Fool's Paradise', *New Statesman*, XLVIII, 1239 (4 Dec. 1954), p. 746. Poem.

C81. [Three Poems], *Listen*, I, 3 (winter 1954), pp. 2-4. Contents: 'Portrait of the Artist as a Farmyard Fowl', 'The Bride of Reason', 'The Gorgon'.

C82. [Review of *Poems: A Selection* by Leonie Adams], *Shenandoah*, VI, 1 (winter 1954), pp. 64-7.

C83. 'The Poet-Scholar', *Essays in Criticism*, V, 1 (Jan. 1955), p. 43. Poem.

C84. *'Poetry, or Poems?', *Twentieth Century*, CLVII, 935 (Jan. 1955), pp. 79-87.

C85. 'Poet and Persona', *New Statesman*, XLIX, 1251 (26 Feb. 1955), p. 295. Review of *Ezra Pound's Mauberley* by John J. Espey.

C86. 'Tuscan Morning', *New Statesman*, XLIX, 1252 (5 March, 1955), p. 329. Poem.

C87. [Three Poems], *Shenandoah*, VI, 2 (spring 1955), pp. 3-5. Contents: 'The Fountain', 'Going to Italy', 'Chrysanthemums'.

C88. [Review of *The Collected Poems of Wallace Stevens*], *Shenandoah*, VI, 2 (spring 1955), pp. 62-4.

C89. 'Entering into the Sixteenth Century', *Essays in Criticism*, V, 2 (April 1955), pp. 159-64. Review of *English Literature in the Sixteenth Century* by C. S. Lewis.

C90. 'Dream Forest', *Spectator*, CXCIV, 6615 (8 April 1955), p. 441. Poem.

C91. 'The Ruins of Rome', *New Statesman*, XLIX, 1260 (30 April 1955), p. 618.

C92. 'Cambridge Frivolity', *Twentieth Century*, CLVII, 939 (May 1955), pp. 447-53.

C93. 'Mickiewicz on Courteous Friendship', *Spectator*, CXCIV, 6624 (10 June 1955), p. 746. Poem.

C94. 'Yeats, Berkeley, and Romanticism', *Irish Writing*, 31 (summer 1955), pp. 36-41.

C95. 'A Dublin Cento', *Shenandoah*, VI, 3 (summer 1955), pp. 36-8. Poem.

C96. 'Elders and Betters', *Essays in Criticism*, V, 3 (July 1955), p. 242. Poem.

C97. 'Wharncliffe', *New Statesman*, L, 1275 (13 Aug. 1955), p. 190. Poem.

C98. [Two Poems], *Irish Writing*, 32 (autumn 1955), pp. 7-8. Contents: 'North Dublin', 'Priory of St Savior Glendalough'.

C99. [Two Poems], *Listen*, I, 4 (autumn 1955), pp. 9-11. Contents: 'The Wind at Penistone', 'Humanist'.

C100. [Review of *Shield of Achilles* by W. H. Auden and *Book of Moments: Poems 1919-1954* by Kenneth Burke], *Shenandoah*, VII, 1 (autumn 1955), pp. 93-5.

C101. 'Yeats and Pound', *Dublin Magazine*, ns. XXXI, 4 (Oct.-Dec. 1955), pp. 17-21. Review of *Autobiographies* and *Classic Anthology Defined by Confucius*.

C102. 'The Poetry of Prince Vyazemsky (1792-1878)', *Hermathena*, 86 (Nov. 1955), pp. 1-19. Introduction and translations.

C103. 'Augustans Old and New', *Twentieth Century*, CLVIII, 945 (Nov. 1955), pp. 464-75.

C104. 'Berkeley and "Philosophic Words" ', *Studies: An Irish Quarterly Review*, XLIV, 4 (winter 1955), p. 319.

C105. 'Reflections of an English Writer in Ireland', *Studies: An Irish Quarterly Review*, XLIV, 4 (winter 1955), p. 439.

C106. 'Great or Major?', *New Statesman*, LI, 1297 (14 Jan. 1956), p. 48. Review of *Collected Poems* by Wallace Stevens.

C107. 'Encomiastic Criticism', *New Statesman*, LI, 1303 (3 March 1956), p. 190. Review of *Predilections* by Marianne Moore.

C108. [Two Poems], *Folio*, XXI, 2 (spring 1956), pp. 21-2. Contents: 'The Nonconformist', 'Heigh-ho on a Winter Afternoon'.

C109. '*Poems and Satires*: Spring Verse Choice', *Irish Writing*, 34 (spring 1956), pp. 57-8. Review of *Ancient Lights: Poems and Satires* by Austin Clarke.

C110. [Review of *The Less Deceived*, Poems by Philip Larkin and *Way of Looking*, Poems by Elizabeth Jennings], *Irish Writing*, 34 (spring 1956), pp. 62-4.

C111. [Two Poems], *Shenandoah*, VII, 2 (spring 1956), pp. 16-18. Contents: 'At the Cradle of Genius', 'The Mushroom Gatherers, after Mickiewicz'.
C112. *'T. S. Eliot: The End of an Era', *Twentieth Century*, CLIX, 950 (April 1956), pp. 350-62.
C113. 'Pleasures of Ruins', *New Statesman*, LI, 1314 (19 May 1956), p. 571. Review of *Marvels of Ancient Rome* by Margaret R. Scherer and *The Shrine of St Peter* by J. Toynbee and J. Ward Perkins.
C114. 'Correspondence', *Delta,* 9 (summer 1956), pp. 27-8.
C115. 'Obiter Dicta', *Listen*, II, 1 (summer 1956), pp. 7-8. Poem.
C116. 'Notes on the Later Poems of Stevens', *Shenandoah*, VII, 3 (summer 1956), pp. 40-1.
C117. 'Off the Assembly Line', *Essays in Criticism*, VI, 3 (July 1956), pp. 319-25. Review of *Pope's Dunciad* by Aubrey L. Williams and *Personification in Eighteenth Century English Poetry* by Chester F. Chapin.
C118. ' "Forma" and "Concept" in Ezra Pound's *Cantos',* *Irish Writing*, 36 (autumn-winter 1956), pp. 160-73.
C119. [Review of *A Summoning of Stones* by Anthony Hecht], *Shenandoah*, VIII, 1 (autumn 1956), pp. 43-4.
C120. 'Adrian Stokes and Pound's *Cantos',* *Twentieth Century*, CLX, 457 (Nov. 1956), pp. 419-36.
C121. 'Poetry's Imaginary Museum', *Spectrum*, I, 1 (winter 1957), pp. 56-60. Review of *The Criterion Book of Modern American Verse* ed. W. H. Auden.
C122. 'Mens Sana In Corpore Sano', *Spectator*, CXCVIII, 6706 (4 Jan. 1957), p. 30. Poem.
C123. 'From an Italian Journal', *Twentieth Century*, CLXII, 960 (Feb. 1957), pp. 125-137.
C124. 'Bedrock', *New Statesman*, LIII, 1356 (9 March 1957), p. 316. Review of *Section: Rock Drill de los Cantares* by Ezra Pound.
C125. 'Derbyshire Turf', *Listen*, II, 2 (spring 1957), p. 7. Poem.
C126. *'Common-Mannerism', *Listen* II, 2 (spring 1957), pp. 20-2. Review of Randall Jarrell's *Collected Poems* and D. J. Enright's *Bread Rather than Blossoms*.
C127. 'Under St Paul's', *Spectrum*, I, 2 (spring-summer 1957), pp. 19-20. Poem.
C128. 'Killala', *Listen*, II, 3 (summer-autumn 1957), p. 7. Poem.
C129. 'On Bertrand Russell's Portraits from Memory', *Sewanee Review*, LXV, 3 (summer 1957), p. 360. Poem.
C130. '*New Lines* and Mr Tomlinson', *Essays in Criticism*, VII, 3 (July 1957), pp. 343-4. Letter in Critical Forum.
C131. 'The Dublin Theatre Festival', *Twentieth Century*, CLXII, 965 (July 1957), pp. 71-3.
C132. *'The Poet in the Imaginary Museum', *Listener*, LVIII, 1476 (11 July 1957), pp. 47-8. Part 1.

C133. *'The Poet in the Imaginary Museum', *Listener*, LVIII, 1477 (18 July 1957), pp. 92-3. Part 2.

C134. 'Looking at Buildings', *Twentieth Century*, CLXII, 966 (Aug. 1957), pp. 164-71.

C135. 'First Fruits: The Poetry of Thomas Kinsella', *Irish Writing*, 37 (autumn 1957), pp. 47-9. Review of *Poems* (Dolmen Press).

C136. 'Introductory Note [to Jean Cocteau's *Leone*, trans. by Allan Neame]', *Spectrum*, I, 3 (fall 1957), pp. 13-15.

C137. *'An Alternative to Pound?', *Spectrum*, I, 3 (fall 1957), pp. 60-3. Review of *The Form of Loss* by Edgar Bowers.

C138. 'Poems in a Foreign Language', *Essays in Criticism*, VII, 4 (Oct. 1957), pp. 440-4. Review of *The Faber Book of Modern American Verse* ed. W. H. Auden.

C139. 'Enigma', *Poetry*, XCI, 1 (Oct. 1957), pp. 56-60. Review of *The Letters of James Joyce* ed. Stuart Gilbert and *Collected Poems* by James Joyce.

C140. 'Common and Uncommon Muses', *Twentieth Century*, CLXII, 968 (Nov. 1957), pp. 458-68.

C141. 'The Waterfall at Powerscourt', *Shenandoah*, IX, 1 (winter 1958), p. 13. Poem.

C142. *'Kinds of Comedy', *Spectrum*, II, 1 (winter 1958), pp. 25-31.

C143. 'Versions from the *Pan Tadeusz* of Adam Mickiewicz (1798-1855)',*Listen*, II, 4 (spring 1958), pp. 11-13. Contents: 'Remembering Lithuania', 'Femme Fatale', 'Extravaganza'.

C144. 'Whitmanesque with a Difference', *Shenandoah*, IX, 2 (spring 1958), pp. 54-7. Review of *Hot Afternoons Have Been in Montana: Poems* by Eli Siegel.

C145. 'From *Pan Tadeusz*, Books 3 & 4, by Adam Mickiewicz', *Spectrum*, II, 2 (spring-summer 1958), pp. 67-82. Introduction and translation.

C146. 'A Book of Modern Prose', *The Use of English*, IX, 4 (summer 1958), pp. 240-3. Review of *Book of Modern Prose* by Douglas Brown.

C147. 'Professional Standards', *New Statesman*, LVI, 1449 (20 Dec. 1958), p. 886. Review of *Poems* by Boris Pasternak and *Back to Life* ed. Robert Conquest.

C148. [Three Poems], *Listen*, III, 1 (winter 1958), pp. 7-9. Contents: 'Hidden Persuaders', 'Anecdote of Transitions', 'Against Confidences'.

C149. 'Doing What Comes Naturally', *Listen*, III, 1 (winter 1958), pp. 24-8. Review of *The Talking Skull* by James Reeves and *The One-eyed Gunner* by Robert Beloof.

C150. 'Ebenezer's Son', *Spectrum*, III, 1 (winter 1959), pp. 58-63. Poem.

C151. 'With the Grain', *Sewanee Review*, LXVII, 1 (winter 1959), pp. 49-51. Poem.

C152. 'Advanced Level', *New Statesman*, LVII, 1454 (24 Jan. 1959),

p. 121. Review of *A Grammar of Metaphor* by Christine Brooke-Rose.

C153. 'Reflections on Deafness', *Critical Quarterly*, I, 1 (spring 1959), p. 33. Poem.

C154. *'See, and Believe', *Essays in Criticism*, IX, 2 (April 1959), pp. 188-95. Review of *Seeing Is Believing* by Charles Tomlinson.

C155. 'Free Thinkers', *New Statesman*, LVII, 1468 (2 May 1959), p. 616. Review of *The Broken Mirror* ed. Pawel Mayewski.

C156. 'Book-Making', *Spectator*, CCII, 6829 (15 May 1959), p. 706. Review of *The Critical Writings of James Joyce*, ed. Ellsworth Mason and Richard Ellmann.

C157. 'Maker and Breaker', *New Statesman*, LVII, 1470 (16 May 1959), p. 695. Review of *The Masterpiece and the Man: Yeats as I Knew Him* by Monk Gibbon.

C158. 'False Harvest', *New Statesman*, LVII, 1471 (23 May 1959), p. 729. Poem.

C159. *'Remembering the Movement',*Prospect*,summer 1959,pp.13-16.

C160. 'Coming to Maricopa', *Delta*, 18 (summer 1959), pp. 4-5. Poem.

C161. 'The Legacy of Fenimore Cooper', *Essays in Criticism*, IX, 3 (July 1959), pp. 222-38.

C162. 'Immoderate Criticism', *Encounter*, XIII, 2 (Aug. 1959), pp. 62-4. Review of *The Tradition of the New* by Harold Rosenberg.

C163. [Review of *Life Studies* by Robert Lowell and *Vision and Rhetoric* by G. S. Fraser], *Twentieth Century*, CLXVI, 990 (Aug. 1959), pp. 116-18.

C164. [Three Poems and an untitled statement], *Universities Quarterly*, XIII, 4 (Aug.-Oct. 1959), pp. 338-42. Contents: 'Old Fort Frontenac', 'The Last Frontier', 'Red Rock of Utah'.

C165. 'Against Confidences',*Spectrum*,III,3(fall 1959),pp.158-9.Poem.

C166. 'Dublin's Swift', *New Statesman*, LVIII, 1493 (24 Oct. 1959), p. 549. Review of *In Search of Swift* by Denis Johnston.

C167. [Two Poems], *Paris Review*, 25 (winter-spring 1960), pp. 54-5. Contents: 'Letter to Curtis Bradford', 'Lasalle and the Discovery of the Great West'.

C168. 'Finnegan Began Again', *New Statesman*, LIX, 1504 (9 Jan. 1960), p. 47. Review of *The Books at the Wake* by James S. Atherton.

C169. [Review of *English Literature in the Early Eighteenth Century* by Bonamy Dobrée], *Listener*, LXIII, 1611 (11 Feb. 1960),p.275.

C170. 'At a Solemn Music', *Listen*, III, 3-4 (spring 1960), p. 3. Poem.

C171. *'Impersonal and Emblematic', *Listen*, III, 3-4 (spring 1960), pp. 31-6. Review of Robert Graves's *Collected Poems*.

C172. 'Cross-Channel Traffic', *New Statesman*, LIX, 1517 (9 April 1960), p. 532. Review of *From Gautier to Eliot* by Enid Starkie.

C173. 'To a Brother in the Mystery', *Encounter*, XIV, 6 (June 1960), pp. 29-30. Poem.

C174. 'John Oldham', *The Times Literary Supplement*, 3052 (26 Aug.

1960), p. 544. Unsigned review of *Poems of John Oldham*.

C175. 'The Importance of Being O'Connor', *Spectator*, CCV, 6909 (25 Nov. 1960), pp. 868-9. Review of *The Lower View* by Philip O'Connor.

C176. 'Polish Baroque', *New Statesman*, LX, 1550 (26 Nov. 1960), p. 843. Review of *Five Centuries of Polish Poetry, 1450-1950*, translated by Jerzy Peterkiewicz and Burns Singer.

C177. 'Literature into Life', *Spectator*, CCV, 6911 (9 Dec. 1960), p. 945.

C178. 'Right Wing Sympathies', *Prospect*, winter 1960, pp. 9-10. Poem.

C179. 'Past and Present', *Critical Quarterly Supplement: Poetry 1960*, p. 17. Poem.

C180. 'Against All Odds: Two Poems', *New World Writing*, 17 (1960), pp. 203-4. Contents: 'On Generous Lines', 'Nineteen Seventeen'.

C181. 'Looking for the Actual', *Spectator*, CCVI, 6915 (6 Jan. 1961), p. 19. Review of *Selected Poems* by John Peale Bishop, *Selected Poems* by e. e. cummings, *E. E. Cummings* by Norman Friedman, *On a Calm Shore* by Frances Cornford, *Country Matters* by Oliver Bernard, *The Only Need* by Brian Higgins.

C182. 'Kinds of Mastery', *Spectator*, CCVI, 6920 (10 Feb. 1961), pp. 193-4. Review of *Imaginings* by David Holbrook, *When That April* by Gillian Stoneham, *Any Day* by K. W. Gransden, *The Rats* by Alan Sillitoe.

C183. 'Designed to be Read as the Bible', *Spectator*, CCVI, 6925 (17 March 1961), pp. 370-1. Review of *The New English Bible: New Testament*.

C184. 'Barnsley and District', *Critical Quarterly*, III, 1 (spring 1961), p. 41. Poem.

C185. 'Australians and Others', *Spectator*, CCVI, 6926 (24 March 1961), pp. 416-7. Review of *Poems* by A. D. Hope, *Once Bitten, Twice Bitten* by Peter Porter, *Heart's Needle* by W. D. Snodgrass, *William Empson Reading Selected Poems*.

C186. 'Verser's Playtime', *Spectator*, CCVI, 6930 (21 April 1961), pp. 575-6. Review of *The Screens, and Other Poems* by I. A. Richards, *Thistles and Roses* by Iain Crichton Smith, *Solstices* by Louis MacNeice, *The Map of Clay* by Jack Clemo.

C187. 'The Writer's Condition in Hungary', *Guardian*, 28 April 1961, p. 9.

C188. 'For Doreen', *New Statesman*, LXI, 1575 (19 May 1961), p. 793. Poem.

C189. 'The Life of Service', *New Yorker*, XXXVII, 16 (3 June 1961), p. 38. Poem.

C190. 'Poets and Improvisers', *New Statesman*, LXI, 1579 (16 June 1961), pp. 958-9. Review of *Collected Poems 1908-1956* by Siegfried Sassoon, *More Poems, 1961* by Robert Graves, *The Bluebells* by John Masefield.

C191. 'Literature and Morality', *Critical Quarterly*, III, 2 (summer 1961), pp. 109-13.

C192. 'A Meeting of Cultures', *Critical Quarterly*, III, 2 (summer 1961), pp. 151-2.

C193. 'Fine Old Eye', *New Statesman*, LXI, 1581 (30 June 1961), pp. 1047-8. Review of *Wilfred Scawen Blunt* by the Earl of Lytton.

C194. 'Model Children', *Twentieth Century*, CLXX, 1010 (July 1961), p. 65. Poem.

C195. 'Poems and Orations', *New Statesman*, LXII, 1584 (21 July 1961), pp. 91-2. Review of *Chronique* by St John Perse, *Weep Before God* by John Wain, *The Last Galway Hooker* by Richard Murphy.

C196. 'A Christening', *New Statesman*, LXII, 1586 (4 Aug. 1971). p. 157. Poem.

C197. 'Insights and Epigrams', *New Statesman*, LXII, 1589 (25 Aug. 1961), pp. 246-7. Review of *The Many Named Beloved* by Samuel Menashe, *Later Poems* by Austin Clarke, *Title Deeds* by Frederick Grubb, *Song for a Birth or a Death* by Elizabeth Jennings.

C198. 'Clear Glass, and Rippled', *New Statesman*, LXII, 1594 (29 Sept. 1961), pp. 435, 438. Review of *A Tropical Childhood* by Edward Lucie-Smith, *Tares* by R. S. Thomas, *Morant Bay* by Francis Berry, *Poisoned Lands* by John Montague.

C199. 'Hardy and the Avant-garde', *New Statesman*, LXII, 1597 (20 Oct. 1961), pp. 560-1. Review of *Some Recollections* by Emma Hardy.

C200. 'Toynbee's Gerontion', *New Statesman*, LXII, 1598 (27 Oct. 1961), p. 615. Review of *Pantaloon* by Philip Toynbee.

C201. 'Snags', *New Statesman*, LXII, 1602 (24 Nov. 1961), pp. 794-5. Review of *Audible Silence* by Lawrence Whistler, *New Poems, 1961—The PEN Anthology*, *The Re-ordering of the Stones* by Jon Silkin, *Time for Sale* by Edward Lowbury, *Johnny Alleluia* by Charles Causley.

C202. 'Frontenac', *Partisan Review*, XXIX, 1 (winter 1962), pp. 92-3. Poem.

C203. *'Nightingales, Anangke', *New Statesman*, LXIII, 1608 (5 Jan. 1962), pp. 20-1. Review of *Collected Poems* by Ronald Bottrall, *Poems in English* by Samuel Beckett, *The Nature of Cold Weather* by Peter Redgrove, *The Bright Cloud* by Christopher Lee.

C204. 'The Irish at Home', *New Statesman*, LXIII, 1614 (16 Feb. 1962), p. 230. Review of *Twice Round the Black Church* by Austin Clarke.

C205. 'Angry Penguins', *New Statesman*, LXIII, 1615 (23 Feb. 1962), pp. 270-2. Review of *The Early Drowned* by Hilary Corke, *Ern Malley's Poems*, *The View from a Blind I* by George Barker.

C206. 'Right Wing Sympathies', *The Review*, 1 (April-May 1962), pp. 4-5. Poem. Reprinted from *Prospect*, winter 1960, pp. 9-10.

C207. 'A. Alvarez and Donald Davie: A Discussion', *The Review*, 1 (April-May 1962), pp. 10-25.

C208. *'Two Analogies for Poetry', *Listener*, LXVII, 1723 (5 April

1962), pp. 598-9.

C209. 'All Wistful', *New Statesman*, LXIII, 1621 (6 April 1962), p. 498. Review of *torse 3* by Christopher Middleton, *The Landfallers* by John Holloway, *A Garland for the Green* by Ewart Milne.

C210. 'Translating Pasternak', *New Statesman*, LXIII, 1622 (13 April 1962), pp. 533-4. Review of *In the Interlude, Poems 1945-1960* by Boris Pasternak, translated by Henry Kamen.

C211. 'So Far', *New Statesman*, LXIII, 1624 (27 April 1962), p. 604. Review of *Robert Lowell, the First Twenty Years* by Hugh Staples.

C212. [Seven Poems], *Poetry*, C, 2 (May 1962), pp. 71-8. Contents: 'In California', 'New York in August', 'Coastal Redwoods', 'Agave in the West', 'On Not Deserving', 'Hyphens'.

C213. 'England as a Poetic Subject', *Poetry*, C, 2 (May 1962), pp. 121-3.

C214. 'The Right Use of Conventional Language', *The Dubliner*, 3 (May-June 1962), pp. 15-28.

C215. [Review of *John Wesley's English* by George Lawton], *Listener*, LXVII, 1727 (3 May 1962), pp. 782-5.

C216. 'Reason Revised', *New Statesman*, LXIII, 1625 (4 May 1962), pp. 639-40. Review of *The New Poetry* selected by A. Alvarez, *Fighting Terms* by Thom Gunn, *The Penguin Book of Russian Verse* ed. D. D. Obolensky, *The Penguin Book of Latin Verse* ed. F. Brittain, *The Penguin Book of Chinese Verse* ed. A. R. Davis, *Rimbaud* translated by Oliver Bernard, *Penguin Modern Poets 1* (Lawrence Durrell, Elizabeth Jennings, R. S. Thomas), *Penguin Modern Poets 2* (Kingsley Amis, Dom Moraes, Peter Porter), *Control Tower* by Richard Kell, *Haste to the Wedding* by Alex Comfort, *Guinness Book of Poetry 5, A Row of Pharaohs* by Patrick Creagh.

C217. 'Use of English', *New Statesman*, LXIII, 1627 (18 May 1962), p. 722. Review of *English in Education* ed. Brian Jackson and Denys Thompson.

C218. 'Poems by Donald Davie', *New Statesman*, LXIII, 1632 (22 June 1962), p. 912. Contents: 'At an Italian Barber's', 'Low Lands', 'Holiday House', 'House Keeping'.

C219. 'Life Encompassed', *Listener*, LXVIII, 1738 (19 July 1962), p. 99. Poem.

C220. *'A'e Gowden Lyric', *New Statesman*, LXIV, 1639 (10 Aug. 1962), pp. 174-5. Review of *Collected Poems* by Hugh MacDiarmid and *Hugh MacDiarmid: a Festschrift* ed. K. R. Duval and Sydney Smith.

C221. 'Hornet', *Listener*, LXVIII, 1744 (30 Aug. 1962), p. 317. Poem.

C222. 'Pasternak: Poems of Dr Zhivago', *Listen*, IV, 1 (autumn 1962), pp. 16-18. Contents: 'Summer in the City', 'Grass and Stone'.

C223. 'A Note on Translating Pasternak', *Listen*, IV, 1 (autumn 1962), pp. 19-23.

C224. 'Ease and Unease', *New Statesman*, LXIV, 1652 (9 Nov. 1962), pp. 672-4. Review of *The Water Beetle* by Nancy Mitford and *Afterthought* by Elizabeth Bowen.

C225. 'Impersonal and Emblematic', *Shenandoah*, XIII, 2 (winter 1962), pp. 38-44. American reprint of review of Robert Graves's *Collected Poems* from *Listen*, III, 3-4 (spring 1960), pp. 31-6.

C226. [Two Poems], *Shenandoah*, XIII, 2 (winter 1962), pp. 45-6. Contents: 'Love and the Times', 'In Chopin's Garden'.

C227. 'House Keeping', *Critical Quarterly Poetry Supplement Number 3: English Poetry Now* [1962], p. 15.

C228. 'Across the Bay', *New Statesman*, LXV, 1660 (4 Jan. 1963), p. 16. Poem.

C229. 'Co-existence in Literature', *New Statesman*, LXV, 1666 (15 Feb. 1963), p. 238. Review of *The Meaning of Contemporary Realism* by George Lukacs.

C230. 'Spender Struggling', *New Statesman*, LXV, 1672 (29 March 1963), p. 465. Review of *Struggle of the Modern* by Stephen Spender.

C231. 'The Feeders', *Spectator*, CCX, 7031 (29 March 1963), p. 406. Poem.

C232. 'Three Poems', *New Statesman*, LXV, 1677 (3 May 1963), p. 679. Contents: 'The Windfall', 'After a Car Smash', 'Between Dead and Alive'.

C233. 'Femme Fatale', *New Statesman*, LXV, 1684 (21 June 1963), pp. 939-40. Review of *My Sister, My Spouse* by H. F. Peters.

C234. [Seven Poems], *Poetry*, CII, 5 (Aug. 1963), pp. 312-16. Contents: 'Autumn Imagined', 'Hot Hands', 'Where Depths are Surfaces', 'Vying', 'Red Mills', 'July', 'Battlefield'.

C235. 'In Dog Days', *New Statesman*, LXVI, 1698 (27 Sept. 1963), p. 414. Poem.

C236. 'The Vindication of Jovan Babic', *The Review*, 9 (Oct. 1963), p. 38. Poem.

C237. *'Mr Eliot', *New Statesman*, LXVI, 1700 (11 Oct. 1963), pp. 496-7. Review of *Collected Poems 1909-1962* by T. S. Eliot.

C238. 'Histories of Desperation', *New Statesman*, LXVI, 1708 (6 Dec. 1963), pp. 845-6. Review of *English Literature, 1815-1832* by Ian Jack and *The Romantic Conflict* by Allen Rodway.

C239. 'Time Passing, Beloved', *Critical Quarterly Poetry Supplement Number 4: Twentieth Century Love Poems* [1963], p. 18.

C240. 'Unsettling Restraint', *New Statesman*, LXVII, 1712 (3 Jan. 1964), p. 14. Review of *Racine: Phèdre and Other Plays* translated by John Cairncross.

C241. 'Hearing Aids', *New Statesman*, LXVII, 1716 (31 Jan. 1964), pp. 175-6. Review of *The Confucian Odes of Ezra Pound* by L. S. Dembo and *A Bibliography of Ezra Pound* by Donald Gallup.

C242. 'Multi-Storey Structures', *New Statesman*, LXVII, 1722 (13 March 1964), p. 406. Review of *Selected Essays* by R. P. Warren.

C243. *'Alan Stephens—A Tone of Voice', *Prospect*, 6 (spring 1964), pp. 38-40.

C244. 'Profits of Curiosity', *New Statesman*, LXVII, 1727 (17 April 1964), p. 607. Review of *In General and Particular* by C.M.Bowra.

C245. 'Drawing the Line', *New Statesman*, LXVII, 1732 (22 May 1964, pp. 810-11. Review of *Montenegro* by Milovan Djilas, translated by Kenneth Johnstone.

C246. 'Reading between the Gists', *Guardian*, 22 May 1964, Review of *Poet in Exile* by Noel Stock.

C247. 'To a Wife in Her Middle Age', *Listener*, LXXI, 1836 (4 June 1964), p. 914. Poem.

C248. 'John Clare', *New Statesman*, LXVII, 1736 (19 June 1964), p. 964. Review of *The Shepherd's Calendar of John Clare, The Later Poems of John Clare, The Life of John Clare* all ed. Eric Robinson and Geoffrey Summerfield.

C249. 'Rodez', *Shenandoah*, XV, 4 (summer 1964), p. 45. Poem.

C250. 'In the Pity', *New Statesman*, LXVIII, 1746 (28 Aug. 1964), pp. 282-3. Review of *English Poetry of the First World War* by John H. Johnston and *Up the Line to Death* by Brian Gardner.

C251. 'Thomas', *New Statesman*, LXVIII, 1750 (25 Sept. 1964), p. 447. Poem.

C252. 'Malchus, the High Priest's Servant', *New Statesman*, LXVIII, 1755 (30 Oct. 1964), p. 664. Poem.

C253. 'Shelley and the Pforzheimer Foundation', *New Statesman*, LXVIII, 1759 (27 Nov. 1964), pp. 840-1. Review of *The Esdaile Notebook* by Percy Shelley ed. Kenneth Cameron.

C254. 'Two Poems', *Critical Quarterly*, VI, 4 (Dec. 1964), p. 339. Contents: 'Postmeridian', 'Abishag a Shunammite'.

C255. *'Two Ways out of Whitman', *The Review*, 14 (Dec. 1964), pp. 14-19. Review of *Pictures from Brueghel* by William Carlos Williams and *The Far Field* by Theodore Roethke.

C256. 'New University of Essex: The Merits of City Culture', *New Statesman*, LXVIII, 1761 (11 Dec. 1964), p. 920.

C257. 'Edward Dorn's *The Rites of Passage*', *Wivenhoe Park Review*, 1 (winter 1965), pp. 112-18.

C258. 'Pietà', *Paris Review*, 33 (winter-spring 1965), pp. 60-1. Poem.

C259. 'The Blank of the Wall', *Agenda*, IV, 1 (April-May 1965), p. 35. Poem.

C260. 'On Translating Mao's Poetry', *The Nation*, CC, 26 (28 June 1965), pp. 704-5. Review of *Mao and the Chinese Revolution* translated by Michael Bullock and Jerome Ch'en.

C261. 'Iowa', *New Statesman*, LXX, 1802 (24 Sept. 1965), p. 440. Poem.

C262. *'After Sedley, After Pound', *The Nation*, CCI, 14 (1 Nov. 1965), pp. 311-13. Review of *All: The Collected Shorter Poems* by Louis Zukofsky.

C263. 'Enjoy the African Night', *New Statesman*, LXX, 1813 (10 Dec. 1965), p. 934. Review of *Young Commonwealth Poets* ed. Peter Brent.

C264. 'Or, Solitude', *New Statesman*, LXX, 1816 (31 Dec. 1965), p. 1032. Poem.

C265. *'Sincerity and Poetry', *Michigan Quarterly Review*, V, 1 (winter 1966), pp. 3-8.

C266. 'The Historical Narratives of Janet Lewis', *Southern Review*, ns. II, 1 (Jan. 1966), pp. 40-60.

C267. 'T. S. Eliot—1928', *Encounter*, XXVI, 2 (Feb. 1966), p. 47. Poem.

C268. 'From the New World', *Listener*, LXXV, 1924 (10 Feb. 1966), p. 211. Poem.

C269. *'A Poetry of Protest', *New Statesman*, LXXI, 1822 (11 Feb. 1966), pp. 198-9. Review of *Geography* by Edward Dorn.

C270. 'The North Sea', *New Statesman*, LXXI, 1827 (19 March 1966), p. 380. Poem.

C271. 'Ode to Reason', *Literary Review*, IX (spring 1966), pp. 487-8. Poem by Istvan Vas, translated by Donald Davie.

C272. 'Argument. 1. Dr Zhivago's Poems', *Essays in Criticism*, XVI, 2 (April 1966), pp. 212-19. Joint author, with John Bayley.

C273. 'Airs', *The Times Literary Supplement*, 3354 (9 June 1966), p. 508. Poem.

C274. 'A Winter Landscape near Ely', *New Statesman*, LXXI, 1840 (17 June 1966), p. 900. Poem.

C275. 'Focus on Translation: Pioneering in Essex', *Author*, 77 (summer 1966), pp. 28-30.

C276. 'Expecting Silence', *Critical Quarterly*, VIII, 2 (summer 1966), p. 179. Poem.

C277. 'Come Rain down Words', *Outposts*, 70 (autumn 1966), pp. 2-3. Poem by Boris Pasternak, translated by Donald Davie.

C278. 'Sylva', *Listener*, LXXVI, 1957 (29 Sept. 1966), p. 465. Poem.

C279. 'A Death in the West', *The Review*, 16 (Oct. 1966), p. 20. Poem.

C280. 'My Father's Honour', *New Statesman*, LXXII, 1859 (28 Oct. 1966), p. 628. Poem.

C281. 'Privately Published', *New Statesman*, LXXII, 1860 (4 Nov. 1966), pp. 672-3. Review of *Briggflatts* by Basil Bunting and *A Range of Poems* by Gary Snyder.

C282. 'Behind the North Wind', *Listener*, LXXVI, 1963 (10 Nov. 1966), p. 687. Poem.

C283. 'What Imagism Was', *Listener*, LXXVII, 1975 (2 Feb. 1967), pp. 172-3. Review of *The Influence of Ezra Pound* by K. L. Goodwin.

C284. 'Jewish Idylls', *New Statesman*, LXXIII, 1888 (19 May 1967), pp. 690-1. Review of *In My Father's Court, Short Friday* and *Satan in Goray* by Isaac Bashevis Singer.

C285. 'Beyond All This Fiddle: A Rejoinder to A. Alvarez', *The Times Literary Supplement*, 3404 (25 May 1967), p. 472.

C286. 'Expostulations of an Old Shaker', *Southern Review*, III, 3 (July 1967), pp. 648-9. Poem.

C287. 'Intervals in a Busy Life', *Listener*, LXXVIII, 2003 (17 Aug.

1967), p. 214. Poem.

C288. 'Honest England', *Listener*, LXXVIII, 2004 (24 Aug. 1967), p. 245. Poem.

C289. 'Arts and Sciences', *Listener*, LXXVIII, 2010 (5 Oct. 1967), pp. 415-16.

C290. 'Out of East Anglia', *Listener*, LXXVIII, 2011 (12 Oct. 1967), p. 473. Poem.

C291. *'A Continuity Lost', *Listener*, LXXVIII, 2018 (30 Nov. 1967), pp. 708-9. Review of *Anna Karenina and Other Essays* by F. R. Leavis.

C292. *'The Translatability of Poetry', *Listener*, LXXVIII, 2022 (28 Dec. 1967), pp. 838-40.

C293. 'Language to Literature: The Long Way Round', *Style*, I (1967), pp. 215-20.

C294. [Two Poems], *Listener*, LXXIX, 2025 (18 Jan. 1968), p. 80. Contents: 'Excellence', 'Essences'.

C295. 'Cowper's "Yardley Oak": A Continuation', *Listener*, LXXIX, 2033 (14 March 1968), p. 344. Poem.

C296. 'Pasternak's Midi', *New Statesman*, LXXV, 1931 (15 March 1968), pp. 342, 344. Review of *Letters to Georgian Friends* by Boris Pasternak, translated by David Magarshack.

C297. 'Views', *Listener*, LXXIX, 2034 (21 March 1968), p. 365.

C298. 'Poems of the Fifties', *Critical Quarterly*, X, 1-2 (spring-summer 1968), pp. 89-94. Contents: 'On Sutton Strand', 'Aubade', 'Dudwood', 'Dublin Georgian', 'Dublin Georgian (2)', 'Eden'.

C299. 'Poets on the Vietnam War', *The Review*, 18 (April 1968), p. 31.

C300. 'Views', *Listener*, LXXIX, 2037 (11 April 1968), p. 461.

C301. 'Epistle; to Enrique Caracciolo Trejo', *The Times Literary Supplement*, 3454 (9 May 1968), p. 486. Poem.

C302. *'Poetry and the Other Modern Arts', *Michigan Quarterly Review*, VII, 3 (summer 1968), pp. 193-8.

C303. *'Landscape as Poetic Focus', *Southern Review*, ns. IV, 3 (summer 1968), pp. 685-91.

C304. 'Views', *Listener*, LXXX, 2049 (4 July 1968), p. 6.

C305. 'No Commentary', *The Times Literary Supplement*, 3465 (25 July 1968), p. 804. Exchange of letters with the Arts Council.

C306. 'Three Poems', *Listener*, LXXX, 2054 (8 Aug. 1968), p. 168. Contents: 'Oak Openings', 'Midsummer's Eve', 'Revulsion'.

C307. 'August, 1968', *Listener*, LXXX, 2060 (19 Sept. 1968), p. 373. Poem.

C308. 'Giorgio Bassani, Three Poems Translated by Donald Davie', *Agenda*, VI, 3-4 (autumn-winter 1968), p. 78. Contents: 'Vide Cor Meum', 'Dream', 'Dawn at the Windows'.

C309. 'On Sincerity, from Wordsworth to Ginsberg', *Encounter*, XXXI, 4 (Oct. 1968), pp. 61-6. British reprint from *Michigan Quarterly Review*, V, 1 (winter 1966), pp. 3-8.

C310. 'Democracy', *Listener*, LXXX, 2064 (17 Oct. 1968), p. 497. Poem.

C311. 'Forgotten Poet', *Listener*, LXXX, 2065 (24 Oct. 1968), pp. 540-1. Review of *Selected Poems of Fulke Greville*, ed. Thom Gunn.

C312. 'Energies', *Listener*, LXXX, 2072 (12 Dec. 1968), p. 786. Poem.

C313. 'Revulsion', *New Republic*, CLIX, 25-6 (21 Dec. 1968), p. 37. Poem.

C314. 'Boyhood Misremembered', *The Times Literary Supplement*, 3487 (26 Dec. 1968), p. 1457. Poem.

C315. 'Reflections on the Study of Russian Literature in Britain', *Association of Teachers of Russian Journal*, 17 (1968), pp. 17-23.

C316. 'Emigrant, to the Receding Shore', *Malahat Review*, 9 (Jan. 1969), pp. 158-9. Poem.

C317. 'Views', *Listener*, LXXXI, 2078 (23 Jan. 1969), pp. 101-2.

C318. 'Oriental Visitor', *The Times Literary Supplement*, 3502 (10 April 1969), p. 382. Poem.

C319. 'Oak Openings', *New Republic*, CLX, 17 (26 April 1969), p. 25. Poem.

C320. 'England', *Listener*, LXXXI, 2092 (1 May 1969), p. 612. A sequence from Book Four of 'England', a long poem in progress.

C321. 'Brantome', *New Republic*, CLX, 25 (21 June 1969), p. 24. Poem.

C322. 'Michael Ayrton's *The Maze Maker*', *Southern Review*, ns. V, 3 (summer 1969), pp. 640-54.

C323. 'From Book Four of "England" ', *Listener*, LXXXII, 2107, (14 August 1969), p. 213. Poem.

C324. 'The Shakespeare of the North', *Listener*, LXXXII, 2112 (18 Sept. 1969), p. 381. Review of *The Achievement of Sir Walter Scott* by A. O. Cockshut and *Sir Walter Scott: The Formative Years* by Arthur Melville Clark.

C325. 'On Hobbits and Intellectuals', *Encounter*, XXXIII, 4 (Oct. 1969), pp. 87-92.

C326. 'To Certain English Poets', *Harpers*, CCXXXIX, 1433 (Oct. 1969), p. 68. Poem.

C327. 'Christopher Smart: Some Neglected Poems', *Eighteenth Century Studies*, III, 2 (winter 1969), pp. 242-64.

C328. 'Cold Spring in Essex', *Harpers*, CCXL, 1437 (Feb. 1970), p. 116. Poem.

C329. 'A First Epistle to Eva Hesse', *London Magazine*, ns. IX, 11 (Feb. 1970), pp. 5-12. Poem.

C330. 'A Second Epistle to Eva Hesse', *London Magazine*, ns. X, 1 (April 1970), pp. 28-37. Poem.

C331. *'The Poetry of Samuel Menashe', *Iowa Review*, I, 3 (summer 1970), pp. 107-14.

C332. 'A Fifth Epistle to Eva Hesse', *London Magazine*, ns. X, 4 (July/Aug. 1970), pp. 35-41.

C333. 'The Failure of a Dialogue', *Listener*, LXXXIV, 2161 (27 Aug. 1970), pp. 272-3.

C334. 'An Appreciation of Canto 110', *Agenda*, VIII, 3-4 (autumn-winter

1970), pp. 19-26.

C335. 'England', *Agenda*, VIII, 3-4 (autumn-winter 1970), pp. 63-77.
       Poem.

C336. 'John Ledyard: The American Traveler and His Sentimental Jour-
       neys', *Eighteenth Century Studies*, IV, 1 (fall 1970), pp. 57-70.

C337. 'To England. Flying In', *Listener*, LXXXIV, 2165 (24 Sept.
       1970), p. 408. Poem.

C338. *'Eminent Talent', *Essays in Criticism*, XX, 4 (Oct. 1970), pp.
       466-72. Review of *Landor's Poetry* by Robert Pinsky.

C339. 'A First Epistle to Eva Hesse', *Quarterly Review of Literature*,
       XVII, 1-2 (1970), pp. 56-63. American reprint from *London
       Magazine*, ns. IX, 11 (Feb. 1970), pp. 5-12.

C340. [Letter to the Editors], *Sad Traffic*, 3 (1970), p. 11.

C341. 'Memories of Russia', *Sad Traffic*, 3 (1970), pp. 12-14.

C342. [Two Poems], *Southern Review*, ns. VII, 1 (Jan. 1971), pp.
       211-12. Contents: 'Idyll', 'Christmas Syllabics for a Wife'.

C343. 'Vancouver', *New Poetry*, XIX, 1 (Feb. 1971), pp. 25-8. Poem.

C344. [Three Poems], *Iowa Review*, II, 2 (spring 1971), pp. 88-90.
       Contents: 'Preoccupation's Gift', 'Commodore Barry', 'Winter
       Landscape'.

C345. 'Two Poems', *Listener*, LXXXV, 2191 (25 March 1971), p. 372.
       Contents: 'Abbeyforde', 'The North Sea in a Snowstorm'.

C346. *'Pushkin, and Other Poets', *Listener*, LXXXV, 2203 (17 June
       1971), pp. 789-90. Review of *Pushkin: A Comparative Commen-
       tary* by John Bayley and *Pushkin on Literature* ed. and translated
       by Tatiana Wolff.

C347. 'An English Couple', *New Poetry*, XIX, 4 (Aug. 1971), p. 8. Poem.

C348. [Review of *The Life of Ezra Pound* by Noel Stock], *New Poetry*,
       XIX, 4 (Aug. 1971), pp. 32-5.

C349. 'Cochrane (and Lady Cochrane)', *The Times Literary Supple-
       ment*, 3624 (13 Aug. 1971), p. 966. Poem.

C350. 'Seeing Her Leave', *Listener*, LXXXVI, 2222 (28 Oct. 1971), p.
       566. Poem.

C351. 'Trevenen', *Atlantis*, 3 (Nov. 1971), pp. 35-43. Poem.

C352. *'The Adventures of a Cultural Orphan', *Listener*, LXXXVI,
       2230 (23 Dec. 1971), pp. 876-7. Review of *Discretions* by Mary
       de Rachewiltz.

C353. *'Hardy's Virgilian Purples', *Agenda*, X, 2-3 (spring-summer
       1972), pp. 138-56.

C354. 'Widowers', *Agenda*, X, 2-3 (spring-summer 1972), p. 157. Poem.

C355. 'Of Graces', *Antaeus*, 5 (spring 1972), pp. 107-8. Poem.

C356. *'The Cantos: Towards a Pedestrian Reading', *Paideuma*, I, 1
       (spring-summer 1972), pp. 55-62.

C357. 'Widowers', *Listener*, LXXXVII, 2248 (27 April 1972), p. 549.
       Slightly different version from that printed in *Agenda*, X 2-3
       (spring-summer 1972), p. 157.

C358. 'Ireland of the Bombers', *Humanist*, XXXII, 4 (July-Aug. 1972), p. 42. Poem.

C359. 'Some Notes on Rhythm in Verse', *Agenda*, X, 4—XI, 1 (autumn-winter 1972-3), pp. 17-19.

C360. 'Reticulations', *Agenda*, X, 4—XI, 1 (autumn-winter 1972-3), pp. 71-9.

C361. 'Poems by Donald Davie', *Critical Quarterly*, XIV, 3 (autumn 1972), pp. 197-8. Contents: 'To a Teacher of French', 'Word-Games'.

C362. 'Eliot in One Poet's Life', *Mosaic*, VI, 1 (fall 1972), pp. 229-41.

C363. 'A Vegetable World', *Shenandoah*, XXIV, 1 (fall 1972), pp. 92-4. Review of *Shagbark* by John Peck.

C364. 'Ed Dorn and the Treasures of Comedy', *VORT*, I, 1 (fall 1972), pp. 24-5.

C365. *'The Rhetoric of Emotion', *The Times Literary Supplement*, 3682 (29 Sept. 1972), pp. 1141—3.

C366. 'Little England', *Essays in Criticism*, XXII, 4 (Oct. 1972), pp. 429-36. Review of *Chaucer and the English Tradition* by Ian Robinson.

C367. 'Panicky and Painful', *Guardian Weekly*, CVII, 18 (28 Oct. 1972), p. 24. Review of *Sincerity and Authenticity* by Lionel Trilling.

C368. 'The Universe of Ezra Pound', *Paideuma*, I, 2 (winter 1972), pp. 263-9. Review of *The Pound Era* by Hugh Kenner.

C369. 'Anglican Eliot', *Southern Review*, ns. IX, 1 (Jan. 1973), pp. 93-104.

C370. 'The Coleridge Conspiracy', *Guardian Weekly*, CVIII, 6 (3 Feb. 1973), p. 27. Review of *Coleridge's Verse: A Selection* by William Empson and David Pirie and *Coleridge: The Damaged Archangel* by Norman Fruman.

C371. *'An Ambition Beyond Poetry', *The Times Literary Supplement*, 3701 (9 Feb. 1973), pp. 151-2. Unsigned review of *Selected Poems* and *The Telling* by Laura Riding.

C372. 'The Morning after the Revolution', *Encounter*, XL, 3 (March 1973), pp. 56-61. British reprint of 'Poetry and the Other Modern Arts' from *Michigan Quarterly Review*, VII, 3 (summer 1968), pp. 193-8.

C373. 'Two Poems', *Listener*, LXXXIX, 2292 (1 March 1973), p. 281. Contents: 'Mandelstam in the Crimea', 'Robinson Jeffers at Point Sur'.

C374. 'The Universe of Ezra Pound', *Critical Quarterly*, XV, 1 (spring 1973), pp. 51-7. British reprint from *Paideuma*, I, 2 (winter 1972), pp. 263-9.

C375. *'Braveries Eschewed', *Shenandoah*, XXIV, 3 (spring 1973), pp. 90-5. Review of *Seascape: Needle's Eye* by George Oppen.

C376. 'Larkin's Choice', *Listener*, LXXXIX, 2296 (29 March 1973), pp. 420-1. Review of *The Oxford Book of Twentieth-Century English*

Verse ed. Philip Larkin.

C377.   'Views', *Listener*, LXXXIX, 2302 (10 May 1973), pp. 610-11.

C378.   'Berryman', *The Times Literary Supplement*, 3721 (29 June 1973), p. 750. Poem.

C379.   *'Robert Lowell', *Parnassus*, II, 1 (fall-winter 1973), pp. 49-57.

C380.   'A West Riding Boyhood', *Prose*, 7 (fall 1973), pp. 61-70.

C381.   'His Themes', *Encounter*, XXXI, 10 (Oct. 1973), pp. 59-60. Poem.

C382.   'Two Poems', *Listener*, XC, 2325 (18 Oct. 1973), p. 510. Contents: 'An End to Good Humour', 'Silver-Tongue'.

C383.   [Two Poems], *London Magazine*, ns. XIII, 5 (Dec. 1973–Jan. 1974), pp. 76-7. Contents: 'Seur', 'A Spring Song'.

C384.   *'Tragedy and Gaiety', *New Statesman*, LXXXVI, 2229 (7 Dec. 1973), pp. 862-5. Review of *Mandelstam* by Clarence Brown, *Selected Poems* by Osip Mandelstam translated by David McDuff, *Selected Poems* by Osip Mandelstam translated by Clarence Brown and W. S. Merwin, *Chapter 42* by Nadezhda Mandelstam with *The Goldfinch* by Osip Mandelstam translated by Donald Rayfield.

C385.   'Notes on George Oppen's *Seascape: Needle's Eye*', *Grosseteste Review*, VI, 1-4 (1973), pp. 233-9. British reprint of 'Braveries Eschewed' from *Shenandoah*, XXIV, 3 (spring 1973), pp. 90-5.

C386.   'Treasure Island', *Meridian*, 1 (1973), p. 10. Poem.

C387.   'Morning', *Poetry Nation*, 1 (1973), p. 15. Poem.

C388.   'A Comment', *Poetry Nation*, 1 (1973), pp. 54-8.

C389.   'At Belleau Wood', *Wave*, 6 (1973). Poem.

C390.   'Poems from the Shires', *Listener*, XCI, 2338 (17 Jan. 1974), p. 82. Contents: 'Middlesex', 'Wiltshire', 'Hertfordshire'.

C391.   'Open Poetry', *Parnassus*, II, 2 (spring-summer 1974), pp. 136-8. Review of *Open Poetry: Four Anthologies of Expanded Poems* ed. Ronald Gross and George Quasha.

C392.   *'An Appeal to Dryden', *Listener*, XCI, 2354 (9 May 1974), pp. 603-4. Review of *In the Trojan Ditch* by C. H. Sisson.

C393.   'After the Calamitous Convoy (July, 1942)', *The Times Literary Supplement*, 3759 (17 May 1974), p. 526. Poem.

C394.   'Transatlantic Exacerbations', *New Statesman*, LXXXVII, 2255 (7 June 1974), pp. 803-4. Review of *Love-Hate Relations* by Stephen Spender.

C395.   *'Slogging for the Absolute', *Parnassus*, III, 1 (fall-winter 1974), pp. 9-22.

C396.   'Hardy's Virgilian Purples', *Arion*, ns. I, 3 (1973-4), pp. 505-26. American reprint from *Agenda*, X, 2-3 (spring-summer 1972), pp. 138-56.

C397.   'From "The Shires" ', *Poetry Nation*, 2 (1974), pp. 3-5. Contents: 'Cheshire', 'Derbyshire', 'Northumberland', 'Staffordshire', 'Westmoreland', 'Lancashire'.

C398.   'The Varsity Match', *Poetry Nation*, 2 (1974), pp. 72-80. Review of *A Poetry Chronicle, Essays and Reviews* by Ian Hamilton.

INDEX